C000116684

WHICH? HOLIDAY DESTINATION

WHICH? HOLIDAY DESTINATION

An A–Z guide to where to go on holiday

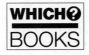

CONSUMERS' ASSOCIATION

Which? Books are commissioned and researched by
Consumers' Association and published by
Which? Ltd, 2 Marylebone Road, London NW1 4DF
Email address: books@which.net

Distributed by The Penguin Group:
Penguin Books Ltd, 27 Wrights Lane, London W8 5TZ

Acknowledgements
Morag Aitken, Ros Belford, Eileen Brennan, Sophie Carr, Jonathan Cox,
Alexander Craig, Mick Diffley, Jan Dodd, Frank Dunne, Caroline Ellerby,
David Else, Anna Fielder, Simon Gaul, Patricia Goldstraw, Emma Gregg,
Emily Hatchwell, Sasha Heseltine, Lucy Hooker, Lindsay Hunt, Roger Larkin,
Julie Lennard, Nicola and Charles Liu, James Lyon, Shereen Makarem,
Fred Mawer, Conor McCutcheon, Ella Milroy, Rob Nash, Helen Oldfield,
Mike Pedley, Polly Phillimore, Tony Pinchuck, Paul Pontone, Gordon Robison,
David Rodwell, Tony Rooney, Lucy Smith, Bob Tolliday, Richard Trillo,
Julia Tweed, Neil Walkling, Kim Winter, Pat Yale, Patricia Yates, Nancy Yuill

Typographic design by Sarah Watson
Cover design by Paul Saunders
Cover photograph by Peter Baker/Photobank

First edition January 1997
Revised edition January 1998
Copyright © 1998 Which? Ltd

British Library Cataloguing in Publication Data
A catalogue record for this book is available from the British Library

ISBN 0 85202 705 2

For a full list of Which? books, please write to
Which? Books, Castlemead, Gascoyne Way, Hertford X, SG14 1LH.

Holiday Which? regularly inspects holiday destinations both in Britain and
abroad, as well as reporting on airfares, hotel safety and other issues of interest to holiday-makers. To keep up to date with the best information, take out
a subscription. For details of a free trial, write to *Holiday Which?*, Consumers'
Association, PO Box 44, Hertford SG14 1SH, tel (01992) 822804.

Typeset by Business Color Print Ltd
Printed and bound by Clays Ltd, Bungay, Suffolk

CONTENTS

INTRODUCTION

Which? Holiday Destination will help you when you are planning your holiday, trying to cut through the brochure hype and decide where to go. It provides, in a nutshell, all the key facts about a wide range of holiday venues around the world. Since its first edition, it has been expanded to include a further 20 destinations, all of them long-haul, reflecting the growing popularity of countries which may take longer, and cost more, to get to but which in many cases offer superb value once you have made the trip.

Our concise overviews of each place highlight what each country or region has to offer the holidaymaker. Each will give you a pretty good idea of whether it is the sort of place that is right for you and the type of holiday you envisage.

The key features of each destination are listed under the following headings, so you can see at a glance whether your own interests are represented:

Beaches Good ones are those with golden sand, preferably gently shelving, with plenty of room for everyone, taking into account the size of the resort or island★

Culture Includes museums, galleries, theatre, music and architecture (Indian temples as well as Roman ruins)

Family holidays Bases for those with young children

Flora Flowers, shrubs and trees, whether in carefully cultivated gardens or in the wild

Food/wine Resorts which offer a wide selection of restaurants serving good-value food, not just expensive gourmet haunts. This category also covers beer as well as wine and fortified wine like port or sherry, including areas where it is produced

History Denotes historically significant sites, e.g. American Civil War battlefields, Hiroshima, the ruins of the Inca civilisation at Machu Picchu

Local colour Places where local traditions and customs still live on – and not just as nightly 'folklore' shows put on for the benefit of tourists

Nightlife If your idea of a holiday is to spend the night on the tiles, the morning in bed and the afternoon recovering on the beach or by the pool, this is the resort for you

Outdoor activities Specialising in one or more sports, such as golf, water sports, walking or trekking, cycling, sailing or diving

Romantic escapism For getting away from it all, avoiding crowds

Scenic landscape Memorable mountains and lakes, desert wilderness, stunning seascapes, good for touring or walking

Shopping For those who need more than a couple of souvenir stalls and postcard stands

Wildlife Including birds, whales and big game.

Cost of living ££ is equivalent to the cost of living in the UK.

For each country we list tour operators offering holidays there, concentrating mainly on smaller specialist operators whose brochures you may not see in a high-street travel agency. All are bonded, so your money is safe if the company goes bust. The tour operators' telephone numbers are listed on pages 496–501.

Where possible, we give the web site addresses of official tourism organisations for specific countries. You may also find it useful to visit the ANTOR UK (Association of National Tourist Offices of the United Kingdom) web site, which represents 88 national and regional tourist offices. For each country you can access useful information, tour operator listings and details of web sites of further interest. The ANTOR UK web site can be found at: http://www.tourist-offices.org.uk/.

We also give advice on getting around independently, whether you need a visa, and whether there are any specific health or safety concerns. Hints on applying for a visa are on page 17. For advice on health and safety, see pages 10–12. A checklist on what to do before you go away is on page 9, and information on how to complain if something goes wrong with your holiday is provided on pages 13–16.

★ Our assessments do not take into account the quality of the bathing water, as this changes from year to year. The European Union awards Blue Flags to beaches in member countries that meet mandatory minimum standards for bacteria and viruses and publishes the results of its surveys every year. For a list of all the European Blue Flag beaches, contact the Foundation for Environmental Education in Europe, Olof Palmes Gade 10, DK-2100 Copenhagen, Denmark.

HOLIDAY CHECKLIST

Health Seek advice about immunisations two months before travel to exotic locations. Take your vaccination certificate with you. Supplement malaria tablets on holiday with use of mosquito nets, repellent and other anti-bite measures, and be sure to complete the course of tablets on your return. Form E111 (available from the post office) entitles you to receive urgent medical treatment on the same basis as a national of the country concerned (free or at reduced cost) while visiting a European Union (EU) member state, Norway or Iceland. The Department of Health produces booklet T5 *Health Advice for Travellers* (updated regularly), available from post offices or via the Health Literature Line, tel (0800) 555777.

House Do your best to make your house look occupied. You could consider getting a house-sitter – a friend or a specialist company such as Homesitters Ltd, tel (01296) 630730 or Housewatch Ltd, tel (01279) 777412 (both operate nationwide). Failing that, set your lights and radio on timers and arrange for somebody to check the house.

Insurance Take out insurance against cancellation (almost one-third of claims are for cancellation). Remember to pack the policy document and your insurer's emergency assistance company's telephone number.

Money For uncommon currencies give your bank or exchange bureau at least 72 hours' notice; choose US$ travellers cheques for the USA as well as countries in Eastern Europe, Latin America and the Caribbean. Local currency cheques are best in France and Germany.

Motoring If you are taking your own car abroad, remember to extend you car insurance cover. Take the vehicle registration document. Check your spare tyre. Adjust your headlamps for driving on the right, with an adhesive or clip-on converter. Some countries require you to carry a warning triangle and/or first aid kit and spare bulb.

Passports and visas The UK Passport Agency aims to process all correct applications for passports within 10 working days. Alternatively, you can hand in your application to main post offices, branches of Lloyds Bank and branches of ARTA WorldChoice travel agents, who, for a small handling charge, will check that your application is correctly completed and deliver it to the Passport Agency for processing; your passport should be returned within four days.

HOLIDAY HAZARDS

YOU DO not have to go on holiday to get ill or be mugged. But unfamiliar surroundings, language problems, strange food and drink, and too much sun can create the risks. Here are some tips to help ensure you have a healthy and safe holiday.

Altitude sickness Altitude sickness, or mountain sickness, can be fatal but is largely avoidable. The best way to prevent it is to ascend gradually. If you are travelling by road, air or rail to high altitudes, you should allow a couple of days for your body to acclimatise. Rest as much as you need, drink plenty of liquids and avoid alcohol.

Animal and insect bites Do not approach any animal if there is a risk of rabies; cover arms and legs (especially at dawn or dusk, when mosquitoes bite). Use insect repellent, spray rooms with insecticides and sleep under nets. Check whether you need to take anti-malaria pills.

Ear infections They can be caused by polluted or warm tropical water – shower in fresh water after swimming and dry the ear canal by shaking the head.

Heat exhaustion and sunburn Stay in the shade or cover up between 11am and 3pm. Wear a broad-rimmed hat and sunglasses. Spread sun cream evenly and thickly and re-apply every two hours.

Lost credit/charge cards Advise the card issuer and inform the police as soon as the theft comes to light to limit your liability for any unauthorised purchases made with your card. Keep the issuer's 'lost card' telephone number to hand and note your card number and expiry date in order to help speed up its cancellation (keep separately from the card). Some card issuers can make cash advances to help tide you over – check that yours offers the facility before departure.

Plane travel Flying can be a health hazard, particularly to long-haul destinations. Side-effects include tiredness, swollen ankles, headache, sore throat, dry or watery eyes and coughing owing to poor ventilation. People with heart, respiratory or neurological problems may suffer from hypoxia (lack of oxygen) owing to atmospheric pressure; symptoms resemble mild drunkenness. Jet lag, which occurs because the body's natural rhythms take time to adjust to a new time zone, can cause tiredness, poor concentration, inability to sleep at night, loss of appetite, bowel problems and headaches (the effects may be worse on eastward flights). For a more comfortable journey, choose a daytime flight to minimise sleep loss and tiredness. Walk frequently around the cabin or exercise in your seat; on long flights, get off at refuelling points for some fresh air and a walk. Avoid alcohol to combat dehydration and maximise your exposure to bright light to help the body clock read-just. If you get air sickness, sit over the wings, where the plane moves least. To avoid painful pressure in the ears, yawn or suck a sweet.

Pregnant travellers Before travelling, check with your GP or a trav-el clinic. Steer clear of places with a high malaria risk such as East and West Africa and Thailand. Beware of horse-riding, mountain climbing and other activities that may cause a fall. Observe the same food pre-cautions as you would at home; in addition, drink only bottled water. For the *Travelling in Pregnancy* brochure from the Royal College of Obstetricians and Gynaecologists, call 0171-772 6275.

Road accidents Check a hired vehicle fully before driving off, espe-cially tyres; make sure you have a spare wheel, test all the lights (espe-cially brake lights) and seat belts. Wear a helmet and protective cloth-ing if riding a motorbike or moped (check first if your holiday insur-ance covers you). Learn the rules of the road and local speed limits.

Sports injuries Check the condition of any equipment you hire or use. Check whether your insurance covers 'hazardous activities'.

Stomach upsets Beware of food left on display uncovered at room temperature. Drink boiled or bottled water or use purifying tablets if you are unsure of the water. Beware of salads, shellfish, ice-cream, and ice-cubes in drinks. The best treatment is rehydration.

Travel Advice Unit

The Foreign and Commonwealth Office (FCO) has set up a Travel Advice Unit offering information on the risks to tourists in differ-ent countries. The information comes from British embassies and consulates and security agencies and is updated as necessary. The FCO also has close links with the travel trade – if it advises against visiting a country, ABTA tour operators will generally pull out and give refunds to people who have already booked. Individual trav-ellers, however, cannot be prevented from visiting a country against its recommendation. The FCO Travel Advice Unit can be contact-ed on 0171-238 4503/4504. Travel advice is also available on BBC2 Ceefax, page 564 onwards, on travel agents' computer sys-tems, and can be accessed on the Internet at:
http://www.fco.gov.uk/reference/travel_advice/index.html

Theft If you must take valuables with you, leave them in a safety-deposit box in your hotel. Lock the doors and windows of your hotel room or apartment securely. Keep the safety chain on in your room, and never open the door unless you know who is there. Get local advice on no-go areas and wear a money belt under your clothes. Hide valuables from view even if you are in the car and do not leave anything in the car overnight. Put personal safety first and if you are threatened, hand over your possessions.

Water sports Do not swim after eating a heavy meal or drinking alcohol. Take note of warning signs or flags on beaches. Check the condition of equipment you are using and insist on a full briefing on unfamiliar equipment and procedures. Always check the depth of the hotel pool before you dive in.

MAKING A CLAIM

Check that you have adequate insurance cover for your possessions. If you are robbed, report the theft to the local police and fill out a report form, keeping a copy to show the insurance company; if something is stolen from your hotel room or apartment, most insurers also require you to notify the hotel manager and tour operator's rep; if the theft occurs during a flight, report it to the airline straight away – some policies will not pay out unless thefts are reported within 24 hours.

IF THINGS GO WRONG

TRAVEL AGENCIES

When you ask a travel agent to book a holiday for you the agent must use reasonable skill and care to book the holiday or travel arrangements you requested. An agent who fails to do this is in breach of contract. If you have special requirements – for example, allocation of a ground-floor room – make them a condition of your booking. This means that if the tour operator fails to take notice of your requirements, he/she is in breach of contract. Put your requirements to the travel agent in writing, and ask for written confirmation that the tour operator has been made aware of your special needs.

If things go wrong
● Write to the agent as soon as possible, referring to both your letter of instruction and the agent's letter confirming your instructions have been acted on. Ask for a reply with settlement proposals within 14 days.
● Clause 1.10 of the ABTA code of conduct obliges agents to acknowledge complaint within 14 days, and to send a detailed response within 28 days. If the agent does not comply, or the response is unsatisfactory, you can complain to ABTA.
● If all else fails, consider going to the small claims court or to arbitration (see below).

BROCHURES

The brochure description plus the associated photographs and any maps are part of the contract between you and the tour operator. If the company fails to deliver what it has promised, you can claim compensation. In addition, the Trade Descriptions Act 1968 makes it a criminal offence for a tour operator to publish a brochure which it knows (or should know) contains false or misleading information.

If things go wrong
● Your local Trading Standards Department can prosecute alleged offenders.
● The Advertising Standards Authority (ASA), 2 Torrington Place, London WC1E 7HW, tel 0171-580 5555, is able to investigate complaints that brochures or other advertising material are dishonest or misleading.
● Always take a copy of the brochure with you on holiday so that you can see what you were promised.

FLIGHTS

If a tour operator tells you that your flight times have been changed, you should check that the booking conditions allow this. In most cases 'minor' changes can be made without any entitlement to compensation; minor in this case usually means up to 12 hours. Clause 2.4 (i) of the ABTA tour operator's code of conduct outlaws major changes within 14 days of your departure date. Where late alterations are made in defiance of the ABTA ban you are entitled to compensation and to a full refund if you decide to cancel.

If things go wrong

● Write to the tour operator immediately, setting out your claim for compensation.

● If the change of flight time leaves you out-of-pocket – for instance, you need to take a taxi to the airport to catch an early-morning flight – your letter to the operator should accept the change under protest and reserve your rights to claim additional compensation beyond that set out in the brochure.

RESORT AND ACCOMMODATION

The first rule of complaining is to do it straight away, and give the hotel or tour operator a chance to sort out your problem. If you do not, the operator — and the court in any subsequent action – may decide that you have 'failed to mitigate your loss' and are entitled to reduced compensation, if any.

If things go wrong

● Ask the management to sort out any problems you encounter.

● Tell your holiday rep of your complaint at the first opportunity. Be polite, but firm. If you feel that the brochure seriously misrepresents the facilities available, show it to the rep and ask to be moved to a hotel or apartment in line with the brochure description. Most reps have the authority to do this on the spot.

● Complete a claims form, and retain a copy for future reference.

● Keep a diary detailing requests to the hotel and rep to put things right and their responses. Note down all meetings, telephone calls and any expenses that you incur.

● Take photographs to back up your case. These are particularly useful if your complaint relates to substandard accommodation and misleading brochure descriptions.

● Write down the names and addresses of any witnesses who can confirm your complaints.

● Think carefully before accepting any offer of on-the-spot compensation. Some companies pay compensation in the resort but require a disclaimer stating that the holidaymaker accepts this in full and final settlement of any claims. It may be easy to undervalue your claim in the heat of the moment.

● Curtail your holiday and return home only as a last resort. If your accommodation is unacceptable, and the rep is unable or unwilling to move you, you should try to arrange a suitable alternative, at a cost and with facilities similar to those originally booked – remember the duty to mitigate your loss. Keep receipts to substantiate your claim to the tour operator when you return.

● List your grievances on any 'welcome home' questionnaire you may be given or sent.

LETTERS OF COMPLAINT

Write to the tour operator as soon as you get home, or at any rate within 28 days of your return, detailing your complaint. Aim to be concise, logical, honest and thorough. Show determination but do not whinge. Your letter should:

● be headed with your name, holiday dates, accommodation booked, and booking reference

● deal with your story chronologically, and give dates, times and names of parties involved

● explain any breach of contract by detailing discrepancies between the brochure description and the actual situation encountered, referring to any special requirements notified and not met

● indicate that photographs and witnesses are available, if this is appropriate

● indicate the amount of compensation claimed, based on the factors below.

The amount of compensation you are likely to recover depends on the impact the deficiencies had on your enjoyment of your holiday. Your claim is made up of three elements:

Loss of value – the difference between the holiday you got and the one you paid for e.g. if you are moved to inferior accommodation due to overbooking this figure will be the difference in the value of the accommodation. Or, if the holiday was a 'complete disaster', this figure will amount to the cost of the holiday.

Loss of enjoyment – compensation for distress, disappointment and inconvenience. This is a difficult figure to assess, but courts often allow very reasonable amounts of compensation for this part of a claim.

Out-of-pocket expenses – the refund of any reasonable extra costs incurred.

Keep a copy of the letter with all subsequent correspondence. Clause 2.9 of the ABTA code of conduct requires tour operators to acknowledge your letter within 14 days, and to send a detailed response within 28 days. Matters should be concluded within 56 days.

COURT OR ARBITRATION?

If your letter fails to win you acceptable compensation you must decide how to proceed with your claim. In this situation you have two options:

The small claims court

This is a cheap, informal procedure designed to let people argue their cases in person, without any need for lawyers, and without the risk of being liable for the tour operator's legal costs if they lose. The maximum sum you can claim in England and Wales is £3,000. The court fee is between £10 and £80, depending on the sum claimed. In Scotland, the upper limit for small claims in the sheriff court is £750, and the fee is up to £35. In Northern Ireland the limit is £1,000 and the fee is up to £50.

Arbitration

The Chartered Institute of Arbitrators runs an independent, legally binding arbitration scheme on behalf of ABTA. This is a documents-only scheme. However, because there is no hearing, the impact of your personal testimony – often a potent consideration in small claims – will be lost. The maximum award is £1,500 per person or, in the case of large parties, £7,500 per booking form. Holidaymakers who use the scheme pay a registration fee of between £65 and £111. Decisions made by the arbitrators are binding on both sides – so you cannot go to the small claims court if you lose. You do have a right of appeal to the courts but this is likely to leave you out of pocket.

In a report in September 1996, *Holiday Which?* compared awards made by district judges and Abta arbitrators and concluded that the arbitration scheme failed to give consumers their due. Abta are currently considering a major overhaul of their arbitration scheme. In the meantime, our advice would be that consumers in England and Wales, at least, are better served by taking their cases to the small claims court.

The ABTA codes of conduct

Many travel agents and tour operators are members of the Association of British Travel Agents (ABTA). Its members agree to comply with a code of conduct which therefore forms part of your contract with the member concerned.

ABTA
68–71 Newman Street
London W1P 4AH
tel 0171-637 2444

APPLYING FOR A VISA

THIS INFORMATION is for holders of British Citizen passports only. Check with the relevant embassy about regulations and always apply well in advance of departure. If booking a late bargain, check with the travel agent that there is enough time to get a visa before you leave. Remember, a visa doesn't guarantee you entry. Any immigration official can refuse to admit you. For more detailed information about individual countries, see the appropriate chapters.

In person The cheapest option, but requires access to an embassy and time to queue. Check payment methods: some embassies prefer cash or postal orders. Also check opening times. The country may have consulates you could visit in UK cities other than London.

By post Apply well in advance: it can take up to six weeks to issue some visas. Phone the consulate to obtain application forms, then send everything by registered mail, enclosing a registered sae. Make sure application forms are completed correctly and check what form of payment is required – credit cards are rarely accepted.

Visa agencies
These add a service charge on top of the basic visa fee. Prices vary enormously and sometimes 'difficult' visas can cost more to procure. Agencies can give discounts for groups and work fairly quickly. The downside is the expense.

Tour operators
Few offer any comprehensive kind of visa procurement service. Most point out clearly in their brochures that it is your responsibility to sort out visas before travelling. Escorted tours are often covered by a group visa: confirm this when you book.

Travel agents
Most do not offer a visa service. Their advice can be at best sketchy, at worst plain wrong and it is wise not to commit yourself until you actually book a holiday and have a contract with the agent or tour operator.

Countries included in this edition which require a visa

Australia, China, Cuba, Dominican Republic (Caribbean), Egypt, India, Jordan, Kenya, Nepal, Oman, Russian Federation, Tanzania (Zanzibar), Turkey, Vietnam

---

AUSTRALIA

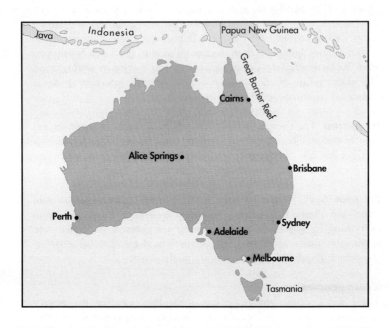

HIGHLIGHTS

Beaches
New South Wales, Queensland

Culture
New South Wales, Outback

Flora
New South Wales, Queensland, Western Australia

Food/wine
New South Wales, Western Australia, Victoria

Nightlife
New South Wales

Outdoor activities
New South Wales, Queensland,

Western Australia, Outback

Scenic landscape
New South Wales, Queensland, Western Australia, Victoria

Shopping
Victoria

Wildlife
New South Wales, Queensland, Western Australia, Outback

NEW SOUTH WALES
Good for beaches, culture, flora, food/wine, nightlife, outdoor activities, scenic landscape and wildlife

OVER A third of Australia's population lives in New South Wales, but it's hardly crowded; the coastline north and south of Sydney is a chain of often empty beaches pounded by Pacific surf; superb World Heritage national parks run the length of the Great Dividing Range. The spectacular valleys and escarpments of the Blue Mountains are in Sydney's backyard, while the Hunter Valley to the north is a must for wine-lovers.

SYDNEY

APART FROM the almost Manhattan-like centre, vibrant, colourful and cosmopolitan Sydney is a beach city *par excellence*, boasting at least a dozen world-famous beaches, such as Bondi and Manly, as well as many excellent but less well-known spots stretching from Palm Beach to Cronulla. The eclectic mix of cultural influences provides a huge choice of restaurants, galleries, museums, pubs and clubs.

BEST SIGHTS
Port Jackson (the harbour area's proper name) has one of the world's great natural settings, giving Sydney its unique and immediately recognisable face. Visit the iconic Sydney Opera House, the Harbour Bridge, the Botanical Gardens and the Rocks, where Sydney put down its roots.

The concrete jungle of Darling Harbour has some excellent museums, including the Maritime Museum and the Powerhouse Museum, as well as the stunning Aquarium, where you can walk beneath stingrays and sharks in long, clear plastic tunnels. For great views, climb the Harbour Bridge, visit Sydney Tower, or take a ferry trip to Manly.

BEST RESORTS
The key to picking the right beach resort for your needs is to decide what nightlife (it varies from wild to non-existent) you prefer.

Byron Bay
● Brilliant beaches and surfing, and laid-back atmosphere.
● Off-beat residents contribute to the distinctive mix of art and crafts shops, veggie and wholefood restaurants.

Coffs Harbour
● Major resort with a wide selection of accommodation suitable for families, and a string of good beaches.

Port Macquarie
- Large, family-oriented resort with various theme parks and river-front area as well as beaches.
- Koalas have quite a presence here, in both the Koala Hospital and Billabong Koala Park.

BEST SCENIC LANDSCAPE

Barrington Tops
Great walking through a Unesco World Heritage Site of rainforest. Bush bungalows are set among beautiful scenery and rivers.

Blue Mountains
The region's vertiginous cliffs, rugged gorges and eucalyptus forest (whose oily haze gives the mountains their name) were impenetrable to early settlers. Today, Sydney residents come for adventure activities. Accommodation to suit all budgets abounds in the main centres of Katoomba, Leura and Wentworth Falls. Jenolan Caves, Australia's best-known limestone caverns with wonderfully surreal rock formations, are worth a visit.

Dorrigo
Just inland from Coffs Harbour, Dorrigo is worth a detour for the drive alone, quite apart from the bushwalking opportunities and the rainforest canopy walks among the orchids of Dorrigo National Park.

Snowy Mountains and Mount Kosciusko National Park
It is possible to ski here from July to September, and in other seasons there is white-water rafting, hiking and beautiful alpine flowers.

BEST EXCURSION

Hunter Valley
Australia's most famous wine region boasts about 50 wineries, many of which welcome visitors for tastings.

QUEENSLAND
Good for beaches, flora, outdoor activities, scenic landscape and wildlife

BEST CITIES

Brisbane
Brisbane has little of Sydney's jet-set image and cosmopolitan nightlife. Colonial architecture is overshadowed by gleaming high-rise towers of concrete and glass, while broad walkways line the river's edge, and several impressive bridges span its muddy reaches. George Street has the

best central colonial buildings, while the excellent art gallery and Queensland Museum are a good way to spend a morning. For great views over the city and Gold Coast head out to Mount Coot-tha park.

Cairns
The main tourist base for exploring the highlights of the rainforest in north Queensland. Downtown are cafés, bakeries, T-shirt shops and cheap hostels and motels, with smarter high-rises along the Esplanade. There is no beach; Palm Cove is the nicest resort north of Cairns.

BEST SCENIC LANDSCAPE
Atherton Tablelands
West of Cairns is a volcanic landscape of crater lakes, splendid water-falls, rich farmlands and quaint little towns such as Yungaburra, where you can spot platypuses in the nearby river. Kuranda's markets are reached via a spectacular railway and cable car, and wildlife cruises on Lake Barrine can often provide sightings of cassowary (a large flight-less bird), eels, pelicans and pythons. The Curtain Fig and the Cathedral Fig are fine examples of strangler figs, while Millaa Millaa is the cen-tre of a series of waterfalls.

Daintree and Cape Tribulation
Plenty of day-tips from Cairns and Port Douglas take in the unique eco-system of rainforest and reef around Cape Tribulation; for a mem-orable experience stay in an eco-lodge. Try Mossman Gorge for swim-ming, rapids or rainforest walks, while Daintree village, on the banks of the eponymous river, is a good base for wildlife cruises.

Further north are superb beaches at Cow Bay, Thornton Beach and Cape Tribulation itself; beyond this point you need a four-wheel-drive vehicle.

BEST RESORTS
Noosa
● A surfers' mecca since the 1960s, this trendy resort has old beach houses, bougainvillea and acacia trees in a gorgeous setting.
● Town centre at Noosa Heads has the vibrant Hastings Street.
● The cape at the northern tip is Noosa National Park, a stunning mix of eucalyptus, rocky coves and sandy bays.

Surfers Paradise and Broadbeach
● Looming skyscraper hotel blocks.
● Tacky shopping malls and pink stretch limousines exude an air of brash wealth.
● Unbeatable for a lively time.

ISLANDS OF THE BARRIER REEF

THE GREAT Barrier Reef has over 600 islands interspersed between the reef formations. Most are uninhabited, but around 20 have resort and hotel facilities.

Dunk Island
Arguably the most attractive of the islands, thanks to dense rainforest, large numbers of birds and butterflies and views from Mount Kootaloo.

Fraser Island
The world's largest sand island, located south of the Great Barrier Reef. Stunning, though crowded.

Great Keppel Island
This large island off the coast at Yeppoon is heavily promoted for its activities and superb beaches.

Green Island
Green Island's Coral Bay is a popular destination for day-trips from Cairns. The island offers Melanesian art and artefacts as well as an underwater observatory.

Heron Island
The huge array of marine life makes it a diver's paradise, while reef herons and other feathered friends are of interest to birdwatchers.

Hinchinbrook Island
A national park with extensive walks. There are also some fine stretches of beach and you can also see fantastic rainforest and wildlife, including crocodiles.

Lady Elliot Island
Shipwrecks and access to reefs direct from the beach make this a hit with divers. A simple, no-frills place, the island has a lighthouse and airstrip.

Lady Musgrave Island
An emerald isle set in a perfect turquoise lagoon. Day-trips or campers only.

Lizard Island
Remote, secluded, and pricey, but for your money you get pristine coral and superb diving as well as fantastic fishing.

The Whitsundays
A group of 70-odd islands, several of which have been developed into resorts. Boats from Shute Harbour serve the islands, although the beaches are uninspiring.

WESTERN AUSTRALIA
Good for flora, food/wine, outdoor activities, scenic landscape and wildlife

MUCH OF this vast region (ten times the size of the UK) is desert; most of the population lives in the south-west. The area is rich in gold and Aboriginal culture, but resorts are scarce – most lie south of Perth.

PERTH AND AROUND

THE WORLD'S most isolated city (1,242 miles from its neighbour Adelaide) offers good beaches and cheap accommodation. The port district of Fremantle is worth a visit for its market and café society, but when the sailors are in town every bar becomes a strip joint. Northbridge has many good restaurants and clubs and Cottesloe boasts a stunning beach. The weekend markets at Subiaco are worth a visit.

Only 11 miles from Perth, Rottnest Island is home to quokkas – small marsupials – and has good snorkelling. From Perth you can also visit the limestone pillars of the Pinnacles Desert, swim with dolphins at Monkey Mia, see wild flowers in the Darling Ranges, travel to Wave Rock or try an Australian white burgundy at the Swan Valley vineyards.

BEST BASES
Albany
A pleasant old whaling settlement surrounded by dramatic scenery, Albany is near two national parks on the coastal route: Cape Naturaliste and Cape Leeuwin.

Broome
Once a pearling centre, Broome has a laid-back yet cosmopolitan charm, with a small Chinatown and a Japanese cemetery testifying to the dangers of pearl fishing. The superb Cable Beach lies nearby.

Esperance
Esperance has a pink lake, day-trips to see the seals and penguins in the wildlife sanctuary of Woody Island, and organised four-wheel-drive trips to Cape Le Grand National Park.

Kalgoorlie
The active gold-mining town that brought prosperity to Western Australia is an inhospitable, barren, forsaken place, interesting but far from pleasurable for tourists – or the native Aboriginal population.

Margaret river
The home of Western Australia's surfers is a good place to relax, play golf, go walking, visit a cave, drink excellent local wine, surf the 'big one' or rent out a horse-drawn gypsy van. Margaret river is often fully booked during the school holidays.

Pemberton
Pemberton has the famous Gloucester Tree, reputedly the highest fire lookout tree in the world (a sunset climb is recommended). Like the rest of the south-west, the area has become a centre for crafts, especially wood-turning.

BEST SCENIC LANDSCAPES
Bungle Bungles
These are extraordinary beehive formations, comprised of sandstone covered in alternating layers of silica and lichen. They are so fragile that climbing is forbidden. Accessible only by helicopter from Kununarra or Turkey Creek or by four-wheel drive from the latter, the Bungle Bungles are worth the journey for the intrepid.

Nearby is the Argyle Diamond Mine, which accounts for about a third of the world's diamonds.

Ningaloo Reef
Less famous but more accessible than its eastern counterpart, the Great Barrier Reef, Ningaloo offers a chance to see humpback whales, turtles and manta rays. Whales and whale sharks are a seasonal attraction.

Reef tours leave from Exmouth, also the starting-point for the area's major diving site, the Peak Islands.

Pilbara and the Kimberleys
Red earth is common to these two vast, hot and underpopulated areas of Western Australia, but green waterways, orange beaches, gorges and boab trees are the main attractions of the Kimberleys.

BEST FLORA
Tall Trees
A tree-top walk along a suspended metal walkway, which meanders through the canopy of tall and extremely rare tingle trees.

OUTBACK AUSTRALIA
Good for culture and outdoor activities

THESE TIMELESS red landscapes of searing bone-dry wilderness hold the key to understanding Australia's soul and the ancient culture of the Aborigines.

BEST SIGHTS

Alice Springs
'The Alice' is a modern town built on a grid layout and is a good base from which to explore the Red Centre, with a range of shops, restaurants, and Aboriginal art and crafts.

Ayers Rock (Uluru) and the Olgas (Kata Tjuta)
The village of Yulara makes a visit to the Uluru National Park an easy prospect. The immense rock is a site of deep religious and cultural significance for the region's Aboriginal tribes. It can be tough to climb – many lose their nerve. The Olgas, or Kata Tjuta ('many heads') are a fragmented version of Ayers Rock and just as impressive in their own way.

Coober Pedy
The name means 'white fellow's hole in the ground'. This is a unique town of opal miners living in underground dug-outs in a post-apocalyptic landscape. Rough, ready and ugly, yet oddly compelling. Try your luck at 'fossicking' for opals.

Kakadu National Park
One of Australia's most famous parks, situated in the Northern Territory bordering Aboriginal Arnhem Land. The location for *Crocodile Dundee*, this vast, varied terrain of wide plains is punctuated with giant rock formations, waterfalls, billabongs (waterholes) and mangrove swamps and is inhabited by snakes and crocodiles.

Rich in Aboriginal rock art, the park boasts Nourlangie, and Ubirr Rock which has about 7,000 paintings dating back 20,000 years. Don't be disappointed if you discover images repainted in the 1960s – it's an Aboriginal tradition to touch up rock art. Boat trips and guided tours highlight the best of the park's wildlife and Aboriginal art.

Katherine Gorge (Nitmiluk National Park)
A chain of red, majestic gorges, linked by a series of rapids. Boat trips and canoeing excursions explore the fiery canyon with its steep-sided escarpments. The rapids are not difficult to negotiate – when the waters are low you may have to carry your canoe over slippery rocks, but the spectacular scenery merits the challenge.

VICTORIA
Good for food/wine, scenic landscape and shopping

THIS IS fast becoming a very fashionable state and has long left behind the rather conservative, agrarian image it had in the past. In recent times the Grand Prix, the Comedy Festival and the Melbourne Cup have brought the state on to the international stage. Fiercely competitive with New South Wales in everything from Australian Rules Football to having the tag of the country's finest city, the 'Garden State' is keen to capture more of the tourist market. Cooler than some other Australian states, Victoria is home to some of the most spectacular but overlooked scenery on the continent.

MELBOURNE

THE STATE'S cultural and demographic heart. Established in the early nineteenth century, the city is located on the immense Port Phillip Bay and has some of the finest restaurants and nightlife in Australia. What it perhaps lacks in terms of sunshine, it more than makes up for in terms of ambience, diversity and charm.

Brunswick Street and St Kilda are two of the most popular thoroughfares in which to linger over a *caffe latte* and watch the world pass by. The latter has an attractive marina and pier. Several popular markets are located around the city as are some excellent galleries, the National Gallery of Victoria being foremost among them. For shopping, head for the centre of town around Elizabeth Street and the South Gate Centre on the Yarra river opposite Flinders Street station. Sports fans will probably wish to savour the legendary environs of the MCG (Melbourne Cricket Ground), and the Botanical and Zoological Gardens located centrally are also worth a visit. However, the city's charm lies in its eateries and the good-natured and unhurried *viveurs* who frequent them.

BEST SIGHTS AND EXCURSIONS

Lakes Entrance
This boating destination is popular with Victorians.

Murray river
The tranquil meanderings of this vast river lie inland, along with the haunting expanse of the Mallee, for those who want to escape the surf.

Twelve Apostles
These towering stacks of limestone, located south-west of Melbourne, rise up from the Great Southern Ocean. They can be accessed from the

Great Ocean Road, which takes you along a magnificent tract of coast.

Wilson's Promontory
A stunning national park three hours' drive south-east of Melbourne, just about close enough for a day visit and perfect for camping.

WHEN TO GO

THE CLIMATE varies from north to south throughout the year, so you should find somewhere to suit you at any time. If travelling the length of the east coast, go in spring or late autumn (Australian seasons).

Festivals are important in the Sydney calendar. The January arts festival features open-air music in the parks. Chinese New Year celebrations occur in January or February, followed by the Gay and Lesbian

Average daily maximum temperature °C											
London	6	7	10	13	17	20	22	21	19	14	10	7
Sydney	26	26	24	22	19	16	16	17	19	22	23	25
	JAN	FEB	MAR	APR	MAY	JUN	JUL	AUG	SEP	OCT	NOV	DEC
Sydney	14	13	14	14	13	12	12	11	12	12	12	13
London	15	13	11	12	12	11	12	11	13	13	15	15
Average number of rainy days per month												

Average daily maximum temperature °C											
London	6	7	10	13	17	20	22	21	19	14	10	7
Perth	29	29	27	24	21	18	17	18	19	21	24	27
	JAN	FEB	MAR	APR	MAY	JUN	JUL	AUG	SEP	OCT	NOV	DEC
Perth	3	3	5	8	15	17	19	19	15	12	7	5
London	15	13	11	12	12	11	12	11	13	13	15	15
Average number of rainy days per month												

Average daily maximum temperature °C											
London	6	7	10	13	17	20	22	21	19	14	10	7
Cairns	32	32	31	29	27	26	26	27	28	30	31	32
	JAN	FEB	MAR	APR	MAY	JUN	JUL	AUG	SEP	OCT	NOV	DEC
Cairns	16	16	19	15	12	10	8	8	7	7	10	12
London	15	13	11	12	12	11	12	11	13	13	15	15
Average number of rainy days per month												

Mardi Gras in March. The Royal Show at Easter has a cattle and rodeo theme, and the rest of the year is liberally sprinkled with many film and arts events, as well as the Sydney-to-Hobart yacht race on Boxing Day.

PACKAGE TRAVEL

ALL THE specialist tour operators offer a great deal of flexibility. The airfare will be a substantial part of the total cost, though some internal flights may be included with your flight to Australia.

As long-distance travel is likely it is wise to organise at least part of your holiday before you arrive. Travel and accommodation passes, car and camper-van hire, coach tours, short stop-over tours, self-drive itineraries, scenic train tours, day trips and adventure tours are all on offer. You can take part in activities such as walking, birdwatching, camping safaris, canoeing and diving on the Great Barrier Reef.

Tour operators

Coach tours: AAT Kings, Australian Pacific Tours **Flora**: Cox & Kings, David Sayers Travel **General and specialist**: Airtours, All-Ways Pacific, Austravel, Australia Affair, Bridge the World, British Airways Holidays, Cosmos, Jetabout, Jetset, Kuoni, Premier, Sunset Travel, Thomas Cook, Thomson, Tradewinds, Trailfinders, Travelbag, Travelmood, Travelpack **Walking/adventure**: Exodus, Explore Worldwide, Ramblers Holidays **Wildlife/birdwatching**: Abercrombie & Kent, Animal Watch, Cygnus Wildlife Holidays, Limosa, Naturetrek, Ornitholidays, Sunbird, Wildlife Worldwide **Wine**: Arblaster & Clarke, Winetrails **Other activities**: Ace Study Tours, Ffestiniog Travel (rail tours), Peregrine (horse-riding)

INDEPENDENT TRAVEL

MANY CHEAP flight deals exist, especially on charter flights (often cramped: you can pay more for leg-room). November to February is the most expensive time; April and May are the cheapest months. If you have lots of spare time, a round-the-world ticket can be an excellent option.

It is easiest to use internal airlines for national travel. Qantas and Ansett Australia are the two main carriers. Advance booking is strongly advised and can save you money, as can airpasses. Some have to be bought in advance before you reach Australia – check with the airlines.

Driving is the best way to appreciate the scale of Australia provided you have enough time and stamina for long stints at the wheel (it is

1,600 miles from Cairns to Sydney). Driving is on the left; a British driving licence with passport is acceptable. In the outback, plan your route carefully and keep to main roads – it's easy to get lost in the bush. Carry plenty of water, and stay with your vehicle if you break down.

The coach network is highly developed and the cheapest means of travelling, though the vast distances mean long hours. Greyhound-Pioneer offers an Aussie Pass giving unlimited travel for up to 60 days.

Railways link the main coastal cities and some inland towns. Trains are comfortable, but often slower and pricier than coaches. Passes are available to overseas travellers; some must be bought before you arrive.

Accommodation is in American-style comfortable hotel and motel chains. Budget backpacking hostels offer a wide accommodation network; standards vary. B&Bs and guesthouses are on offer, mostly in the south and east. In the outback, bush camping may be the only option.

RED TAPE, HEALTH AND SAFETY

BRITISH TOURISTS need a visa, which is free for visits of less than three months. Your travel agent should be able to arrange this for you, alternatively apply to the Australian High Commission in London (open 9am to 1pm, Monday to Friday) or the Consulate in Manchester (open 8.30am to 1pm, Monday to Friday). You will need a valid passport and should allow three to four weeks for processing.

No vaccinations are necessary, but take care in the sun (Australian rays are far stronger than those in northern Europe, and the country has one of the world's highest incidences of skin cancer). Flies and mosquitoes can be constant irritants during the summer: cover up arms and legs, especially at dusk and dawn, and take plenty of repellent. A sting from the poisonous box jellyfish can be fatal – steer clear of the beach when it is around (generally November to March, north of the Tropic of Capricorn).

MORE INFORMATION Australian Tourism Commission, Gemini House, 10–18 Putney Hill, Putney, London SW15 6AA, tel 0181-780 2227, web site: http://www.aussie.net.au

Australian High Commission, Australia House, Strand, London WC2B 4LA, tel 0171-887 5698, visa information (0891) 600333 (premium rate number)

Australian Consulate, Chatsworth House, Lever Street, Manchester M1 2QL, tel 0161-228 1344

COST OF LIVING £–££

AUSTRIA

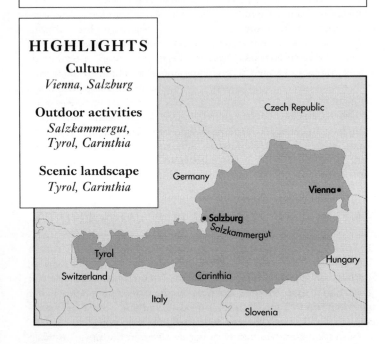

VIENNA
Good for culture

STATELY AVENUES, squares, palaces and museums make Vienna an excellent city for sightseeing. Many of Vienna's great cultural attractions – and traditional coffee houses – line the Ringstrasse (or Ring), a grand boulevard that follows the line of the former medieval city walls.

BEST SIGHTS

As well as the traditional 'sights' there are events such as the opera, and performances by the Vienna Boys' Choir and the Spanish Riding School. Getting tickets can be complicated, however: contact the tourist office for advice.

Belvedere
Baroque summer palace housing three museums: works by *Jugendstil* (Viennese art nouveau) artists such as Klimt, Schiele and Kokoschka in the Upper Belvedere; the Austrian Baroque Museum in the Lower Belvedere; and a good collection of medieval art in the Orangery.

Hofburg
The state rooms of this huge imperial palace recall Franz Josef's reign (1848-1916) – among them, his wife Elisabeth's 'gymnasium' appears incongruous. The Albertina has superb graphic art by Dürer, Klimt, Schiele and Rubens, while the *Schatzkammer*, or Treasury, displays the Crown of the Holy Roman Empire. The chapel is best seen during Sunday morning Mass, when the Vienna Boys' Choir sings. Alternatively, watch the Spanish Riding School in the Hofburg on Sunday morning.

Kunsthistorisches Museum
One of the world's greatest art collections, housed in one of a pair of monumental domed buildings on the Ring. The galleries contain paintings by Rubens, Cranach, Dürer and Holbein, and an excellent Italian section. On the ground floor are the Egyptian antiquities.

Schönbrunn Palace
The Habsburgs' summer palace, 20 minutes by underground or tram from the centre, has beautiful gardens. Tours of the state apartments cover 40 of the 1,500 rooms, including the Long Gallery and Hall of Mirrors.

Stephansdom
The cathedral's Gothic spire and roof of coloured tiles soar above the city at the heart of the Ring. The towers give great views; the north one allows a close-up look at the roof tiles. Below are the fascinating catacombs, where the intestines of the Habsburgs are stored.

SALZBURG
Good for culture

A BEAUTIFUL baroque city in a dramatic mountain setting, Salzburg is the product of 700 years of ecclesiastical rule, and its attractions are mainly architectural and cultural. It is also a paradise for music-lovers, as Mozart's birthplace and the home of the renowned Salzburg Festival.

BEST SIGHTS
Cathedral and Dommuseum
The stern stone exterior of the first Italianate baroque church north of the Alps belies the marble and stucco fripperies of the vast interior. Art-lovers should visit the Dommuseum, which has rare treasures ranging from an eighth-century Northumbrian cross to Gothic altarpieces.

Hellbrunn
About 15 minutes from the centre, Hellbrunn's main claim to fame is the water-spraying trickery of the fountains in its baroque garden.

Aquatic gags abound as the tour guides pull levers and press buttons to unleash the superb intricacies of the seventeenth-century plumbing.

Mönchsberg and the Hohensalzburg Fortress
One of the most pleasant ways of spending the day, in fine weather, is to take the funicular up the Mönchsberg cliff and visit the fortress, and then walk along the top where there is a path to the lift.

Mozart's birthplace
In a third-floor apartment on Getreidegasse, Mozart's birthplace is more a place of pilgrimage than a museum, with its stone stairway, a simple cold kitchen and barren floorboards. Family portraits and a few exhibits, including the violin he played as a child, are on display.

Residenz
The remains of the art collection of the Prince-Bishops contains paintings of the seventeenth- and eighteenth-century European schools hung in a classical setting of grand rooms. Guided tours of the state rooms are monotonous unless you have a good grasp of German.

SALZKAMMERGUT
Good for outdoor activities

THE SALZKAMMERGUT area, 12 miles east of Salzburg, is a region of gentle mountains and glistening lakes. It is easy to visit on day-trips from Salzburg – there are plenty of excursions, and public transport to the area is efficient.

BEST RESORTS
Hallstat
● Neatly tiered houses crowd the hillside and a sliver of flat land by a lake ringed by mountains.
● The town is a good base for exploring the Dachstein massif.

St Gilgen
● Pretty old town with painted stucco buildings and haphazard layout.
● Horses and traps whose drivers wear traditional dress are a feature.

BEST SIGHTS AND EXCURSIONS
Churches
The church at Mondsee, nicknamed 'Salzkammergut's Cathedral', merits a visit for its 13 superbly ornate altars, while that at St Wolfgang has an exquisitely carved winged altar by Gothic master Michael Pacher.

Dachstein Caves
Reached by cable-car, the caves are full of wonderful formations of stratified ice, including a complete ice chapel. Take a sweater.

BEST MOUNTAIN TRIPS

Dachsteinbahn
The cable-car to the glaciers rises in a single, unsupported loop to the top station on the rocky pinnacle of the Hunerkogel mountain.

Schafberg
The cog railway to the top of the Schafberg gives superb views over the lakes; the lovely walk back down takes about three hours.

TYROL
Good for outdoor activities and scenic landscape

MANY RESORTS are in the less beautiful eastern Tyrol, among bland towns such as Soll and Kirchberg. West of Innsbruck are higher and more spectacular mountains, emptier roads and undeveloped villages.

BEST RESORTS

Alpbach
● Peaceful, notably pretty resort bursting with flowers.
● Located in a rural valley near the rugged Kitzbüheler Alps.

Kitzbühel
● A large, busy town with solid, well-established hotels, picturesque churches and a skiing museum that is a shrine to local heroes.
● A chairlift and cable-car network provides easy access to the uplands.

Mayrhofen
● Big resort with large hotels, glossy shops and breathtaking scenery.

Obergurgl
● Quirky mix of traditional Tyrolean charm and hi-tech sophistication in the shape of gleaming hotels and futuristic cable-car stations.

BEST SIGHTS

Innsbruck
Stroll around the old centre, and watch for the shimmering Gothic 'Golden Roof' of copper tiles and the extravagantly rococo Helblinghaus. The Hofkirche houses 28 giant copper and bronze statues. The Tyrolean Folk Museum recreates old pine-panelled rooms and tiled stoves.

Rattenberg
Top of the tourist itinerary for its glassworks and the Höfemuseum, showing the different styles of building in the Tyrolean regions.

Schwaz
You can tour the remains of the silver mines – an entertaining two-hour trip on an electric train into the mountain through a tiny tunnel.

BEST MOUNTAIN TRIPS

Nordketterbahn
At the top you can look down to the man-tamed landscape of the Inn valley or north across the uninhabited Karwendelgebirge massif.

Pitztaler Gletscherbahn
You can reach the top of the Hinterer Brunnenkogel via cable-car and funicular for views of the Wildspitze, the highest mountain in the Tyrol.

Zugspitze
Staggering views down into Germany, where the Eibsee is a glistening mass of constantly changing colour.

CARINTHIA
Good for outdoor activities and scenic landscape

AUSTRIA'S SOUTHERNMOST province is an oval basin, its central lakes rimmed by mountains. Visit Romanesque churches, hill fortresses and Roman remains, or try Carinthia's ample outdoor sports facilities.

BEST RESORTS

Bad Kleinkirchheim
● High-altitude spa/ski resort, a refreshing change from lakeside resorts.

Millstatt
● Resort on the northern shore of Millstättersee, geographically divided in two by its small and intimate abbey.
● Quiet, yet very close to the motorway – a good base for touring.

Pörtschach
● On the largest lake of Wörthersee, Pörtschach is on a promontory.
● An attractive lakeside promenade is lined with hotels and restaurants.

St Veit an der Glan
● Peaceful fortress city with a medieval street plan and old town wall.
● The ornate town hall inhabits the main square.

BEST SIGHTS AND EXCURSIONS

Friesach and Gurk

The slopes around the town of Friesach contain many ruined churches and castles; Gurk's onion-domed cathedral is one of Austria's best-known Romanesque buildings.

Grossglockner Hochalpenstrasse

One of the first commercial Alpine roads to be built, this gives magnificent views of glacial scenery on a fine day.

Hochosterwitz

This imposing hilltop fortress with 14 towered gates contains displays of weapons and armour – be prepared for a stiff climb up to it.

Magdalensburg

At this excavated Roman settlement you can see remains of public baths, temples and a centrally heated villa. There is also a museum.

Maria Wörth

This small promontory, with two pretty churches on its tip, is popular as a photographic subject. Just south is the peak of Pyramidenkogel.

Spittal an der Drau

In the centre stands the Italianate Schloss Porcia, whose inner courtyard contains three tiers of superb Renaissance arcades.

WHEN TO GO

MAY, JUNE and September are good months to visit Vienna. In July and August you will miss the Spanish Riding School, the Vienna Boys' Choir and the opera. In winter it is easier to get tickets for the opera and other attractions, but be prepared for very cold weather.

Book accommodation early for the Salzburg Festival (late July–August) and for the similar, smaller-scale Easter and Whitsun Festivals.

Average daily maximum temperature °C											
London	6	7	10	13	17	20	22	21	19	14	10	7
Vienna	1	3	8	15	19	23	25	24	20	14	7	3
	JAN	FEB	MAR	APR	MAY	JUN	JUL	AUG	SEP	OCT	NOV	DEC
Vienna	15	14	13	13	13	14	13	13	10	13	14	15
London	15	13	11	12	12	11	12	11	13	13	15	15
Average number of rainy days per month											

In the high Alps, many hotels and facilities close after the skiing season (which lasts from December to early April), open in late May and close again in early October.

PACKAGE TRAVEL

THERE IS a wide choice of packages to resorts in the Tyrol, Carinthia and Salzkammergut. Single or two-centre holidays in mountain villages and towns let visitors make the most of facilities in the local area or use good public-transport links to explore further afield. Resorts offer a range of sporting activities, including organised walks, so unless you want a specialist holiday you will not necessarily need to book an activity package. Fly-drive packages and car hire can be arranged. Tour operators may use Munich airport as well as Innsbruck for holidays in the Tyrol. Accommodation is in hotels, guesthouses and self-catering farmhouses.

Most city-break tour operators go to Vienna and Salzburg; a few also feature Innsbruck and Graz in their brochures. Vienna can also be combined with other central European cities such as Budapest and Prague. Activity holidays focus on cycling, walking, music and birdwatching.

Tour operators

Birdwatching: Ornitholidays, Sunbird **Camping**: Canvas, Eurocamp, Eurosites, Keycamp, Select Sites **City breaks**: Bridgewater Travel, British Airways Holidays, Cresta, Crystal, DER, Hungarian Air Tours, Inghams, Made to Measure, Moswin, Osprey, Sovereign, Thomson, Time Off, Travelscene **Coach tours**: Bowens, Cosmos, Excelsior, Saga, Shearings, Travelsphere, Wallace Arnold **General and specialist**: Airtours, Austria Travel, Cosmos, Crystal, First Choice, Lakes & Mountains, Inghams, Thomas Cook, Thomson **Walking**: Exodus, HF Holidays, Inntravel, Ramblers Holidays, Sherpa, Waymark **Other activities**: Ace Study Tours, Anglo Dutch (cycling), Martin Randall (cultural), Prospect (music), Solo's Holidays (singles), Travel for the Arts (opera)

INDEPENDENT TRAVEL

IT IS easy to organise your own holiday. Scheduled flights go to Vienna and Salzburg, but western Austria is also easily reached via Munich in Germany, which has a bigger (and cheaper) choice of flights.

Taking your own car is quite feasible – the crossings to Belgium or Holland are the most convenient. Main roads are reliable, but tolls exist on many tunnels and on some scenic mountain roads. Many mountain passes are narrow and twisting, and may be barred to cars towing caravans. If taking your car over in spring, check its tyres, as some roads may still be snowy and icy. Use of seat-belts is compulsory, and drivers must carry a first-aid kit and warning triangle. All petrol is unleaded. If you are hiring a car, an international driving licence is recommended.

Electrified rail lines connect the main cities, and branch lines (some narrow-gauge and privately owned) run up side valleys. Trains are clean, comfortable and punctual, though fast expresses are few. Fares are high, but several value-for-money train passes are available – some give unlimited travel for a set number of days, others allow a set number of kilometres (useful if you intend to do only a few day-trips).

Even small villages usually have a yellow postbus service, to access the remotest corners, although long delays over short distances are common.

Standards of accommodation are high (though cheap city hotels can be basic). Hotels are graded from one to five stars, less formal guesthouses (*Gasthäuser*) from one to three stars. In country areas many hotels are built in an informal chalet style, but will often have up-to-date facilities such as swimming-pools and saunas. Pensions are graded separately from hotels, at one to three stars. They do not usually serve meals. Best value of all are rooms in private houses and farmhouses (look for *Zimmer frei* signs, or book through tourist offices).

Self-catering consists mainly of apartments in chalet-style buildings. Local tourist offices have lists. Campsites are usually well organised, with good facilities, though those near popular resorts can get very crowded.

RED TAPE, HEALTH AND SAFETY

BRITISH PASSPORT-HOLDERS do not need a visa.

Austria has no particular health or crime problems: just take the usual precautions (see pages 10–12).

MORE INFORMATION Austrian National Tourist Office, 30 St George Street, London W1R 0AL, tel 0171-629 0461, web site: http://austria-info.at/

COST OF LIVING £££

BELGIUM

North Sea

Netherlands

• Bruges   • Antwerp

• Ieper   • Ghent

• Tournai   • Brussels

France

Ardennes

HIGHLIGHTS

Culture
Brussels, Antwerp, Bruges

Family holidays
Ardennes

Food/wine
Brussels

History
Ieper

Local colour
Bruges, Ghent, Tournai

Nightlife
Antwerp

Outdoor activities/ scenic landscape
Ardennes

BRUSSELS
Good for culture and food/wine

DESPITE BRUSSELS' reputation as a dull centre of commerce and bureaucracy, the city contains some fine museums, a beautifully preserved medieval centre and some of Europe's best restaurants.

BEST SIGHTS

Cathedral
This fine Gothic church was begun in 1220 and has been restored many times. The wonderful stained glass in the transepts is sixteenth-century.

Grand Place
The indisputable centre of Brussels, this magnificent square was once a market-place. The elaborate façades of guildhouses and the Gothic

Hôtel de Ville make a great backdrop for a drink in one of the over-priced cafés.

Musées Royaux des Beaux Arts
Belgium's best fine-art collection occupies two linked museums: the Musée d'Art Ancien has works by Bruegel, Rubens and Cranach; the Musée d'Art Moderne has Belgian Surrealists Delvaux and Magritte.

Musée Victor Horta
This house, designed by Belgium's most famous architect, Victor Horta, is a marvellously fluid, sensuous example of art nouveau.

BRUGES
Good for culture and local colour

EVEN THOUGH Bruges heaves with tourists during the summer, its gloriously preserved medieval buildings and winding streets make it an unmissable destination.

BEST SIGHTS
Groeninge Museum
An outstanding collection of Flemish paintings. The early works, plus several paintings by Jan van Eyck, who lived and worked in Bruges, are the best of the collection.

Hans Memling Museum
The fifteenth-century artist's works are in the church of St Jan's Hospital.

Markt and Burg squares
These adjacent squares are the old town's focus. The Markt is lined with gabled buildings and the thirteenth-century Belfry; in the smaller Burg the Heilig Bloed Basiliek contains a phial of Holy Blood.

Onze Lieve Vrouwekerk
Huge church with a marble Madonna and Child by Michelangelo.

GHENT
Good for local colour

ALTHOUGH NOT as compact or well-preserved as nearby Bruges, Ghent has character, some fine medieval buildings and far fewer tourists than its neighbour.

BEST SIGHTS
St Baaf's Cathedral
Mostly Gothic church with a priceless early fifteenth-century altarpiece.

's Gravensteen
The imposing twelfth-century 'Castle of the Counts' is complete with battlements, arrow slits, narrow winding corridors and a dungeon.

ANTWERP
Good for culture and nightlife

ONCE ONE of the busiest ports in Europe, Antwerp is a gritty, lively city that has several excellent museums and an outstanding cathedral.

BEST SIGHTS AND EXCURSIONS
Museum voor Schone Kunsten
Eclectic collection housed in huge neo-classical building. Among the most important works are paintings by Rubens, Van Eyck and Matsys.

Onze Lieve Vrouwe Cathedral
One of Belgium's finest Gothic churches dates mainly from the fifteenth century and has a beautiful nave. Four works by Rubens hang here.

Rubenshuis
Impressively restored house of painter Peter Paul Rubens (1577-1640).

TOURNAI
Good for local colour

A RELAXED, low-key town dominated by its superb cathedral.

BEST SIGHT
Cathédrale Notre Dame
A wonderful, five-towered twelfth-century church, probably Belgium's finest example of Romanesque-Gothic architecture. It features exquisite transepts, some glorious paintings and an interesting treasury.

IEPER
Good for history

IEPER (YPRES), a once-prosperous medieval town, was ruined in the First World War. Some important old buildings have since been rebuilt.

BEST SIGHTS AND EXCURSIONS

First World War battlefields

The 43-mile '14-'18 Route takes in museums and many battle sites. However, beautifully kept cemeteries (like Tyne Cot near Zonnebeke) provide the most moving testament to the scale of the slaughter.

THE ARDENNES

Good for family holidays, outdoor activities and scenic landscape

A WORLD away from the flat industrial north and west, the Ardennes is a sparsely populated region of wooded hills and peaks, stunning river valleys and wild beauty. The Hohes Venn is the highest part, but the most popular, attractive areas and famous cave systems lie further west.

BEST SIGHTS

Dinant

This town is a centre for boat trips along the Meuse and for canoeing on the wilder Lesse. Its much fought-over citadel now contains a historical museum. The nearby Parc National de Furfooz is worth visiting.

Namur

The 'gateway to the Ardennes' is a pleasant town with several museums and the region's liveliest nightlife. A citadel stands where the Meuse and Sambre rivers meet. Its three main sections are the Terra Nova bastion, the imposing Donjon, and the Mediane works – part of a citadel to the east, including the stronghold of the Counts of Namur.

BEST RESORTS

Bouillon

● Resort attractively sited in a loop of the River Semois.
● Stunning castle, modified by Louis XIV's military engineer, Vauban.

Han-sur-Lesse

● Site of the most spectacular cave system in the Ardennes.
● Plenty of accommodation and restaurants but overrun in summer.
● In one of the region's most beautiful areas, offering great walking.
● Near a wild animal reserve with bison, bears and boar, the Belgian space and satellite station at Lessive and a château at Lavaux Ste-Anne.

La Roche-en-Ardenne

● A picturesque summer resort hidden away in the hills. It can be over-crowded with tourists in season.
● Topped with a ruined castle and at the centre of dramatic scenery.

Rochefort
● Less touristy than Han, with its own caves and access to country-side.

St-Hubert
● Popular resort in the most densely forested region of the Ardennes.
● Good base for gentle hiking and for a wild animal reserve (Parc à Gibier), an open-air museum of rural life and the Euro Space Centre.
● Fine sixteenth-century Gothic basilica.

Stavelot
● Small, pretty town in the eastern Ardennes, dominated by its abbey, and site of a lively annual carnival (third weekend before Easter).
● Close to famous (though not very interesting) health resort of Spa.

WHEN TO GO

CITY BREAKS are popular at any time of year. The Ardennes is crowded in July and August, when you should book accommodation in advance.

		Average daily maximum temperature °C											
London	6	7	10	13	17	20	22	21	19	14	10	7
Brussels	4	7	10	14	18	22	23	22	20	15	9	6
	JAN	FEB	MAR	APR	MAY	JUN	JUL	AUG	SEP	OCT	NOV	DEC
Brussels	21	17	17	18	16	15	17	18	13	17	20	19
London	15	13	11	12	12	11	12	11	13	13	15	15
		Average number of rainy days per month											

PACKAGE TRAVEL

MOST TOUR operators to Belgium offer city breaks to Bruges and Brussels for any number of nights by air, ferry, coach or rail (including Eurostar). Other choices outside the cities include self-catering holiday in a holiday park, B&B in the Ardennes, coach tours and accommodation in hotels and guesthouses throughout the country. Activity holidays include art and music tours, battlefield tours and wine tours.

Tour operators

City breaks: British Airways Holidays, Cresta, Crystal, Inghams, Kirker, Made to Measure, Osprey, Sovereign, Time Off, Travelscene, VFB **Coach tours**: Cosmos, Crusader, Excelsior, Leger, Shearings, Wallace Arnold **Special interest**: AA Motoring (hotel touring), Arblaster & Clarke (wine), Ffestiniog Travel (rail tours), Holts' Tours (battlefields), Inter-Church Travel (pilgimage), Martin Randall (art), Prospect (art, music) **Specialists**: Belgium Travel Service, Stena Line Holidays

INDEPENDENT TRAVEL

FREQUENT FLIGHTS run to Brussels from the UK, but it is easy (and cheap) to go via the Channel Tunnel on Eurostar. There are also ferry connections via Ostend.

The best way to explore Belgium is by train. The country's small size and the efficient and relatively cheap rail network mean that few places are more than a couple of hours from Brussels. Bruges, for example, is only one hour away. If you intend to travel extensively by train, a range of rail passes is available. In contrast, buses are mainly useful for travel within the towns and in some remoter parts of the Ardennes.

Travellers without a car will have most difficulty getting around in the Ardennes. Rail links are few, and sporadic bus services are often the only option. Cycling is a possibility. If you do not take your own cycle you can follow an excellent scheme run by Belgian railways that allows you to hire a bike from one railway station and return it to any other of your own choosing.

Car hire can be expensive. A British driving licence is accepted by car hire companies. Signposts can cause confusion, as all towns are referred to in Flemish in the north of the country and in French in the south.

In addition to hotels, cheaper private accommodation is also sometimes available and an extensive network of official and unofficial youth hostels operates, many with private and family rooms. Camping is a popular alternative: there are many well-equipped campsites in Belgium. These are graded from one to four stars. Another option is working holidays on farms. Tourist offices can supply leaflets on all these options and will book accommodation for you, usually without charge.

RED TAPE, HEALTH AND SAFETY

YOUR PASSPORT must be valid for three months beyond your date of departure from Belgium.

Belgium has no particular health or crime problems: just take the usual precautions (see pages 10–12).

MORE INFORMATION Belgian Tourist Office,
29 Princes Street, London W1R 7RG, tel 0171-629 1988, brochure line (0891) 887799 (premium rate number)

No tourist office web site exists, but you can access information about Belgium at: http://www.tourist-offices.org.uk/Belgium/index.html

COST OF LIVING £££

BOLIVIA

HIGHLIGHTS

Culture
Sucre, Potosi

History
Tiahuanaco

Romantic escapism
*The Yungas,
Lake Titicaca,
Salar de Uyuni*

Local colour
La Paz

Shopping
La Paz

Scenic landscape
*The Yungas,
Lake Titicaca,
Salar de Uyuni*

LA PAZ
Good for local colour and shopping

THE FIRST impression of La Paz is unforgettable, with the snow-capped Andean peaks in the distance and the pastel–coloured houses climbing up the edge of the steep canyon in which the city nestles. It provides a wonderful introduction to this diverse country, and is a good place in which to spend a few days acclimatising to the altitude – simply wander around and absorb the bustling atmosphere.

BEST LOCAL COLOUR

The market is a fine spot to observe local life. Traditionally dressed Indian women in bowler hats sell a wide range of Bolivian handicrafts.

BEST SIGHT
Museo Nacional de Arte
Housed in a beautiful Baroque palace, the museum boasts works of contemporary local artists as well as an impressive collection of colonial paintings. The city contains many other museums, two of which exhibit some of the best statues from the ancient site of Tiahuanaco.

TIAHUANACO
Good for history

TIAHUANACO IS thought to have been an Aymara ceremonial complex which existed at the heart of a large empire around the ninth century AD.

THE YUNGAS
Good for romantic escapism and scenic landscape

FOR THOSE adventurous enough to brave the terrifying roads leading to Coroico or Sorata, this lush mountainous region, verging on the edge of the Amazon basin, is a tranquil haven. It is a place to relax, admire the wonderful views and enjoy the semi-tropical climate. Many pleasant walks can be taken through the orange and banana groves that cover the mountainside.

LAKE TITICACA
Good for romantic escapism and scenic landscape

THIS CALM, beautiful inland sea, at a height of nearly 13,000 feet, is the highest navigable water in the world. From the pleasant town of Copacabana, boats take visitors out to the unspoilt Islas del Sol and de la Luna where you can spend the night. The tranquillity and the vistas across the still blue waters which reflect the distant mountains are magical.

SUCRE
Good for culture

NAMED IN 1825 after the first president of the new Republic, Sucre is the official capital of Bolivia. It is a pretty city where all the buildings in the centre are traditionally painted white.

BEST SIGHTS

Casa de la Libertad
Elegant buildings surround the central square, where Bolivia's Declaration of Independence was signed in 1825.

Ecclesiastical buildings
Sucre's cathedral and the monasteries of La Recoleta and San Felipe Neri are worth a visit.

POTOSI
Good for culture

THIS PICTURESQUE city has narrow, winding streets, much colonial architecture and Baroque churches. You can visit the Mint here.

BEST SIGHT

Potosi mines
The mines have been worked since the sixteenth century, yielding silver, copper, lead and now mostly tin. Meet the miners and witness the harsh conditions endured by many of Potosi's inhabitants – it is a fascinating, if rather disheartening and claustrophobic experience.

SALAR DE UYUNI
Good for romantic escapism and scenic landscape

EMERGING FROM this vast and surreal dried-up salt lake, or *salar*, are curious 'islands' covered in giant cacti.

BEST EXCURSION

An extraordinary four-day journey from Uyuni by jeep past the *salar,* onward through phenomenal scenery to the Chilean border and back. The trip across the desert takes in salt flats, geysers, volcanoes and the startling jade-coloured Laguna Verde and Laguna Colorado, dotted with hundreds of pink flamingoes. Conditions are harsh: go well-prepared with plenty of food, water, warm clothes and good company.

WHEN TO GO

THE BEST time to visit Bolivia is from May to November during the dry season. June and August are the coldest months. Warm clothing is essential at all times of year, and you should always be prepared for the drastic changes in temperature, which can plummet as low as -25°C.

		JAN	FEB	MAR	APR	MAY	JUN	JUL	AUG	SEP	OCT	NOV	DEC
Average daily maximum temperature °C													
	London	6	7	10	13	17	20	22	21	19	14	10	7
	La Paz	17	17	18	18	18	17	17	17	18	19	19	18
		JAN	FEB	MAR	APR	MAY	JUN	JUL	AUG	SEP	OCT	NOV	DEC
	La Paz	21	18	16	9	5	2	2	4	9	9	11	18
	London	15	13	11	12	12	11	12	11	13	13	15	15
Average number of rainy days per month													

PACKAGE TRAVEL

ONLY A few specialist tour operators offer a variety of holidays in Bolivia. Most feature the country as part of a two-week tour in combination with Peru and/or Chile, allocating around four or five days for exploring the north of the country including La Paz, the Inca ruins by Lake Titicaca, the Island of the Sun and Copacabana.

Specialists offer tailor-made tours with suggested itineraries that include Sucre, Potosi and the Yungas region. Spectacular rail journeys from Santa Cruz to the Brazilian border and four-wheel-drive exploration of the salt flats around Uyuni can also be arranged as inclusive tours.

Accommodation ranges from de luxe city hotels and comfortable town hotels to very basic accommodation with primitive facilities and camping on more adventurous trips. Special interest holidays include mountain biking, trekking, wildlife and adventure camping trips.

Tour operators

Adventure: Encounter Overland, Kumuka Expeditions **General**: Bales Tours, Cox & Kings, Kuoni, Voyages Jules Verne **Mountain biking**: KE Adventure **Specialists**: Austral Tours, Journey Latin America, Nomadic Thoughts, Passage to South America, South American Experience, Travel South America, Union Castle Travel **Walking**: Exodus, Explore Worldwide, Guerba **Wildlife**: Animal Watch

---

INDEPENDENT TRAVEL

BOLIVIANS ARE not the friendliest or most helpful of South Americans and as a tourist you will often encounter an aloof, disinterested manner in the people you come across. However alienating this may be, it can come as a welcome change to the constant attention one tends to attract in most other countries on the continent. An even greater advantage is the distinct sense of safety their indifference generates. Bolivia not only *feels* safe but *is* one of the safest countries in South America.

Bolivia is extremely popular with travellers since it is cheap and relatively easy to get around. Many buses ply between the main tourist destinations, and although the roads are poor (especially during the rainy season), the scenery is breathtaking and the distances endurable. Train routes connect Bolivia with neighbouring Brazil, Argentina and Chile. Flights are cheap, but since much of Bolivia's appeal lies in the dramatically changing landscape, overland travel is really the only way to appreciate the country.

Simple accommodation is easy to find in most places, but more upmarket hotels should be booked in advance.

RED TAPE, HEALTH AND SAFETY

WITH THE exception of Canadian and French citizens, most nationalities do not require a visa and will be granted three months on entry into Bolivia.

The main health complaint suffered by travellers is caused by the altitude and it is vital on arrival in the Andes to take time to acclimatise and not over-exert yourself – see page 10 for hints on combating the symptoms. To avert stomach problems be sure to avoid tap water, ice and salads at all times.

Inoculations against typhoid and hepatitis are recommended, as are malaria tablets if you are visiting the lowlands. Yellow fever inoculations are also required if you arrive from an 'infected' country (not if you go direct from the UK).

MORE INFORMATION Tourist Department, Bolivian Embassy, 106 Eaton Square, London SW1W 9AD, tel 0171-235 4248/2257

COST OF LIVING £

BRAZIL

HIGHLIGHTS

Beaches *Rio de Janeiro, North-east Brazil*	**Scenic landscape** *Rio de Janeiro, Iguaçu Falls*	**Culture** *Rio de Janeiro, Ouro Prêto, Salvador, Olinda*	**Flora/ wildlife** *The Amazon, the Pantanal*
Local colour *North-east Brazil*	**Nightlife** *Rio de Janeiro*	**Food/wine** *North-east Brazil*	**Romantic escapism** *Ouro Prêto, Praia do Forte*

RIO DE JANEIRO
Good for beaches, culture, nightlife and scenic landscape

THE BUZZING atmosphere on the streets is one of Rio's biggest attractions – never more so than during the February carnival. As the archetypal city of extremes, however, Rio is not for the faint-hearted.

BEST SIGHTS AND EXCURSIONS
Folklore Museum
A small but excellent museum devoted to folk art from all over Brazil.

Santa Teresa
This hilltop district contains lovely colonial architecture, and is blissfully quiet by Rio standards. The tram ride through cobbled streets to get there is part of the fun.

Viewpoints
Sugar Loaf Mountain and the Corcovado (crowned with the much-photographed statue of Christ) are the two places that every tourist visits – for their superb views over the city. Expect crowds unless you go early or late in the day.

BEST BEACHES
Copacabana
The beach at Copacabana is not so much the focal point as the setting: this is a place to people-watch as much as swim or sunbathe – as long as you can cope with the hawkers. At night, Rio's most outrageous nightclubs come into their own.

Costa Verde
If you want to escape the hubbub of Rio, there are lovely beaches along the Costa Verde to the west.

Ipanema and Leblon
These adjacent beaches are more chic but not as fun as Copacabana. The sand is cleaner and the atmosphere more relaxed.

THE SOUTHERN INTERIOR
Good for culture, flora, romantic escapism, scenic landscape and wildlife

BEST SIGHTS
Brasilia
Brazil's space-age capital is a curiosity rather than a must-see destination. Located miles from anywhere, it might appeal to those interested in 1950s architecture but is otherwise best left alone.

Ouro Prêto
The best of a remarkable group of colonial towns set in the lush hills of Minas Gerais state, Ouro Prêto is chock-a-block with beautifully preserved mansions and churches and was once a gold and diamond mining centre. While dangerously close to being a living museum, with its lovely hotels and restaurants Ouro Prêto is a relaxing place to stay and a good base for exploring the nearby towns.

BEST SCENIC LANDSCAPE
Iguaçu Falls
These magnificent waterfalls spanning the Brazilian–Argentinian border are higher than Niagara and broader than the Victoria Falls. The best overall view is on the Brazilian side, but for a close-up view of the Falls and surrounding jungle you should nip over to Argentina. The Falls are at their most dramatic in summer.

BEST WILDLIFE
The Pantanal
This vast swamp has more wildlife than anywhere else in Brazil, and it is pleasantly easy to observe. The birdlife is particularly rich, including everything from macaws to emus. Safaris are by truck, foot, canoe or horseback, and sleeping arrangements are usually very basic.

NORTH-EAST BRAZIL
Good for beaches, culture, food/wine and local colour

BEST SIGHTS AND EXCURSIONS
Cachoeira
An easy overnight excursion from Salvador, Cachoeira is one of Brazil's most atmospheric colonial towns – thanks partly to its state of picturesque decay.

Olinda
This delightful place, overlooking the ocean near Recife, boasts some of the nation's best-preserved colonial architecture. Would-be guides pester tourists, but they do not ruin the place.

Salvador
The African flavour is strong in Salvador, visible in the city's music and dance, religion and wonderful food. Tourists pour in to explore its cobbled streets and admire its colonial architecture, but this city is as chaotic as it is entrancing, and some people find it unnerving.

BEST BEACHES
Fine sandy beaches line much of the north-east coast, but many have not been developed for tourism. Salvador and Fortaleza offer about the liveliest beach scene in the north-east, but if you are more interested in the quality of the sand and peace and quiet, head out of the cities.

Ilha de Tinharé
South of Salvador, this island's magnificent beaches are among the best in Brazil. The growing crowd of trendy Brazilians and foreign tourists

mostly gather around the once quiet fishing village of Morro de São Paulo.

Praia do Forte
North of Salvador, Praia do Forte has miles of glorious beaches and is perfect for a week away from it all – particularly with the improved facilities of the developing resort.

BEST CARNIVAL
Rio's carnival is best-known, but experts assert that carnival is better in Salvador, Recife and Olinda – thanks to the strong African influence.

THE AMAZON
Good for flora and wildlife

YOU SHOULD not go to the Amazon just for the varied scenery or for guaranteed sightings of exotic wildlife or indigenous people. Go expecting an adventure and a taste of the mystery of Amazonia and you should not be disappointed.

BEST BASES
Belém
The departure point for boat services up the Amazon River, Belém is the most attractive city in the Amazon and deserves a day's exploration.

Manaus
The only reason to go to Manaus, a shabby, million-strong city in the heart of the Amazon, is to organise a trip into the rainforest (though many Brazilians come for the duty-free shops). You need at least four days to make a jungle trip worthwhile.

WHEN TO GO

IN THE Amazon it is hot and wet most of the year, but it is the high humidity which causes most discomfort. The seasons are much more defined in the southern states, where summers are hot and winters cool. It can rain at any time, but the wettest months are between October and April (during the Brazilian summer). The incessant rains and extreme heat make the Pantanal off-limits during the peak of the wet season. Generally, though, Brazil is a year-round destination.

Many Brazilians are on holiday from December to February, when seats on planes and buses get booked up.

Anyone thinking of visiting in February but who is not interested in the carnival should consider changing their plans: during the carnival chaos reigns, hotels are full and flights are heavily oversubscribed.

	Average daily maximum temperature °C											
London	6	7	10	13	17	20	22	21	19	14	10	7
Rio de Janeiro	29	29	28	27	25	24	24	24	24	25	26	28
	JAN	FEB	MAR	APR	MAY	JUN	JUL	AUG	SEP	OCT	NOV	DEC
Rio de Janeiro	13	11	12	10	10	7	7	7	11	13	13	14
London	15	13	11	12	12	11	12	11	13	13	15	15
	Average number of rainy days per month											

PACKAGE TRAVEL

GENERAL TOUR operators offer holidays in Rio de Janeiro with excursions to the Iguaçu Falls, or two-week tours of Brazil's highlights also taking in Manaus and maybe Brasilia, Salvador or the Pantanal close to the western border of Brazil. Specialists offer more flexibility and more options such as two or three days in jungle lodges around Manaus observing wildlife, the colonial mining town of Ouro Prêto, exploring offshore islands around Paraty, or breaks to Natal beach.

Accommodation varies considerably according to budget, from luxurious, colourful *pousadas* (guesthouses) to simple or basic accommodation in jungle lodges. Activity holidays include walking, cruising expeditions on the Amazon, birdwatching and wildlife holidays in the Pantanal swamplands or Amazon jungle.

Tour operators

Adventure: Explore Worldwide, Guerba **Birdwatching**: Limosa **Cruising**: Abercrombie & Kent **General**: Bales Tours, British Airways Holidays, Cox & Kings, Hayes & Jarvis, Kuoni **Inclusive**: Club Med **Specialists**: Journey Latin America, Nomadic Thoughts, Passage to South America, South American Experience, Travel South America, Union Castle Travel **Wildlife**: Animal Watch, Wildlife Worldwide

INDEPENDENT TRAVEL

THERE ARE direct flights to Rio from the UK, but you can save money by taking an indirect route – by changing, for example, in

Madrid or a US city. Flights direct to Recife are worth considering if you are interested only in the north-east.

Brazil covers an area larger than Europe so flying is the only sensible way to get around if you are not planning a one-centre holiday. Air passes cut the price of internal flights, but these must be purchased outside Brazil. Shop around if you are buying individual fares, and you will get a better deal if you buy ahead. Brazil has a couple of scenic train rides, but otherwise rail services are minimal. The buses, on the other hand, are excellent. Services between cities are frequent and often non-stop, and there are sleeper (*leito*) services too, which are worth considering for long journeys. Think carefully before hiring a car. In the big cities, traffic and theft are real problems. The main roads are generally in reasonable shape, particularly along the coast and in the south.

There are scheduled boat services along the Amazon between Belém and Manaus. These provide a glimpse of life on the river, but to really explore the Amazon you must go on an organised trip. In Manaus umpteen agencies and guides compete for tourists' custom, so it is a good idea to get a recommendation. Organised trips are the best option in the Pantanal too.

The words 'hotel' and '*pousada*' (guesthouse), the most common forms of lodgings in Brazil, are used to describe anything from a smart resort hotel to a fleapit. In cities with beaches, the hotels in the beach areas tend to be more expensive but are closer to bars and restaurants. Some surprisingly comfortable lodges are on offer in the Amazon, but normally you will have to sleep in a hammock or in a simple shelter.

RED TAPE, HEALTH AND SAFETY

UK CITIZENS do not require a visa but must show on arrival: a passport valid for six months; a return or outward ticket; and proof of means of subsistence.

The chief health risks are malaria (which affects inland areas including the Amazon, the Pantanal and the Iguaçu Falls), dengue fever and yellow fever. See your GP or a travel clinic before departure and ensure that you are inoculated against hepatitis A, polio and typhoid. In the coastal cities, the main threat to your health is from the tap water – especially in the north-east – so drink bottled water. Also in the northeast, watch out for *bichos de pé*, which are small parasites that live in the sand and burrow into people's feet.

Petty theft is a problem in all the large Brazilian cities – especially Rio, Salvador and Manaus – and you should be particularly watchful on city buses and on the beach. Follow the precautions on page 12 and take particular care during carnival time.

MORE INFORMATION Tourist Information Department, Brazilian Embassy, 32 Green Street, London W1Y 4AT, tel 0171-499 0877 ext. 218, web site: http://www.embratur.gov.br

COST OF LIVING £

BRITAIN

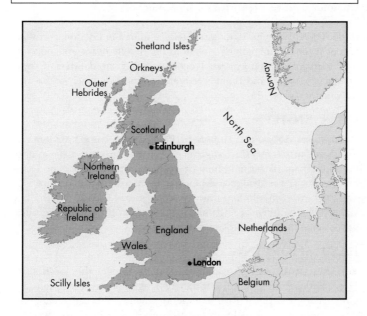

HIGHLIGHTS

History
*Stonehenge,
Hadrian's
Wall, Midlands*

Beaches
*Brighton,
Bournemouth,
Torquay,
Scarborough*

Nightlife
London

Culture
*London,
southern
England,
central and
northern
England, Wales*

**Outdoor
activities**
*Eastern and
northern
England*

**Family
holidays**
*Southern
England*

Flora
*Eastern
England*

Wildlife
*Eastern
England,
Scotland*

**Scenic
landscape**
*Lake District,
Yorkshire
Dales, west
coast of
Scotland,
Cotswolds,
Scilly Isles,
Wales*

Shopping
London

SOMETIMES IT is all too easy to overlook the possibilities on our own doorstep when we are trying to decide on a holiday destination. The pages that follow are a brief reminder of some of them.

LONDON
Good for culture, nightlife and shopping

FOR ANYONE who is not afraid to be a tourist in London, Piccadilly Circus is the hub of activity – right in the middle of theatreland, close to the major shopping areas, Regent Street, Oxford Street, Covent Garden, Piccadilly and Bond Street, and within easy reach of the capital's major sights.

BEST SIGHTS
Westminster Abbey, the Houses of Parliament, Nelson's Column in Trafalgar Square and Buckingham Palace (for the daily Changing of the Guard) are all within a mile or so of Piccadilly Circus. The Tower of London, Tower Bridge and Docklands are a short bus or tube ride away. Art lovers should find time for the National Gallery and the Tate Gallery. Kew Gardens, a few miles south-west of the city centre, offers green acres and a superb plant collection.

BEST SHOPPING
You can walk from Piccadilly to Knightsbridge, the location of Harrods department store, through two of London's prettiest parks: Green Park and Hyde Park. For trendy, slightly alternative shopping head south from Knightsbridge to the Kings Road, or west to Kensington High Street. The Natural History Museum with its spectacular dinosaurs and whales is also in this area.

SOUTHERN ENGLAND
Good for beaches, culture and family holidays

THE SOUTH of England has a fair number of elegant cities, rolling countryside and resorts.

BEST RESORTS
Summer visitors might choose to visit Bournemouth, Brighton or Torquay, or seek out the beaches of Cornwall or the Scilly Isles for a longer stay at the seaside.

BEST TOWNS
Bath
The Romans developed baths from springs discovered here by the Celts. Georgian architects later embellished this spa town with sandstone terraces and Palladian façades. Its elegant shops are another attraction.

Winchester

Once Alfred the Great's capital, this serene city has medieval buildings, Georgian streets and a superb cathedral, the site of Jane Austen's grave.

Windsor

For royal enthusiasts, Windsor, with its castle and extensive park, merits a visit. Just a short walk across the river Thames lies Eton College, one of the oldest schools in Britain.

BEST SIGHT

Stonehenge

Europe's most famous prehistoric site is in Wiltshire, and is thought to date from about 3000 BC. Its origins and its enormous scale have amazed and baffled historians and visitors for centuries. If you are fascinated by prehistoric man, Avebury Stone Circle, Old Sarum and Silbury Hill are other ancient sites worth visiting in the region.

SOUTHERN CENTRAL ENGLAND
Good for culture and scenic landscape

THIS AREA of great variety is ideally suited to touring.

BEST SIGHTS

Blenheim Palace

Not far from Oxford on the edge of the small town of Woodstock stands Blenheim Palace, home of the Duke of Marlborough and birthplace of Sir Winston Churchill. This superb baroque palace, designed by Vanbrugh, is surrounded by a vast park and gardens.

Oxford

Oxford makes an excellent base for the area and is worth a couple of days sightseeing itself. The university colleges are magnificent buildings dotted around the city dating from the fifteenth century. The town also boasts excellent shops and museums.

BEST SCENIC LANDSCAPE

The Cotswolds, a band of gently rolling limestone hills that cut across Gloucestershire, offer a very English experience of picturesque, manicured villages, teashops and beautiful countryside. Many houses are built of the attractive local honey-coloured stone. Hotels and restaurants abound throughout this area.

EASTERN ENGLAND
Good for flora/wildlife, outdoor activities and scenic landscape

EAST ANGLIA is a region often bypassed by tourists but has much to offer. The north coast of Norfolk is popular with birdwatchers, while the Norfolk Broads offer one of the largest inland boating areas in Britain.

BEST TOWNS
Cambridge
Take a punt out on the river Cam to enjoy views of the city's 31 university colleges. Peterhouse is the oldest, dating from the thirteenth century, and the most recent, Robinson, was built in 1979. A tour of the colleges is an instructive architectural experience.

Norwich
From the soaring grandeur of the cathedral to the microcosm of world art at the Sainsbury Centre, this fine ancient city is well worth a visit.

BEST SCENIC LANDSCAPE

John Constable, one of England's most famous landscape artists, lived and took inspiration from the countryside around Dedham and Colchester in Essex. Further north, in Suffolk, villages such as Lavenham and Southwold, once at the heart of the country's old wool trade, are some of the prettiest in Britain.

NORTHERN ENGLAND
Good for culture, outdoor activities and scenic landscape

THE NORTH of England contains the country's wildest scenery, interspersed with the major industrial cities.

BEST RESORT
Scarborough
This handsome Regency/Victorian town is 25 miles north-east of York. A popular seaside resort, it offers:
● a sandy beach with full resort amenities at the South Bay
● the quieter, more genteel North Bay.

BEST CITIES
Bradford
In this gruff industrial city, now becoming rejuvenated, explore the quirky high-tech museums and the Victorian village, or sample the famous Indian restaurants.

Leeds

England's third-largest city has a proud industrial past, reflected in its handsome civic buildings. It boasts impressive art galleries and museums and houses the Royal Armouries collection.

York

If time is short, head straight for York. The glorious York Minster dominates this ancient and beautiful city. A tour of the city walls shows you the Roman, Anglo-Saxon and Viking elements of the city. Two of the best of many excellent sights are the National Railway Museum and the Jorvik Viking Centre.

BEST SIGHT

Hadrian's Wall

The Roman emperor Hadrian constructed the wall in AD 120 to keep out the wild Northern tribes. It stretches a remarkable 73½ miles from the River Tyne in Newcastle to the Solway Firth in Cumbria, effectively dividing Scotland from England.

BEST SCENIC LANDSCAPE

Lake District

In the north-west is the Lake District, a 30-mile-long tract of lake and fell-land offering some of the most rewarding and beautiful walking, boating and touring in England. The area was a source of inspiration for William Wordsworth and other Romantic poets.

North York Moors

Head north to the wild expanses of the North York Moors and relish the views from the Cleveland Way path. Further west, the Yorkshire Dales offer gentler landscape. Throughout North Yorkshire, charming market towns and villages, splendid houses, castles and gardens blend with the magnificent scenery, making this a great touring destination.

THE MIDLANDS
Good for culture, history and scenic landscape

THE MIDLANDS area saw the birth of the Industrial Revolution, but its many historic towns are never far from superb countryside.

BEST TOWNS

Ludlow

Shropshire's most prominent town grew up around a Norman fortress. The surrounding area is rich in hill-top settlements and castles, dating from the Iron Age to medieval times.

Stratford-upon-Avon

This town of half-timbered buildings, giftshops and tea-rooms enthusiastically exploits its connection with William Shakespeare. Visit the playwright's birthplace and Anne Hathaway's cottage, or see a play at the Royal Shakespeare Theatre, if tickets are available.

BEST SIGHT

Ironbridge Gorge

Ironbridge Gorge played an important role in the Industrial Revolution. The Ironbridge Museum (a total of seven sites spread over seven miles) is outstanding and should not be missed.

BEST SCENIC LANDSCAPE

The Peak District National Park

The Park, spanning Staffordshire and Derbyshire, offers a wonderful variety of landscapes: the Dark Peak on the eastern side occupies three-quarters of the Park with its tracts of lonely moorland and craggy heights, while the softer White Peak in the south is limestone country. Dales and river valleys cut into the rolling hills and small grey-stone villages dot the landscape.

Just outside Bakewell, magnificent Chatsworth House, home of the Duke of Devonshire, can be visited in summer.

WALES
Good for culture and scenic landscape

WALES HAS a distinct heritage and language, rooted in the country's Celtic past. English occupation in the Middle Ages bequeathed a string of castles, and the superb scenery extends from the industrialised valleys of the south to the mountains of Snowdonia.

BEST SCENIC LANDSCAPE

Welsh Marches

The border country between England and Wales is known as the Welsh Marches. It is marked for some of its length by Offa's Dyke, built between AD 757 and 796 by the King of Mercia. Langollen, at the northern end of the marches, is an attractive town bisected by the River Dee and the venue for the annual International Eisteddfod in August – a music competition of global renown. Look out for the remarkable Pontcysyllte Aqueduct a few miles south-east.

Further south, Hay-on-Wye is a mecca for book-lovers with 25 bookshops and allegedly over 21 miles of shelving. Tintern Abbey, immortalised by William Wordsworth, is one of the furthermost landmarks of the southern marches just north of Chepstow.

Snowdonia

The mountains of Snowdonia are some of the highest and most dramatic in the country, but surprisingly accessible. You could stay in the refined resort of Llandudno yet be in the heart of Snowdonia within the hour. For history, head for the Menai Straits and Caernarfon. The castle built by Edward I is the traditional site of investiture of the Princes of Wales; Prince Charles was enthroned here in 1969.

SCOTLAND
Good for scenic landscape and wildlife

THE TWO obvious destinations in Scotland – and you can fly to both – are the country's major cities: Edinburgh and Glasgow.

Exploring central Scotland will reveal the story of Scotland's turbulent past. However, if you seek the wild, sometimes desolate beauty of Scotland, you should head for the west coast and follow it all the way up to Cape Wrath. If you take the train to Fort William and set off towards the Kyle of Lochalsh you can now drive straight on to the Isle of Skye.

BEST CITIES
Edinburgh
Edinburgh, predominantly medieval and Georgian in architecture, is traditionally the more attractive and refined city, but its supremacy in the arts has recently been challenged by Glasgow. Edinburgh's annual international arts festival, both mainstream and fringe, attracts thousands of visitors every August. The excellent National Gallery of Scotland and the National Gallery of Modern Art are both here.

Glasgow
Glasgow, a Victorian industrial town voted European City of Culture in 1990, has a number of exceptional museums; the Burrell Collection a few miles from the centre and the Kelvingrove Gallery housed within the University are two of the best.

BEST SIGHTS
Dundee
For anyone keen on industrial history, Dundee is one of the most interesting Scottish cities. The manufacture of jute and jam contributed great riches to the city and its inhabitants in the Victorian era.

Perth
Perth, a Roman city, is about 25 miles north-west of Stirling. It is built around the River Tay with pedestrianised areas and renovated Georgian

terraces. Its historical significance is reinforced by the proximity of Scone Abbey, where generations of Scottish kings were crowned.

Stirling
Stirling has an imposing castle and a memorial to Robert Bruce, who perpetrated his famous victory against the forces of Edward II at near-by Bannockburn.

BEST SCENIC LANDSCAPE
Handa Island
Handa Island, a must for ornithologists, is reached by tiny ferry from Tarbet a few miles north of Scourie. Walks from Kinlochbervie, the most northern fishing port on this coast, bring you to some stunning beaches, the somewhat inaccessible Sandwood Bay being the best.

Outer Hebrides, Orkneys and Shetlands
A trip from the mainland to the Outer Hebrides, the Orkneys or the Shetland Islands requires a little extra planning, but their windswept appeal is irresistible. Orkney and Shetland are rich in prehistoric sites and seabird colonies. Some crofters still follow a traditional farming lifestyle, and local crafts include silverwork and knitwear.

Skye
A beautiful island but best seen in clear weather, so if the elements are against you head on to the Applecross Peninsula for some memorable views.

Ullapool
Ullapool is an attractive centre on the way north and the last reason-able-sized town on the west coast. From here on the roads become narrower and the scenery increasingly dramatic. A detour not to missed is the road out to Achiltibuie and the Summer Isles; then snake on round the coast joining the main road at Lochinver.

THEME PARKS IN BRITAIN

BRITAIN NOW has over 30 theme parks, and the six listed below are particularly worth a visit.

Alton Towers, Staffordshire
Alton Towers is one of Britain's largest theme parks, with over 125 rides and attractions in beautiful grounds, including Nemesis, the Black Hole, the Corkscrew and the Log Flume. The park has tamer rides for children and those with weaker stomachs, also a show on ice and a 3D cinema.

Blackpool Pleasure Beach, Lancashire

One of Europe's biggest theme parks, Blackpool Pleasure Beach has over 150 rides, including the terrifying Big One rollercoaster, Swamp buggies and the Grand National.

Crinkley Bottom at Cricket St Thomas, Somerset

As well as a wildlife park, Crinkley Bottom also includes a heavy horse centre, playground and woodland railway. Children will enjoy Blobbyland.

Oakwood Adventure Park, Dyfed

As well as mini-golf and a bobsleigh ride, Oakwood Adventure Park also has a play area with bouncers, slides and a spider's web, plus Jake's Town with goldmine, trading post and music hall.

Thorpe Park, Surrey

Thorpe Park is the home of Depth Charge, the UK's first four-lane waterslide, as well as the Flying Fish rollercoaster and Carousel Kingdom.

Wonderwest World, Strathclyde

This Butlins-owned theme park features Wondersplash sub-tropical waterworld and over 25 funfair rides.

Average daily maximum temperature °C

	JAN	FEB	MAR	APR	MAY	JUN	JUL	AUG	SEP	OCT	NOV	DEC
London	6	7	10	13	17	20	22	21	19	14	10	7
Edinburgh	6	6	8	11	14	17	18	18	16	12	9	7
Edinburgh	17	15	15	14	14	15	17	16	16	17	17	18
London	15	13	11	12	12	11	12	11	13	13	15	15

Average number of rainy days per month

Average daily maximum temperature °C

	JAN	FEB	MAR	APR	MAY	JUN	JUL	AUG	SEP	OCT	NOV	DEC
London	6	7	10	13	17	20	22	21	19	14	10	7
Cardiff	7	7	10	13	16	19	20	21	18	14	10	8
Cardiff	18	14	13	13	13	13	14	15	16	16	17	18
London	15	13	11	12	12	11	12	11	13	13	15	15

Average number of rainy days per month

CANADA

HIGHLIGHTS

Beaches
*British
Columbia,
Atlantic
provinces*

**Flora/
wildlife**
*British
Columbia*

Culture
*Ontario,
Quebec,
Atlantic
provinces*

**Outdoor
activities**
*British
Columbia*

Nightlife
*Ontario,
Quebec*

**Family
holidays**
*British
Columbia,
Ontario,
Quebec*

Food/wine
Quebec

**Scenic
landscape**
*British
Columbia,
Atlantic
provinces*

BRITISH COLUMBIA
**Good for beaches, family holidays, flora, outdoor activities,
scenic landscape and wildlife**

BRITISH COLUMBIA (BC) advertises its attractions as 'Super
Natural British Columbia'. With over 16,000 miles of coastline and
countless inland lakes and rivers, boating, canoeing, fishing, cruising,
and just plain sightseeing are easy and affordable practically anywhere.

You can also experience the peace of the great forest on the plentiful hiking trails. Just driving up the main highway east to Alberta, on
the first stretch of the 4,970-mile Trans-Canada Highway through the
Fraser River Canyon, will give you an idea of the majestic landscape.

BEST SIGHTS

Banff and Jasper National Parks

The former is Canada's oldest national park. It is as large as Lincolnshire, while the even bigger Jasper, at 4,000 square miles, is less crowded and developed. The main attractions here are scenic: majestic mountains, lakes and valleys. Wildlife-spotting is good too, with bighorn sheep frequently on the road and mountain goats on the peaks. Deer, bear, moose and eagles are among the fauna you can, and must, admire from a distance. The Columbia Icefields straddle both parks, and you can travel on these huge glaciers by snowcoach.

The province of Alberta is Canada's Wild West. Its major cities, Edmonton and Calgary, are nearby and worth visiting for the former's Klondike Days and the latter's famous Stampede.

Vancouver

Canada's third-largest city – its most booming by far – enjoys a dramatically scenic location between the imposing Rockies and the outlet of the Fraser River into the Pacific Ocean. A bus or trolley tour will show you the main attractions, such as the photogenic inlet of Kettle Creek, the expanding Chinatown, the trendy village of Gastown, and the sandy beaches of Spanish Banks. At the scenic campus of the University of British Columbia on Point Grey Cliffs, the Museum of Anthropology is the finest research collection of aboriginal artefacts in North America, including a captivating assembly of heavily carved totem poles and ceremonial masks.

Only five minutes from downtown lies Stanley Park, one of North America's finest natural parks with lots of amusements for children. Both adults and children will enjoy a drive over Lions Gate Bridge or a trip on the SeaBus to North Vancouver, and then a ride on the tram up to the top of Grouse Mountain.

Victoria

The car ferry from Vancouver to the provincial capital on Vancouver Island is an excellent trip in its own right, meandering between the beautiful Gulf Islands. Once in Victoria, see the Parliament Buildings, the Empress Hotel, and the Royal British Columbia Museum. Then tour the beautiful Butchart Gardens and the gardens of Government House, open year-round because of the mild climate.

ONTARIO
Good for culture, family holidays and nightlife

ALTHOUGH THE province is four times the size of Britain, the north is a virtually untouched vastness, and most inhabitants live in the south, a varied area of rich farmland and prosperous small towns, with all sorts of reconstructed settlements, restored villages, recreational trails and museums. Algonquin Provincial Park, near Ottawa, is even larger than Banff National Park, and offers many wild lakes and forests, rivers, cliffs and beaches: you can reach large parts only on foot or by canoe. Ontario also borders four of the five Great Lakes.

BEST SIGHTS

Niagara Falls
More film is used here than at any other location in the world – from the roadside or from cruise boats, such as the famous *Maid of the Mist*. Only a 20-minute drive away, at Niagara-on-the-Lake, the Shaw Festival has presented world-class international theatre every summer since 1962. The even older Stratford Festival is only two hours away by car.

Ottawa
The nation's capital, well-cared for by federal funds, is a graceful, elegant city. Most of the architecture is traditional, as you will see if you walk around the compact downtown area. The House of Commons and the Senate are contained in the Gothic Revival buildings overlooking the Ottawa River. The Château Laurier and the National Arts Centre are perched on the Rideau Canal (which becomes the world's longest skating-rink in winter).

Two excellent, very modern, museums are the Art Gallery of Canada and the Museum of Civilisation.

Toronto
The Harbourfront Centre, a complex of theatres, galleries and shops, is a leading cultural attraction, along with the Art Gallery of Ontario and the Royal Ontario Museum. You can stroll around the huge yet charming campus of the University of Toronto, right beside Queens Park, where the large, impressive, provincial Parliament stands. City Hall in Philips Square is also interesting. The CN Tower is worth going up, either for the revolving restaurant, or just to look down over Toronto and across Lake Ontario to Niagara Falls and Buffalo, New York.

You can tour the harbour on a yacht, or take the ferry that goes every half-hour to the Toronto Islands with their amusement park, lagoon with waterfowl, and bikes, quadracycles and canoes to rent. Children will also enjoy the zoo and the Ontario Science Centre uptown, and lakeside Ontario Place, an imaginative park with a panorama of attractions and activities.

QUEBEC
Good for culture, food/wine and nightlife

BEST SIGHTS
Montréal
The world's second-largest French-speaking city is popular with American tourists because it is old, exotic and safe. The old port, recently refurbished, consists mostly of seventeenth- to nineteenth-century buildings and offers many summer festivities and activities. You can tour the old fort and huge modern casino on the adjacent islands. The Can Centre for Architecture has a stark yet serene elegance and puts on important exhibitions from its own collection and elsewhere. Don't miss the architectural park across the street.

Downtown you can climb Mount Royal by car or foot, and stroll around the McGill campus, where you will find the McCord Museum, devoted to Canadian history. The nearby Musée des Beaux Arts is worth a visit.

Built for the 1976 Olympics, the stadium and its huge leaning tower are not as interesting as the nearby Botanical Gardens or the Biodôme: the latter re-creates four ecosystems, from polar to tropical, presenting 1,000 types of fish, amphibians, reptiles, birds and mammals in their natural habitats.

Quebec City
The only walled city in America north of Mexico looms on the cliffs above the St Lawrence river, where Wolfe beat Montcalm in 1759 to ensure that Canada remained British rather than French. Walk around its historic buildings and museums, and see them again from the river as you cruise to the Ile d'Orléans. The city has excellent facilities for all winter sports and a huge winter carnival. Good restaurants abound.

ATLANTIC PROVINCES
Good for beaches, culture and scenic landscape

NEWFOUNDLAND, MAINLAND Nova Scotia and New Brunswick each have lots to offer – an almost endless variety of bays, coves, beaches, scenic drives and vistas, charming villages and fresh seafood. Halifax, Nova Scotia, is the regional capital. An important and historic port, it makes an ideal base.

BEST RESORTS
Cape Breton Island
● Dramatic vistas of cliffs and oceans open before you along the 186-

mile Cabot Trail through the Cape Breton Highlands National Park.
● Major attractions include the Alexander Graham Bell National Historic Site in Baddeck and the massive fortress of Louisbourg, restored to replicate everyday life in 1744, when the island was France's major North American stronghold; there is so much to see here that you should devote the best part of a day to it.

Prince Edward Island (PEI)
● Known as 'Garden of the Gulf' (of the St Lawrence), PEI is popular with Japanese tourists because *Anne of Green Gables* is compulsory reading for Japanese girls.
● All round the island, which in 1997 was joined to the mainland New Brunswick by an eight-mile causeway, are beautiful unspoilt beaches and attractive farming country.
● Rent bikes or drive round the charming rustic roads, set in the red clay earth of Canada's potato capital: there's a potato museum here.

WHEN TO GO

MUCH OF Canada has year-round tourism, but most activities for visitors run from June to August. The autumn foliage season, mid-September to mid-October, is worthwhile too. You can ski in Quebec and the Rockies from November to May, but the best period is December to March.

Average daily maximum temperature °C											
London	6	7	10	13	17	20	22	21	19	14	10	7
Montréal	-6	-4	2	11	18	23	26	25	20	14	5	-3
	JAN	FEB	MAR	APR	MAY	JUN	JUL	AUG	SEP	OCT	NOV	DEC
Montréal	17	15	15	14	13	12	13	10	13	12	15	17
London	15	13	11	12	12	11	12	11	13	13	15	15
Average number of rainy days per month											

Average daily maximum temperature °C											
London	6	7	10	13	17	20	22	21	19	14	10	7
Vancouver	6	7	10	14	17	20	23	22	19	14	9	7
	JAN	FEB	MAR	APR	MAY	JUN	JUL	AUG	SEP	OCT	NOV	DEC
Vancouver	20	16	17	13	10	10	7	7	10	15	18	21
London	15	13	11	12	12	11	12	11	13	13	15	15
Average number of rainy days per month											

PACKAGE TRAVEL

TOUR OPERATORS offer a choice of eastern or western seaboard holidays and tours, with a few whistlestop trans–Canadian tours by rail, coach or air for those who want to sample all the highlights of Canada.

Fly-drive packages or self-drive tours by car, motor home or even motorbike give you the flexibility to set your own pace. You can also travel by rail through the Rockies or cruise along the Inside Passage. Inland, you can stay in lodges or hotels in the mountains and tour by car. City breaks are offered to Montréal and Toronto.

Canada also offers a wide variety of activity holidays. They include grizzly bear tours, polar bear adventures, whale watching, cycling, ranching, river-rafting, canoeing, wagon trekking and trail riding.

Tour operators

Birdwatching: Limosa, Ornitholidays **Camping/adventure**: American Adventures, Trek America **City breaks**: British Airways Holidays, Cresta, Crystal, Inghams, North American Travel Service, Sovereign, Time Off, Travelscene **Coach and rail tours**: APT International, Bales Tours, Cosmos, Explorers Tours, Page & Moy, Saga, Titan HiTours, Travelsphere **Specialists**: British Airways Holidays, Canadian Connections, Hamilton Travel, Jetsave, Jetset, Just America, Kuoni, Lakes & Mountains, NAR, Vacation Canada **Walking**: Explore Worldwide, Ramblers Holidays, Waymark **Wildlife**: Animal Watch, Discover the World, Wildlife Worldwide **Other activities**: American Round-Up (ranch riding), Anglers World (fishing), Arctic Experience (Arctic wilderness), Peregrine (horse-riding), Solo's Holidays (singles)

INDEPENDENT TRAVEL

IT IS best to choose one of three options – British Columbia and the Rockies, Ontario and Quebec, or the maritime provinces.

Hiring a car is by far the best way of getting around. Both cars and petrol are comparatively cheap. The Canadian Automobile Association (the CAA) works very closely with its US counterpart, the AAA, and has reciprocal agreements with both the AA and the RAC. The CAA, which also acts as a travel agency, can provide information on accommodation, restaurants and attractions, and offers maps and trip kits (excellent custom-made detailed road-maps). Get other useful information from local libraries and chambers of commerce as well as the ubiquitous tourist information centres.

You can no longer cross the country on a single train, but VIA Rail offers 50 per cent discounts, seven days a week, as well as a runabout ticket. Children can sometimes travel free.

You can rent bikes, tents and even motor homes. (Ask the rental agency which hotels in major cities are best for parking them.)

Like other Canadian cities, Montréal offers museum passes (for 19 museums in Montréal). There are also passes that are valid for 1-3 days on the buses or speedy metro, for individuals or families.

Comfortable accommodation of all kinds abounds. Prices, like those of most goods and services, are very reasonable by British standards. For accommodation in Ontario, phone toll-free 1-800-ONTARIO; in Quebec, use toll-free Hospitality 1-800-665-1528. Budget travellers should check out university and college accommodation, particularly during vacation periods.

RED TAPE, HEALTH AND SAFETY

BRITISH VISITORS do not need a visa to visit Canada. Check US visa requirements if you are thinking of dropping into the US, the border of which is often very close.

There are no particular health or crime problems: just take the usual precautions (see pages 10–12).

MORE INFORMATION Visit Canada Centre, 62-65 Trafalgar Square, London WC2N 5DY, tel (0891) 715000 (premium rate number), web site: http://info.ic.gc.ca/Tourism

COST OF LIVING £

THE CARIBBEAN

HIGHLIGHTS

Beaches
*Bahamas,
Barbados,
Caymans,
Dominican
Republic,
French
Antilles,
Jamaica,
Leewards,
Tobago,
British and US
Virgin Islands*

Local colour
*Trinidad and
Tobago*

Food/wine
French Antilles

**Romantic
escapism**
*Bahamas,
French
Antilles,
Leewards,
Tobago, British
Virgin Islands*

Nightlife
*Barbados,
French
Antilles, US
Virgin Islands*

**Outdoor
activities**
*Bahamas,
Barbados,
Caymans,
French
Antilles,
Jamaica,
Trinidad and
Tobago,
Windwards,
British and US
Virgin Islands*

**Scenic
landscape**
Dominican

*Republic,
Jamaica,
US Virgin
Islands*

**Flora/
wildlife**
*Caymans,
Dominican
Republic,
Trinidad and
Tobago,
Windwards,
US Virgin
Islands*

BAHAMAS
Good for beaches, outdoor activities and romantic escapism

BEST ISLANDS

Abaco Islands
The best beach is on Great Guana Cay; the islands offer many peaceful sandy stretches while calm waters provide fine sailing. You can hire boats in Hopetoun, Marsh Harbour and Treasure Cay.

Andros
Find sheltered beaches in the east, or dive at resorts near Andros Town.

Berry Islands
Popular with anglers, the islands provide fantastic diving facilities at the underwater cliffs around Tongue of the Ocean.

Bimini Islands
Ernest Hemingway's favourite islands have the best deep-sea fishing areas in the world. Trips are arranged from Alice Town.

Eleuthra
This is a long, thin island with sandy beaches along the sheltered west coast. On the windward side the waves are big enough for surfing. Tiny Harbour Island is famous for Pink Beach on the east coast.

Exuma Cays
The area is mostly uninhabited. Some stunning beaches are located at Elizabeth Harbour and Stocking Island, a short sail away.

Grand Bahama
Freeport/Lucaya boasts hotels, beaches, casinos, marinas and shops. The best beaches outside Freeport include William's Town to the south, remote Barbary Beach, and Gold Rock Beach on the south coast. Trails in the Lucayan National Park lead to limestone sinkholes.

New Providence
Nassau, the Bahamian capital, is the centre of the island's nightlife, with lots of American-style bars, clubs and restaurants. The main tourist enclaves are Cable Beach and Paradise Island, the latter a thin sandy strip noteworthy for its wonderful beaches. Many beaches are private; exceptions include Lighthouse, Adelaide and South beaches.

Rum Cay
Rum Cay numbers a tiny village, a few bars, palms and endless beaches.

BARBADOS
Good for beaches, outdoor activities and nightlife

BEST BEACHES AND WATER SPORTS

A continuous strip of beach winds along the protected west coast, north of Bridgetown. Try Paradise Beach and Mullins Bay. For peace and local colour, explore Maycock's Bay north of Speightstown. On the south coast the sand is pink. Bottom Bay is pretty. The Atlantic coast is spectacular, but swimming is largely prohibited because of rough seas. Picnic on the rocky beaches from Ragged Point to Gay's Cove.

Try windsurfing around Silver Sands beach (popular with local Bajans) on the south coast, where the tradewinds stream in. There is good reef diving in the Folkestone National Marine Park (near Holetown).

BEST SIGHTS

St Nicholas Abbey, Francia Plantation House and Villa Nova recall Barbados's colonial past under British rule. Rum enthusiasts should tour Mount Gay Visitors' Centre or the West India Rum Refinery. Andromeda Gardens has orchids and banyan trees; nearby, the Flower Forest leads through swathes of tropical breadfruits, mangoes and spices.

BEST NIGHTLIFE

Head for Bridgetown or St Lawrence Gap for rum shops, wine bars, restaurants and clubs to suit all tastes.

CAYMAN ISLANDS
Good for beaches, flora, outdoor activities and wildlife

BEST ISLANDS
Cayman Brac and Little Cayman
Seven miles apart, smaller and less developed than Grand Cayman, these islands suit serious divers. The main underwater attraction is Bloody Bay, north of Little Cayman. Little Cayman also has Booby Pond, home to red-footed booby birds as well as whistling ducks and snowy egrets.

Grand Cayman
The largest and most developed island also has the best stretch of sand, Seven Mile Beach. Behind this are most hotels and condominiums. Queen Elizabeth II Botanic Park is an excellent woodland trail where you might spot parrots or agouti among the air plants and trees. Suitable diving sites are too numerous to list; the most famous is Stingray City, where the eponymous fish eat squid from divers' hands.

DOMINICAN REPUBLIC
Good for beaches, flora, scenic landscape and wildlife

BEST BEACHES

In the remote northern area around the Haitian border, the superior beaches are at Luperon and Cofresi. In the east, resorts are more developed; head for Playa Dorada, three miles east of Puerto Plata, for most water-sports facilities. Round the eastern tip of the island, the beaches at Las Terrenas rank highly. The one at Cabo Francés Viejo is quiet, but the waves are big and the undertow is strong.

Boca Chica, the closest resort to Santo Domingo on the south-east coast, is one to avoid at weekends, when everybody abandons the city. Escape instead to remote Bayahibe Beach, or head to Playa Catalina from La Romana. The windsurfing beach is at Cabarete, on the north coast, served by strong winds coming off the Atlantic.

BEST SIGHTS

Santiago, the republic's second city, has a rather grand, quiet air, with some ornate town-houses, contrasting with the frenetic activity of Santo Domingo. There is a great view from the obelisk commemorating a battle in 1844, and a small museum of folklore in the centre.

At the end of the Samana peninsula, humpbacked whales occupy the Bahia de Samana in winter. Boat trips to see them are pricey.

BEST SCENIC LANDSCAPE

The interior landscape ranges from plantations to mountains. Four national parks can be visited with a guide – Isla Cabrito, Armando Bermúdez, Los Haitises and the National Park of the East. Permission to visit comes from the Department of Ecotourism in Santo Domingo. Take food and water, as the parks have few facilities.

FRENCH ANTILLES
Good for beaches, food/wine, nightlife, outdoor activities and romantic escapism

BEST ISLANDS

Guadeloupe

Of the island's two 'wings', Grande Terre has the sandiest beaches: Caravelle Beach is crowded, but beyond St-François, the Plage des Salines is often deserted. Strong currents prohibit swimming on the east coast. To the north of Basse Terre, the gold sand is granulated. Windsurfing boards can be hired on the south coast of Grande Terre, yachts from Pointe Pitre and Deshaies. Jacques Cousteau's marine reserve on Ilet de Pigéon is a must for divers. Deep-sea fishing trips are arranged in St-Anne and St-François. In Basse Terre's national park, trails meander through rainforest, and there are walks to La Soufrière (an active volcano), its lava flows and nearby waterfalls. Grande Terre resounds nightly to the sounds of *zouk* music, with hundreds of clubs and bars along the south coast. For romantic escapism, La Désirade, Marie-Galante and Les Saintes are almost deserted, with glorious beaches and bays.

Martinique
The best beaches are on the St-Anne peninsula; Grande Anse des Salines is packed at weekends, as is Point de Marin, while Grande Terre and the remote Baie des Anglais are tranquil. Cap Chevalier is good for windsurfing and L'Anse d'Arlets is ideal for snorkelling. The Musée Gauguin, the island's main sight, is worth a visit as is Habitation Clement, near Vauclin, one of the West Indies' finest plantation houses. Superb local restaurants serve up a happy blend of French and Creole.

St-Barthélémy
This island is the amazingly expensive playground of France's elite. Beaches are busiest on the south coast and quieter to the north. Gentle seas at Anse de Flamands and Lorient are ideal for children. Gustavia and St-Jean, the main towns, support clusters of tax-free French boutiques around their marinas. St-Barthélémy's nightlife is low-key.

St-Martin
Baie Longue and Duck Bay are the best beaches on the island's built-up east coast; windsurfing is popular at Galion Bay. Offshore cays offer seclusion. St-Martin's reefs are protected, hence its pristine coral.

JAMAICA
Good for beaches, outdoor activities and scenic landscape

BEST RESORTS AND BEACHES
Montego Bay
● Close to the airport, with family hotels and water-sports facilities.
● The loud beaches at Doctor's Cave and Cornwall charge admission.
● Burwood Beach is quieter, and a favourite with windsurfers.

Ocho Rios
● To escape the crowds and jet skiers, head west for Mammee Bay.
● At nearby Port Maria beaches are sheltered and uncrowded.

Port Antonio
● Air of faded grandeur and an incomparable setting between two bays.
● Renowned for deep-sea fishing.
● For beaches take the ferry to Navy Island, or search out Dragon Bay and the deserted beaches beyond Long Bay.

Other beaches
● Kingston's Port Henderson beach, which gets crowded with locals, is the ultimate Jamaican experience and has live music most weekends.
● On the western tip of Jamaica, Negril stretches along miles of sandy beaches and cliffs. Just south lie Bloody Bay and pretty Miskito Cove.

BEST SIGHTS AND EXCURSIONS

Jamaica is scattered with plantation houses; Devon House is in the sub-urbs of Kingston, Harmony Hall near Ocho Rios, Rose Hall and Greenwood close to Montego Bay. Noel Coward's house, Firefly, perches high above Port Maria. Reggae fans seek the Bob Marley Museum in Kingston and his birthplace in Nine Mile.

Trails cross the Blue and John Crow Mountains. Climb the 7,400-foot Blue Mountain Peak (take a guide and go before dawn). Bamboo Avenue leads to Black River, where boat trips visit Great Morass swamp.

Dunn's River Falls, south of Ocho Rios, tumble 600 feet. Visit Rockland Bird Sanctuary at feeding time in the afternoon. Tropical gardens are at Hope, on the outskirts of Kingston, and Castleton in the Wag Valley. The Enchanted Gardens and Coyaba are south of Ocho Rios.

LEEWARD ISLANDS
Good for beaches and romantic escapism

BEST ISLANDS

Anguilla
Anguilla's beaches are arguably the finest in the world. Shoal Bay in the north is the busiest, while to the west Mead's Bay and Shoal Bay West are quieter. Misanthropes head north-east, to a series of tiny coves and Captain's Bay. Uninhabited cays can be visited by arrangement with local fishermen. You can enjoy snorkelling at Little Bay on the west coast.

Antigua
Beaches get busy north of Saint John's; those at Ffrye's Bay and Darkwood Beach are more remote. Try visiting sandy inlets like Galleon Bay by water-taxi. Windsurfers can head for Dickenson Bay on the east coast, and sailors will be able to hire yachts in English Harbour and Parham Harbour. Eighteenth-century military forts abound to keep historians happy: Fort James and Fort Barrington are in St John's

Harbour, Monks Hill Fort is in Falmouth and Johnson Point Fort is in the south-west.

Barbuda
Near-deserted beaches and few hotels characterise Barbuda; petrol is still hand-pumped. Millions of frigate birds occupy Codrington Lagoon.

Nevis
Nevis has a slow, stately charm: little major development occurs outside private resorts. The best beach is Pinney's, on the west coast, while Oualie Beach to the north has golden sands and views across the Narrows to St Kitts. Many plantation houses in the hills have now been converted to splendid, pricey hotels.

St Kitts
St Kitts is busier than Nevis, possessing more hotels and water-sports facilities. Friar's Bay is an exceptional sandy beach on the south coast. You can hire water-sports equipment at neighbouring Frigate Bay; catamaran and deep-sea fishing charters are also booked here. Take a walking trip up 4,000-foot Mount Liamuiga, or tour old plantation houses (some of the island's best hotels are in renovated plantation houses). Take a guide if venturing up into the hills.

TRINIDAD AND TOBAGO
Good for beaches, flora, local colour, outdoor activities, romantic escapism and wildlife

BEST BEACHES
Sleepy Tobago is home to splendid sandy beaches, sheltered by palms and ringed with reefs, with the occasional shack for refreshments.

Trinidad has comparatively few quality beaches, although the sand along the east coast is soft. The remote coves at Balandria and Salibia bays look out towards Tobago. The capital, Port of Spain, is quite far from the sea; most trippers go to Maracas Beach on the north coast. Inland, try river bathing at the Maracas Falls, north of St Joseph.

BEST LOCAL COLOUR
On Trinidad, Port of Spain's 500,000 inhabitants have Indian, Chinese, South American, Asian, African and European origins. The resulting cultural pandemonium of music, architecture, religion and style has produced a vibrant city bursting with calypso, reggae and steel-pan music, notably during the world-famous carnival in the first week of Lent. Pubs and clubs buzz all year round – but take extra care after dark.

BEST NATURAL HISTORY

Although quite heavily industrialised, Trinidad boasts the Caribbean's best flora and fauna. Aficionados should seek out the Royal Botanical Gardens in Port of Spain's Savannah Park and the Asa Wright Nature Centre above Arima. There is a bird sanctuary at Caroni Swamp, and the Pointe-à-Pierre Wildfowl Trust. North of the Oropouche river, turtles creep up the beach at Matura Bay. An amazing natural sight is Pitch Lake, which has produced bitumen for roads all over the world.

BEST FOR ROMANTIC ESCAPISM

For escapism, seek Castara and Englishman's Bay on the north coast of Tobago, and stay in a traditional hideaway. For more action, Pigeon Point and Store Bay have beach bars, and are popular with the locals.

BEST WATER SPORTS

Tobago is a water-sports haven. Hire gear and boats from Pigeon Point. Buccoo Reef is popular with snorkellers and scuba divers, but is damaged; try beautiful less-visited reefs off the eastern coast. Water-sports facilities on Trinidad are not top-notch, but you can hire boats, boards and fishing lines around Bayshore in Port of Spain and from larger hotels.

WINDWARD ISLANDS
Good for flora, outdoor activities and wildlife

BEST ISLANDS
Dominica
The poorest of the group, Dominica has craggy, cloud-topped slopes. As the beaches are mostly volcanic black sand, river bathing on the Rosalie river and at Trafalgar Falls is popular. Much of the interior is national park, with walking trails through the rainforest, which is home to 150 species of bird and rare iguanas. Between May and October, whale-watching is a popular tourist activity off the west coast.

Grenada
The capital, St George's, is the prettiest town in the Caribbean. Beaches and coves dot Grenada's coastline, with most hotels located around Grand Anse. Water-sports equipment can be hired here. For privacy, try Dr Groom or Magazine Beach to the west. Sailors could potter around the inlets of the south coast or cruise up to the Grenadines. Bareboat charters are available in L'Anse aux Epines. Organised walks explore rainforest in the National Park. Join a trek to the volcanic lake of Grand Etang, or try an easier hike to Concord Falls.

St Lucia

The most developed of the Windwards, St Lucia boasts white sandy beaches on its leeward coast and a tradition of delicious Creole food, thanks to the French. The most popular beach here is Reduit; the tranquil La Toc lies south of Castries. The best windsurfing is off beaches to the south of the island. Divers' choice on St Lucia is Anse Chastanet, a grey sand cove on the west coast.

St Vincent and the Grenadines

Like several other islands among this incredibly unspoilt group, Mustique is an exclusive retreat of the rich and famous. On St Vincent, walkers can attempt the three-hour climb up the Soufrière (take a guide) or follow the gentler Vermont Nature Trails. The islands are a sailing paradise, with clear seas, a backdrop of volcanic peaks on the horizon, and playful dolphins. Divers and snorkellers should head for Bequia, which is surrounded by reefs, or the Tobago Cays, five deserted islands encircling a protected reef.

BRITISH VIRGIN ISLANDS
Good for beaches, outdoor activities and romantic escapism

BEST ISLANDS

Anegada

Lying less than 35 feet above sea-level, Anegada has miles of sandy beaches. There is a big scuba and snorkelling centre on the reef, with over 300 wrecks to explore. You can hire equipment from the Anegada Reef Hotel.

Jost van Dyck

A great place for escapists, the island has strips of idyllic beach and few hotels. The best beaches are at Great Harbour and White Bay on the south coast, or try Sandy Spit (off Green Cay) with its palm trees and white sands.

Tortola

Tortola's sandiest beaches are on the north coast; try Cane Garden Bay or Smuggler's Cove, the best on the island. Scuba divers should head for the wreck of the *Rhone* off Salt Island, while snorkellers should try the coral reefs. The Sage Mountain National Park has trails through rainforest. You can charter bareboats in Roadtown, Nanny Cay and West End.

Virgin Gorda

The most popular beaches are in the south-west. From Mad Dog Bar, footpaths lead to the Baths, with deep sand and clear water. To the north, Spring and Trunk bays are popular with yachtsmen, and Long Bay has views to Tortola. Bareboat charters can be picked up at North Sound and the main yacht harbour. Hire water-sports gear from sailing clubs and hotels. It is expensive to dive here.

US VIRGIN ISLANDS
Good for beaches, flora, nightlife, outdoor activities and wildlife

BEST ISLANDS
St Croix
The least developed island of the group and a laid-back holiday location, St Croix features beaches in isolated coves. In the north-east Isaac's Bay, off the road, is good for snorkelling. In the south-west, head for Sandy Point between May and July to see leatherback turtles laying eggs. On the northern coast, the shallow waters of sandy Chenay Beach are ideal for children. Water-sports equipment can be hired.

St John
With tranquil white beaches lining the north-west coast from Trunk Bay to Francis Bay, St John is another snorkellers' mecca. Two-thirds of the island is national park and paths criss-cross the rainforest. Guides lead tours which include picnic and snorkelling stops (5,600 acres of the park cover offshore reefs).

St Thomas
Hotels and private resorts fringe St Thomas's coastline. For tax-free shopping, head downtown and make tracks for Havensight Mall in Charlotte Amalie. At night, Charlotte Amalie and Frenchtown buzz; tastes are eclectic, with sushi bars ranged alongside piano bars and nightclubs. The most popular beach is Magen's Bay on the north coast; you can hire water-sports equipment here. For total seclusion, sail south to Buck Island. Now a national park, it is guarded by a vast reef and snorkelling here is superb.

WHEN TO GO

THE OFFICIAL hurricane season in the Caribbean runs from 1 June to 30 September, though recent hurricanes have struck between the end of August and mid-September.

Carnival is the main celebration in the Caribbean; although this is traditionally a pre-Lenten festival, some of the smaller islands alter the dates of festivities to avoid competing for performers and visitors. Thus,

	Average daily maximum temperature °C											
London	6	7	10	13	17	20	22	21	19	14	10	7
Bridgetown	28	28	29	30	31	31	30	31	31	30	29	28
	JAN	FEB	MAR	APR	MAY	JUN	JUL	AUG	SEP	OCT	NOV	DEC
(Barbados)	13	8	8	7	9	14	18	16	15	15	16	14
London	15	13	11	12	12	11	12	11	13	13	15	15
	Average number of rainy days per month											

	Average daily maximum temperature °C											
London	6	7	10	13	17	20	22	21	19	14	10	7
Kingston	30	30	30	31	31	32	32	32	32	31	31	31
	JAN	FEB	MAR	APR	MAY	JUN	JUL	AUG	SEP	OCT	NOV	DEC
(Jamaica)	3	3	2	3	4	5	4	7	6	9	5	4
London	15	13	11	12	12	11	12	11	13	13	15	15
	Average number of rainy days per month											

for example, Trinidad, Dominica, St Lucia and most of the French islands celebrate in February or March; Barbados and St Vincent in July; Anguilla and Grenada in August; Montserrat and St Kitts in December.

PACKAGE TRAVEL

MOST TOUR operators feature packages to hotel complexes with the emphasis on relaxation and water sports. The Caribbean is notable for the number of all-inclusive holidays on offer. These vary slightly in what is covered, but generally all meals, entertainment and sporting activities are included in the price. In some packages drinks are also thrown in. Some hotels are for couples only, others have more of a family appeal. All-inclusive holidays save money, but encourage guests to stay in the hotel rather than exploring the island they are staying on.

Self-catering on the popular islands is in apartments and also in purpose-built villas. Several operators offer private villas. These tend to be at the upper end of the market, with private pools and maid service (sometimes even fully staffed). Two-centre and island-hopping holidays are also available; the latter will be more expensive than a standard package.

Activities on offer include sailing, scuba diving and deep-sea fishing. You can charter bareboat (crewless) or crewed sailing boats and pick your own route or join a sailing trip as part of your holiday. Cruising can be on a four-masted sailing ship or on a full-size cruise ship. Birdwatching holidays are on offer in Trinidad and Tobago, and walking in Jamaica.

Tour operators

Birdwatching: Abercrombie & Kent, Cygnus Wildlife, Limosa, Ornitholidays, Sunbird, Wildlife Worldwide **General**: Abercrombie & Kent, Airtours, Airwaves, British Airways Holidays, Caribbean Connection, Caribtours, Club Med, Cosmos, CV Travel, First Choice Holidays, Harlequin, Hayes & Jarvis, Hermis, Kestours, Kuoni, Made to Measure, Meon, Silk Cut Travel, Simply Caribbean, Simply Tropix, Sunset Travel, Thomas Cook, Thomson, Tradewinds, Tropical Places, Unijet, VFB, Virgin Holidays **Walking**: Explore Worldwide

---

INDEPENDENT TRAVEL

LONDON AND Paris are the main European gateways for flights to the Caribbean; otherwise you can transit through the United States. If you have lots of time to spare, a 'banana boat' cargo ship might appeal.

LIAT is the main airline providing connections between the islands, and offers a range of discounts and passes. Smaller airlines, like Winair or Air Guadeloupe, cover more limited areas or island groups.

Ferries, catamarans and cargo boats are options, or you can charter bareboat or crewed yachts. It is easiest to sail north to south, with the prevailing winds; some yacht charter companies allow you one-way hire.

Buses are a cheap mode of transport on individual islands. The word 'bus' also covers vehicles such as minivans or pick-up trucks. Taxis are also cheap and offer more comfort. If you plan to hire a car, you may have to buy a temporary local driving permit. Driving is on the left on former British islands, and on the right on former French and Dutch islands.

RED TAPE, HEALTH AND SAFETY

EACH OF the islands has its own entry rules and regulations – check with the appropriate tourist office or your tour operator, and with your GP or travel clinic for health advice.

Most visitors to the Caribbean enjoy trouble-free holidays (but note months affected by the hurricane season under 'When to go'). The Foreign Office Travel Advice Unit issues notices about various islands, particularly Jamaica and Trinidad and Tobago. Leave valuables and large amounts of cash in your hotel, do not carry packages for strangers if you do not know their contents, do not resist if threatened with a weapon, and take local advice on areas to avoid, especially at night. For further advice see page 12.

MORE INFORMATION Caribbean Tourism Organisation, 42 Westminster Palace Gardens, Artillery Row, London SW1P 1RR, tel 0171-222 4335, web site: http://www.caribtourism.com

Individual offices

Anguilla Tourist Office
3 Epirus Road, London SW6 7UJ
tel 0171-937 7725

Antigua & Barbuda Tourist Board
15 Thayer Street, London W1M 5LD
tel 0171-486 7073

Bahamas Tourist Office,
3 The Billings, Walnut Tree Close
Guildford, Surrey GU1 4UL
tel (01483) 448900

Barbados Tourism Authority
263 Tottenham Court Road
London W1P 9AA
tel 0171-636 9448

Cayman Islands Department of
Tourism, 6 Arlington Street
London SW1A 1RE
tel 0171-491 7771

Dominica Tourist Office
1 Collingham Gardens
London SW5 0HW
tel 0171-835 1937

Grenada Board of Tourism
Address: as Dominica Tourist Office
tel 0171-370 5164

Jamaica Tourist Board
1–2 Prince Consort Road
London SW7 2BZ
tel 0171-224 0505

St Kitts & Nevis Tourism Office
10 Kensington Court
London W8 5DL
tel 0171-376 0881

St Lucia Tourist Board
421A Finchley Road
London NW3 6HJ
tel 0171-431 3675

St Vincent & the Grenadines
Tourist Office
10 Kensington Court
London W8 5DL
tel 0171-937 6570

Trinidad & Tobago Tourism
International House
47 Chase Side, Enfield
Middlesex EN2 6NB
tel 0181-367 3752

US Virgin Islands Tourist Office
Molasses House, Clovehitch Quay
Plantation Wharf, London SW11 3TW
tel 0171-978 5262

COST OF LIVING ££-£££

CHINA

HIGHLIGHTS
Culture
Beijing, Sichuan province, Xi'an, Shanghai, Nanjing

Food/wine
Sichuan province

Nightlife
Shanghai

Scenic landscape
Guilin, Hangzhou, Sichuan province, Suzhou

Shopping
Shanghai

BEIJING
Good for culture

BEIJING (PEKING), the power base of modern China and its ancient northern capital, lies at the heart of the Middle Kingdom and is not to be missed. A visit to this extraordinary city also offers a chance to sample typical northern food (try the Mongolian hotpot and steamed dumplings, or *jiaozi*).

BEST SIGHTS
Forbidden City
The massive, sealed quarters of the emperors of China, just off Tiananmen Square, date back to the fifteenth century and provide a perfect example of classical Chinese architecture (Bertolucci's *The Last Emperor* was filmed here). Allow a day for this and neighbouring sights around the square.

Great Wall and the Ming Tombs

Construction of the Great Wall began in 221 BC. You can escape the many visitors by walking far enough along from its Badaling access point to be afforded spectacular mountain views. Then visit the nearby Ming Tombs, especially for the ancient spirit walkway.

Summer palaces

The summer palace (Yiheyuan) in Haidian district is set in an exotic lakeside royal garden, with temples, pavilions and bridges. It can be crowded, hot and tiring in the summer, but in midwinter when the lake freezes it is pleasant to watch the skaters. Or try the old summer palace (Yuanmingyuan) nearby. Looted by Europeans in 1860, the melancholy ruins and tranquil gardens provide a haven from modern China.

Tiantan Park

Home to the Temple of Heaven, this is a favourite spot for local city-dwellers, with lots of greenery and trees. The temple, with its blue-tiled roof and white marble terrace, the 'altar of heaven', is the central attraction. Nearby is an excellent silk shop.

XI'AN
Good for culture

XI'AN WAS the imperial capital (Changan) during the Tang dynasty (AD 618-907). It has the best-preserved city walls in China and many interesting historical sites. See in particular the Shaanxi History Museum on Xiaozhai Road; the nearby Big Wild Goose Pagoda (seventh century); the Banpo neolithic village in the eastern suburbs; and the Great Mosque in the old Muslim quarter. And fit in a visit to the forest of stone steles (tall, thin gravestones), housed in a former Confucian temple at the Shaanxi Provincial museum. Nearby is the Bell Tower and a market selling local food.

BEST SIGHTS

Huashan Mountain

One of China's sacred mountains, this lies 75 miles east of Xi'an at Huayin. Allow half a day to climb its extremely steep slopes. Daoist temples abound. It is not suitable for sufferers of vertigo or inexperienced walkers, but provides an excellent antidote to city blues. (And it could inspire you to seek out China's other sacred mountains: Hengshan, south of Datong; Songshan, home to the Shaolin Temple in Henan province; Taishan, north of Qufu in Shandong province, birthplace of Confucius; Emeishan, in Sichuan; and Huangshan – perhaps the most beautiful mountain in China – in Anhui province.)

Qin terracotta army

Twenty-five miles north-east of Xi'an in Lintong county lies one of China's most famous sights. An army – over 2,000 years old – of 6,000 life-sized terracotta warriors form an eternal imperial guard for the Emperor Qin Shi Huangdi. The exhibit lives up to all the hype – it is an extraordinary glimpse of China's past. Inevitably, it's crowded. Nearby, the thermal complex of Huaqing hot springs dates back to the Tang dynasty.

SICHUAN PROVINCE
Good for culture, food/wine and scenic landscape

CHENGDU IS the capital of Sichuan, whose people have a reputation for a fierce intelligence; many of China's ancient heroes come from this enclosed land. The food is superb – but be warned, it is spicily hot.

BEST SIGHTS

Chengdu

The ancient city of Chengdu is famous for its bamboo tea-houses and Du Fu, one of China's great Tang poets and a son of Sichuan (you can visit the shrine where his house used to stand).

Chengdu is also a good base for excursions – maybe to the Dujiangyan Dam (31 miles north-west), an irrigation project engineered in 306 BC but still in operation today; the sacred mountain of Emeishan (100 miles south); or the Wolong panda reserve.

Chongqing

Chongqing was the wartime capital of the Nationalist (Guomindang) government in the 1940s; today it is the main base for trips down the Yangtze river. It is a fascinating place of mists, steep streets and houses that cling to the hills, but scorching summer temperatures make it one of the 'fiery ovens' of China. Sit by the docks and sample the air, attempt a cable-car crossing of the Yangtze, or rest at Pipashan Park (in the south-west) and the northern hot springs (in the north-west).

Yangtze

From Chongqing you can travel down the Yangtze ('Changjiang') and its gorges by boat. Do it now, while it is still there. There are plans to drown the gorges under a 370-mile reservoir, part of an ambitious – and contentious – dam project under way. Take a book and some food to supplement what's on offer and enjoy a two- or three-day journey through beautiful surroundings. After the spectacular Qutang Gorge you carry on through Wu and Xiling gorges, as far as Yueyang, Wuhan or Shanghai. But if you like the rapids and can afford the pricey fare, leave the boat at Wushan and try the small gorges of the Daning River.

GUILIN
Good for scenic landscape

A LANDSCAPE fit for poets, artists and the gods, consisting of lime-stone hills, networks of caves and clear waterways, all to be explored by boat or raft. Especially worth visiting are the Reed Flute Cave, Fuboshan Mountain and Elephant Trunk Hill (Xiangbishan).

Take a boat trip 37 miles down the Li river to Yangshuo, to absorb the scenes that inspired Chinese poets and painters of old. You can travel back by bus to get a feel for the countryside. Guilin is filled with the scent of cassia trees in the autumn (but it is stifling in summer). The area is, sadly, in danger of becoming overdeveloped.

HANGZHOU
Good for scenic landscape

HANGZHOU'S WEST Lake is a 'pearl in the city', a place of bridges, pavilions, causeways and islands, again at risk of being overwhelmed by tourism. The carved laughing Buddha at Feilai Feng (the 'peak that flew from afar') is one of 380 sculptures dating from the tenth to the fourteenth centuries. Combine this with a visit to Lingyin Si (the Temple of Spiritual Retreat). Or step on a pleasure boat or gondola and sail away into a Chinese scroll painting. Hangzhou is also famous for its silk and its Dragon Well tea; the silk factories are good value.

Further afield, the village of Meijiawu (20 minutes by car heading south) and the mountain Moganshan (37 miles to the north) offer a chance to escape the crowds. Boat trips down the Grand Canal to Suzhou offer the experience of 'a slow boat in China'.

SUZHOU
Good for scenic landscape

'IN HEAVEN there is Paradise, on earth there is Suzhou', according to a Chinese saying. Suzhou is given over to gardens and canals. Chinese gardens encapsulate harmony, poetry and water, tree and stone: they attempt to create the universe in a small space. See especially the Xi Yuan Garden (with a temple filled with 500 Buddhist Luohan statues at its heart), the Liu Yuan Garden (200 designs of window) and the Zhuozheng Yuan Garden (where water reigns). In summer the Wangshi Yuan Garden remains open in the evening and traditional Chinese music is played.

SHANGHAI
Good for culture, nightlife and shopping

SHANGHAI – THE Paris of the Orient – is one of the great cities of the world: huge, phenomenally crowded and with a past that speaks of glamour, danger and excitement. But it is not the best place to take young children (too busy, too tiring). Nor should it be your first taste of the country – visit it after northern or central China.

Much of Shanghai's waterfront architecture (along the Bund) is rooted in European tradition: China's history of colonisation is there for all to see. Shanghai was, and is, a capitalist's dream (and a communist's nightmare), with a sophisticated identity of its own (as the Shanghainese love to remind other Chinese). And the shopping is all-consuming.

NANJING
Good for culture

ONCE THE south's ancient capital, Nanjing is a civilised city of maples, chrysanthemums and mausoleums – or rather, one mausoleum. The tomb of the 'father of modern China' and its first President, Sun Yatsen, is worth a visit. Also interesting are the Linggu Temple, the Confucius Temple and Chaotian Palace. Enjoy views from the cable-car as it ascends the purple-and-gold mountains, and visit the lake at Xuanwu Park. Another of China's 'fiery ovens', Nanjing is very hot in summer.

WHEN TO GO

IF YOU are planning to visit both northern and southern China, spring or autumn are the best times to avoid extremes of temperature. Spring Festival, or Chinese New Year, is a three-day celebration in January or February, depending on the lunar calendar, and is best avoided, as transport is even more crowded than usual.

Average daily maximum temperature °C											
London	6	7	10	13	17	20	22	21	19	14	10	7
Guangzhou	17	17	21	25	30	31	33	33	32	28	25	21
	JAN	FEB	MAR	APR	MAY	JUN	JUL	AUG	SEP	OCT	NOV	DEC
Guangzhou	5	8	11	12	15	17	16	13	10	4	3	5
London	15	13	11	12	12	11	12	11	13	13	15	15
Average number of rainy days per month											

	Average daily maximum temperature °C											
London	6	7	10	13	17	20	22	21	19	14	10	7
Shanghai	8	8	13	19	25	28	32	32	28	23	17	12
	JAN	FEB	MAR	APR	MAY	JUN	JUL	AUG	SEP	OCT	NOV	DEC
Shanghai	6	9	9	9	9	11	9	9	11	4	6	6
London	15	13	11	12	12	11	12	11	13	13	15	15
	Average number of rainy days per month											

	Average daily maximum temperature °C											
London	6	7	10	13	17	20	22	21	19	14	10	7
Tientsin	1	4	11	20	27	32	32	31	26	20	9	2
	JAN	FEB	MAR	APR	MAY	JUN	JUL	AUG	SEP	OCT	NOV	DEC
Tientsin	1	<1	2	2	4	6	10	9	4	1	2	1
London	15	13	11	12	12	11	12	11	13	13	15	15
	Average number of rainy days per month											

PACKAGE TRAVEL

MOST PACKAGES featured in brochures are two- or three-week escorted tours starting from Beijing and including internal coach, rail and air travel. A 10- or 12-day tour may include Beijing, Chengdu, Xi'an, Guilin, Suzhou and Shanghai. Longer tours could also include Nanjing and Hangzhou or you could follow the old Silk Route. A three-week tour may also include a five-day cruise on the Yangtze river from Chongqing to Wuhan. Alternatively, go for a two-centre stay based in Beijing – with day-trips to sights such as the Great Wall – and Shanghai, or combine China with destinations such as Hong Kong, Bali or Penang.

Tour operators

Activities: Exodus (trekking), Explore Worldwide (trekking), Holts' Tours (battlefields), Ramblers Holidays (walking), Solo's Holidays (singles), Sunbird (birdwatching) **General**: Abercrombie & Kent, Airwaves, Asiaworld Travel, Bales Tours, British Airways Holidays, Cosmos, Dream Journeys, Far East Gateways, Hayes & Jarvis, Jasmin Tours, Jetabout, Kuoni, Premier Holidays, Saga, Thomas Cook, Tradewinds, Travelsphere, Voyages Jules Verne **Specialists**: China Travel Service

Specialists such as China Travel Service also include the Trans-Siberian Express travelling from Moscow to Beijing independently or travelling into Tibet from Chengdu. Activity tour operators offer adventure and trekking tours, birdwatching, battlefield tours and rail tours.

INDEPENDENT TRAVEL

DIRECT FLIGHTS run from London to Beijing; other destinations involve stopovers. Many people enter China via Hong Kong, by train or boat; the truly adventurous can take the Trans-Siberian Express, the Karakoram Highway from Pakistan, or cross the border from Vietnam.

If you decide to go it alone – without guide, coach and trappings – then do research first, and at all times take it easy. Independent travel in China brings an exhaustion quite different from package holiday 'hotel fatigue'. But the sense of achievement along the way is wonderful. The chances of having an unforgettable holiday shoot up if you go it alone.

Language is unlikely to be a problem, provided you speak English and have a bilingual phrase-book of even the most basic kind. A smattering of Chinese (far easier to pick up than it sounds) will open unexpected doors. When you are trying to communicate, politeness and patience win every time. Smile frequently and learn some courtesy phrases. The new entrepreneurial spirit sweeping China means that there should be no shortage of people willing to help you. However, beware of overcharging.

Train and aeroplane ticket prices are still higher for visitors than for most Chinese. Train tickets can be harder to come by, but be persistent, because a train journey is an excellent way to get a feel for the real China. Ask for *ying wo* (second-class with a berth) and bring your own mug. Look out especially for the local food sold on train stations.

You can also get around China by bus and boat. Try, for example, the boat from Shanghai up to Qingdao in Shandong (and from there to Qufu, to see the grave of Confucius, or to Taishan to climb the sacred mountain). Study your maps and guide books before you go: varying journeys can reveal different glimpses of China. A little courage, a little luck... and, if Buddha smiles on you, China will show her best face.

RED TAPE, HEALTH AND SAFETY

ALL BRITISH passport-holders, including transit passengers, require a visa to enter China. Tour groups will probably travel on a group visa; individual travellers should contact the Chinese Embassy, which will supply an application form. To obtain a visa you must submit a completed form, a valid passport and one passport photograph, plus evidence of booked accommodation in China and a return ticket. Apply in person between 9am and 12pm Monday to Friday or courier your application to the Visa Section at the Chinese Embassy enclosing a strong sae. A single-entry tourist visa is valid for four months and costs £25 (cash or postal order) to personal applicants, £35 to postal applicants who must add £10 extra towards handling charges; a double-entry tourist visa costs £50. You must enter China within three months of issue.

The Chinese swear by garlic to fend off stomach upsets brought on by food or water contaminated with bacteria – or simply by a diet your digestive system is not used to. Don't let this put you off sampling local restaurants. It is unlikely that you will catch anything serious, as long as you are as careful as you would be in your own country. Hotel food does not have the same cachet, and is far more expensive. The fastidious among the urban Chinese use *gao meng suan jia* (potassium permanganate) to wash fresh fruit before they eat it; you can buy it at any pharmacy.

It is worth noting that hard toilet paper is the norm in China (apart from in the major hotels), so if you regard soft paper as a must, you can buy a roll in any shop. (Sanitary towels and tampons are widely available.)

A final word of warning: China is more dangerous for independent travellers than it used to be. Be on your guard, as anywhere, and keep your money, passport and other valuables out of sight. For the latest advice, contact the Foreign Office Travel Advice Unit (see page 11).

MORE INFORMATION China National Tourist Office, 4 Glentworth Street, London NW1 5PG, tel (0891) 600188 (premium rate number)

No tourist office web site exists, but you can access information about China at: http://www.tourist-offices.org.uk/China/index.html

Chinese Embassy, 31 Portland Place, London W1N 3AG, tel 0171-631 1430, visa information (0891) 880808 (premium rate number)

COST OF LIVING £

COSTA RICA

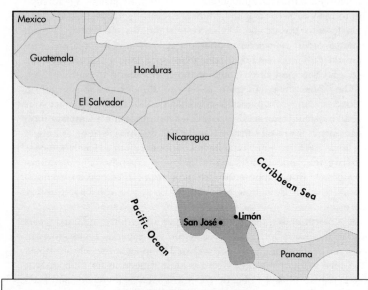

HIGHLIGHTS

Beaches
Manuel Antonio National Park, Nicoya Peninsula

Flora
Braulio Carillo National Park, Santa Rosa National Park

Outdoor activities
Braulio Carillo National

Park, Tortuguero National Park, Pacuare river

Romantic escapism
Tortuguero National

Park, Nicoya Peninsula

Wildlife
Monteverde Cloud Forest Reserve, Tortuguero National Park

THE NATIONAL PARKS
Good for beaches, flora, outdoor activities, romantic escapism and wildlife

---

THE NATURAL world is the big attraction in Costa Rica, almost 30 per cent of which is protected. Much of the countryside is stunningly beautiful and home to an amazing abundance of wildlife, and there are great beaches too. This is not a place for culture vultures, although the capital, San José, has a couple of excellent museums.

BEST WILDLIFE

Corcovado National Park
This park on the Osa Peninsula is very remote but is home to an astounding array of wildlife.

Monteverde Cloud Forest Reserve
Costa Rica offers the best chance to see the elusive, resplendent quetzal, and this reserve has the highest density of this bird in the world.

Santa Rosa National Park
Santa Rosa, in the north-west, has glorious beaches and abundant wildlife which is easy to spot.

Tortuguero National Park
Few people would venture over to the Caribbean coast if it weren't for Tortuguero. It is inaccessible by road, and the boat ride through jungle from Limón is part of the attraction. The park is named after the sea turtles which come ashore to lay eggs on the beach.

BEST VOLCANOES

Poás and Irazú volcanoes in the Central Valley are both easily accessible by road from San José and offer good views inside their craters and of the landscape below. The most dramatic of Costa Rica's volcanoes, the Arenal, is best seen from a distance: its constant emissions of white-hot ash and lava light up the sky at night.

BEST RESORTS AND BEACHES

Cahuita National Park
● A small resort on the north coast with a Caribbean atmosphere.
● The town is off the main tourist route.
● There are gorgeous palm-fringed beaches and a coral reef within swimming distance of the shore.

Manuel Antonio National Park
● Contains some of the most accessible rainforest in Costa Rica but many people – locals and tourists – come just for the beaches.
● The area possesses the largest concentration of smart resorts in Costa Rica, so you will not be alone.

Nicoya Peninsula
● Not the most scenic part of the country, but boasts some of Costa Rica's best beaches.
● Tamarindo is developed but not spoiled.
● Montezuma is popular with backpackers.
● Nosara, Samara and Carrillo are other good resorts.

BEST OUTDOOR ACTIVITIES

You don't have to walk anywhere to enjoy the scenery, but hiking will enable you to see the most pristine areas, where you will have minimal human company. The national parks and other areas of natural beauty offer a range of sporting opportunities.

Braulio Carrillo National Park
The park contains Costa Rica's most rugged countryside, with densely forested mountains cut through by countless rivers.

Cerro Chirripó National Park
A mix of tropical forests and peaks, including the nation's highest mountain, Cerro Chirripó (12,500 feet).

Reventazón and Pacuare rivers
Rafting is the most popular adventure sport in Costa Rica. The River Reventazón is ideal for beginners, while the River Pacuare is more challenging.

Rincón de la Vieja National Park
Trails run deep into the forest, where there are springs, waterfalls and a volcano to climb.

Tortuguero National Park
Costa Rica is well known for its blue-water fishing: sporting anglers flock to the Pacific coast, and some say the waters around Tortuguero National Park provide the best tarpon fishing in the world – the large, silvery fish are common in tropical waters.

WHEN TO GO

THE INLAND valleys and Pacific coast have two distinct seasons: dry, from December to April; rainy, from May to November. Costa Rica is at its most lush and beautiful during the wet season, and the short

	Average daily maximum temperature °C											
London	6	7	10	13	17	20	22	21	19	14	10	7
San José	24	24	26	26	27	26	25	26	26	25	25	24
	JAN	FEB	MAR	APR	MAY	JUN	JUL	AUG	SEP	OCT	NOV	DEC
San José	3	1	2	7	19	22	23	24	24	25	14	6
London	15	13	11	12	12	11	12	11	13	13	15	15
	Average number of rainy days per month											

downpours every afternoon are predictable enough to be tolerable – at least outside the wettest months of September and October. You will be lucky to avoid rain along the Atlantic coast, where the two short dry seasons are barely discernible. The climate in the mountains is often pleasantly cool – and chilly at night – with temperatures rising significantly along the coast.

PACKAGE TRAVEL

A GOOD range of tours making the most of the remarkable diversity of the country are available through tour operators, visiting the many national parks and reserves that constitute around 20 per cent of Costa Rica. A typical escorted tour would start from San José, visiting the Poás volcano, the Monteverde Reserve and the Tortuguero National Park with perhaps a couple of days on the Caribbean or Pacific coast exploring the parks, cruising the offshore islands or staying in a beach hotel. Specialists offer tailor-made itineraries and escorted tours.

Accommodation varies from top-of-the-range to basic. At the reserves accommodation is usually in lodges and the beach hotels on offer are of a good standard.

The diversity of birdlife makes Costa Rica a popular destination for specialist birdwatching and wildlife tour operators. Other activities include trekking, white-water rafting, camping and mountain biking.

Tour operators

Adventure: Exodus, Explore Worldwide, Guerba, Journey Latin America **Birdwatching**: Abercrombie & Kent, Animal Watch, Limosa, Naturetrek, Ornitholidays, Sunbird, Wildlife Worldwide **General**: Airtours, Bales Tours, British Airways Holidays, Cox & Kings, Cricketer, Hayes & Jarvis, Kuoni, Sunvil, Voyages Jules Verne **Specialists**: Journey Latin America, Nomadic Thoughts, South American Experience, Travel South America, Trips Worldwide, Union Castle Travel **Walking**: Exodus, Explore Worldwide, Guerba, Journey Latin America

---

INDEPENDENT TRAVEL

NO DIRECT scheduled flights are available from the UK. The best connections are via Miami, Amsterdam or Madrid.

Costa Rica is small – just twice the size of Scotland – but getting around can be time-consuming owing to the topography. Specialist tour operators in the UK can arrange Central American air passes, fly-drive and hotel voucher schemes for travellers in advance.

Internal flights are worth considering if you have a tight schedule. The couple of train services are entertaining but slow. Bus services are efficient along the Pan-American Highway and other main routes and within the Central Valley, but are otherwise patchy. If you are dependent on local transport you will have a hard time getting to and from most national parks. Many visitors opt to take a tour, and the many agencies in San José offer a wide choice. You can hire a car for a moderate cost; some agencies hire out camping gear too. The topography can make for some dramatic journeys, but keep your eye on the road: Costa Rica has the highest road accident rate in Central America.

As wealthy North Americans love to escape to Costa Rica, there are plenty of good-quality hotels. You will find conventional luxury hotels in San José, but outside the city – mainly along the Pacific coast – the good hotels are usually small, tasteful, wood-built affairs set in lovely grounds. You can expect more basic facilities in areas where Americans do not go. While the most visited national parks have comfortable lodges, most others have either simple refuges or camp sites.

RED TAPE, HEALTH AND SAFETY

BRITISH PASSPORT-HOLDERS do not need a visa and can stay in Costa Rica for three months.

The tap water is safe to drink in the main towns, and the healthcare is the best in the region. There is a risk of dengue fever in Puntarenas, the Pacific coast, Guanacaste and Limón. Ensure that your hepatitis A, polio and typhoid inoculations are up to date and consult your GP or a travel clinic for further health advice.

Take strict precautions against the 'aedes aegypti' mosquito and use lots of repellent. It is unlikely you will encounter one of Costa Rica's poisonous snakes, of which there are several varieties, but because so much of the countryside is accessible they are a potential danger.

Costa Rica likes to promote itself as a peaceful, 'civilised' place, but the country has its fair share of crime. You should take the same care in San José and the port of Limón as you would in any big city (see page 12), and do not presume that your belongings are safe in the beautiful surroundings of a national park.

MORE INFORMATION Tourist Information, Costa Rican Embassy, 14 Lancaster Gate, London W2 3LH, tel 0171-706 8844 (*please send an A4 sae with four first-class stamps*)
Web site: http://www. embcrlon.demon.co.uk

COST OF LIVING £

CUBA

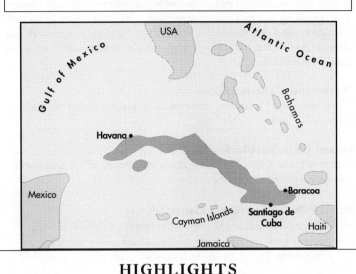

HIGHLIGHTS

Beaches
*Cayo Largo,
Varadero, Cayo
Coco, Cayo
Guillermo,
Playa Santa
Lucía,
Guardalavaca,
Baracoa*

**Scenic
landscape**
Viñales Valley,

*Baracoa,
Sierra Maestra*

Culture
*Havana,
Trinidad,
Santiago de
Cuba*

Nightlife
*Havana,
Santiago de
Cuba*

**Outdoor
activities**
*Cayo Largo,
Isla de la
Juventud,
Varadero,
Cayo Coco,
Cayo
Guillermo,
Playa Santa
Lucía,
Guardalavaca*

Local colour
*Havana,
western, central
and eastern
Cuba*

**Romantic
escapism**
*Viñales Valley,
Remedios,
Baracoa*

HAVANA
Good for culture, local colour and nightlife

CUBA'S CAPITAL was once Spain's most important colonial port and from the 1930s to 1950s was a Mafia-run prostitution and gambling den. Now it is a cocktail of decrepit seediness and architectural splendour, at times overpoweringly romantic, at times frustrating and exhausting.

OLD HAVANA

Mostly very dilapidated but gradually being restored, colonial Havana is as rewarding for its grand palaces and dusty backstreets as for any individual sights. Its showpiece squares are Plaza de la Catedral and Plaza de Armas; the finest thoroughfare is the Prado, lined with gaily painted mansions.

Morro and Cabaña castles

These imposing fortresses commanding Havana's harbour deliver magnificent views over the city.

Museo de la Revolución

Everything you wanted to know about the history of Castro's revolution (and a lot more besides).

Palacio de los Capitanes Generales

Havana's grandest palace, the former residence of Cuba's colonial governors, is now the city museum. The sumptuously furnished galleries remember Cuba's nineteenth-century independence heroes.

NEW HAVANA

Cementerio de Colón

An enormous, dreamy marble city of the dead, with giant mausoleums and poignant tombs.

Museo Hemingway

This country house at the edge of Havana's suburbs is furnished much as it was when the American writer Ernest Hemingway lived here on and off between 1939 and 1960; sadly, you can only peer through the windows.

Partagás cigar factory

The country's biggest cigar factory; tours look at the whole process of cigar-making, from sorting and rolling the tobacco leaves to bundling and banding the cigars.

Plaza de la Revolución

Cuba's governmental hub is a vast square surrounded by ugly ministry buildings and a towering obelisk which is 460 feet high – a lift goes to the top. At its base is an exhibition to José Martí, Cuba's most important independence hero.

BEST NIGHTLIFE

Cuba's most famour bar/restaurants are the plush El Floridita, noted for its daiquiris, and the graffiti-scrawled El Bodeguita del Medio. The Tropicana lays on showily kitsch open-air cabaret extravaganzas. For a less touristy experience, catch top contemporary Cuban salsa bands at the Palacio de la Salsa or the Casa de la Música.

BEST HOTELS

Some of Havana's hotels are sights in their own right. They include the ostentatious Nacional, emblematic of the Mafia era, and half-a-dozen historic places in Old Havana such as the opulent Santa Isabel, the Sevilla (with Graham Greene associations) and the Inglaterra, the island's oldest hotel which opened in 1875.

WESTERN CUBA
Good for beaches, local colour, outdoor activities, romantic escapism and scenic landscape

BEST RESORTS

Cayo Largo
● This small island, devoted exclusively to tourism, has six mediocre hotels and Playa Sirena, one of Cuba's best beaches.
● Boredom may soon set in, however.

Isla de la Juventud
● Backwoods island with little to offer except the best diving in Cuba (from the Hotel Colony).

Varadero
● Far and away Cuba's largest resort, comprising a ribbon of massive hotel complexes along a 12-mile-long beach.
● Drawbacks are the continuing construction work, the lack of a real centre, limited entertainment outside hotels, and sulphurous wafts from nearby oil wells at its western end.
● Pluses are a dazzling, white-sand beach, comfortable accommodation, super water sports and excursions to almost everywhere in Cuba.

BEST SIGHTS AND EXCURSIONS

Playa Girón
The failed US Bay of Pigs invasion landed here on the coast of the vast Zapata swamp in 1961; a good (if one-sided) museum tells the story.

Viñales Valley
Tobacco fields ploughed by oxen, and giant limestone outcrops covered in thick vegetation (called *mogotes*) define this romantic, peaceful idyll; it has two memorably sited hotels.

CENTRAL CUBA
Good for beaches, culture, local colour, outdoor activities and romantic escapism

BEST RESORTS

Cayo Coco and Cayo Guillermo
● Isolated islands, linked to the mainland by a causeway, being rapidly developed for tourism with outsize, luxury hotel complexes.
● Fantastic beaches and excellent water sports, but nothing else to do.

Playa Santa Lucía
● Five moderate hotels strung out along a fine beach providing super diving.
● Three miles away is the memorable beach of Playa Los Cocos.

BEST SIGHTS AND EXCURSIONS

Camagüey
Aside from its clutch of crumbling Baroque churches, Cuba's third largest city has more sombre architecture than Havana or Santiago. However, it is also far less touristy and an ideal place in which to immerse yourself in day-to-day Cuban life. Its most picturesque square is Plaza San Juan de Dios.

Remedios
This often overlooked colonial backwater has a stunning main square and church.

Trinidad
Cuba's most touristy but also most complete small colonial town, designated a UNESCO World Heritage Site, has beautifully restored mansions (now museums) and sleepy, cobbled backstreets.

EASTERN CUBA
Good for beaches, culture, local colour, nightlife, outdoor activities, romantic escapism and scenic landscape

BEST RESORTS

Guardalavaca
● Cuba's prettiest resort, surrounded by verdant countryside, has half-a dozen hotels along a scenic, shady beach.
● Two further smart hotels sit next to smaller, but equally lovely, Playa Esmeralda a few miles west.

BEST SIGHTS AND EXCURSIONS

Around Guardalavaca

Close to the resort lie: Chorro de Maíta, a well-presented excavated Indian burial ground; Gibara, a little port with tumbledown colonial buildings; and a moving memorial at Bahía de Bariay, where Columbus landed in 1492 while seeking a new trade route from Europe to Asia.

Baracoa

Remote and magical, this little-altered, languorous colonial port sits ensconced in cocoa and coconut groves. There are a couple of memorable, simple hotels, and magnificent beaches nearby such as Maguana.

Santiago de Cuba

Cuba's laid-back, number-two city has bewitching, lazy backstreets. It also offers some superb music: try the Casa de la Trova, where bands play all day. The top historic sights are: Casa de Velázquez, said to be the oldest house in the Americas; the Moncada Barracks, against which Castro launched an unsuccessful attack in 1953; and Cementerio Santa Ifigenia, where many Cuban heroes are buried. José Martí, Cuba's famous nineteenth-century hero, has a moving Art Deco mausoleum.

Sierra Maestra

Cuba's largest mountain range is wild and very impressive. Treks are normally possible (with guides) from Santo Domingo. The new coastal road skirting the mountains from Marea del Portillo to Santiago de Cuba is the country's most stunning drive.

WHEN TO GO

THE BEST time to travel is from November to April, when the temperature is normally pleasantly warm and there is little rain. In summer, it is too hot and humid for energetic sightseeing, tropical thunderstorms are frequent, and hurricanes a distinct possibility. Santiago hosts Cuba's most famous carnival around 26 July.

	Average daily maximum temperature °C											
London	6	7	10	13	17	20	22	21	19	14	10	7
Havana	26	26	27	29	30	31	32	32	31	29	27	26
	JAN	FEB	MAR	APR	MAY	JUN	JUL	AUG	SEP	OCT	NOV	DEC
Havana	6	4	4	4	7	10	9	10	11	11	7	6
London	15	13	11	12	12	11	12	11	13	13	15	15
	Average number of rainy days per month											

PACKAGE TRAVEL

THE MOST popular packages to Cuba involve a stay-put beach holiday, often on an all-inclusive basis. Caribbean sun-and-sand holidays are available in sanitised but comfortable resorts with superb beaches, mainly in and around Varadero.

Specialists offer a wider choice of options and generally stay away from the more commercialised beach resorts. Fortnight-long coach tours (sometimes also involving internal flights) visit places such as Havana, Santiago de Cuba, Trinidad, Cienfuegos and the Viñales Valley. Many companies combine a week on the beach with a week-long cultural tour.

A number of themed specialist packages are also on offer, from cigar tours and Hemingway tours to politically oriented holidays that visit hospitals and schools. Fly-drive holidays also feature, as do activity holidays including scuba diving, steam train tours, cycling and multi-activity breaks.

Tour operators

General and specialist: Archers, Bales Tours, Cox & Kings, Cricketer, Hayes & Jarvis, Holiday Place, Journey Latin America, Regent Holidays, Saga, Special Places, Sunvil, Travelcoast, Travelsphere **Tailor-made specialists**: Interchange, South American Experience, Trips Worldwide **Other activities**: Aquatours (scuba diving), Bike Tours, Exodus (cycling),Club Med (multi-activity), Railtours (rail tours), Sunbird (birdwatching)

INDEPENDENT TRAVEL

CHEAPEST SCHEDULED flights are with Cubana, three times a week from Gatwick to Havana and once a week from Manchester to Havana.

The tourist industry in Cuba is geared towards package holiday-makers, but no restrictions are imposed on independent travellers. That said, dealing with Cuba's often infuriating bureaucracy and the limitations of its decrepit transport system can be very trying. However, you'll only learn what Cuba is really like if you leave the confines of package hotels and explore without a tour guide. Outside the resorts, conditions are generally far more primitive, but compensations include superb Spanish colonial buildings, a rich musical heritage and a fascinating culture little changed since the late 1950s when Fidel Castro imposed communism on the island. For example, classic American Cadillacs and horse-and-carriages are typical forms of transport. Some Spanish is a great advantage: away from hotels, English is spoken only sporadically.

The best way to get around is to take internal flights (cheap and fairly reliable) and hire a car. Though car hire is relatively expensive and vehicles are often in dubious condition, roads are blissfully empty and you'll meet hordes of Cubans if you give lifts – hitching is ubiquitous. The only decent train service runs from Havana to Santiago (about 14 hours). Buses are horrifically overcrowded and infrequent, and seats on long trips can be hard to come by. Though it is illegal, many Cubans drive tourists around for the day in their old Cadillacs.

Most resort accommodation is prohibitively expensive for independent travellers. However, there are affordable, atmospheric hotels in Havana and Santiago, and cheap hotels in all the other cities. The cheapest accommodation is renting a room in a private house – a practice legalised in 1997. To avoid immigration hassles on arrival at the airport, it is best to pre-book accommodation for your first few nights.

Independent travellers can also experience *paladares* – mini family-run restaurants where you eat very inexpensively in someone's living room. Service, atmosphere and food are usually far better than in state-run restaurants.

RED TAPE, HEALTH AND SAFETY

BRITISH HOLIDAYMAKERS need a tourist card to enter Cuba; these are available from tour operators, specialist travel agencies and the Cuban Embassy. The card is valid for 30 days and must be used within six months of issue. It costs £15 and is extendable once in Cuba.

Vaccinations are recommended against typhoid, tetanus, polio and hepatitis A. Dengue fever is reported in Santiago and southern Cuba – use mosquito repellent and cover your arms and legs between dusk and dawn. Take all medicines and bathroom essentials with you from home, as they are expensive and/or hard to come by locally.

Tourists use US dollars in Cuba. Go with as much cash as possible, plus some dollar travellers cheques and a credit card: neither can be American Express because of the US embargo against Cuba.

Though crime is on the increase, Cuba is still a very safe destination compared with many developing countries. While crime against the person is virtually unheard of, bag-snatching and pickpocketing have become problems in parts of Old Havana (particularly south of Calle Obispo), in the district called Centro, and at festivals. Bigger problems include being harrassed by locals for money, gifts and the purchase of black–market cigars, and above all being pestered by pros-titutes, who are especially prolific in Havana.

Foreign tourists have been targeted by a terrorist group responsible for planting several bombs in hotels and restaurants between April and September 1997; one explosion at a Havana hotel killed an Italian. The Cuban government has blamed anti-Castro groups. For the latest advice contact the Foreign Office Travel Advice Unit (see page 11).

MORE INFORMATION Cuba Tourist Board, 167 High Holborn, London WC1V 6PA, tel 0171-240 6655
Web site: http://www.caribtourism.com/

Cuban Embassy, 167 High Holborn, London WC1V 6PA, tel 0171-240 2488

Also helpful are specialist tour operators such as: Regent Holidays, tel 0117-921 1711; and South American Experience, tel 0171-976 5511

COST OF LIVING £-££

CYPRUS

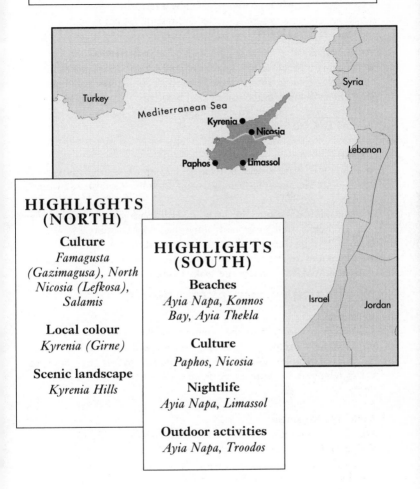

HIGHLIGHTS (NORTH)

Culture
Famagusta (Gazimagusa), North Nicosia (Lefkosa), Salamis

Local colour
Kyrenia (Girne)

Scenic landscape
Kyrenia Hills

HIGHLIGHTS (SOUTH)

Beaches
Ayia Napa, Konnos Bay, Ayia Thekla

Culture
Paphos, Nicosia

Nightlife
Ayia Napa, Limassol

Outdoor activities
Ayia Napa, Troodos

A BUFFER zone (the 'Green Line') patrolled by the UN has split Cyprus since the 1970s. The Greeks control the island south of this line and the Turks the north. Northern Cyprus is not recognised by any country except Turkey, which makes it less accessible than the south.

Hostility runs deep, and free movement across the Line is forbidden. If you visit Northern Cyprus, ask the officials to stamp your entry visa on a separate sheet of paper, as you may otherwise be forbidden entry to southern Cyprus and possibly mainland Greece.

SOUTHERN CYPRUS

BEST RESORTS

Ayia Napa
● The superb beach of fine sand prompted speedy development of this sleepy fishing village into a tangle of souvenir shops, bars and banks.
● Night-owls loiter in the squares and busy bars.
● If you hire transport, you can explore smaller, quieter beaches like Konnos Bay and Ayia Thekla.

Paphos
● The local market and historic sights attract tourists, but good beaches are lacking (the nearest decent stretch is Coral Bay, 14 miles away).
● Waterside cafés along the harbour do a roaring trade, while huge package hotels stretch eastwards along the rocky coastline.
● Over 20 third-century mosaics were discovered here in 1962.
● Excavations also continue on the Tombs of the Kings, a vast necropolis hollowed out beneath the rocky landscape.

BEST SIGHTS AND EXCURSIONS

Curium
On a high promontory lie the extensive Greek and Roman remains of the town of Curium, notable for its theatre and mosaics. The nearby Sanctuary of Apollo, destroyed by an earthquake in AD 76-7, has been partly rebuilt. A museum in Episkopi shows items retrieved from the votive pit.

Folk Art Museum
Housed in an eighteenth-century stone house in Yeroskipos is a variety of Cypriot implements and crafts.

Kykko
The most famous monastery on the island feels more like a showpiece than a religious centre. The tomb of Archbishop Makarios, who fought against British rule, is nearby.

Limassol
Good for shopping and strolling along the seafront, Limassol also has a small archaeological museum, and a twelfth-century castle housing Venetian stone engravings and medieval buckles. Alternatively, you can take a guided tour of the local brewery.

Makheras
This photogenic monastery nestles against the steep side of a wooded mountain and offers imposing views.

Nicosia
The city is encircled by vast sixteenth-century walls stamped with the Venetian lion. The Cyprus Archaeological Museum gives pride of place to the eighth-century BC contents of the Salamis royal tombs, including a throne decorated with gold; rulers were buried with their chariots and horses in Greek epic tradition. There is a small museum at Salamis itself. In the Byzantine Museum, 144 icons from churches throughout Cyprus have been gathered for safe keeping. The Leventis Museum charts Nicosia's history, while the National Struggle Museum records the struggle for independence from Britain in the 1950s.

Panayia Angeloktistos
The main focus of attention in this light stone, domed church is the miraculously preserved Byzantine mosaic of the Virgin and Child.

Panayia Khrysorroyiatissa
Founded in 1152 by a monk, Ignatius, the monastery commands lovely views over the hills. You can buy wines from the vineyards.

Troodos Mountains
A cool day in the mountains comes as a relief after the baking coastal heat. A leisurely stroll around villages like Omodhos, Phini and Kato Platres reveals a way of life unchanged for centuries. The best walking base in the mountains is Troodos, at the foot of Mount Olympus. Nature-trails are signposted through forests of black pine and cypress.

NORTHERN CYPRUS

BEST RESORT
Kyrenia
● The main base for visitors to Northern Cyprus, Kyrenia has a picturesque fishing harbour ringed with outdoor cafés.
● A Venetian castle overlooks the harbour.
● The Shipwreck Museum has the oldest wreck ever to be recovered.

BEST SIGHTS AND EXCURSIONS
Famagusta
The city's impressive Lusignan-Venetian walls failed to keep out the Ottomans, but inside them is a thriving centre with business conducted

in and around the narrow streets that separate the ruins. The attractive Lala Mustafa Pasa Camii (St Nicholas Cathedral) was where Lusignans were crowned honorary kings of Jerusalem.

Outside the walls, in Famagusta new town, the beach hotels of Varosha have been deserted since 1974. View this crumbling embryonic Benidorm from the Palm Beach Hotel.

Kyrenia Hills
The ruined abbeys and Crusader castles in the Kyrenia Hills are best explored by car. St Hilarion is the best-preserved; Buffavento is the hardest to reach and has the most extensive views; Kantara is more accessible, with fine views over the Karpas peninsula. Bellapais, a hill village dominated by a ruined Gothic abbey, was the home of writer Lawrence Durrell in the 1950s, immortalised in his novel *Bitter Lemons*.

North Nicosia
Despite the blight cast by the wall dividing it from South Nicosia, sleepy North Nicosia is worth visiting for its medieval churches (now mosques) and small museums. The best sights are Selimiye Camii (Church of Aya Sofya), the lovely French-Gothic cathedral where Lusignan kings were crowned kings of Cyprus, and the Ethnography Museum (the actual collection is of limited interest but is housed in a seventeenth-century lodge where dervishes whirled until 1954). Finally, the Turkish bath of Buyuk Hamam is worth frequenting if you are not visiting mainland Turkey.

Salamis
These extensive Roman ruins lie within a taxi-ride of Famagusta. At the nearby Royal Tombs horses were sacrificed, as described by Homer.

WHEN TO GO

IN JULY and August Cyprus is extremely hot; June and September are better months in which to visit. North Cyprus is not as crowded as the rest of the Med, but temperatures at these times are more comfortable.

Average daily maximum temperature °C											
London	6	7	10	13	17	20	22	21	19	14	10	7
Nicosia	15	16	19	24	29	34	37	37	33	28	22	17
	JAN	FEB	MAR	APR	MAY	JUN	JUL	AUG	SEP	OCT	NOV	DEC
Nicosia	14	10	8	4	3	1	<1	<1	1	4	6	11
London	15	13	11	12	12	11	12	11	13	13	15	1
Average number of rainy days per month											

PACKAGE TRAVEL

Southern Cyprus

All the major tour operators to southern Cyprus offer one- or two-week packages to the main coastal resorts of Limassol, Paphos, Protaras, Larnaca and Ayia Napa in either hotels or apartments. Some combine a week on the coast with a week in a resort-style hotel in the Troodos mountains, or with a week staying in simple village houses. Purpose-built villas with pools in the hill villages are available only through a handful of tour operators. Car hire is sometimes included in the package price. If not, budget for it, as public transport is limited.

If you want to explore, several companies offer self-drive tours where you stay in pre-arranged hotels, or if you want more freedom you can take a fly-drive package and make your own way around the island. Mini-cruises to Israel and Egypt lasting from two to seven nights are on offer from many tour operators, and a couple combine a holiday in Cyprus with a trip to Jordan.

Specialist activity holidays to Cyprus feature birdwatching (the best time is in the spring), walking, cycling, scuba diving, golf, botany and cultural tours.

Northern Cyprus

Few tour operators include Northern Cyprus in their brochures, and lack of competition rules out rock-bottom prices. Most packages are based in Kyrenia.

Tour operators

Birdwatching: Birding, Cygnus Wildlife, Naturetrek, Ornitholidays, Sunbird **Cultural**: Andante, Prospect **Diving**: Airglobe, Inspirations, Sunvil **Flora**: Cox & Kings, David Sayers Travel, Naturetrek **General and specialist**: Airglobe, Airtours, Amathus, Anemone, Argo, Aspro, Aztec, Best of Greece & Cyprus, Cadogan, Cosmos, Cyplon, Cyprair, Delta, First Choice, Greece & Cyprus Travel Centre, Golden Sun, Intersky, Inspirations, Magnum, Manos, Pan Atlas, Price Right, Rendezvous, Skytours, Sovereign, Sunvil, Sunworld, Tapestry, Thomas Cook, Thomson, Travel Club of Upminster **Walking**: Alternative Travel Group, Exodus, Explore Worldwide, Waymark **Other activities**: Anglers World (fishing), Inter-Church Travel (religious tours), Solo's Holidays (singles), Wildlife Worldwide (wildlife) **Northern Cyprus**: Andante, Prospect, Regent Holidays, Tapestry

---

INDEPENDENT TRAVEL

Southern Cyprus

In southern Cyprus you are unlikely to save money by going independently, and accommodation can be difficult to find, as it will invariably be fully booked by tour operators.

Large towns are linked by regular bus services and shared taxi services, but to explore extensively you will need to hire a car. Stick to the main roads, as minor ones can be lethal, and do not be afraid to use the horn (except at night). Driving is on the left-hand side of the road.

You will find well-equipped, self-contained hotel complexes, and plenty of villas and apartments. Some smaller tour operators offer 'agro-tourism' programmes on the Akamas peninsula and in the Troodos mountains, where you can stay in traditional village houses, mixing with local people and experiencing their way of life.

Northern Cyprus

In Northern Cyprus, provided you do not want to stay in the few resort-class hotels, it can be cheaper to make your own arrangements. The international boycott means that flights to Nicosia's Ercan airport have to transit Turkey; with time to spare the cheapest way to reach North Cyprus is to fly to Istanbul and then take a 'domestic' flight to Ercan or a bus south to Alanya, Tasucu or Mersin and the Kyrenia ferries. Kyrenia, Nicosia and Famagusta are linked by cheap, shared taxis called *combos*. For reaching outlying sites, ordinary taxis are a godsend.

The international car rental companies do not operate in Northern Cyprus. Not all hire cars are well maintained; look them over carefully before accepting one.

Hotels are not officially graded and standards are generally lower than in the south. Kyrenia has plenty of clean and well-run pensions. Elsewhere, they may double as homes-from-home for Turkish soldiers.

RED TAPE, HEALTH AND SAFETY

UK PASSPORT-HOLDERS do not require a visa to visit southern Cyprus, but your passport must be valid for three months after your date of departure. Visitors to Northern Cyprus have their passports stamped with an entry visa when they arrive: ask for it to be stamped on a separate piece of paper, if you want to visit southern Cyprus or mainland Greece on a future occasion.

Sensitivity about the Green Line runs deep, and trouble occasionally flares up. It is advisable to pay attention to signs forbidding access, photography, etc. For the latest advice contact the Foreign Office Travel Advice Unit (see page 11).

No vaccinations are required. Tap water is safe to drink, but the water in the south-eastern part of the island has a slightly funny taste, and even the locals drink bottled water here.

MORE INFORMATION

Southern Cyprus
Cyprus Tourism Organisation, 213 Regent Street,
London W1R 8DA, tel 0171-734 9822
Web site: http://www.cyprustourism.org/

Northern Cyprus
North Cyprus Tourist Office, 29 Bedford Square,
London WC1B 3EG, tel 0171-631 1930

COST OF LIVING £

CZECH REPUBLIC

HIGHLIGHTS

Culture
Prague, Tabor, Telč

Local colour
Moravia

Scenic landscape
Bohemia, Giant Mountains and Český Ráj, Šumava National Park, Moravský Kras

PRAGUE
Good for culture

THE HEART of historic Bohemia, Prague is one of the world's most beautiful cities. An incredible mix of Gothic, Romanesque, baroque and art nouveau architecture forms the backdrop to an unbeatable literary and musical calendar. Its popularity, however, means that over-crowding can detract from the fairy-tale delicacy of the main sights.

BEST SIGHTS

Hradčany (castle district)
The largest ancient castle in the world is Prague's biggest crowd-puller – go early or late to avoid crowds. It dates from the ninth century and incorporates a series of courtyards with fascinating chapels, halls, gateways and gardens. Do not miss St Vitus Cathedral with its spectacular stained-glass windows, and the historic Old Royal Palace.

Beyond the castle walls, Hradčany teems with palaces. The main trio are the Sternberg, Schwarzenberg and Archbishop's. In Loretánské Náměstí, visit the impressive Loreta and Chapel of Our Lady of Sorrows with its treasury. Malá Strana is a picturesque area for a stroll.

Tourists, hawkers and buskers (and pickpockets) pack the Charles Bridge (Karlův Most) for the best views of the city from the river.

Staré Město (old town)
Staroměstské Náměstí, the Old Town Square, is significant in Czech history and a focal point today. Look out for the Astronomical Clock, with its hourly show, the baroque façade of St Nicholas Church, and the towers of the Gothic Týn Church. The old Jewish quarter of Josefov has an important museum and a unique multi-level cemetery.

BOHEMIA
Good for culture and scenic landscape

BEST TOWNS AND VILLAGES
Český Krumlov
Fairy-tale streets lined with baroque and Renaissance façades and a grandiose castle put Český Krumlov on UNESCO's World Heritage list.

Kutná Hora
Once a wealthy town with grand palaces and churches, due to its now defunct silver mines, Kutná Hora resembles Prague on a friendlier, more accessible scale. St Barbara's Cathedral is the highlight.

Loket nad Ohří
This medieval walled village in a splendidly romantic setting was one of Goethe's favourite spots for courting. The castle, altered over the centuries but still magnificent, gives great views over the countryside.

Tabor
Tabor's gorgeous winding streets, the former stronghold of the revolutionary anti-Catholic Hussites, are fronted by Gothic and Renaissance houses. Tour the underground passages linking their cellars.

BEST SCENIC LANDSCAPES
Giant Mountains (Krkonoše)
The highest peak on the border with Poland in Eastern Bohemia is Sněžka, at over 4,800ft. Skiing (in winter) and walking are good, although the forests have suffered from acid rain. Accommodation is not very high-quality in the resort centres. In the foothills lies Český Ráj, or 'Czech paradise', a surreal sandstone landscape with a web of walking trails, and the interesting 'rock villages' of Prachovské Skaly and Hrubá Skala. Their sandstone labyrinths of caves, towers and passageways are unmissable. Bring your own camping gear on longer hikes.

Šumava National Park
Attractions of this thickly forested, mountainous area are walking and

cross-country skiing in pristine forest, untouched by pollution. Boubin Forest, designated a UNESCO protected landscape, is particularly prized.

BEST SPA TOWNS

The Czech Republic's famous trio of spas, Karlovy Vary (Karlsbad), Mariánské Lázně (Marienbad) and Františkovy Lázné (Franzenbad), were, in their heyday, the playgrounds of Goethe, Kafka, Wagner, Schiller, Beethoven and Gogol. Nowadays overweight German tourists flock there for the cure, and even if you are not there to ingest noxious fumes and sulphurous waters, great pleasure can be found in the spas' sedate and dignified ambience. Of the three, Karlovy Vary is the most magnificent – and the most overrun with tour groups.

BEST BEERS

České Budéjovicé

At the heart of this town is a gorgeous arcaded square with baroque, Gothic and Renaissance façades. The Budvar, or Budweiser, brewery is outside the centre and runs tours for six or more people.

Plzeň

This industrial town with some Renaissance houses is home to Pilsner, and has enough historical interest for a day-trip. The Prazdroj (Urquell) Brewery and beer museum explain the brewer's ancient and noble art.

BEST CASTLES

Karlštejn

Renovated in the nineteenth century, pristine Karlštejn is a favourite with day-trippers from Prague. The castle is best seen from outside.

Krivoklat

Worth a visit for the train trip along the forested Berounka valley and mostly free of tour groups, Krivoklat's Gothic features are more evocative than Karlštejn's remodelled face.

Rožmberk

A romantic fusion of Gothic and Renaissance styles, Rožmberk's interior is stuffed with fascinating furniture, porcelain and sculpture.

MORAVIA
Good for local colour and scenic landscape

BEST SIGHTS

Moravské Slovácko

This region of south-east Moravia is a suitable place to sample local folk traditions including colourful costumes, singing and dancing, and painted houses. The best-known festivals are held at Strážnice, Blatnice and Vlčnov. The local wine is also the best in the Republic.

Pernštejn Castle
A well-preserved thirteenth-century castle near Brno, enlarged and rebuilt several times. The tour includes library, chapel and knights' room.

Rožnov pod Radhoštěm
This resort town is home to one of the country's best open-air museums, including a reconstructed Wallachian shepherds' village and pub.

Telč
Founded in the thirteenth century, Telč's pastel gingerbread façades, centred on a square which has remained unchanged for centuries, qualify it to be a UNESCO World Heritage Site.

BEST SCENIC LANDSCAPE
Moravský Kras
The Moravian karst lies to the north of Brno. It is a hilly area slashed by canyons and porous with hundreds of caves, the most spectacular of which are Punkevni and the Macocha Abyss. A boat tour on the underground river is an eerie and popular way to see these caves. The karst formations are hewn by acidic rainwater passing through limestone, resulting in wonderfully coloured stalactites and stalagmites.

WHEN TO GO

IF YOU intend to focus on Prague, any time of year is suitable. The crucial factor will be your tolerance of crowds, which are worst from May to August, at Easter and over the Christmas/New Year period, when Austrians, Germans and Italians take over Prague and the mountains. November to April is distinctly chilly, with snow on the ground in higher regions, though you will avoid crowds and rip-off prices.

Average daily maximum temperature °C											
London	6	7	10	13	17	20	22	21	19	14	10	7
Prague	0	1	7	12	18	21	23	22	18	12	5	1
	JAN	FEB	MAR	APR	MAY	JUN	JUL	AUG	SEP	OCT	NOV	DEC
Prague	13	11	10	11	13	12	13	12	10	13	12	13
London	15	13	11	12	12	11	12	11	13	13	15	15
Average number of rainy days per month											

Prague's major cultural event is the Spring International Music Festival in May through to June, when concerts are held in the city's historic churches and palaces.

Easter and Christmas have shed most of their religious significance thanks to the Communist era, but are still major holidays.

PACKAGE HOLIDAYS

MANY TOUR operators offer city breaks to Prague (some in combination with other central European cities such as Budapest and Vienna) in a choice of accommodation ranging from five-star hotels to one-star pensions, apartments or rooms in private homes.

Specialists such as Cedok offer the widest choice of holidays outside Prague, including visits to the spa towns of Bohemia such as Karlovy Vary or Mariánské Lázně, Brno in Moravia and the mountain and lake resorts north of Prague. Self-catering houses in the countryside, self-drive tours and coach tours are also on offer. Coach tours from the UK offer holidays based in a hotel (usually within striking distance of Prague) and include daily excursions.

Activity holidays include battlefield tours, birdwatching, cultural, music and study tours, walking, horse-riding and golf.

Tour operators

City breaks: British Airways Holidays, Cresta, Crystal, Inghams, Made to Measure, Osprey, Sovereign, Thomson, Time Off, Travelscene **Coach tours**: Crusader, Leger, Shearings, Travelsphere **Cultural/music/study tours**: Ace Study Tours, Martin Randall, Prospect, Travel for the Arts **Specialists**: Bridgewater, Cedok, Danube Travel, Hungarian Air Tours, Intra Travel, Lanzotic Travel, Peltours, Regent Holidays, Travellers Czech **Walking**: Exodus, Explore Worldwide, HF Holidays, Ramblers Holidays, Sherpa **Other activities**: Alternative Travel Group (cycling), Cedok (horse-riding, golf), Inter-Church Travel (pilgrimage), Midas (battlefields), Ornitholidays (birdwatching), Solo's Holidays (singles), Sunbird (birdwatching)

INDEPENDENT TRAVEL

PRAGUE IS well served by scheduled and charter flights, and has regular internal connections to Brno and Ostrava. You can go from London to Prague by rail in about 36 hours.

There are car rental agencies in the Czech Republic, but it is cheaper to book before you arrive. A UK or European licence plus passport are all you need. Seat-belts are compulsory. On-the-spot fines are levied for speeding and other minor offences. If you want to use toll roads you must pay in advance for a sticker, valid for one year, that you must display on your windscreen. You can buy stickers at petrol stations, border crossings and various retail outlets. Unleaded petrol is widely available. Be warned if you plan to take your own car: a thriving market in stolen Western cars with foreign numberplates operates, especially in Prague.

The Czech Railways network is extensive, covering most of the country. Fares are cheap by Western standards. You can also buy a regional or network ticket valid for a week, a month, or a year, for the whole network or for Bohemia or Moravia and Silesia. To buy a pass you need your passport and a photo. You can also buy passes before you arrive.

Book accommodation well ahead at all times and especially for the spring music festival, when Prague is overflowing. B&B in private homes is the best budget option, as Prague hotels tend to be expensive. Accommodation agencies can find you flats or rooms in central Prague. Most will have photos of the room and show you the address on a map. It is best to book for one night and then, if you like it, to negotiate directly with the owner. Or look out for *Zimmer frei* signs.

RED TAPE, HEALTH AND SAFETY

BRITISH PASSPORT-HOLDERS do not need a visa to visit the Czech Republic for visits of up to 90 days.

Petty theft is common, especially in Prague: watch out for pickpockets around Charles Bridge, the castle area, Wenceslas Square, Old Town Square and the Jewish Cemetery. Thieves also operate on trains and trams and around the main railway station. Leave valuables in a hotel safe and carry a photocopy of your passport for identification purposes. For the latest information contact the Foreign Office Travel Advice Unit (see page 11).

MORE INFORMATION Czech Tourist Authority, Czech Centre, 95 Great Portland Street, London W1N 5RA, tel 0171-291 9925

No tourist office web site exists, but you can access information about the Czech Republic at:
http://www.tourist-offices.org.uk/ Czech_Republic/index.html

COST OF LIVING £

DENMARK

Sweden

Jutland

Copenhagen

Funen

Zealand

Germany

COPENHAGEN
Good for culture, family holidays and nightlife

DENMARK'S CAPITAL is a charming and likeable city. Its compact centre is pedestrian-friendly, its people are welcoming and its attractions include excellent museums, lively nightlife and the best value for money of any of the Scandinavian capitals.

BEST SIGHTS

National Museum
Fascinating displays on Danish history, including Viking exhibits.

Ny Carlsberg Glyptotek
The city's best gallery contains a tremendous selection of ancient artefacts, particularly Etruscan, as well as important works by Gauguin, Degas and Rodin.

Rosenborg Castle
This castle is a medley of Dutch gables, fancy brickwork and polygonal green spires. The Danish Crown Jewels are kept in the basement treasury.

Strøget
This series of cheerful pedestrianised streets lined with shops, bars and restaurants is liveliest between Nytorv and Gammeltorv squares, where there is a daily market and some interesting churches.

Tivoli Gardens
Copenhagen's famed amusement park (open in 1843) has fairground rides, ice-cream stalls and other attractions. Although rather over-priced, it is fine for carefree strolling and great fun for children.

ZEALAND
Good for beaches and culture

BEST SIGHTS

Helsingør
The best-known sight in this prosperous port is the sixteenth-century castle, which inspired Elsinore Castle in Shakespeare's *Hamlet*.

Hillerød
Most visitors to this busy town come to admire the many towers, spires and Gothic arches of Frederiksborg Castle, largely the work of Christian IV's extensive rebuilding in the early seventeenth century. The interior is a museum devoted to Danish history.

Humlebaek
This charming old fishing village houses one of Denmark's most famous galleries, Louisiana, which harmoniously combines modern art, architecture and sculpture. American works are particularly well represented.

Roskilde
This ancient town, once capital of Denmark, is an appealing, laid-back place. Its Domkirke is a mixture of architectural styles; the Royal Chapels house the coffins of Danish kings and queens. Other attractions include five different types of Viking boat in the Viking Ship Museum, and the fascinating reconstruction of a Danish Iron Age village at the Lejre Archaeological Research Centre, just outside Roskilde.

Rungsted
Opposite the busy yachting harbour sits an inspiring museum which is dedicated to Karen Blixen, author of *Out of Africa*.

BEST BEACHES AND ISLANDS
Bornholm
A popular holiday island (nearer to Sweden than Denmark) which offers excellent beaches in the south and good walking in the woods and along the cliffs of the north.

Møn
The most interesting of the islands off the south coast of Zealand is known for its white chalk cliffs and neolithic burial sites.

Northern Zealand
A series of fine beaches and sleepy villages – such as Hornbaek and Gilleleje – stretch along the peninsula west of Helsingør and are ideal for a couple of days' relaxation.

FUNEN
Good for beaches

BEST SIGHT
Odense
Denmark's third largest town is the only sizeable settlement on the agricultural island of Funen. The cathedral, the only purely Gothic church in the country, dates mainly from the late thirteenth century and contains the eleventh-century skeleton of King Knud II. Hans Christian Andersen, the author of The Little Mermaid, The Ugly Ducking and other famous fairy tales, was born in Odense. His childhood home has now become a museum. You can watch ancient trades being practised at the careful reconstruction of the nineteenth-century Funen Village.

BEST BEACHES AND RESORTS
Aerø
● The most interesting island off Funen's south coast.
● Excellent beaches and ancient burial places as well as a fine medieval town, Aerøskøbing.

Southern Funen
● Known for its many inviting, sandy beaches (which can become uncomfortably crowded in summer).
● Best bases are Svendborg and Fåborg. The latter is generally quieter and contains the excellent Museum of Funen Painting.

JUTLAND
Good for culture, family holidays, nightlife, outdoor activities and scenic landscape

BEST SIGHTS

Aalborg
The major city of northern Jutland is a lively, likeable place with hand-some buildings and access to the wild far north of the peninsula. The North Jutland Art Museum is one of Denmark's best modern art collec-tions, with works by Warhol, Le Corbusier and Claes Oldenburg. Near the city, the atmospheric Viking and Iron Age burial ground of Lindholm Hoje includes rare 'ship monuments' – stones laid in the shape of a ship.

Århus
Denmark's second city is compact and lively, with some superb buildings and a thriving nightlife. The Domkirke is a huge, mainly fifteenth-cen-tury church that replaced the twelfth-century original. The area around the cathedral is the centre of city life and is filled with numerous well-preserved buildings containing shops, cafés and bars. A collection in the Århus Art Museum gives an overview of Danish art from the late eigh-teenth century. Den Gamle By successfully recreates a traditional Danish town, with more than 60 houses from all over the country reassembled.

Ribe
Remarkably preserved medieval town dominated by its enormous twelfth-century cathedral.

Silkeborg
This smart town in an area of lakes and woodland called the Lake District is a good base for walking. Its Culture Museum contains the famed Tollund Man, the superbly preserved body of an Iron Age man found in a nearby bog.

Skagen
A popular holiday town of bright houses perched on top of the windswept peninsula. Its museum has work by the 'Skagen Artists'.

Vejle
This neat town on a fjord is well sited for nearby Legoland and Jelling. Legoland has made the village of Billund a major tourist destination – children love the buildings, animals and machines made of almost 40 million Lego bricks. Jelling is an ancient pagan festival site. The tomb of tenth-century King Gorm and his wife was discovered here, and old runic stones stand in the church.

Viborg

At the centre of Denmark's region of rolling hills, wind-ravaged heaths and wooded valleys, Viborg makes a convenient base for walking. The town itself has some interesting churches and a pleasant old quarter.

WHEN TO GO

COPENHAGEN IS best visited during the Tivoli season, which lasts from May to September. Summer is the best time for the rest of the country too; temperatures are similar to those of southern England, but Denmark is noticeably sunnier – and slightly wetter.

Copenhagen's carnival, with flowers and processions, is held in early June. It is fun, but makes it difficult to see or do anything else for the duration.

	Average daily maximum temperature °C											
London	6	7	10	13	17	20	22	21	19	14	10	7
Copenhagen	2	2	5	10	16	19	22	21	18	12	7	4
	JAN	FEB	MAR	APR	MAY	JUN	JUL	AUG	SEP	OCT	NOV	DEC
Copenhagen	17	13	12	13	11	13	14	14	15	16	16	17
London	15	13	11	12	12	11	12	11	13	13	15	15
	Average number of rainy days per month											

PACKAGE TRAVEL

TOUR OPERATORS offering Denmark tend to concentrate on city breaks in Copenhagen and visits to Legoland although there are also the options of self-drive tours, Hans Christian Andersen themed tours and self-catering cottages or chalets and camping. Activity tour operators offer battlefield tours, fishing, cultural and study tours.

INDEPENDENT TRAVEL

SEVERAL FLIGHTS run every day between Britain and Denmark and regular ferry crossings from Harwich and Newcastle to Esbjerg.

Trains and buses within Denmark are frequent, efficient and cheap, and because the country is small, travelling times are short. Cycling is very popular and, with about 6,000 miles of signed cycle routes, often the best way to appreciate the mainly flat countryside. Bikes can be hired at most tourist offices, youth hostels and bike shops. A useful publication is *CykelGuide*, available from bookshops or Sustrans, tel 0117-929 0888.

Car hire is expensive. A UK driving licence is adequate.

The Copenhagen Card, available from tourist offices, provides free transport and entrance to all the city's museums. The Use-It centre in Copenhagen is a good source of information on budget accommodation, transport and entertainment.

Accommodation in Denmark is cheaper than in the rest of Scandinavia but still a major expense. It is worth looking around for pensions and country inns, which often offer similar facilities to hotels but are cheaper. Rooms in private houses are a good-value alternative. Camping is cheap, and campsites abound – some have cabins, which are excellent value for several people sharing. Hostel, also plentiful, are the next-cheapest option. Many have private rooms. Tourist offices have English-speaking staff who can book accommodation for you.

Tour operators

Birdwatching: Limosa, Ornitholidays, Sunbird **City breaks**: British Airways Holidays, Cresta, Crystal, Inghams, Osprey, Premier Holidays, Time Off, Travelscene **Specialists**: Colour Line, Finlandia, Inntravel, SAS Holiday World, Scandinavian Seaways, Scandinavian Travel Service, ScanMeridian, Scantours, Sovereign Scanscape, Specialised Tours, Taber **Walking**: Explore Worldwide, Headwater, Ramblers Holidays, Waymark **Other activities**: Ace Study Tours, Anglers World (fishing), Discover the World (wildlife), Eurocamp (camping), Holts' Tours (battlefields), Solo's Holidays (singles)

RED TAPE, HEALTH AND SAFETY

BRITISH PASSPORT-HOLDERS do not need a visa to visit Denmark.

There are no particular health or crime problems in Denmark. Just take the usual precautions (see pages 10–12).

MORE INFORMATION Danish Tourist Board, 55 Sloane Street, London SW1X 9SY, tel 0171-259 5959
Web site: http://www.dtb.dt.dk

COST OF LIVING £££

ECUADOR

HIGHLIGHTS

Culture
*Cuenca,
Ingapirca, Quito*

Flora
The Oriente

Local colour
*Cuenca, Quito,
Otavalo, Saquisilí*

Outdoor activities
*Avenue of the
Volcanoes, Baños,
the Amazon*

Scenic landscape
Andes, the Sierra

Wildlife
*The Oriente,
Galapagos Islands*

THE ANDES
Good for culture, local colour and scenic landscape

BEST CITIES

Cuenca
This is Ecuador's prettiest colonial city and a well-sited base for exploring the surrounding area, which includes the Inca ruins of Ingapirca (the best in Ecuador), traditional villages and national parks.

Quito
Much of the capital of Ecuador is dirty and ramshackle, but it has a gorgeous setting and Old Quito boasts lovely colonial architecture. Its museums are a good introduction to the rest of the country.

BEST LOCAL COLOUR

Otavalo
Tourists pour into the home of Ecuador's most famous market, to

admire the local Indians dressed in their colourful traditional clothes. Although the market is geared mainly to the sale of livestock, a few craft stalls cater for the tourist trade.

Saquisilí
The Thursday market in Saquisilí, south of Quito, is rated by many to be the country's best − both commercially for the locals and for its tourist colour and interest − but it does not attract as many people as Otavalo's market.

BEST SCENIC LANDSCAPE

The magnificent scenery of the Andes, above all the so-called Avenue of the Volcanoes south of Quito, can be enjoyed from the road or as a backdrop to the towns of the Sierra.

You need to be a serious climber to tackle the highest peaks, including Cotopaxi (19,500 feet) and Chimborazo (20,700 feet). The easiest volcano to climb is Tunguruhua (16,500 feet), which is accessible from Baños.

THE ORIENTE
Good for flora, outdoor activities and wildlife

ECUADOR'S MAGNIFICENT and varied landscapes, abundant wildlife and rich indigenous culture have made it one of the top destinations in South America. Two-thirds of Ecuador, the so-called Oriente, forms part of the Amazon basin.

BEST WILDLIFE
The Amazon
There is little virgin jungle within easy reach, but you can see lovely birds and flowers.

Podocarpus National Park
In the far south of Ecuador, this national park's varied habitats provide some of the best chances to see native mammals and birds.

GALAPAGOS ISLANDS
Good for wildlife

LOCATED 600 miles off the South American coast, these volcanic islands are prized for their unique wildlife, which seems to show no fear of humans. The cost of the trip doesn't deter visitors, the number of whom is limited by the government to 40,000 a year.

WHEN TO GO

THE COASTAL, mountain and jungle regions of Ecuador each have a very different climate. The Amazon is hot and wet all year round, and roads may close after heavy rain. In the Andes, on the other hand, temperatures can fluctuate enormously during a single day, and the sudden changes in weather conditions are a potential hazard for climbers. Quito is pleasantly fresh all year round and is cool at night. The weather should cause minimal disruption whatever time you go. The period from June to October is the driest in many areas.

	Average daily maximum temperature °C											
London	6	7	10	13	17	20	22	21	19	14	10	7
Quito	22	22	22	21	21	22	22	23	23	22	22	22
	JAN	FEB	MAR	APR	MAY	JUN	JUL	AUG	SEP	OCT	NOV	DEC
Quito	16	17	20	22	21	12	7	9	14	18	14	16
London	15	13	11	12	12	11	12	11	13	13	15	15
	Average number of rainy days per month											

PACKAGE TRAVEL

AN IMPRESSIVE variety of package holidays is available. You can journey from Ecuador's tropical coastline high up into the Andes and back down into the jungle, staying in all manner of accommodation from upmarket city hotels to jungle lodges. Travel choices range from public transport to coach, boat or raft.

Tour operators

Adventure: Adrift, Dragoman, Encounter Overland, Exodus, Guerba **Birdwatching/wildife**: Abercrombie & Kent, Animal Watch, Cox & Kings, Kuoni, Limosa, Sunbird **Cruising the Galapagos Islands**: Explore Worldwide, Journey Latin America, Noble Caledonian, South American Experience, Travel South America, Worldwide Journeys **General**: Hayes & Jarvis, Sunvil, Titan HiTours, Voyages Jules Verne **Specialists**: Journey Latin America, Passage to South America, South American Experience, Travel to South America **Tailor-made specialists**: Nomadic Thoughts, Scott Dunn World, Union Castle Travel **Trekking**: KE Adventure

Specialists offer flexibility with tailor-made tours and suggested itineraries. A tour starting from Quito might include a visit to the market at Otavalo, the Cotopaxi National Park, the spectacular train journey down to Guayaquil and a cruise to the Galapagos Islands.

Nearly all the tour operators offer cruises to the Galapagos Islands, either as part of a tour or on their own. Specialist cruises suiting a range of budgets from economy to luxury and catering for groups of 15 to 90 people visit a selection of islands; most vessels have naturalists and guides on board.

Activity holidays include wildlife and birdwatching, adventure, trekking and white-water rafting.

INDEPENDENT TRAVEL

THERE ARE no direct flights to Ecuador from the UK, but there are numerous routes via European and US cities. Demand is high, however, so if you plan to travel in the high season (June to August and December to January), book your flight at least three months in advance.

Ecuador's comparatively small size makes the country easy to explore. Internal flights are reasonably frequent, but almost always originate either in Quito or Guayaquil. Trains are a fine way to travel if you want a long, slow look at the scenery – the ride from Riobamba to Guayaquil is one of the most dramatic in the world. Buses are faster and serve most towns, while glorified trucks operate along minor routes. Hiring a car is expensive compared with most things in Ecuador, and can be more of a worry than an asset in such a poor country. Many national parks are difficult to reach by public transport, but you can normally arrange trips in the nearest town or in Quito.

Most people go on organised trips to the Galapagos Islands, but it is possible to plan a tour once in Ecuador. It is important to book your flight to the islands in good time: i.e. before you leave home.

Accommodation tends to be simple, although the rise in tourism means that guesthouses are more comfortable than previously. If you have your heart set on a particular place, book ahead, but otherwise rooms are easily found on the spot – although they will be in short supply the day before and after market days, or big festivals.

RED TAPE, HEALTH AND SAFETY

BRITISH PASSPORT-HOLDERS do not need a visa and can stay for three months in Ecuador. When entering the country, you must show a passport valid for six months and a return ticket.

Parts of Ecuador, including the northern Oriente, have a reputation for a particularly virulent form of malaria, and the whole country lies within a yellow fever zone. Altitude sickness can affect people in the Sierra, and you should take time to acclimatise before attempting any big mountain climbs.

Crime is a big problem in Quito, and you must guard against bag snatchers and pickpockets in the old city; evenings here are best spent in the new city. Do not venture down any dark streets at night and try to avoid walking alone – a rule which applies to all Ecuadorean cities. Visitors to the Ashvar Territories of the Oriente should beware of kidnapping. For a permit to enter Ashvar territory, contact FINAE or CANODROS. The Ecuador/Peru border is open but sensitive: stay on well-marked paths, as there are still mines in the area. For up-to-date information, contact the Foreign Office Travel Advice Unit (see page 11).

MORE INFORMATION Tourist Information, Embassy of Ecuador, Flat 3B, 3 Hans Crescent, London SW1X 0LS, tel 0171-584 1367 (*please send an sae with two first-class stamps*)
Web site: http://www.ecuaworld.com

FINAE tel 03 883827 (in Pastaza province)
CANODROS tel 04 2855711 (in Guayaquil)
CANODROS tel 02 454586 (in Quito)

COST OF LIVING £

EGYPT

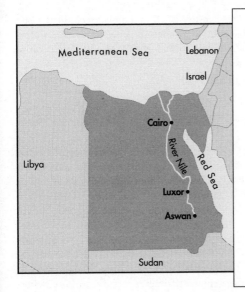

Mediterranean Sea
Lebanon
Israel
Cairo •
River Nile
Red Sea
Libya
Luxor •
Aswan •
Sudan

CAIRO
Good for culture and local colour

THE LARGEST city in Africa, Cairo is a frantic, teeming metropolis. Its noise and bustle make it hard to love, but the medieval quarter is worth a visit to sample the street life of the famous Khan el-Khalili bazaar – or see some of the many hundreds of mosques and minarets. The Christian (Coptic) quarter makes a quieter, pleasant diversion from the constant rush elsewhere.

BEST SIGHTS

Museum of Egyptian Antiquities
The greatest collection of Pharaonic art in the world includes the treasure hoard from Tutankhamun's tomb – try to spend an hour or two here on your own; the guided tours only point out the highlights.

Pyramids at Giza
Cairo's uninspiring suburbs now sprawl right up to the foot of the Pyramids, which are best seen from the desert side. It is only when you stand right underneath them that you appreciate them fully. The Sphinx

crouches a short distance away amid a complex of ruins of indeterminate appearance. There is a sound and light show most evenings.

Saqqara

It was at Saqqara in the 27th century BC that the first pyramid, the Step Pyramid of King Zoser, was built. Numerous other tombs and monuments are dotted around the site, which is most easily visited on an organised tour from Cairo.

LUXOR
Good for culture

THE MODERN town of Luxor stands on the site of ancient Thebes, Egypt's capital for 15 dynasties. It is an ideal base for visiting the necropolis on the west bank, where the tombs of hundreds of ancient Egypt's pharaohs and noble families lie.

BEST SIGHTS
Queen Hatshepsut's Temple

An amphitheatre of bare cliffs provides a spectacular setting for the colonnaded terraces of the temple of Egypt's only female pharaoh. Some of the lively carvings depict a trading expedition to Punt, whose fat queen you can see standing behind a thin king.

Temple of Karnak

The scale of this temple is immense. Most imposing is the colossal Hypostyle Hall, where 134 massive stone pillars sprout into capitals shaped like palm-fronds, papyrus buds and lotus flowers.

Valley of the Kings

Only a small number of the 60 or so rock-hewn sepulchres are open to the public, and it is difficult to predict which ones you will be able to see. Steep steps descend into burial chambers whose wall paintings depict detailed instructions for the journey to the hereafter.

ASWAN
Good for flora and local colour

BIGGER AND busier than Luxor, Aswan is nevertheless an appealing place in which to spend a few days. It is a handy spot for taking a *felucca* (small sail boat) ride to some of the nearby islands – perhaps Kitchener's Island, which has a fine botanic garden with many rare tropical species and strutting, gargling egrets.

BEST SIGHTS

Abu Simbel

A 30-minute flight south of Aswan, the temple of Abu Simbel had to be re-sited after the rising waters of Lake Nasser threatened to submerge it. It is a stunning site: four giant seated figures of Rameses II look out over the lake, while a smaller temple is dedicated to Nefertari – the only Egyptian temple built for a pharaoh's wife.

High Dam

Completed in 1971, the dam has helped Egypt avoid famines like those in other parts of Africa. On the other hand, because the Nile no longer floods its banks, leaving a rich alluvial silt, farmers are becoming more dependent on chemical fertilisers, and the water table is rising, seeping into the walls of many ancient temples.

RED SEA

Good for beaches and outdoor activities

THE MAIN interest of the Egyptian coastline is the coral reefs that lie very close to the shore. The range of aquatic life around the reefs and the clear water make it one of the most attractive places in the world for scuba diving and snorkelling.

BEST RESORTS

Hurghada

● Hurghada, with its straggle of low-rise modern buildings, is the main coastal resort on the Gulf of Suez.

● Learn scuba diving or snorkelling.

● Take boat trips out to the reefs and islands just offshore.

Sharm el Sheik

● On the tip of the Sinai peninsula, another popular divers' haunt, with fine sandy beaches and an increasing amount of accommodation.

● The resort is backed by spectacularly desolate mountain scenery.

● A good base from which to visit the Greek Orthodox monastery of St Catherine, supposedly the spot where Moses saw the Burning Bush.

WHEN TO GO

IF POSSIBLE, go between October and March, when it is pleasantly warm – though nights can be chilly. From April onwards, daytime temperatures soar, and sightseeing is pushed towards the very beginning or end of the day. Air-conditioning is essential from April to September. In late spring the *khamseen* wind blows clouds of dust in from the desert; take antihistamines if you are allergic to dust. In the holy month of Ramadan, shops may open at odd hours or not at all, and there is much less nightlife.

Average daily maximum temperature °C												
London	6	7	10	13	17	20	22	21	19	14	10	7
Aswan	24	26	30	35	40	42	42	42	40	37	31	26
	JAN	FEB	MAR	APR	MAY	JUN	JUL	AUG	SEP	OCT	NOV	DEC
Aswan	<1	<1	<1	<1	<1	0	0	<1	<1	<1	<1	<1
London	15	13	11	12	12	11	12	11	13	13	15	15

Average number of rainy days per month

Average daily maximum temperature °C												
London	6	7	10	13	17	20	22	21	19	14	10	7
Cairo	19	21	24	28	32	35	35	35	33	30	26	21
	JAN	FEB	MAR	APR	MAY	JUN	JUL	AUG	SEP	OCT	NOV	DEC
Cairo	3	2	1	1	1	0	0	0	<1	1	1	2
London	15	13	11	12	12	11	12	11	13	13	15	15

Average number of rainy days per month

PACKAGE TRAVEL

MOST PEOPLE take packages to Egypt, for several reasons: a tour leader eases your way through the bureaucracy by a well-judged distribution of small amounts of money (small-scale bribery is part of Egyptian life); it can be exhausting and time-consuming to make your own arrangements, and Egypt is a country where first-time travellers may feel less confident. Most package holidays also provide Egyptian guides, whose standards vary. The more scholarly tours provide specialist lecturers as well.

A Nile cruise is a unique and very relaxing part of most Egyptian holidays, and it is the easiest way to see the temples at Esna, Edfu and Kom Ombo, between Luxor and Aswan. However, all the other major sights can be seen from comfortable land bases at Cairo, Luxor and Aswan. Hotel rooms are usually larger than the often cramped cruise boat cabins, and the food is often safer.

Most tour operators offer Nile cruises or the resorts of the Red Sea as part of a package to Egypt. Typically, cruises last from four to seven days. Cruise boats are often luxurious and air-conditioned, though travel by *felucca* (small sail boat) is also available on a package. Luxor and Aswan are the main starting points for cruises and some operators offer cruises on Lake Nasser.

You can extend your holiday on the banks of the Nile or add on a trip to Cairo or the Red Sea resorts of Hurghada, Sharm el Sheik and Dahab. When comparing brochure prices look out for 'optional excursions', which can add a lot to the basic cost of a package. Activity holidays include desert safaris in the Sinai, birdwatching and adventure tours. Many specialists offer diving packages in the Red Sea, based in hotels or on live-aboard vessels, or camping safaris along the coast.

Tour operators

General and specialist: Abercrombie & Kent, Airtours, Bales Tours, British Airways Holidays, Cosmos, Egyptian Encounter, Goldenjoy, Guerba, Hayes & Jarvis, Infinity Tours, Jasmin Tours, Kuoni, Peltours, Saga, Seafarer, Skybus, Somak, Thomas Cook, Thomson, Tradewinds, Voyages Jules Verne **Scuba diving**: Destination Red Sea, Explorers Tours, Oonas Divers, Regal Holidays, Speedwing **Other activities**: British Museum Traveller (archaeology), Exodus (walking), Explore Worldwide (adventure, walking), Holts' Tours (battlefields), Peregrine (horse-riding), Solo's Holidays (singles), Sunbird (birdwatching)

INDEPENDENT TRAVEL

TRAVELLING INDEPENDENTLY in Egypt is a lot more hassle, but you have more control over the sights you see and how long you take about it. Both British Airways and Egypt Air fly from London to Cairo; Egypt Air has a monopoly of internal air services (except to the Sinai), and all major centres, like Luxor and Aswan, are connected. Demand exceeds capacity, and flights are often overbooked. Book well ahead, from the UK if you can. Charter flights go to Luxor and Red Sea resorts.

There are frequent train services from Cairo to Alexandria and up the Nile valley as far as Aswan. Fares are cheap by UK standards. For reasonable comfort and air-conditioning, travel first-class.

Long-distance buses and coaches serve all major tourist sights and are much cheaper than organised excursions (choose air-conditioned transport). Service taxis are good value. These operate on regular routes, and you pay a flat fare no matter how many passengers turn up. You need an international driving licence to hire a car. The Egyptian inter-pretation of the highway code is somewhat irregular, to say the least.

Nile trips on luxury cruise boats are pricey; you can negotiate *felucca* trips for much less. If going a long way by *felucca*, take a sleeping bag.

Five-star international chain hotels are plentiful, but pleasant mid-range or budget accommodation is scarce. Many hotels in central Cairo suffer from traffic noise. Those near the Pyramids in Giza are quieter, but the five-mile journey into town can take over an hour in heavy traffic.

RED TAPE, HEALTH AND SAFETY

BRITISH PASSPORT-HOLDERS need a visa to enter Egypt. Tourist visas are valid for one month. Either get a visa before you go (two passport photos are needed) or at the airport in Egypt (pay in sterling or dollars, no photo required). Your passport must be valid for six months after the date on which you plan to leave Egypt. For more information contact the Egyptian Consulate.

Upset stomachs are the commonest problem – avoid drinking tap water (clean your teeth in bottled water too), and go for freshly cooked food rather than buffets. Avoid ice in drinks, salads, shellfish, and any fruit that you cannot peel yourself. Get advice from your GP about what vaccinations you need.

Since 1992 extremists have conducted a campaign of violence against the Egyptian government and have warned tourists not to visit Egypt. The Egyptian authorities attach the highest priority to protecting visitors. But security cannot be guaranteed. Contact the Foreign Office Travel Advice Unit for the latest advice before you go (see page 11).

MORE INFORMATION Egyptian Tourist Board, Egyptian House, 170 Piccadilly, London W1V 9DD, tel 0171-493 5282, web site: http://touregypt.net/

Egyptian Consulate, 2 Lowndes Street, Knightsbridge, London SW1X 9ET, tel 0171-235 9777, visa information (0891) 887777 (premium rate number)

COST OF LIVING £

FIJI

THOUGH FIJI has certainly caught the attention of both Antipodean tourists and transpacific fliers keen to break up their journeys, it remains a relatively unsullied and fascinating paradise. Development has largely been focused on the southern coast of the main island, Viti Levu, and on the smaller islands just off its western seaboard. For anyone willing to travel further afield, the scattered islands which make up this welcoming nation offer some of the most dramatic and enticing scenery in the Pacific. Geography and a strident cultural identity have ensured that much of Fiji's charm remains intact. However, despite the staggering natural beauty on offer, the country's real asset is its people. Generous, spirited and often delightfully eccentric, they offer the visitor a warm and engaging introduction to Melanesian culture and lifestyle.

VITI LEVU
Good for culture, outdoor activities and scenic landscape

THIS IS the more developed of the two main islands, the other being Vanua Levu to the north. Lautoka on the western seaboard is the departure point for several popular island chains such as the Mamanuca and Yasawa groups. Nadi is a bustling town awash with touts and vendors who will compete vigorously for your attention. Most people enter and depart Fiji from the airport at Nadi and cruises around the popular island chains pick up passengers from hotels here.

BEST SIGHTS
Coral coast
Travelling south from Nadi, the Queen's Road winds its way east through Sigatoka and along Viti Levu's stunning southern coastline, the Coral Coast. The region offers a concentration of both beauty and resorts which should cater for most preferences and pockets.

Nananu-i-Ra
Nananu-i-Ra is a beautiful, compact little island fringed by coral reef on the King's Road, north of Lautoka. Access is by boat from Rakiraki.

Suva
Suva, the capital, is in the south-east of the island. It is both the cultural centre of Fiji and the main port for other islands, such as Kadavu. The excellent museum includes among its artefacts many items of cutlery, such as brain forks, used in the ritualised cannibalism which was widely practised until the turn of the century.

VANUA LEVU
Good for scenic landscape

THIS IS the second largest island after Viti Levu and is much less developed. Tourism has secured a foothold here but is localised to certain areas and is still a long way from the developed resorts of its southern neighbour.

BEST BASE
Savusavu
Savusavu, the largest town on Vanua Levu, is the main point of entry located on the south of the island. It is a colourful, though quite small and underdeveloped town. It is really a base for diving and exploring the rest of the island.

OTHER ISLANDS
Good for beaches and outdoor activities

DIVING AND snorkelling are excellent throughout the various island groups, and water sports abound. These activities can be arranged through specialist diving shops and most local hotels.

Kadavu

Fast becoming one of the premier diving spots in Fiji owing to the spectacular Astrolabe reef, this island is located to the south of Viti Levu and accessed primarily either by air from Nadi or by boat from Suva. Check the timetable if you intend to arrive by sea.

Mamanuca Islands

Several boat trips arrive here from Lautoka, taking advantage of the islands' perfect setting for laid-back cruising and water sports. The Mamanucas are more expensive than other island groups.

Ovalau

Ovalau is part of the Lomaiviti Islands. Its main town, Levuka, is the old capital of Fiji. It boasts one of the oldest and most charismatic hotels in the South Pacific, the Royal Hotel. Here complimentary Kava (a mildly intoxicating brew made from a ground root) is served daily.

The Lovoni Valley is one of the island's most scenic locations. From Ovalau, you can venture further on to other more isolated islands, such as Caquelai, where the snorkelling and beaches are superb.

Yasawa Islands

This group of islands, which runs roughly north to south to the west of Viti Levu, forms an ideal South Pacific paradise. Unspoilt stretches of pristine sand and translucent water are punctuated by lush headlands: each island has its own character and unhurried charm. It was just off the northern extreme of the Yasawas that Captain Bligh, adrift after the mutiny on the *Bounty*, was almost captured and eaten by irate locals before escaping through a gap in the reef.

Cruise ships regularly stop off at the islands. For most independent travellers, however, arriving by boat from Lautoka is the favoured approach. Be prepared for rudimentary facilities on board.

WHEN TO GO

THE IDEAL time to visit is during the drier and cooler months, which run from early summer through to November. Outside this period the humidity, temperatures and rainfall can all be uncomfortably high, especially at the beginning of the year.

Average daily maximum temperature °C												
London	6	7	10	13	17	20	22	21	19	14	10	7
Suva	29	29	29	29	28	27	26	26	27	27	28	29
	JAN	FEB	MAR	APR	MAY	JUN	JUL	AUG	SEP	OCT	NOV	DEC
Suva	18	18	21	19	16	13	14	15	16	15	15	18
London	15	13	11	12	12	11	12	11	13	13	15	15
Average number of rainy days per month												

PACKAGE HOLIDAYS

FOR THE UK holidaymaker, Fiji is generally featured as a popular stopover destination on round-the-world flights to or from Australasia rather than as the place for a two-week holiday. Consequently, there are few specialist brochures. As Fiji is marketed as somewhere to escape the rigours of intercontinental travel, all arrangements can be tailor-made to suit your requirements.

Most tour operators offer a choice of hotels on Viti Levu – either close to the airport at Nadi or on the Coral Coast, about an hour and a half away. Resorts like Castaway, Treasure and Breakaway Islands are easily accessible from the airport by plane, helicopter or boat, and transfer times are often quicker than to the Coral Coast. Study the resort details carefully to ensure you choose the right island for your requirements. Two-, three- or six-night cruises throughout the islands are also available. Specialist options include tall ship cruising and scuba diving.

Accommodation is usually upmarket and of decent quality, with lots of facilities laid on – particularly water sports. Entertainment is low-key and generally hotel-based.

Tour operators

Cruising: Noble Caledonian **General**: Airwaves, Asiaworld Travel, Austravel, Cadogan, East Travel, Elegant Resorts, Jetabout, Kuoni, Sunset Travel, Tradewinds, Trailfinders, Travel 2, Travelpack **Sailing**: Explore Worldwide **Specialists**: Anderson's Pacific Way, All-Ways Pacific, Destination Pacific

INDEPENDENT TRAVEL

THERE IS a wide range of accommodation on Fiji, ranging from dormitory beds for backpackers to very upmarket hotels. The tourist desk at the airport in Nadi is a useful source of information.

Roads through the lush interior of Viti Levu are limited and if you are driving you should exert extreme caution as the highways, especially the northern loop, are notoriously chaotic. Buses run between Nadi and Suva.

RED TAPE, HEALTH AND SAFETY

VISAS CAN be obtained on entry and extended while in Fiji.

Tropical diseases present in Fiji include hepatitis A, dengue fever, polio and typhoid. If you are arriving from a country where yellow fever is present, immunisation against the disease is essential. Tourists should consult their doctor or a travel centre before travelling to Fiji.

Shark attacks, bites from venomous snakes and stings from cone shells are relatively rare. Seek local advice when you are snorkelling or diving if unsure of currents, rips and other considerations.

Fiji is no more or less dangerous than elsewhere in the South Pacific, although petty theft is not uncommon. The main urbanised areas, such as Suva, are where you are most likely to encounter crime.

MORE INFORMATION Fiji High Commission, 34 Hyde Park Gate, London SW7 5DN, tel 0171-584 3661, web site: http://www.fijifvb.gov.fj (North America: http://www.FijiIslands.org)

COST OF LIVING £

FRANCE

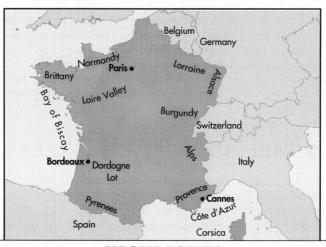

HIGHLIGHTS

Beaches
*Brittany,
South of
France,
Corsica*

**Family
holidays**
*Ile-de-France,
Brittany,
Atlantic coast*

History
Normandy

Food/wine
*Paris,
Loire valley,
Burgundy,
Brittany,
Normandy,
Alsace,
Dordogne,
Atlantic coast,
South of
France*

**Nightlife/
shopping**
Paris

Culture
*Paris,
Ile-de-France,
Loire valley,
Burgundy,
South of
France*

Local colour
Alsace

**Outdoor
activities**
*Alps, Brittany,
Normandy,*

*Alsace,
Dordogne,
South of
France,
Pyrenees,
Corsica*

**Scenic
landscape**
*Dordogne,
South of
France,
Pyrenees,
Corsica*

PARIS
Good for culture, food/wine, nightlife and shopping

SAUNTERING IS the best way to sample the city, whether strolling
the riverside embankments or simply 'licking the panes' (*lèche-vitrines*),
as the French call window-shopping.

BEST SIGHTS

If you have been to Paris before, you will have your own ideas about exploring – perhaps the mansions and antique shops of the Marais, or even a tour of the Paris sewers. For first-timers, however, the attractions listed below are unmissable.

Some museums and local shops close on Mondays.

Eiffel Tower

The top viewing platform of this '300-metre flagpole', as Eiffel himself called it, is accessible only by lift, and there are hour-long queues in the middle of the day – visit early or late.

Louvre

Star exhibits include the *Mona Lisa* and the *Venus de Milo*. Use the leaflets explaining the layout of the museum to pinpoint what you want to see – or you will never get out.

Musée d'Orsay

This turn-of-the-century station picks up French art from 1848, where the Louvre stops. As well as the Impressionists, it displays sculpture by Rodin, art nouveau glass and furniture.

Notre Dame

This beautiful Gothic cathedral is mirrored in the water of the Seine and lit by the searchlights of passing boats. If you are feeling strong, you can tackle the 402 steps to the top of the towers.

Pompidou Centre

The main interest inside the centre is the Modern Art Museum, where canvases by Picasso, Bonnard, Léger and Matisse dominate the huge galleries.

ILE-DE-FRANCE
Good for culture and family holidays

MANY ATTRACTIONS, including Disneyland Paris, can be visited on day-trips from the capital via public transport, while Chantilly and Fontainebleau are excellent bases for drivers.

BEST SIGHTS
Chantilly

The château contains an excellent art collection, while the stables now house a Horse and Pony Museum.

Chartres
The cathedral is a masterpiece of Romanesque and Gothic carving and sumptuous stained-glass. Use binoculars to appreciate details close-up and climb the New Tower for unrivalled views.

Fontainebleau
Lively town with royal château used as base by French kings hunting in surrounding forest. Highlights include the Farewell Court, where Napoleon said goodbye to his soldiers before exile in Elba.

St-Denis
The world's first Gothic cathedral contains the tombs of all but three of the kings of France.

St-Germain-en-Laye
The château where Louis XIV was born houses the excellent National Museum of Antiquities.

Vaux-le-Vicomte
Finely restored château and gardens built by Louis XIV's ambitious Minister of Finance, Nicolas Fouquet.

Versailles
Most visitors tour the grandiose state apartments and the Hall of Mirrors – but do not neglect the gardens, which are particularly stunning when the fountains are switched on (summer Sunday afternoons).

BEST THEME PARKS

Disneyland Paris
Smaller and more manageable than its American counterparts, Disneyland recreates the familiar concept of five themed 'lands'. Most of the queues – and several good attractions – are sensibly under cover. There are plenty of attractions for younger children.

Parc Astérix
Themed park and Disney alternative based on the popular comic strip set in ancient Gaul. Most of the rides are gentle.

LOIRE VALLEY
Good for culture and food/wine

THE REGION'S undisputed magnets are the châteaux. These fanciful Renaissance palaces, severe medieval fortresses and sumptuous classical mansions saw the high life and scurrilous deeds of France's aristocracy.

BEST CHATEAUX

Chambord
The château is covered with carved salamanders – the insignia of
François I – and is remarkable for its astonishing skyline.

Chenonceau
The most romantic château, reflected in the Cher.

Langeais
This comprehensive collection of late medieval furnishings is intensely
atmospheric.

Plessis–Bourré
The bawdily decorated guard room is one of the highlights of this
lesser-known château.

Villandry
A subdued house surrounded by magnificent gardens, renowned for
their topiary.

BEST BASES

Chinon
This is a riverside town of narrow streets where oriel and bay windows overhang the cobbled paths below the ruins of a medieval
château.

Loches
Cafés and gift shops occupy houses on cobbled lanes winding
up towards the walls of an intact medieval city. A rampart walk
connects the château at the northern end with the eleventh-century
keep.

Vendôme
The old town is enclosed within a bend in the Loir, and channels from
the river run between the streets of small stone and half-timbered
houses.

BURGUNDY
Good for culture and food/wine

TO APPRECIATE the beauty of the wine villages, take the side road
designated the Route du Vin running parallel to the N74. Here the
signposts read like an exclusive wine list. There are around 750 miles of
navigable waterway in Burgundy, so it is a good place for a boating

holiday. The most scenic routes are the Canal du Nivernais, which cuts through the Yonne valley from Auxerre to Decize, and the Canal de Bourgogne, from Migennes to the Sâone plain.

BEST SIGHTS

Ancy-le-Franc
This sober, classical Renaissance château has a superb interior by Italian artists Primaticcio and Niccolo dell'Abate.

Beaune
Capital of the wine trade, and a perfect base for touring the famous wine villages. Sample some wine at the Marché aux Vins. The Hôtel-Dieu contains Van der Weyden's *Last Judgement* polyptych.

Dijon
The Dukes of Burgundy ruled from this capital for 500 years. John the Fearless and Philip the Bold's tombs occupy the Musée des Beaux-Arts, surrounded by Renaissance courtyards and half-timbered houses.

Fontenay Abbey
The finest surviving example of a Cistercian monastery.

Tanlay
Château notable for its exterior, more interesting architecturally than that of its neighbour at Ancy-le-Franc.

Vézelay
This outstanding Romanesque building has a lofty interior striped with Moorish bands. The pillar capitals depict gruesome allegories.

THE ALPS
Good for outdoor activities

THE MONT Blanc area is a summer playground for climbers, walkers and cable-car riders. More peaceful are the Queyras region and the Vercors; to escape further, try the national parks of Vanoise or Ecrins.

BEST LAKESIDE RESORTS

Annecy
● A fashionable town with good shops and ancient Savoyard houses.

Meillerie
● A small fishing village off the tourist track in a prime site on Lac Léman (the French shore of Lake Geneva).

Talloires
● Village with superb views, well placed for watching sunsets.
● Prestigious hotels line the waterfront.

BEST EXCURSIONS

Chambéry
Chambéry consists of a network of tunnels and lanes, with a castle at its heart. The cathedral displays extraordinary *trompe l'œil*.

Manigod
This tiny village in the most alluring of the valleys makes a good excursion from Lac d'Annecy. From the Col de la Croix-Fry the peaks of Chaîne des Aravis can be seen.

BEST MOUNTAIN BASES

Chamonix
Crowded, sunny, fashionable Chamonix – a mountain activity base – has a nineteenth-century core of pastiche alpine village style.

Pralognan
This steeply enclosed climbers' and hikers' village just on the edge of the Vanoise National Park offers guided excursions.

St-Gervais
Despite a traffic-ridden main street, St-Gervais is surrounded by unspoilt countryside.

St-Véran
One of the highest villages in Europe (6,600 feet), St-Véran is a delightful combination of resort and rustic village in the Queyras Regional Park. Excellent walks and views to Italy.

Valloire
Traditional alpine village and all-year resort in the Ecrins.

Villard-de-Lans
Sprawling resort in the pre-alpine massif of the Vercors that caters for recreational tastes both leisurely and energetic.

BEST MOUNTAIN TRIPS

Aiguille du Midi
This spectacular cable-car trip from Chamonix provides stunning views of the peaks. A further cable-car takes you over the wastes of snow behind Mont Blanc to Helbronner on the Italian frontier.

Mer de Glace
A rack railway from Chamonix leads you to a cave in the glacier, where sculptures include a bathroom complete with ice lavatory.

Mont Blanc tramway
An old rack railway ascends a spur of Mont Blanc from St-Gervais to reach the Nid d'Aigle (eagle's nest) peak on the edge of the snow line.

Vercors massif
A limestone plateau ringed by fearsome vertical cliffs on all sides. The Gorges de la Bourne, the Grands Goulets and the Combe Laval all involve driving alongside hair-raising chasms.

BRITTANY
Good for beaches, family holidays, food/wine and outdoor activities

ITS 1,000-PLUS miles of sandy coastline make Brittany a good choice for quiet family and beach holidays, especially for campers and self-caterers. By French standards, sightseeing could be limited, and the cuisine, notable for seafood and crêpes (pancakes), uncomplicated.

BEST RESORTS
Beg-Meil peninsula
● Excellent camping area. Sandy stretches and charming coves surround the Cap-Coz promontory, Beg-Meil and Pointe de Mousterlin.

Bénodet
● The south-west's popular yachting centre, ranged picturesquely around the mouth of the Odet estuary.
● Good beaches and plenty of boat trips.

Carantec
● A sleepy peninsular resort with reasonable beaches.
● There is a large nautical club.

Dinard
● Sophisticated town that is host to an annual film festival.
● It also offers a big beach, water sports and boat trips.

Pink Granite Coast
● Weird shoreline rock formations from Perros-Guirec to Ploumanach.

BEST SIGHTS AND EXCURSIONS

Medieval inland towns
Dinan boasts fine half-timbered houses,Vitré and Josselin have conical-towered castles, while Fougères has an awesome medieval fortress.

Medieval ports
St-Malo's ramparts enclose the old town, destroyed in the Second World War and now sensitively rebuilt; at low tide, walk across the sands to islets. The huge fishing port of Concarneau has a fortified old quarter.

Parish closes
North-western Brittany has a concentration of unique sixteenth- and seventeenth-century ecclesiastical architecture. Do not miss the parish closes at Lampaul-Guimiliau, Guimiliau and St-Thégonnec.

Prehistoric sites
Southern Brittany is awash with monuments dating from around 5000-2000 BC: amazing rows of *menhirs* (long stones) and a prehistory museum at Carnac, and a fine *dolmen* (tomb) on Gavrinis Island.

NORMANDY
Good for food/wine, history and outdoor activities

THE MOST varied of France's northern coastal regions is also of great architectural and historical interest. In the countryside, cider and calvados complement the rich, dairy-based cuisine. The region has a history of invasions, from the Norsemen to D-Day.

BEST BASES

Les Andelys
Town comprising Petit and Grand Andelys; the former is one of the prettiest spots on the Seine above Rouen and packed at weekends.

Barneville-Carteret
This small fishing port on the west coast of the Cotentin peninsula lies within reach of deserted sand dunes and spectacular beaches.

Clécy
Rarely overcrowded village in the heart of lovely Suisse Normande. Canoeing and walking are the main activities.

Dieppe
Attractive port with a bustling fishmarket. Shops line the Grand Rue, while the castle museum contains an exquisite ivory collection.

Etretat
Popular French family resort with spectacular cliff scenery. It is lively in season, and has a fair range of facilities.

Honfleur
Boudin and Monet both worked here and are commemorated in the Boudin Museum. Artists still thrive and several galleries exist.

BEST SIGHTS AND EXCURSIONS
Bayeux
Bayeux is most famous for its striking tapestry (actually embroidery) commemorating the Norman invasion of England in 1066.

Coutances
The big draw here is the cathedral, widely held to be a masterpiece of Norman Gothic architecture, with soaring lines and clusters of turrets.

Deauville
Deauville has turn-of-the-century neo-rustic villas and the smartest hotels, shops, nightlife and people.

Giverny
See the famous bridge at Monet's house, now housing Japanese prints.

Jumièges Abbey
The ruins of the Romanesque abbey church loom over the peaceful green lawns where the monks once had formal gardens.

Mont St-Michel
Abbey, fortress and natural curiosity atop a granite mound in the marshy mouth of the Couesnon river. Invariably crowded.

Rouen
Half-timbered houses, energetic street life and magnificent churches, including the cathedral. Best museums are the Musée des Beaux-Arts; Musée le Seq-des-Tournelles (a collection of wrought iron-work); and the Musée Flaubert (the novelist's house, now a medical museum).

BEST D-DAY MUSEUMS AND MEMORIALS
On 6 June 1944 all five designated Normandy beaches – Sword, Juno, Gold, Omaha and Utah – were taken by the Allies. From this base they went on to liberate the rest of Europe.

American Normandy Cemetery
The largest of the war cemeteries. Many buried here were killed during the assault on 'bloody Omaha', the most difficult of the landings.

Arromanches
See the remains of the Mulberry Harbour, built in Britain for troop embarkation in the Normandy landings. The museum shows an explanatory film.

Normandy Memorial at Caen
This huge modern complex traces the history of the last war, with films of the D-Day landings and hopes for future peace. Unmissable.

Pegasus Bridge and Café Gondrée
The first building in France liberated by the Allies. Small museum.

Pointe du Hoc
With its battery in a bunker surrounded by shell craters, this was the scene of an extraordinary D-Day assault by American Rangers.

ALSACE AND LORRAINE
Good for food/wine, local colour and outdoor activities

ALSACE HAS singular traditions and character. The streets and houses gleam with Teutonic spruceness, and hearty local dishes delight in Germanic names such as *bäckeoffe* (meat and potato hotpot) and *ziwelküeche* (onion tart). France's prettiest wine route stretches for about 113 miles from Marlenheim in the north to Thann in the south.

The neighbouring *département* of Lorraine is much less attractive to tourists, but Nancy and Verdun are well worth visiting.

BEST BASES
Strasbourg
The seat of the Council of Europe is excellent for weekend breaks. The River Ill surrounds the old centre with its magnificent cathedral. Château Rohan contains three museums, the best of which is the Museum of Applied Arts. The Alsace Museum explains local traditions.

Wine Road (Route du Vin)
Practically any of the prosperous medieval villages on the Wine Road would be a suitable base for exploring. Ribeauvillé offers enticing shops; Riquewihr is one of the most attractive walled towns; tiny Eguisheim is surrounded by ramparts.

Wissembourg
Right on the German border, Wissembourg has a charming centre with bridges over branches of the River Lauter, and a Gothic church.

BEST SIGHTS AND EXCURSIONS

Château du Haut-Koenigsburg
Rebuilt by Kaiser Wilhelm at the turn of the century to his idea of a medieval castle, the château contains neo-Gothic panelling and frescos.

Colmar
Main administrative focus of Alsace's wine trade with unspoilt centre. The Unterlinden Museum has work by Schongauer and Grünewald.

Ecomusée d'Alsace
Half-timbered houses from all over Alsace have been reconstructed to form a working village at this open-air museum.

Nancy
Capital of Lorraine, noted for baroque buildings, fountains and iron-work. Art-nouveau buffs should visit the Musée de l'Ecole de Nancy.

Route des Crêtes
Road along the ridge of the Vosges. Superb views of glacial lakes, rolling pastures and gulleys from the Grand Ballon and the Hohneck.

Verdun
Over half a million soldiers died in the Battle of Verdun (1916). Visit a memorial museum, defensive forts and the Ossuary.

DORDOGNE AND LOT
Good for food/wine, outdoor activities and scenic landscape

SUNNY, RURAL France at its best, this popular region is small enough for most sights to be seen in a day's drive. Farmhouse-style *gîtes* for self-catering are widely available. Properties here get booked up quickly.

BEST BASES

Brantôme
Hugging the Dronne, the 'Venice of Périgord' has narrow streets with open spaces filled by riverside cafés and bars, and a lovely abbey.

Carjac
This large village is well organised for tourism but manages to feel relaxed and friendly. It is a good base for exploring the Lot valley.

Domme
Well positioned for exploring the chief sights of the Dordogne valley, this beautiful fortified town looks best in quiet mornings and evenings.

Martel
This medieval town surrounded by attractive countryside features magnificent houses, and is an ideal spot from which to explore the Upper Dordogne.

Montignac
Characterful small town, a good base from which to visit nearby prehistoric sights. Self-caterers favour the pretty countryside to the east.

Puy l'Evêque
The town is medieval and full of character; it is also well placed for exploring the Cahors vineyards and hidden countryside to the north.

Ribérac
This town on the Dronne is renowned for its market. The gentle countryside to the north-west is a popular self-catering area.

BEST SIGHTS AND EXCURSIONS

Caves
The prehistoric paintings in the brilliant reproduction cavern of Lascaux II and the genuine Font-de-Gaume are unmissable. Pech-Merle is also fascinating. Rise early to get one of the (limited) tickets.

Châteaux
Most French châteaux are best seen from the outside; Dordogne exceptions include Hautefort, Montal, Castelnaud and Castelnau-Bretenoux. Particularly scenic examples are at Belcastel, Beynac and Montfort.

Churches and abbeys
The abbey church of St-Amand-de-Coly has fortress-like walls. Beaulieu and Carennac have two of the best examples of the region's Last Judgements and Christs in Glory carved above the doorway.

Towns and villages
Visitors throng the charming domestic areas, particularly the honey-pot villages of La Roque-Gageac and Domme on the Dordogne and St-Cirq-Lapopie on the Lot. Pretty Autoire and Limeuil are less crowded. The towns of Périgueux and Brantôme north of the Dordogne are worth exploring. Sarlat is touristy, but its architecture is worth a visit.

153

ATLANTIC COAST
Good for family holidays and food/wine

ENDLESS SANDY beaches on which Atlantic rollers break form the backdrop for family beach and camping holidays. Most resorts are straightforward and unsophisticated; sightseeing trips often involve a considerable drive inland. Bordeaux and its surrounding châteaux provide an alternative focus for wine buffs.

BEST RESORTS

Arcachon
● Large, lively and smart with a promenade and a casino.
● The beaches are muddy.

Bayonne
● Appealing port on the Nive; the old town lies below the cathedral.
● The Musée Léon Bonnat has an excellent art collection.

Biarritz
● Big and ritzy, Biarritz attracts surfers, families and the smart set.
● Splendid beaches, promenades and gardens.

Maubisson
● Good sports activities at this lively, well-maintained little resort.
● Sited in a corner of the huge Etang d'Hourtin-Carcans.

La Rochelle
● Handsome port, now a popular yachting centre.
● Medieval towers guard the harbour; the old quarter is lively.

Les Sables d'Olonne
● A modern family resort with a sandy beach.
● Apartment blocks, hotels and older villas line the wide promenade.

St-Jean-de-Luz
● Popular, stylish fishing port with traditional Basque houses.
● Good swimming in the sheltered bay.

St-Martin-de-Ré
● A lively little port surrounded by seventeenth-century ramparts.

BEST SIGHTS AND EXCURSIONS

Bordeaux
Central Bordeaux has grand eighteenth-century architecture, seen best

around the Place de la Bourse. The old town has elegant shopping areas. The Musée des Beaux-Arts contains a fine collection, while the Maison du Vin offers tastings and information on vineyard visits.

Poitiers
Though not conspicuously charming, Poitiers has some fascinating churches including the Baptistery, Notre-Dame-la-Grande and St-Hilaire-le-Grand. Futuroscope is the jazzy theme park of the cinema.

Saintes
An architectural foretaste of the coastal style, Saintes offers a river cruise on the Charente and a well-preserved Roman amphitheatre.

Vineyards
To get a feel for the region and its history it is best to join one of the vineyard tours organised by the tourist office. Commentary in both French and English explains wine-tasting and wine-making. Book at least a day in advance, either directly with the châteaux or through the tourist office. The prettiest wine town is St-Emilion.

SOUTH OF FRANCE
Good for culture, beaches, food/wine, outdoor activities and scenic landscape

TRAFFIC JAMS, crowds and high prices are the hazards of a holiday on the glamorous Côte d'Azur – to the west, the purpose-built resorts of Languedoc are aimed more at the family self-catering and camping market. Inland, the most visited area is round the Lubéron and Mont Ventoux. If you really want to get away from it all, head for the Alps, for stupendous valley views and bracing alpine air.

BEST RESORTS
For a seaside holiday, choose a resort west of Cannes. Most beaches here are public, with good sand; some are on splendid bays.

Argelès-Plage
● Central beach with smart collection of hotels and apartments bordering boulevard of palms, pines and gardens.
● Greater number of campsites than at any other resort in France.

Canet-Plage
● One of the best of Languedoc's purpose-built resorts, with plenty of bars and a degree of sophistication.
● Three museums and a tropical aquarium.

Cassis
- Most picturesque little resort west of St-Tropez.
- Boat trips explore the fjord-like inlets known as *calanques*.

Juan-les-Pins
- Popular package destination for the young and lively.
- Long narrow strip of sand, mostly divided up into pay beaches.

Le Lavandou
- On wooded Maures massif, which has good long sandy beaches and hills shaded by umbrella pines and cork oaks.
- Small streets and shaded squares extend from the old port.
- Very busy, but with pleasant family atmosphere.

St-Tropez
- In season, the port cafés and boutiques are crammed with people; the back streets are full of trend-setting shops and galleries.
- Good modern art museum.
- Main beaches on the Ramatuelle peninsula are spacious, shady and sandy, but some distance from main road and charge hefty entrance fee.

Ste-Maxime
- More relaxed and less ostentatious than its famous neighbour.
- Resort beach is mostly public, with fine clean sand; there is another long public beach to the west.
- Palmy promenade and port lined with simple, colourful houses.

NICE

THOUGH NO longer the super-fashionable resort of the British *beau monde*, Nice is still prosperous. It combines the charm of an old Italian port town with parks and flowers and candy-floss architecture from the Riviera's *belle époque*, despite traffic and high-season crowds.

BEST SIGHTS

Splitting the city into four distinct areas can be helpful when you are planning your sightseeing. Diverting museums and galleries abound in the modernist 'new town'. In contrast, the dense old town has baroque chapels, small squares, colourful market stalls and pavement cafés. The outstanding Matisse and Marc Chagall Museums are in the smart Cimiez suburb, once the Roman settlement of Cemenelum. Back in town, Nice's most famous landmark, the Promenade des Anglais, edges the Bay of Angels.

BEST COASTAL EXCURSIONS

Abbaye de Fontfroide
Restored Cistercian abbey, a good place to escape the tourist bustle.

Antibes
The Grimaldi château houses one of the finest collections of Picasso's works. The old town is full of life and has a very colourful market.

Cannes
The gleaming Boulevard de la Croisette promenade stretches from the festival and conference centre to the summer casino. Behind its gardens is a succession of villas, large hotels and shops.

Cathar hillforts
The Cathars, an unorthodox Christian sect, were condemned as heretics by the Pope. Among fortresses the Cathars built as refuges, Carcassonne was reconstructed in the nineteenth century. while the most spectacular are Peyrepertuse and Quéribus.

Collioure
The port is overlooked by the Château Royal, the beaches by the pink-domed church. Steep alleys house artists' studios and shops.

Corniche roads
Of the three coast roads, the Corniche Inférieure runs its length, serving all the resorts, inadequately. The exciting, precipitous Grande Corniche is the far-from-straight Roman road from Nice to Genoa. The Moyenne Corniche gives the best sea views and access to Eze, an astonishing perched village with a castle and exotic cactus garden.

Menton
Attractively Italianate old town; the new town resembles a spa town.

Monaco
This tiny principality occupies less than a square mile of ground. Touristy old Monaco boasts a miniature palace; Monte Carlo, the principality's playground, has a casino, luxury hotels and exclusive shops.

St-Paul
This artists' village is a tasteful tourist trap, full of smart little galleries. The Maeght Foundation is an excellent collection of modern art.

BEST SIGHTS

Abbeys
Three Cistercian abbeys are the splendidly isolated Abbaye de

Sénanque, the Abbaye de Silvacane above the River Durance and the Abbaye du Thoronet, offering insights into monks' lives.

Aix-en-Provence
The fascinating old town has a colourful flower market. Artists can seek out Cezanne's studio and the Vasarély Foundation.

Arles
The site of Van Gogh's last years, Arles has a Roman arena, an older ruined theatre and the beautiful church of St-Trophime.

Avignon
An exciting and cosmopolitan city, especially during the summer arts and music festival, Avignon is renowned for its Popes' Palace.

Les Baux
The 'dead' village is an atmospheric ruin providing a glorious panorama; the 'living' village's narrow streets are lined with expensive shops.

Nîmes
Chic and stylish, Nîmes' centre is pedestrianised. The Maison Carrée is a perfect Roman temple; there is also an amphitheatre. The Pont du Gard, a spectacular Roman aqueduct, straddles the Gard 14 miles away.

Orange
Orange's unique theatre is the best-preserved of all Roman theatres.

Vaison-la-Romaine
Extensive Roman remains include a theatre, houses and an elegant portico. A small museum houses excellent mosaics.

Verdon
At the Grand Canyon, cliffs up to 2,300ft high plunge down to the river. Here you can canoe, walk or raft; by car, the best views are from the Belvedere Trascaire, Balcons de la Mescla and the Pont de l'Artuby.

BEST TOURING
Alpes-Maritimes
For real escapists, a remote and adventurous landscape of imposing gorges and plunging valleys. Barcelonnette is a lively town, while St-Martin-Vésubie is a good base for walkers, riders and canoeists.

The Camargue
A harsh, uncompromisingly beautiful triangle of reedy marsh,

the Camargue is ideal to explore in one or two days. The main resort is Stes-Maries-de-la-Mer – a lively outpost with an attractive square.

Lubéron and Vaucluse plateau
The Petit Lubéron's gentle hills cradle fetching villages such as Bonnieux, Lacoste and Ménerbes. The wooded Vaucluse plateau hides a network of underground caves and passages, notably the Fontaine-de-Vaucluse. Attractive villages are Gordes, Roussillon and Rustrel.

Tarn gorges
The forested gorges of the Tarn, Jonte and Dourbie are popular with walkers, canoeists and climbers. Base yourself in Meyrueis or Ste-Enimie, or, for more seclusion, in the Cévennes. Aven Armand is an enormous cavern filled with a forest of stalagmites, while Montpellier-le-Vieux is a fantastic jumble of limestone outcrops sitting above the Dourbie.

Var
This forested area gives way to vineyards and olive groves. Attractive villages are Moissac Bellevue, Fox-Amphoux, Cotignac and Tourtour.

Mont Ventoux
Highest mountain between the Alps and the Pyrenees.

PYRENEES
Good for outdoor activities and scenic landscape

THE CENTRAL Pyrenees have the highest and most spectacular scenery, while the east and west are best for attractive touring.

BEST BASES

Lescun
Pleasantly sleepy village in the mountains, a good base for walking.

Luchon
Fashionable, lively Pyrenean spa in a wide flat bowl surrounded by mountains. Its waters are the most radioactive in France.

Luz-St-Saveur
Combined spa resort and old village in a beautiful mountain valley.

Pau
This cosmopolitan and relaxed regional capital has an imposing château and famous views of the mountains.

St-Jean-Pied-de-Port

St-Jean-Pied-de-Port, a popular stopping-place for pilgrims *en route* to Santiago since medieval times, has a pretty, if rather touristy, old town.

BEST SIGHTS

Caves

Niaux's cave paintings rival those at Lascaux in the Dordogne, but numbers are strictly limited and you may have to reserve a place in advance. See vast groups of stalagmites and stalactites at Lombrives and Labouiche (the latter involves a magnificent underground boat trip).

Romanesque churches

The fine abbeys of St-Michel-de-Cuxa and St-Martin-de-Canigou, both near Vernet-les-Bains, date from the ninth and tenth centuries. St-Martin is remarkably sited on top of a rocky crag.

BEST TOURING

Cirque de Troumouse

Vast amphitheatre of snow-patched rocky peaks, more coming into view as you ascend numerous hairpin bends.

Col d'Aubisque

Lovely col curving along a long, smooth ridge with views across the peaks. Spectacular Cirque de Litor and pretty Col de Soulor.

Col d'Erroymendi

Winding up through forest from Larrau, you reach open slopes and a plateau with splendid views.

Col de Tantes

You can look down on Spain from the top of this col. Climb the grassy knoll of Pic des Tantes for wide views of the cirque and valley.

Col de Tourmalet

Vast grassy slopes with rocky outcrops. The col seems rather Scottish in character.

Gorges de Galamus

Spectacularly steep and narrow chasm, with rock overhanging the road in parts. Steps down the rockface lead to the hermitage of St-Antoine.

Haute Vallée de l'Aude

From Quillan to Mont-Louis the road passes between sheer rock walls, then through wild wooded scenery with several lakes.

Route du Pic du Midi de Bigorre
Narrow road climbing above the snowline by steep hairline bends.
Stupendous views of a forest of jagged peaks, and the plain of Gascony.

CORSICA
Good for beaches, outdoor activities and scenic landscape

THE MOST mountainous Mediterranean island combines dramatic landscapes and good beaches. Nationalist protests about over–development have prevented most of the building-site eyesores, but there have been stories about (rare) attacks on holidaymakers.

BEST RESORTS
Bonifacio
● Attractive, bustling port with a dramatic harbour set in a fjord.
● Boat trips are available. You need transport to get to a beach.

Calvi
● Good for a stay-put holiday, with a long beach and interesting shops.
● Excursions are available on land and sea. The citadel is impressive.

Porticcio
● Porticcio, with its excellent beach, is rapidly developing.
● Vegetation shrouds slopes rising gently to the peak of Monte Rosso.

Porto-Vecchio
● Peaceful town near superb beaches at Palombaggia and Santa-Giulia.
● Olive groves divide old town from modern harbour.

BEST SIGHTS AND EXCURSIONS
Ajaccio
The old town, with its waterfront cafés, feels more French than anywhere else on the island. Napoleon's birth house disappoints, but Cardinal Fesch's museum contains an excellent art collection.

Les Calanche and Gorges of Spelunca
From Piana the road to Porto snakes through Les Calanche: misshapen towers and stacks of pink granite. From Porto to Evisa the road hugs the Gorges of Spelunca. Ample stopping places to view the precipices.

Col de Bavella
The D638 from Porto-Vecchio to Zonza passes cork groves and pine forests. From the Col de Bavella the dramatic Aiguilles de Bavella seem to glow in the sunshine.

Corte

The former capital of Corsica is on a gigantic outcrop, encircled by peaks that provide challenging terrain and picturesque backdrops for walkers. Narrow stairways lead up to the belvedere, a dramatic look-out point.

Filitosa

A row of five 4,000-year-old statue-*menhirs* has faces, swords and belts eroded but still visible. They are the first Western European representations of human portraiture in stone.

Gorges of Asco

The road narrows and climbs along the cleft forged by the Asco beneath the sheer crags on either side. After Asco it widens as it runs up to Haut-Asco, the starting point for some tough mountain walks.

WHEN TO GO

FRANCE HAS something to offer most times of the year. If you are looking for out-of-season sunshine, the south coast has the mildest climate, and the Riviera resorts are lively from March to October. The time to avoid is the French peak holiday period of late July and early August. The same advice applies to Paris, which looks its best in spring and autumn (though September sees a lot of trade fairs); in July and August many restaurants and museums are closed.

Average daily maximum temperature °C												
London	6	7	10	13	17	20	22	21	19	14	10	7
Paris	6	7	12	16	20	23	25	24	21	16	10	7
	JAN	FEB	MAR	APR	MAY	JUN	JUL	AUG	SEP	OCT	NOV	DEC
Paris	17	14	12	13	12	12	12	13	13	13	15	16
London	15	13	11	12	12	11	12	11	13	13	15	15
Average number of rainy days per month												

Average daily maximum temperature °C												
London	6	7	10	13	17	20	22	21	19	14	10	7
Nice	13	13	15	17	20	24	27	27	25	21	17	13
	JAN	FEB	MAR	APR	MAY	JUN	JUL	AUG	SEP	OCT	NOV	DEC
Nice	9	7	8	9	8	5	2	4	7	9	9	9
London	15	13	11	12	12	11	12	11	13	13	15	15
Average number of rainy days per month												

PACKAGE TRAVEL

WELL OVER 150 tour operators feature France in their brochures – far too many to list here. The very useful *Reference Guide for Travellers in France,* published by the French Government Tourist Office, has a comprehensive list of tour operators with a region-by-region break-down of types of holiday featured. A selection of tour operators is listed to get you started. The variety of holidays and activities in France is enormous, ranging from cookery courses and gastronomy tours, naturist and golfing holidays to multi-activity sporting holidays in the Alps.

Tour operators

Activity holidays: Action Vacances (multi-activity), Belle France (cycling), French Country Cruises (boating), French Golf Holidays (golf), LSG Theme Holidays (multi-activity), Susi Madron's (cycling), Unicorn Holidays (château stays), VFB (walking) **Boating**: Blakes, Hoseasons **Camping**: Canvas Holidays, Carisma, Club Cantabrica, Eurocamp, Eurosites, French Country Camping, Keycamp, Sandpiper, Select France, Solaire **City breaks**: Airtours, British Airways Holidays, Cresta, Crystal, Inghams, Kirker, Made to Measure, Osprey, Thomson, Time Off, Travelscene **Cultural**: Andante, British Museum Traveller, Cox & Kings, Martin Randall, Prospect, Travel for the Arts **Self-catering gîtes, villas & apartments**: AA Motoring, Air France, Allez France, Bladon Lines, Bowhills, Brittany Direct, Club Cantabrica, Collineige, Corsican Affair, Corsican Places, Cresta, Crystal, Destination Provence, Dominiques Villas, Drive France, Driveline Europe, Eurovillages, Fourseasons, French Affair, French Impressions, French Life, Headwater, Inghams, Inntravel, Interhome, Just France, Lagrange, Lakes & Mountains, Meon, Motours, Normandie Vacances, P&O European Ferries, Palmer & Parker, Prima Villas, Sally Holidays, Simply Corsica, Sandpiper, Something Special, Sovereign, Stena Line, Sunselect, Travelscene, Vacances en Campagne, VFB, Vintage Travel, Voyages Ilena **Walking**: Exodus, Explore Worldwide, Headwater, HF Holidays, Inntravel, Naturetrek, Ramblers Holidays, Sherpa, Waymark **Wildlife/birdwatching**: Animal Watch, Limosa, Ornitholidays, Sunbird, Wildlife Worldwide **Wine**: Arblaster & Clarke, Winetrails

INDEPENDENT TRAVEL

THERE ARE direct flights from Britain to many French airports, and ferry/catamaran/hovercraft services from Dover to Calais; Ramsgate to Dunkirk; Folkestone to Boulogne; Newhaven to Dieppe; Portsmouth to Le Havre, Caen, Cherbourg and St Malo; Southampton to Cherbourg; Poole to St Malo; and Plymouth to Roscoff. Ferry fares are grouped into bands that depend on the time of day, time of year, and day of the week you intend to travel. To find the best possible deal you need to travel outside July and August, but if you are tied to school holidays it is wise to avoid Friday and Saturday departures and Saturday and Sunday returns.

Le Shuttle transports cars from Folkestone to Calais; foot passengers can take Eurostar from London Waterloo or Ashford to Paris Gare du Nord.

France is quite well served by its motorway system, though tolls make motorways expensive. N-roads (similar to British A-roads) link the main towns and cities but can become clogged by lorries using them as toll-free options. In contrast, D-roads are usually empty, fast and often arrow-straight. Official *Bison Futé* motoring maps, indicating major bottlenecks and alternative routes, are available from the French Government Tourist Office or from service stations in France. Seatbelts are compulsory in France, and you must carry a warning triangle unless your car has hazard warning lights. You are also obliged to carry your vehicle registration document, full driving licence and current insurance certificate. The minimum driving age is 18. Unleaded petrol is widely available; petrol stations on motorways are usually more expensive.

Rail travel is an efficient and fast alternative to taking your own car. Eurodomino Rover Tickets offer unlimited travel on any three, five or ten days in one month. There are few long-distance buses; local services are run by SNCF and link with trains.

Hotels are officially graded from one up to four stars, with a four-star luxury category. Probably the best-known guide to hotels and restaurants is the *Michelin Red Guide*, but a good source of information on cheap, family-run hotels is the *Logis de France* guide, available from the French Government Tourist Office, which also publishes a guide to *Café Couettes* (B&B accommodation).

Self-catering accommodation ranges from simple country cottages to modern purpose-built blocks.

Camping and caravan sites are graded from one to four star. Those in the main seaside areas are often large and organised, with lots of facilities. Sites in rural areas are usually smaller and simpler.

RED TAPE, HEALTH AND SAFETY

BRITISH PASSPORT-HOLDERS do not need a visa to visit France. Mainland France does not have any particular health or safety problems – just take the usual precautions.

Bomb attacks, mainly on public buildings, continue throughout Corsica. Take care in town centres and near public buildings, and look out for suspicious packages. There have been some attacks on British-registered yachts. For the latest advice contact the Foreign Office Travel Advice Unit (see page 11).

MORE INFORMATION French Government Tourist Office, 178 Piccadilly, London W1V 0AL, tel (0891) 244123 (premium rate number), web site: http://www.franceguide.com

COST OF LIVING £££

GAMBIA

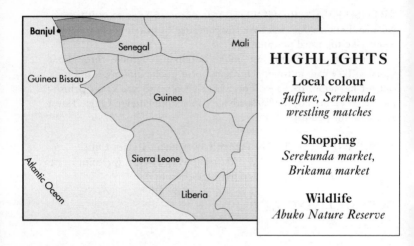

Banjul •

Senegal

Guinea Bissau

Guinea

Mali

Sierra Leone

Atlantic Ocean

Liberia

HIGHLIGHTS

Local colour
*Juffure, Serekunda
wrestling matches*

Shopping
*Serekunda market,
Brikama market*

Wildlife
Abuko Nature Reserve

FOR THOSE looking for a taste of Africa with minimal hassle, the Gambia has the advantages of being English-speaking, accessible (direct flight time from London is under six hours, with no time zone change), and affordable. Tourist development has progressed at the laid-back pace that characterises the Gambian way of life. Even the most visited areas are relatively unspoilt but facilities can be basic.

BEST RESORTS

● Most tourists stay at beach hotels in **Bakau**, **Kotu** or **Fajara**, on the palm-fringed Atlantic coast immediately south of the Gambia river.

● There is little to choose between the resorts: hotels are small-scale, with buildings set in lush gardens with birds and tropical flowers.

● Beaches outside resort areas stretch for 25 miles, wild and deserted.

● The run-down capital, **Banjul**, is a relic of colonial days with little to offer tourists.

● Many hotel tour programmes include a cruise up the Gambia river by motor-powered *pirogue* (dug-out canoe). The river banks are almost completely undeveloped and home to a vast bird population.

BEST SIGHTS AND EXCURSIONS

Abuko Nature Reserve

This is a small but rewarding forest reserve to explore on foot. Families of monkeys, including patas, green monkeys and red colobus, are easy to spot in the trees, and with a little patience you should also see many migrant and resident birds, including parrots, kingfishers and sunbirds.

Boat trips

Record-breaking catches of barracuda, shark and marlin have been made off Cape Point, east of Banjul, and several charter companies will provide anglers with a fully-equipped ocean-going boat with skipper and crew for full-day or half-day sport fishing trips.

For those who prefer calmer waters, the maze of mangrove creeks at the mouth of the Gambia river is a paradise for birdwatchers, and the fishing here is so plentiful that even a novice stands an excellent chance of hauling in a ladyfish, butterfish or grouper. Fishing boats and tackle can be hired through hotel representatives or direct from the handful of private operators at Oyster Creek, off the highway outside Banjul.

Juffure

Many hotels offer a *Roots* tour to this, the supposed birthplace of Kunta Kinte, the Mandinka ancestor of the African-American writer Alex Haley. Juffure is a simple village of thatched, mud-brick huts, just off the north bank of the Gambia River. Present-day members of the Kinte family will allow visitors to take photos, for a fee.

Markets

The market at Serekunda, the Gambia's largest town, is a maze of rick-ety stalls and makeshift pitches selling everything from palm oil by the cupful to chickens by the crateful. Colourful but chaotic and definite-ly not for the faint-hearted, this is an excellent hunting-ground for batik cloth, beads and locally made jewellery. Banjul's Albert Market is smaller and tamer, good for cheap tapes of West African music. For woodcarvings, musical instruments and antique masks, the market at Brikama, a small town south of Serekunda, is worth a visit.

Wrestling

Late in the afternoon on Saturdays and Sundays, lively inter-tribal wrestling matches take place in open-air arenas in Serekunda. Cheering on contestants as they strut around the arena accompanied by teams of whistlers and drummers is all part of the ritual.

WHEN TO GO

THE GAMBIA'S main tourist season runs from October to April, with almost guaranteed sunshine by day, and cool nights. Although the Gambia is a predominantly Muslim country, enthusiastic Christmas celebrations, with music and processions, take place in Banjul and on the coast. The rainy season is from June to September, bringing oppres-sively humid weather broken by sudden downpours. The brilliant dis-plays of fresh green growth are more than adequate compensation, and most of the rain falls at night. Late September and October are hot and dry, like a Mediterranean summer.

	Average daily maximum temperature °C											
London	6	7	10	13	17	20	22	21	19	14	10	7
Banjul	30	31	32	30	30	31	31	30	31	32	32	30
	JAN	FEB	MAR	APR	MAY	JUN	JUL	AUG	SEP	OCT	NOV	DEC
Banjul	<1	1	0	1	1	7	17	22	18	9	1	1
London	15	13	11	12	12	11	12	11	13	13	15	15
	Average number of rainy days per month											

PACKAGE TRAVEL

FOR RESORT-BASED beach holidays, the best deals are to be had by booking packages from the UK. The main options in the brochures are a beach holiday or a birdwatching holiday, both in the winter months (October to April).

Tour operators

Beach packages: Airtours, Cosmos, First Choice, Gambia Experience, Sunworld, Thomas Cook, Thomson **Birdwatching**: Cygnus Wildlife, Limosa, Ornitholidays, Sunbird

---

INDEPENDENT TRAVEL

IF YOU prefer to rough it in simpler accommodation, or to tour independently, you can choose between a scheduled flight or a flight-only charter deal from Gatwick or Manchester.

Many visitors come here purely to soak up the winter sun (and enjoy the riotous sunsets), barely venturing outside the immediate surroundings of their hotel, but the more adventurous can head inland to explore the Gambia's open bush country and sample something of traditional village life.

The Gambia has a few car-hire firms in the Banjul and coastal areas; rates are high. If you plan to venture up-country in the rainy season a four-wheel-drive vehicle is essential. Private taxis can be hired by the half-day or day. The main hotels have their own taxi ranks and discourage guests from using 'unauthorised' taxis for security reasons.

Local transport by bus or bush taxi (shared cars, minibuses or vans which travel along fixed routes) can be uncomfortable but is very cheap. The transport hub for inland destinations is Serekunda. The bush taxi stands are near the market; touts round up travellers and collect fares for their vehicles, which leave when full.

The atmosphere and quality of accommodation at package resort hotels vary a great deal, with some catering predominantly for young singles and couples (offering water sports and nightlife), some geared to families (though none has much in the way of facilities for very young children), and some more sedate in style. All the larger hotels stage regular evenings of traditional music (*balafon*, *kora* and drumming) and tribal dancing. There is no official hotel grading system, and standards are generally more modest than those of European hotels – only the top hotels have air-conditioning, fridges, telephones or televisions.

Although you will not find them in the package tour brochures, the Gambia also has a good choice of small, simple guesthouses, catering for independent travellers, expatriate volunteers and locals.

RED TAPE, HEALTH AND SAFETY

NO VISA is required by British nationals staying for less than three months. Airport tax of £10 is levied on travellers leaving by air.

Visitors are strongly advised to take anti-malaria tablets – see your GP or a specialist travel clinic for advice on what tablets to take as well as other recommended vaccinations. Anti-malaria tablets do not, however, provide total protection against infection, and it is best to avoid being bitten by using insect repellents, electric vaporisers and mosquito nets, and covering up arms and legs, especially at dawn and dusk.

One of the Gambia's greatest assets is the genuine warmth and hospitality of its people. Newcomers should, however, bear in mind that this is a Third World country, and outside wealthier residential and hotel areas the gulf between tourists and local people can be acutely felt. Hustlers – young locals who make a living by badgering tourists to buy souvenirs or drugs, change money, or employ them as a guide – can be a nuisance. It is unwise to walk along empty stretches of beach alone, and inadvisable to venture far outside your hotel compound after dark without a trusted driver or guide. Women travelling alone may feel particularly vulnerable. For the latest Foreign Office advice see page 11.

MORE INFORMATION The Gambia National Tourist Office, 57 Kensington Court, London W8 5DG, tel 0171-376 0093, web site: http://www.thegambia-touristoff.co.uk

COST OF LIVING £

GERMANY

HIGHLIGHTS

Culture
*Berlin, Munich,
Bavaria,
eastern Germany*

Nightlife
Berlin

Local colour
*Bavaria,
northern Germany*

Outdoor activities
*Bavaria,
Black Forest*

Scenic landscape
*Bavaria, Rhineland,
Black Forest*

BERLIN
Good for culture and nightlife

BERLIN, THE focus of Germany's reunification since 1989 when the wall erected during the Cold War was torn down, still seems like a fairly divided city, though new construction is levelling out the differences.

BEST SIGHTS

Brandenburg Gate
When the Wall existed, the area round the Brandenburg Gate was part of no-man's-land, and sealed off. Today this imposing edifice is the centre of a trade in alleged bits of Wall and military memorabilia.

Checkpoint Charlie Museum
This vivid, if partisan, history of the Wall includes accounts of escape schemes. To the west is a chunk of the real Wall, painted by local artists.

Dahlem
Berlin's best-known museums are housed in an enormous complex

south-west of the city. Highlights include the Museums of Oriental Art, Ethnology and Islamic Art, and the Picture Gallery.

Museum Island
Formerly in East Berlin, the Pergamon is a superb collection of Greek, Roman and Mesopotamian antiquities. Other collections include the Egyptian Museum and the Early Christian and Byzantine exhibits.

MUNICH
Good for culture

MUNICH IS a great cultural centre for film, art, theatre and music. Its *Oktoberfest*, a two-week beer festival in late September, is famous abroad.

BEST SIGHTS
Alte and Neue Pinakothek
The 'old' collection has fine Dutch and Flemish works, Bruegel's *Land of Cockayne*, and Dürer's Christ-like self-portrait. The 'younger' collection includes sculpture by Rodin and some of Goya's Black Paintings.

Dachau
The former concentration camp in this market town ten miles from Munich is overwhelmingly flat and grey: 28 of the 30 barrack blocks have been flattened and all that remains are numbered beds of gravel.

Nymphenburg Palace
Rococo palace in a formal park that includes botanical gardens. In the grounds is the blue-and-white hunting lodge of Amalienburg.

St John Nepomuk Church
A superb Bavarian baroque church which resembles an opera house.

BAVARIA
Good for culture, local colour, outdoor activities and scenic landscape

FLYING THE blue-and-white regional flag, Bavaria retains a strong independent identity, flaunting the national dress of *Lederhosen* and *Dirndl* and celebrating with legendary drinking sessions.

BEST SIGHTS AND EXCURSIONS
Augsburg
Grand Renaissance mansions line Augsburg's main street, symbolic of the

city's former wealth. To the east is the Fuggerei, the world's first social housing project for the poor.

Bamberg
This gem of a city on the River Regnitz has an eighteenth-century town hall at its base. An imposing Gothic cathedral stands high above the town.

Bayreuth
Wagner's house is now a museum. The spartan *Festspielhaus*, acoustically perfect, is packed each August during the Bayreuth Festival.

Oberammergau
Famous for its Passion Play, staged every ten years, the village is attractive, but the shops selling woodcarvings make the biggest impression.

Ottobeuren Abbey
This extravagant baroque church is a profusion of sugar almond, pink and yellow, with arches decorated with gold and white stucco.

Passau
This cathedral city sits on a narrow neck of land where the Rivers Inn and Ilz meet the Danube. The old town is a cheerful jumble of stone houses and towers; boats on the quay take trippers on pleasure cruises.

Regensburg
The knobbly twin towers of Regensburg's cathedral dominate huddled medieval stone houses. Ludwig I set up Walhalla, an unnerving shrine of 118 marble busts just outside the city, to honour German heroes.

Rothenburg ob der Tauber
So perfect it is almost a parody: the medieval town centre, surrounded by ramparts, has remained completely untouched. Charming, less-famous Dinkelsbühl and Nördlingen are similarly pristine.

Royal castles
Between 1864 and 1886 Bavaria's mad King Ludwig II spent vast amounts of state funds to build three fantastic castles. Neuschwanstein, bristling with white turrets and never finished, was designed by a stage painter; its interior is painted with heroic scenes. Linderhof, a smaller, completed rococo castle, has lovely grounds containing a Moorish pavilion with cascades of water. Uncompleted Herrenchiemsee was to have been the grandest, a replica of Versailles, but money ran out. Opposite Neuschwanstein is Hohenschwangau, where Ludwig grew up.

Würzburg

The baroque *Residenz*, once home to the prince-bishops, has a fine chapel, a magnificent two-tier staircase and also a huge ceiling fresco by Tiepolo. Würzburg is also the centre of Franconian wine production.

BEST RESORTS

Berchtesgaden

● Facing the peaks of the Watzmann, Berchtesgaden is in the most beautiful region of the German Alps.

● Go boating on the ice-green waters of nearby Königssee.

● Take a bus trip up the spectacular road to Kehlstein, or Eagle's Nest, built for Hitler on his fiftieth birthday.

Garmisch-Partenkirchen

● A busy town with smart shops and hotels, lying below the Zugspitze.

● On offer are mountain rides and easy walks.

Lindau

● Small island in the Bodensee with a relaxing harbourside promenade.

● Steamers carry day-trippers to Switzerland.

RHINELAND
Good for scenic landscape

ONE OF the great transport arteries of Europe, the Rhine valley can be disappointing, heavily industrialised and traffic-ridden. But the tributaries, such as the Mosel and the Nahe, have some attractive scenery.

BEST SIGHTS

Cologne (Köln)

See the city best from the river, where the twin spires of the Gothic cathedral dominate the skyline. Next door is the Roman-Germanic Museum, built around a Dionysos mosaic. The Wallraf-Richartz Museum has modern sculpture and pop art as well as Cologne masters.

Heidelberg

Heidelberg's romantic Neckar valley setting, its part-ruined castle and informal student bars attract many tourists. The courtyard and gardens are the best parts of the castle. Take the Philosopher's Path for fine views.

Mainz

The Gutenberg Museum houses the famous bible, also the hand press used to print it. Mainz also has a reconstructed Romanesque cathedral.

Trier
Birthplace of Karl Marx, Trier has some unmissable Roman remains: the Porta Nigra, an arcaded gate, and the Kaiserthermen, a heated bathing complex.

Worms
The cathedral's western chancel is a celebration of Rhineland Romanesque style, while the Luther Monument commemorates the city's association with the great Protestant reformer.

BEST CASTLES

Many of the Rhine's castles are best regarded as part of the scenery, and in most cases do not merit the uphill trek which their closer investigation usually requires.

Eltz
A nest of sharply pointed turrets rising from an outcrop in the Eltz valley. In the treasure chamber is a glittering array of gold and silver drinking vessels.

Marksburg
The only medieval castle on the Rhine never to be blown up or stormed stands above Braubach, on a narrow cone of rock.

Rheinfels
This desolate rambling ruin is a good spot for watching the barges manoeuvring around the Lorelei rock.

Stolzenfels
Rebuilt in the 1830s by Friedrich Wilhelm IV, the castle attempts an interesting, if self-conscious, recreation of the spirit of the Middle Ages.

BEST TOURING

Ahr valley
A smaller Rhine valley, with vineyards and castles. The prettiest scenery is at Altenahr, the most dramatic between the Ahr valley and the Mosel.

Lahn valley
The least crowded of the Rhine's tributaries enjoys tranquil countryside. Bad Ems, a sedate riverside spa, was Kaiser Wilhelm's favourite resort. Limburg is a medieval town, now encircled by modern development.

Mosel valley
Between Trier and Koblenz the Mosel river curves through a valley of terraced vineyards. The landscape is broken by wine villages and the

occasional ruined castle. Bernkastel is a handsome old town, packed with wine cellars.

Rhine gorge
A V-shaped furrow in the schist massif, the Rhine gorge is the most beautiful and most crowded area. To escape take the Rheingoldstrasse, a scenic route linking Boppard, St Goar, Oberwesel and Bacharach.

BLACK FOREST
Good for outdoor activities and scenic landscape

FOR A civilised break combining spa baths and gentle woodland walks, a holiday in the Black Forest is hard to beat.

BEST BASES
Baden–Baden
The resort centres on a park and an avenue of plane trees. Visit ornate nineteenth-century buildings, an art nouveau *Trinkhalle* where you can taste saline waters, and a sumptuous neoclassical *Kurhaus* and casino.

Freiburg
A 370-ft cathedral spire dominates this city, spiritually ruled by its university. Near the cathedral are medieval and eighteenth-century houses and terrace cafés. The Augustiner Museum houses religious art.

BEST SIGHTS AND EXCURSIONS
Furtwangen
The Black Forest, not Switzerland, is the home of the cuckoo clock – a fact celebrated in this collection of over 1,000 timepieces.

Gutach
Sixteenth-century local buildings have been reassembled in an open-air museum.

Triberg
The Heimatsmuseum is a collection of pianolas and organs. It displays mannikins which burst into life when you put a coin in the slot.

NORTHERN GERMANY
Good for local colour

FEW OF the bigger cities in this area have much charm. The real gems are the small historic towns, not visited by many foreign tourists.

BEST SIGHTS

Bremen
The focus of the city is the market square: a large, irregular, cobbled area bordered by ornate medieval town-houses and the massive, twin-towered Romanesque cathedral.

Goslar
The medieval old town is finely preserved, with fan-shaped carvings, oriels and crooked arcades adorning streets of half-timbered houses.

Lübeck
This medieval town of gateways, red-brick houses with stepped gables, intimate courtyards and fine churches makes for enjoyable exploring; the soaring Gothic Marienkirche is a particular highlight.

EASTERN GERMANY
Good for culture

BEST SIGHTS

Potsdam
About 12 miles south-west of Berlin, the summer retreat of the Prussian kings contains many houses and villas. Best are Frederick the Great's Sans Souci Palace, with fine marquetry, and the grotto of the Neue Palace.

Weimar
Weimar is a picturesque town with museums commemorating the German cultural giants – from Goethe and Schiller onwards – who graced its heyday.

WHEN TO GO

ROSENMONTAG, THE day before Shrove Tuesday, is celebrated with huge carnivals in the Rhineland area around Cologne and Mainz.

	Average daily maximum temperature °C											
London	6	7	10	13	17	20	22	21	19	14	10	7
Berlin	2	3	8	13	19	22	24	23	20	13	7	3
	JAN	FEB	MAR	APR	MAY	JUN	JUL	AUG	SEP	OCT	NOV	DEC
Berlin	17	15	12	13	12	13	14	14	12	14	16	15
London	15	13	11	12	12	11	12	11	13	13	15	15
	Average number of rainy days per month											

	JAN	FEB	MAR	APR	MAY	JUN	JUL	AUG	SEP	OCT	NOV	DEC
Average daily maximum temperature °C												
London	6	7	10	13	17	20	22	21	19	14	10	7
Munich	1	3	9	14	18	21	23	23	20	13	7	2
Munich	16	16	13	15	15	17	16	16	13	13	15	15
London	15	13	11	12	12	11	12	11	13	13	15	15

In August and early September, wine festivals abound throughout the same region. Munich is perhaps best known for its *Oktoberfest*, which usually takes place in the second half of September. In December, nearly every large town holds a Christmas fair, with decorated stalls and carol-singing.

PACKAGE TRAVEL

PACKAGES ARE by air, rail or ferry. Many of the UK tour operators to Germany are coach tour operators offering stay-put holidays with daily excursions or coach tours of the Rhine and Mosel valleys, the Black Forest or Bavaria.

Other ways to get about include booking rail passes, arranging accommodation in advance, or following one of the self-drive itineraries – for instance the Romantic Road, which runs south from Würzburg in the north of Bavaria to Schwangau in the Alps along the Austrian border, or alternatively exploring the wine regions of the Mosel and the Rhine.

Accommodation includes holiday parks, self-catering apartments, staying with a family, farm-stays, guesthouses and hotels.

Tour operators

Battlefields: Holts' Tours, Midas **City breaks**: British Airways Holidays, Cresta, Crystal, Inghams, Made to Measure, Osprey, Scandinavian Seaways, Sovereign, Stena Line, Time Off, Travelscene **Coach tours**: Armchair, Bowens, Crusader, DA Tours, Excelsior, Leger, Shearings, Travelsphere, Wallace Arnold **Specialists**: DER, Moswin, Taber **Walking**: Bents, Ramblers Holidays, Sherpa, Waymark **Other activities**: Ace Study Tours, Anglo Dutch (cycling), Arblaster & Clarke (wine), Bents (cycling), Ffestiniog Travel (rail tours), KD Cruises (river cruising), Martin Randall (opera), Prospect (cultural), Swan Hellenic (river cruising), Travel for the Arts (cultural)

Activities include cruises on the Rhine and Danube, walking, sailing, cycling, canoeing, cultural and music tours, and wine and beer festivals.

Most city breaks offer Berlin and Munich for one or more nights, but a few operators also go to Cologne, Dresden, Frankfurt and Hamburg.

INDEPENDENT TRAVEL

THE COUNTRY is easy to reach from any of the eastern Channel ports, and reduced short-break ferry fares are good value. The major German airports are Berlin, Frankfurt and Munich. The extensive internal air network is expensive.

Walkers and cyclists can use the wide-ranging and efficient rail network – various rover tickets are available. There are few long-distance bus services; most buses run between towns and villages not linked by rail. The exceptions are some scenic routes, such as the Romantic Road.

The Germans are wedded to their cars, and the network of motorways (*Autobahnen*) and other roads is good, except for some secondary roads in eastern Germany. No tolls are levied at the moment, though the idea is being discussed. Unleaded petrol is available everywhere. The speed limit of 80mph on *Autobahnen* is only a recommendation: that speck in your mirror is, within seconds, a Porsche three feet from your bumper. Overtake with extreme care, and be well insured. Seat-belts must be worn in the front and back, and children under 12 must sit in a special seat in the back. On-the-spot fines can be imposed for speeding.

Larger hotels tend to be characterless and unfriendly. The best-value accommodation is in smaller pensions and B&Bs, which offer spotless rooms and hearty breakfasts. Look out for signs saying *Zimmer frei*.

RED TAPE, HEALTH AND SAFETY

BRITISH PASSPORT-HOLDERS do not require a visa to visit Germany. The country has no particular health or safety problems: just take the usual precautions (see pages 10–12).

MORE INFORMATION German National Tourist Office, Nightingale House, 65 Curzon Street, London W1Y 7PE, tel 0171-493 0080, brochure line (0891) 600100 (premium rate number), web site: http://www.germany-tourism.de
Proceeds from the premium-rate number go towards postage and packing; people writing in are asked for £1.50.

COST OF LIVING £££

GREECE

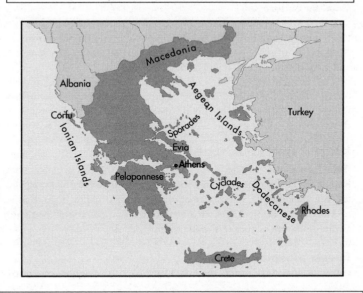

HIGHLIGHTS

Beaches
*Macedonia,
Cyclades,
Ionians,
Sporades,
Crete,
Dodecanese,
north–east
Aegean*

Culture
*Athens, Attica,
Peloponnese,
central Greece,
Macedonia,
Cyclades,
Crete,
north–east
Aegean*

**Family
holidays**
*Macedonia,
Cyclades,
Ionians,
Sporades,
Crete,
Dodecanese*

Local colour
*Peloponnese,
central Greece,
Cyclades,
Sporades,
Crete,
Dodecanese*

Nightlife
*Macedonia,
Cyclades,
Ionians,
Sporades,
Crete*

**Outdoor
activities**
*Peloponnese,
central Greece,
Cyclades,
Ionians,
Sporades,
Crete,
north–east
Aegean*

**Romantic
escapism**
*Central Greece,
Sporades,
Dodecanese,
north–east
Aegean*

**Scenic
landscape**
*Peloponnese,
central Greece,
Cyclades,
Ionians,
Evia,
Crete,
Dodecanese,
north–east
Aegean*

ATHENS
Good for culture

IT IS polluted and noisy, the traffic is impossible and the view from the Acropolis is of shabby blocks and TV aerials. Yet Athens' ancient sites and museums are vital viewing for classical civilisation buffs.

Greece's main port, Piraeus, is connected to Athens by metro or by bus 040 from Filellinon off Syntagma Square. All ferries and the hydrofoil to Aegina leave from the main harbour; other hydrofoils leave from the smaller Zea harbour on the east of the peninsula.

BEST SIGHTS AND EXCURSIONS

The Acropolis
Highlights of this complex, on a rocky outcrop at Athens' heart, include the Erectheion, with replica caryatids, and the Parthenon, main temple to Athena. The original decorative sculpture is in the Acropolis Museum, at the south-east corner of the Acropolis.

Benaki Museum
Fabulous collection, from Mycenaean jewellery to regional costumes.

Byzantine Museum
The only European museum to cover solely Byzantine art.

Greek Agora
Just the foundations of Athens' ancient market-place remain, but acquire a plan and visit the museum first, and the site will come to life.

Museum of Cycladic and Ancient Art
A collection of Cycladic sculptures from 3000 BC – abstract figurines that influenced Picasso, Modigliani and Henry Moore.

National Archaeological Museum
Greece's best museum of antiquities. Highlights include Cycladic and Mycenaean pieces, a fifth-century BC Poseidon and frescos (1500 BC).

Roman Agora
Relics of the Roman market include a public lavatory and the Tower of the Winds, a first-century BC octagonal tower that held a water clock.

Theatre of Dionysos
A fourth-century theatre carved into the Acropolis hill, where the tragedies of Aeschylus, Sophocles and Euripides were first performed.

ATTICA
Good for culture

ATTICA IS unappealing, and none of the resorts along the Apollo Coast is recommendable. There are, however, some sights worth a look.

BEST SIGHTS AND EXCURSIONS

Daphni
Eleventh-century monastery with mid-Byzantine mosaics.

Eleusis
Pilgrims were initiated in the Eleusinian Mysteries at this shrine.

Sounion
One of Greece's celebrated sights: a temple to Poseidon, 200 feet above the sea, on the jagged tip of the Attic peninsula. Best seen at sunset.

THE PELOPONNESE
Good for culture, local colour, outdoor activities and scenic landscape

THE FOUR-CLAWED Peloponnese peninsula is not only peppered with ancient sites, but has some of the loveliest landscapes in Greece.

BEST SIGHTS AND EXCURSIONS

Ancient Corinth
Riotous in ancient times, Corinth today consists of a ruined hilltop acropolis and a Roman town below, with an excellent museum.

Epidavros
This fascinating sanctuary dedicated to Asklepios, god of healing, boasts a famous theatre. A list of miracle cures performed stretches credulity.

Mistra
Byzantine outpost set on a lovely hill crowned by a Frankish fortress.

Mycenae
The evocative ruins of the 3,000-year-old royal palace from which Helen ran off with Paris and provoked the ten-year-long siege of Troy.

Nestor's Palace
To get the most out of these ruins, reputedly visited by Telemachus in *The Odyssey*, stop off at the museum in the nearby village of Hora first.

181

Olympia
Site of the original Olympic Games. Visit the gymnasium, the palaestra with baths and massage parlour, the stadium and an excellent museum.

Tiryns
A well-preserved and rarely visited Mycenaean fortress.

BEST RESORTS
Methoni
● Small coastal market town, with Venetian houses and fortress-walls.
● The beach, used as a road by some traffic, is popular with wind-surfers. Good beaches north beyond Pylos at Gialova and Petrochori.

Porto Heli
● Large resort, with poor beaches, much used by tour operators.
● Good for sailing and water sports, bad for sunbathing.

Stoupa
● A recently developed resort of low-rise, whitewashed apartments, with three golden sandy beaches.
● Well-placed for touring the Mani peninsula.

Tolon
● Good for family holidays, with lots of water sports too.
● Largest resort in the region, with a sheltered beach between two promontories. The sands are soft to the south, but skimpy to the north.
● Lots of seasonal cafés, tavernas, cocktail bars and discos.

BEST BASES
Areopolis
The Mani peninsula's major resort. Stay in converted tower houses.

Kardamili
With its charming, flower-scented village of fine old houses, Kardamili makes a good low-season base (in summer it gets very crowded). The beach is pebbly, but there is excellent swimming.

Monemvasia
A rock connected to the mainland by a causeway. The walled, medieval town, deserted after the nineteenth-century War of Independence against the Turks, was recently renovated. Transport is by donkey. The nearest suitable beach is on the mainland at Epidavros Limera.

Nafplion
This delightful Venetian coastal town is well placed for ancient sites.

From May to September, hydrofoils run to the Peloponnese islands and Piraeus. Try Karathona's good beach, with picnic and parking areas.

Pylos
This stylish, attractive town has great views over Navarino Bay. Fine beaches are to be found to the north, at Gialova and Petrochori.

BEST ISLANDS
Aegina, Hydra, Spetses and Poros are all connected by hydrofoil with Athens and Nafplion and tend to get overrun with day-trippers in high season.

Hydra
The main village, Hydra, is pretty but very crowded in summer. Though no beaches exist, swimming off the rocks is enjoyable. To avoid crowds stay at Kamini, a half-hour's walk west of the port.

Kithira
The island is difficult to reach, and visited mostly by Australian *emigrés*. Villages are mostly inland; the prettiest is blue-and-white Kithira town. The modern port of Kapsali boasts a good, gently shelving beach. Market days – Saturday at Kalamos, Sunday at Potamos – are lively.

Spetses
The main port in Spetses town is crowded, but you will find pleasant villas in the upmarket area by the old harbour, Paleo Limani. Most beaches are shingle. The best out-of-town beach is Agia Anargyri, where some accommodation is available.

CENTRAL GREECE
Good for culture, local colour, outdoor activities, romantic escapism and scenic landscape

CENTRAL GREECE is a vast area with some magnificent sights and remarkable landscapes, though they are widely scattered.

BEST SIGHTS
Delphi
Ruined shrine of the most famous oracle of the ancient world, set on pine-clad slopes. It overlooks a huge sweep of olive groves.

Dodona
Not quite as perfect as Epidavros, the theatre of Dodona stands in a remote mountain valley and is rarely visited by tourists.

Ioannina

This undistinguished lakeside town boasts a superb archaeological museum and a folk art collection in a former mosque. In 1822, the monastery on the lake-island of Nissa was the scene of the assassination of tyrant Ali Pasha.

Meteora monasteries

Dating from the fourteenth century, these are fused to the summits of rock pillars on the Trikkala plain. You can visit Great Meteoron (the first established) and Varlaam; go early to avoid crowds, then try quieter Agios Nikolaos and Roussanou. Stay overnight in Kalambaka village.

Necromanteion of Ephyra

Ancient pilgrims hoping to consult the spirits of the dead here were duped: excavations found traces of lupin seeds and Egyptian jonquil (to induce hallucinations and giddiness), and a windlass for raising 'ghosts'.

Ossios Loukos

Tenth-century monastery with magnificent mosaics. Visit early.

Perama Caves

Caves discovered during the Second World War by locals sheltering from bombs. Impressive stalactite and stalagmite formations.

BEST BASES

Metsovo

On the slopes of a ravine, Metsovo is Epirus' most attractive town. People wear traditional costumes; some hotels exist in village houses.

Pilion peninsula

A lush, hilly peninsula with good beaches and picturesque villages; many traditional houses are now hotels. Best inland bases are Visitsa and Makrinitsa. For a seaside base, try Milopotamos or Chorefto.

Zagorahoria

Beautiful villages in mountain scenery. The Vikos Gorge is popular for hiking locally. Stay in converted traditional houses at Megalo Papingo.

BEST RESORT

Parga

● Red-roofed village on a castle-crowned hill with a harbour.

● Lower part of village is extremely commercialised and gets very busy in high season; upper village is virtually untouched by tourism.

● Beaches of Valtos and Lichnos are better than main beach. To escape the crowds in summer, take a land- or water-taxi to Loutsa.

MACEDONIA AND THRACE
Good for beaches, culture, family holidays and nightlife

THIS IS not a notably scenic area. Most people come to see the region's ancient Macedonian sites, or visit the Halkidiki peninsula on package holidays.

BEST SIGHTS
Halkidiki
A three-pronged peninsula offering different experiences: Kassandra, the westernmost prong, is most developed. Package hotels are often miniature resort complexes, charmless but with ample facilities. Sithonia, the central prong, is the prettiest. Vouvourou has a lovely sandy beach and good rooms to rent. For nightlife head for Nea Marmaras, with a crowded beach and ample rented accommodation. The third prong, Mount Athos, is a self-governing monastic state. Women are banned; men with a genuine interest in monastic life can apply for a visitor's permit from the British Consul in Athens.

Pella
Alexander the Great grew up in Pella. The town's white columns and mosaic floors recall its former elegance. The best mosaics are displayed in the museum.

Thessaloniki
You can see unmissable treasures from the Macedonian tombs at Vergina (where they are housed in the Archaeological Museum) and visit fine Byzantine churches here.

THE CYCLADES
Good for beaches, culture, family holidays, local colour, nightlife, outdoor activities and scenic landscape

THE LARGEST group of islands at over 30, the archipelago is great for island-hoppers (Naxos and Paros are superb for ferry connections).

BEST ISLANDS
Amorgos
The island of Amorgos is popular with hippies, hikers and intellectuals. Though its beaches are poor, both the villages and the landscape are extremely lovely. The best places to stay are the lively port of Katapola, or picturesque Hora.

Andros

A wealthy island with a pleasant resort, Batsi, and a fashionable yacht club. Andros town has a superb archaeological museum.

Ios

Hordes of backpackers are attracted to this rocky island, with only one village, because it has a couple of great beaches. Ios suffers high rates of theft and vandalism.

Mykonos and Delos

These islands are predominantly young, noisy, trendy, narcissistic and gay. The picturesque main town has good shops and pricey food. Visit some brilliant beaches (Paradise and Super Paradise), or make an excursion to Delos, birthplace of Apollo (take a picnic).

Naxos

The best place to stay is in the old part of Naxos town. Though the town beach is poor, good beaches lie a bus-ride away to the south. Many of the island's attractive villages are unaffected by tourism.

Paros

Parikia, the island's main town and port, is popular with backpackers and has lots of young, lively discos and bars. The second port of Naoussa does not have a beach, but you can find excellent ones near-by. The overdeveloped islet of Antiparos is not particularly interesting.

Santorini/Thira

Red-and-black beaches feature on this volcanic island, whose resorts are mostly sub-standard. The main town of Thira is spectacularly sited on the lip of a crater; most of the town was reconstructed after the earthquake of 1956. The town of Ia also has a clifftop site, with much accommodation in restored houses. Fine remains are visible at Akrotiri, buried by volcanic ash in 1500 BC.

Serifos

An island popular with backpackers in high season: come in spring or autumn, and hire a jeep to explore remote beaches along unmade tracks. The best beaches are Psilli Ammos, just over a mile along a rough track from the port, and Agios Iannis, just beyond.

Sifnos

Wealthy Europeans holiday on Sifnos. Visit the inland village of Apollonia, more pleasant and stylish than the port/resort of Kamares. The island is reputed to produce the best cooks in Greece – Apostoli restaurant, on Stylianou Prokou in Apollonia, is truly outstanding.

Tinos
Around 25 March and 15 August the island is overrun with pilgrims. Tinos town is very commercialised. Stay at Kolimbithra, with two sandy beaches, or Panormos, a fishing village with a small beach.

Remote islands
Avoid the islands of **Kouffonissi** and **Folegandros** in high season, as they become overcrowded. **Shinoussa** is not especially attractive, and is becoming commercialised. True islophiles should try heading for **Iraklia** and **Dhonnoussa**.

IONIAN ISLANDS
Good for beaches, family holidays, nightlife, outdoor activities and scenic landscape

TOURISM ON the Ionian islands is overwhelmingly British, and package holidays predominate – though it is possible to escape the crowds, even on the most 'packaged' islands of Corfu and Zante. The islands are not ideal for island-hopping: most ferry connections are to the mainland, although summer links between Lefkas, Ithaca, Zante and Cephalonia now exist.

BEST ISLANDS
Cephalonia
A large island with attractive scenery but few picturesque villages. The best area for touring is the beautiful northern peninsula. Assos and Fiskardo are lovely villages, but offer little to do. There are beaches within walking distance of Fiskardo, and you can use a boat to reach quality beaches a little further afield.

Corfu
Only 25 miles of Corfu's 125-mile coastline have been irreversibly ruined (the area around Corfu town). Avoid this region if you hate clubbing or drinking all night. Corfu town has a lovely Venetian centre and some interesting museums. The most spectacular scenery is in the centre of the west coast: Paramona is a quiet resort here. To the south-west lie mile upon mile of empty sands.

Ithaka
Mostly modern buildings occupy Ithaka, which has a few good beaches, accessible by boat. The nicest place to stay is peaceful Kioni, which retains some character. It is developing as a villa and flotilla resort.

Lefkas

Connected to the mainland by a causeway, Lefkas is convenient for Preveza airport. Day-trips to Ithaka and Cephalonia are possible by ferry. Vassiliki (a windsurfers' mecca) and Agios Nikitas are pleasant resorts. There are some excellent out-of-town beaches.

Paxos

Most accommodation is in villas, booked through small UK tour operators, with the option of renting a dinghy. Day-trippers from Parga and Corfu crowd the villages of Gaios and Lakka. The beaches on Paxos are mostly pebbly; you will find some good ones on the satellite island of Antipaxos.

Zante (Zakinthos)

The main package resort is Laganas, which boasts a long, sandy beach. Quieter options are Cape Gerakas, with sandy beaches and some accommodation, and Agios Nikolaos, with a hotel and sandy beach. Boat trips take in the justly named Blue Grotto (good for snorkelling).

EVIA AND THE SPORADES

Good for beaches, family holidays, local colour, nightlife, outdoor activities, romantic escapism and scenic landscape

EVIA'S BEACHES and resorts are not notably attractive, excluding the spa town of Loutra Edipsos, but the landscape is gorgeous: mountains, farmland, lush valleys and tracts of uncharted coast. More part of the mainland than an island, Evia – linked to Athens by bridge and motorway – is more popular with Greeks than foreigners. The Sporades are fertile, close-knit islands with fine beaches, ideal for flotilla holidays.

BEST ISLANDS

Alonnisos

Quietest of the Sporades, Alonnisos has a small, scruffy modern port, Patitiri, sited in a lovely bay. It also boasts a pleasant part-ruined village, Palaia Alonnisos, and a dreary holiday development at Votsi. The best-quality hotels in Patitiri are on the clifftops. An arty crowd have started to restore ruined houses in Palaia Alonnisos. Most beaches are small and stony, but peaceful and rather pretty. The west coast is good for snorkelling, but watch out for dangerous currents.

Evia

Loutra Edipsos sits on a sweeping bay, with a long beach. The town is quiet and sedate, with few non-Greek visitors. Captivating landscapes are to be found in the lush river valley between Prokopi and

Mantoudi. There are two good, secluded beaches near the port of Marmari.

Skiathos

Skiathos is the smallest, the most charming and the busiest of the Sporades, largely for its abundance of good beaches. Koukounaries is the most popular, a long arc of fine, yellow sand backed by pine trees and a lagoon. Other good beaches are Kanapitsa, Asselinos, Mandraki (Elias), Koutsouri and Krassas — also known as Banana Beach and now mainstream despite a reputation as the island's nudist spot. Busy Skiathos town sees much noisy international beer-swilling. It is, however, a pleasant place to stay in low season.

Skopelos

Skopelos town is outstandingly beautiful. Package tourism is a fairly recent arrival, and of an exceptionally high standard. The atmosphere in town is restrained and civilised. The island's most popular beach is Stafilos, two and a half miles from Skopelos. For more space go to Velanio, or Limnonari and Milia (via tracks). Water sports are in evidence on many beaches.

Skyros

Tourism here is muted (most accommodation is in rooms), but Skyros is one of the Aegean's most trendy, offbeat destinations and, in keeping with the New Age ethos, the island is equipped with two holistic centres. Below the picturesque main hill-town is a fine long sandy beach. There is a beach with dunes at Agios Petros, and a pebble beach at Agios Fokas (within walking distance of the holistic centre at Atsitsa). Local crafts include sandal-making and ceramics.

CRETE

Good for beaches, culture, family holidays, local colour, nightlife, outdoor activities and scenic landscape

CRETE, GREECE'S largest island, has a mountainous backbone. In the north, gentle slopes cradle large towns; in the south the mountains drop sharply into the sea. Much of the north coast is built-up, but the south coast is less spoilt, and the far east and west are virtually wild.

BEST RESORTS

Agia Galini
● The pick of Crete's British package-holiday resorts.
● Pretty harbour, compact village-style layout, good tavernas and discos.
● Poor beach.

Chania
- A beautiful old port, the second largest town in Crete.
- Can be rough, with large numbers of soldiers and backpackers.
- To the west is a new town, Neo Hora, with beaches and restaurants.

Elounda
- A collection of hotels in grounds outside Elounda village.
- Small sandy beach and swimming from ladders fixed to the rocks.
- Lively village square opening on to the harbour in Elounda itself.
- Small hotels and rooms to rent, but no adequate local beaches.

Paleohora
- Not eyecatching, but far from the major resorts, Paleohora lacks large hotels, and has a good coarse sand beach with lively windsurfing.
- Popular with Greek families and foreign backpackers.

Rethymnon
- Interesting town with a mosque and minaret, Venetian fortress, fine old houses, sleepy waterside and, sadly, a scruffy, slum-like new annexe.
- Most visitors stay on the coastal strip: a long beach lined with hotels.

Sitia
- Peaceful, terraced town and a lively harbourfront with French and Italian tourists, tavernas and a quay where ships collect local sultanas.
- Coarse sand beach, mid- to lower-range hotels.
- Vai beach nearby, with a famous palm grove, is superb but crowded.

BEST SIGHTS AND EXCURSIONS
Gorge of Samaria
In summer, thousands tramp through the spectacular gorge daily. The hike is tough-going – so wear stout shoes and carry plenty of water.

Gortyn
This appealing Graeco-Roman site stands on the fertile Messara plain. Most of the ruins are enclosed, but others are scattered nearby.

Gournia
Interesting remains of a Minoan town with narrow cobbled streets.

Heraklion
The Archaeological Museum of this noisy city contains Minoan finds.

Knossos
Most famous Minoan palace and mythical home of the Minotaur, excavated and partly rebuilt by Sir Arthur Evans in the early 1900s.

Melidoni Cave
Against a backdrop of stalactites and stalagmites, altars commemorate 300 local people massacred here by Turks during the wars of the 1820s.

Phaistos
A Minoan palace atop a low hill. There has been no reconstruction, and although the ruins are complex, they are more rewarding than Knossos.

Valsamonero Monastery
A medieval monastery with early fifteenth-century frescos.

THE DODECANESE
Good for beaches, family holidays, local colour, romantic escapism and scenic landscape

TUCKED UP along the Turkish coast are the Dodecanese. Some islands, like Rhodes and Kos, are hugely commercialised; others, like Astypalia, Nisyros and Tilos, are still unspoilt. Ferry links are fairly regular, and cheap charter flights leave frequently for Kos and Rhodes, making the Dodecanese an ideal choice for a varied island-hopping holiday.

BEST ISLANDS
Astypalia
A remote island shaped like a butterfly with an indented coast. The dazzling white village of Hora has a disco, a bouzouki club and great fish tavernas. Most tourists are Athenians who have holiday homes on the island. The best beach is at Livadia, where lush trees fringe the shingle and tavernas offer rooms to rent. Water sports are available. A wider range of beaches is accessible by boat.

Chalki
Tiny Chalki is a barren, rocky island with no fresh water. The harbour and only settlement is idyllic Emborio, with windmills, fishing boats and a few tavernas. The main beach, Pondamos, is ten minutes' walk away. Fishermen can take you to other beaches. In August many Chalkiots return to the island, and it can be difficult to find accommodation.

Karpathos
Dramatically beautiful, with crags looming over pine-forested slopes, Karpathos has a mountainous northern spine. The best places to stay at are Amopi, a growing resort, with beaches on serrated coastline; Finiki, a fishing village with a pretty harbour, a few tavernas and rooms to rent; and Lefkos, three bays of white sand reached via a rough road.

191

Olympos was cut off from the rest of the island until recently, when a road was built. Village people still speak an ancient form of Greek, and adopt traditional dress and customs. There are a few rooms to rent.

Kos

Kos has a fascinating town of minarets, ancient sites, mountains and fine beaches – and has embraced mass tourism. Best beaches are along the eastern side of Kefalos Bay, and east of Mastichari on the north coast.

Rhodes

Splendid medieval Rhodes town and large coastal areas are touristy, but unspoilt villages and beaches (on the west coast) exist. Archeangelos is the largest village; with its golden beach and rooms to let, it is a good base for family holidays. Haraki, a developing fishing village, has tavernas, self-catering accommodation and views down its shingle beach to Lindos. Vliha Bay has a sandy beach, tavernas and water sports. Steps of Lindos and Lindos Mare Hotels have family facilities. At Lindos houses like sugar cubes tumble down a hill, but the village is grossly over-commercialised and packed in high season. Lardos is a smart village. The bay below has mile upon mile of shingle and dunes.

Symi

The layers of neo-classical houses make Symi's harbour, Gialos, one of the most beautiful of any Greek island. An influx of day-trippers (between 10am and 3pm in high season) shatters the calm, but other-wise the island is very laid back. Labyrinthine Chorio, the ancient cap-ital, is linked to Gialos by a vast staircase. Caiques run between the peb-ble and shingle beaches at Marathorinta, Nanon and Georgios. The shingly sand at Nimborio is also accessible via a coastal path from the harbour.

Minor islands

Craggy, remote **Kasos** has few beaches or tourists but good walking. Try accommodation at Phry, a charming port with a few tavernas. **Kastellorizo** (setting of the film *Mediterraneo*) is near Turkey. Yachtsmen visit its magnificent natural harbour. No real beaches exist; you swim from hotel steps or rocks. The main village, Mandraki, has some pensions. Lovely, prosperous **Nisyros** has cube houses, fruit groves and a volcanic crater which draws a regular stream of day-trippers. Beaches are black volcanic sand, or pebble, and often empty even in summer. **Patmos** was home to St John, and is where his Revelation occurred. Except for the busy monastery of St John, a quiet island (beaches are poor). Rugged **Tilos** has quiet beaches. Stay in the main town, pretty Livadia, inland at the island capital, Megalo Chorio, or at Eristos.

NORTH-EAST AEGEAN ISLANDS
Good for beaches, culture, outdoor activities, romantic escapism and scenic landscape

BEST ISLANDS

Chios

This beautiful island sees relatively few tourists, perhaps because it has no quality beaches. The main town, Chios, is large, ugly and modern but very lively. You could stay in the Villa Argentikon, maybe Greece's most exclusive hotel. Inland are fascinating fortified villages built for mastic-growers. Accommodation is available in Pirgi, the prettiest (and busiest) of them.

Ikaria

A wonderful place for Grecophiles who have enough Greek to appreciate the eccentricity of the island. Ikaria is a stronghold of the Left; you may meet Stalinists in village *kafeneions* and, on asking the price of a room, be asked what you can afford. A brilliant sand beach is to be found at Armenistis, and a small, mostly modern whitewashed village with rooms and tavernas is nearby. Lots of mountain villages can be explored.

Lesbos

A large island, peaceful even in summer, when the islanders head for shanty holiday colonies on the coast. The main resort, Molivos, is a perfectly restored fortified village of timbered mansions. Nearby is a pebbly local beach, while sand and pebble beaches are further afield. Eressos, birthplace of Sappho, has a cheerful resort on a vast sandy beach. It is popular with lesbians and families of all nationalities. Sigri, a fishing harbour with a sandy crescent and tavernas, is a Greek resort used by some UK specialist operators. Many good local beaches exist here.

Limnos

The main town, Myrina, bustles above a fortified acropolis. Accommodation here is of a high standard. Some excellent sandy beaches are sited near the town, while good, undeveloped ones are on the outskirts. Outside Myrina, most of Limnos is dominated by the army. Specialist archaeological sites are to be found at Hefestia, Kavirio and Poliochni.

Samos

Samos has few established resorts. Most tourism involves package accommodation. The port/resort of Vathi is known for its fine archaeological museum. Pythagorion, the main resort, is focused on the harbour. Kokkari is the island's third resort. To the west, the coast and hills are enchanting. Tzamadou is a popular pebble beach. Stay at Ormos Marathokampos or find accommodation along the miles of beach to the west. The hills offer fine touring and walking.

Thassos
Traditionally popular with Greeks, Thassos is also used by UK tour operators. Accessible from mainland Kavala, it is not linked with other islands. A beautiful place of pine-covered mountains, its coastline fills up with campers and beach holidaymakers. Beware the vicious local mosquitoes. Potamios Bay has a long, sandy beach, pebbly in the middle. For great beaches, try Aliki and Potos, both busy with accommodation. Skala Potamios, a village with an excellent beach, makes a good base. Few people head inland. Theologos is the most charming village.

Samothraki
Accessible only by ferry from Alexandroupolis on the mainland, this is an island of woods, waterfalls and towering mountains. Long, sandy Ammos is the only beach. The ruins of the Sanctuary of the Great Gods are impressive. Find accommodation at the port, Kamariotissa (lively but not pretty) or at the spa town of Therma, which attracts a mix of elderly Greeks and young hippies. Lots of remote places allow for free camping.

WHEN TO GO

APRIL, MAY and October are good months to visit the islands in peace and quiet, but even in July and August one can find empty or near-empty beaches on the remoter islands. Between November and March ferry schedules are skeletal. In August the Aegean islands are swept by the *meltemi* wind, which can affect hydrofoil services.

Athens is a better autumn/winter destination, as the air quality gets appalling when the heat rises. The climate is hottest in Halkidiki and Athens, next hottest are the Ionian and east Aegean islands.

	Average daily maximum temperature °C											
London	6	7	10	13	17	20	22	21	19	14	10	7
Athens	13	14	16	20	25	30	33	33	29	24	19	15
	JAN	FEB	MAR	APR	MAY	JUN	JUL	AUG	SEP	OCT	NOV	DEC
Athens	16	11	11	9	8	4	2	3	4	8	12	15
London	15	13	11	12	12	11	12	11	13	13	15	15
	Average number of rainy days per month											

Average daily maximum temperature °C												
London	6	7	10	13	17	20	22	21	19	14	10	7
Heraklion	16	16	17	20	23	27	29	29	27	24	21	18
	JAN	FEB	MAR	APR	MAY	JUN	JUL	AUG	SEP	OCT	NOV	DEC
Heraklion	14	9	10	6	4	1	<1	<1	2	6	11	14
London	15	13	11	12	12	11	12	11	13	13	15	15
Average number of rainy days per month												

The best pre-Lenten carnival celebrations take place on Skyros, Cephalonia and in the port of Patras. There are scores of local saint's-day festivals (all of which are celebrated the previous evening). St George's festival (23 April) is noted on Skyros and in the village of Arahova near Delphi.

PACKAGE TRAVEL

ALL THE mass-market tour operators go to Greece, often with a large programme in a dedicated brochure. Hotels, self-catering and simple rooms are on offer in mainland resorts and on the islands. Greek specialists are listed below.

Charter and scheduled flights to Thessaloniki are used for packages to northern Greece and Halkidiki. Athens is the charter and scheduled flight airport for the Peloponnese and the islands. The larger islands of Corfu, Crete and Rhodes and the smaller islands

---

Tour operators

Birdwatching: Limosa, Naturetrek, Ornitholidays, Sunbird, Wildlife Worldwide **Pilgimage**: Highway, Inter-Church Travel, McCabe, Pilgrimage **Specialists**: Airtours, Amathus, Argo, Best of Greece, Catherine Secker (Crete), Club Cantabrica, Corfu à la Carte, Cosmos, CV Travel, Filoxenia, First Choice, Golden Sun, Greece & Cyprus Travel Centre, Greek Islands Club, Greek Sun, Ilios Island Holidays, Inghams, Kosmar, Laskarina, Paxos, Planos, Pure Crete, Simply Simon, Simply Travel, Skiathos Travel, Skopelos Villas, Sunvil, Sunworld, Thomas Cook, Thomson, Unijet, Voyages Ilena **Walking**: Explore Worldwide, Ramblers Holidays, Sherpa, Waymark **Other activities**: Ace Study Tours, Cox & Kings (flora), Martin Randall (cultural), Midas (battlefields), Peregrine (horse-riding), Propect (cultural), Solo's Holidays (singles), Swan Hellenic (cultural cruises) which have direct flights from the UK tend to be the busier island destinations.

Packages range from a one- or two-week stay-put hotel or self-catering holiday, to a two- or three-centre or a more active island-hopping holiday. Special-interest holidays include archaeological tours, island cruises, birdwatching, walking, cultural tours and sailing.

INDEPENDENT TRAVEL

DIRECT CHARTER flights (usually from May to October) go to many islands, including Corfu, Crete, Karpathos, Kos, Lesbos, Limnos, Mykonos, Rhodes, Samos, Santorini, Skiathos and Zante, as well as Athens, Kalamata, Kavala, Preveza and Thessaloniki on the mainland. All scheduled flights involve changing planes at Athens or Thessaloniki.

For island-hoppers, the best choices are well-connected islands such as the Cyclades or Dodecanese. The Sporades and Peloponnese islands also have regular hydrofoil and ferry services. It is best to 'hop' in May, June or September: in high season accommodation is scarce. Ferry timetables are unreliable (though improving), so keep a flexible itinerary. Internal Olympic Airways flights cover 30 island and mainland airports.

Car hire is expensive – rates do not include insurance and local tax, and the final bill may be double what you expect. What is more, even the international companies rent out cars in poor condition. Collision damage waiver (CDW) is usually included in pre-booked cars, but you may have to cover costs up to a certain amount. Car undersides are not insurable because of poor road surfaces, and the CDW will often also exclude windscreen and tyre damage. Many local firms do not offer CDW.

Fly-drive deals can often be cheaper than flying and adding on the cost of car hire. That said, rates charged by local rental firms are nego-tiable, especially in low season, so haggle.

All but the remotest islands have moped/motorbike operators. No one bothers with a helmet, and no questions are asked as long as you pay in advance, leave your passport as a deposit, and show you can ride a few yards. The accident rate is huge, and even if you are confident on a bike in the UK, you may come a cropper on Greece's rutted, pot-holed roads. Most injuries, however, are cuts and bruises, avoidable by wearing jeans and a long-sleeved shirt.

Taxis are cheap. You can negotiate a fixed rate with a driver for a day or half-day out – which can work out reasonably for a group. Also, the best taxi drivers make great guides, and if you hit it off they may even take you to a favourite remote beach, or to see their country relatives.

The railway network is limited, and trains are very slow. Long-distance buses are faster, and usually air-conditioned. The bus network is vast; and even remote villages are regularly served. On islands and in rural areas buses also deliver the post and supplies. On local buses, pay the driver. For long-distance buses it is wise to buy your ticket in advance in high season and on popular routes. Seats are numbered.

Haggling is still the norm – so in low season, or on islands experiencing a lull in tourism, you can get good deals on accommodation in rooms. Try bargaining even in summer, although on oversubscribed islands such as Paros, Mykonos and Ios discounts are unlikely.

Greek hotels are officially graded from E-category up to A and L (luxury). Rooms fall into three classes: A, B and C. Rooms in D- and E-class hotels can be as cheap as room-only accommodation; conversely, facilities in rooms can be as good as in an A- or B-class hotel. Fascinating ethnic village houses, restored to hotels or holiday homes by the National Tourist Board of Greece, can be found at Papingo (Epirus), Monemvasia, Vathia, Areopolis (Peloponnese), Makrynitsa, Vizitsa (Pilion), Mestá (Chios), Psara (Chios) and Ia (Santorini).

Hundreds of campsites exist, from basic pitches to those with bungalows, huts, restaurants, beach bars and sports facilities. Camping outside official campsites is illegal, and local police are now vigilant about moving people on, especially if there are vacant rooms or hotels. However, on the really remote islands (perhaps with no accommodation anyway), the locals will usually accept you, if you live cleanly and modestly. Even in summer you will probably need a sleeping bag if sleeping under the stars on a beach, as nights can be quite cold.

RED TAPE, HEALTH AND SAFETY

BRITISH PASSPORT-HOLDERS do not need a visa to visit Greece.

There have been problems with boat thieves in Corfu, and a UK resident of Corfu was shot and killed in Gouvia in September 1996 by criminals attempting to steal a boat. British citizens visiting Corfu by boat should stay overnight in harbours where the boat can be guarded. The Foreign Office advises holidaymakers to avoid marinas between midnight and 6am; for further advice see page 11.

MORE INFORMATION National Tourist Organisation of Greece, 4 Conduit Street, London W1R 0DJ, tel 0171-734 5997

No tourist office web site exists, but you can access information about Greece at: http://www.tourist-offices.org.uk/Greece/index.html

COST OF LIVING £-££

197

GUATEMALA

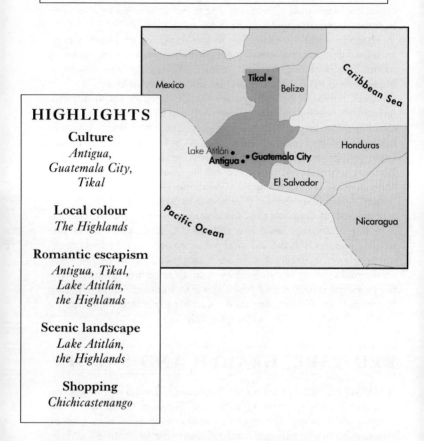

HIGHLIGHTS

Culture
Antigua,
Guatemala City,
Tikal

Local colour
The Highlands

Romantic escapism
Antigua, Tikal,
Lake Atitlán,
the Highlands

Scenic landscape
Lake Atitlán,
the Highlands

Shopping
Chichicastenango

Map labels: Mexico, Tikal, Belize, Caribbean Sea, Lake Atitlán, Antigua, Guatemala City, Honduras, El Salvador, Pacific Ocean, Nicaragua

MUCH OF the interest of Guatemala lies in the rich culture of its people, 50 per cent of whom are indigenous – descendants of the ancient Maya civilisation. But it is also an astonishingly beautiful country.

GUATEMALAN CITIES
Good for culture and romantic escapism

Antigua
This peaceful colonial gem is firmly on the *gringo* trail (young travellers come here to learn Spanish) but is still a delight. There are good places to sleep, drink and eat, making Antigua an excellent base.

Guatemala City

The vast Guatemalan capital is an unsavoury place, but it is worth staying at least a day to visit the fine museums. The excellent Museo Popol Vuh has a superb Mayan collection, while the Indian weavings and costumes at the Museo Ixchel merit a browse.

Tikal

The greatest Mayan city, where towering pyramids poke up above the canopy, attracts hordes of tourists to the remote Petén region. However, it is easy to lose the crowds in the jungle, where you are more likely to have parakeets and howler monkeys for company.

SOUTHERN AND EASTERN GUATEMALA
Good for romantic escapism and scenic landscape

BEST SCENIC LANDSCAPE
Lake Atitlán
Surrounded by volcanoes, Lake Atitlán is the most beautiful spot in Guatemala. The resort of Panajachel is totally dominated by tourism but is a relaxed enough base for exploring the Indian villages around the lake – the main attraction after the scenery.

Río Dulce
Boat trips up the Río Dulce from Livingston on the Caribbean coast to Lake Izabal take you through lush jungle scenery and away from the normal tourist route.

THE HIGHLANDS
Good for local colour, romantic escapism, scenic landscape and shopping

BEST LOCAL COLOUR

The highland villages are fascinating places to observe the rich culture of the local people with their colourful clothes, religion and festivals.

Chichicastenango
'Chichi' is too much on the tourist trail for some people's tastes, but Guatemala's most famous market attracts traders from all over the highlands. There is also bizarre pagan-style worship in the local church.

Todos Santos
The inhabitants of this remote village in the western highlands wear

particularly distinctive traditional clothes (the men's costume is said to have been inspired by that of Spanish noblemen), which you can see and buy at the weekly market.

Zunil

People in this small, friendly town follow the curious cult of Maximón, a saint whose favourite gifts are cigarettes and alcohol. A visit to his shrine is an unforgettable experience.

WHEN TO GO

GUATEMALA HAS a rainy season (May to October) and a dry season (November to April). The latter is a good time to be in the highlands, when temperatures are warm and the skies clear. The nights are usually fairly cool all year round. In the Petén, it can rain solidly all day (even out of the peak of the wet season), making the paths around Tikal very slippery. Visitor numbers increase during the usual peak winter and summer periods, but generally booking flights and hotels is not a problem – except during big festivals such as Holy Week.

Every town and village has its own special festival, but some are particularly famous. At Easter, Antigua hosts Guatemala's most celebrated Holy Week processions; in mid-August Joyabaj holds a festival of traditional dances rarely seen elsewhere; on All Saints Day (31 October) a chaotic horse race occurs in Todos Santos; on the Day of the Dead (1 November) giant kites are flown at Santiago Sacatepequez; and in mid-December a festival of dancing, worship and processions takes place in Chichi.

	Average daily maximum temperature °C											
London	6	7	10	13	17	20	22	21	19	14	10	7
Guatemala City	23	25	27	28	29	27	26	26	26	24	23	22
	JAN	FEB	MAR	APR	MAY	JUN	JUL	AUG	SEP	OCT	NOV	DEC
Guatemala City	4	2	3	5	15	23	21	21	22	18	7	4
London	15	13	11	12	12	11	12	11	13	13	15	15
	Average number of rainy days per month											

PACKAGE TRAVEL

ONLY A handful of tour operators offer holidays in Guatemala on its own. The country is mostly offered as part of a two-week tour visiting the Mayan sights of central America which combines Mexico and/or Belize with around five days in Guatemala. Tours usually take in

Guatemala City, Lake Atitlán, Chichicastenango, Antigua and Tikal. Accommodation is generally in hotels of reasonable quality.

Special interest holidays include adventure tours such as camping, walking, minibus or truck travel, or public transport tours.

Tour operators

Adventure: Dragoman, Encounter Overland, Exodus, Explore Worldwide, Guerba, Travelbag, Trips Worldwide **Cultural**: Ace Study Tours, Prospect **General**: Bales Tours, Cox & Kings, Kuoni, Sunvil **Specialists**: Cathy Matos, Journey Latin America **Tailor-made specialists**: Passage to South America, Scott Dunn World

---

INDEPENDENT TRAVEL

IN THE absence of direct flights from the UK, the best links to Guatemala City are via Amsterdam or Madrid, although you can also get good deals via Miami; Mexico City and Cancún are also possible changeover places. Once in Guatemala, there is only one internal air route, from Guatemala City to Tikal, which is how virtually everyone travels to the Petén. Rail services are limited, so most people rely on the buses. Public buses can be poorly maintained and dangerous. The services along or close to the Pan-American Highway are reasonably good, and you can reach most main towns easily; you can also flag down buses from the side of the road but you will probably have to stand once on board. First-class buses (which are faster and more comfortable) are available along some routes. Car hire is not particularly expensive and is worth considering if you want to time your trip like clockwork. The main roads are generally good, but surfaces deteriorate rapidly as you head into remoter areas. Security will be a worry wherever you are.

There are international-standard hotels in the capital, Chichicastenango, Antigua, Panajachel and around Tikal, and reasonable hotels or guesthouses in towns used to putting up tourists – but you should always ask to see the room before committing yourself. In remoter villages, guesthouses will be very basic. The price for accommodation, as for most things in Guatemala, is exceptionally low.

RED TAPE, HEALTH AND SAFETY

NO VISA is required by British passport-holders. On arrival in Guatemala, you must show a passport that is valid for six months. This will be stamped allowing you to stay for 90 days in the country.

Have yourself immunised against yellow fever, hepatitis A, polio and typhoid. Take anti-malaria pills if you plan to travel to jungle regions such as the Petén. The main problem most visitors face is a bout of diarrhoea: the best protection is to follow the advice on preventing stomach upsets on page 11.

Pickpocketing and bag-snatching are common on the streets of Guatemala City, particularly in the downtown district known as Zone 1. Petty thieves also operate in popular tourist centres such as Chichicastenango, Lake Atitlán and even Tikal (cling on to your belongings carefully in markets).

Guatemala has a long history of civil war, and while peace accords have been signed between the government and Indian guerrillas, the situation has not been resolved. You are strongly advised not to go off hiking in remote highland areas, where bandits have occasionally attacked travellers. There is little public transport on the road after 7pm – an unofficial curfew that has not ceased with the end of the war. Violent and armed crime is common throughout Guatemala. Visitors are advised to register with the British Embassy in Guatemala City on arrival (tel 3321601) for an update on the latest situation. Specific, current information is available from the Foreign Office Travel Advice Unit (see page 11), and specialist travel agencies should also know the latest situation.

MORE INFORMATION Tourist Information, Guatemalan Embassy, 13 Fawcett Street, London SW10 9HN, tel 0171-349 0346, web site: http://www.travel-guatemala.org.gt

COST OF LIVING £

HUNGARY

HIGHLIGHTS

Food/wine
Eastern and southern Hungary

Flora/ wildlife
Great Plain

Family holidays
Western Hungary

Outdoor activities
Western Hungary

Nightlife
Budapest

Scenic landscape
Eastern and southern Hungary

Culture
Budapest, Danube Bend, eastern and southern Hungary

BUDAPEST
Good for culture and nightlife

YOU CAN visit the main tourist sights of both Buda and Pest in two days. But Hungary's lively capital repays closer attention. Trace the history of the region in its streets, from Ottoman thermal baths to bullet marks in the walls from the uprising in 1956. The capital boasts plenty of reasonably priced restaurants, bars, cafés and night-clubs. In many of these, gypsy musicians play.

BEST SIGHTS

Coffee houses
Three fine examples of the turn–of–the–century coffee-house culture

have survived: Café Gerbeaud, Müvész Kávéház, and New York Kávéház. Drink coffee, eat cream cakes, and make intellectual conversation in great central European tradition.

Fisherman's Bastion
These man-made, stone-turreted ramparts on Castle Hill attract many buskers and entertainers, and were designed to give idyllic views down the Danube. They surround the neo-Gothic Matthias Cathedral, with its unusual Turkish and Hungarian-style painted interior.

National Gallery
Part of a pleasant museum complex on Castle Hill, this is the only place displaying a good-sized collection of Hungarian painting.

Opera House
This grand venue, built at the end of the last century, is best experienced during a performance. Budapest has an impressive musical heritage: Liszt, Bartók and Kodály were all Hungarian.

Parliament building
You can take a guided tour around the excessively ornate parliament next to the Danube. Modelled on Westminster, it was built to mark Hungary's increased independence from Vienna 100 years ago. The red star that capped the spired dome was removed in 1990.

St Stephen's Basilica
Splendid nineteenth-century Catholic basilica in central Pest.

Thermal Baths
Budapest's many natural thermal baths vary greatly in atmosphere and clientele. The most picturesque are in Secessionist style: in the Gellért Hotel, and the Széchényi Fürdõ outdoor pool in the City Park, where wide-girthed men soak and play chess.

DANUBE BEND
Good for culture

JUST NORTH of Budapest, where the Danube curves through a narrow valley, is a trio of historic towns and ruins that make a long but interesting day-trip out from the city.

BEST SIGHTS
Esztergom
Hungary's first capital is dominated by a huge domed Catholic cathedral.

Szentendre and Visegrád

Szentendre, the traditional home of Hungary's creative types, attracts thousands of tourists to its well-preserved nineteenth-century streets with folk arts and crafts sales. Visegrád boasts an impressive ruined castle atop a hill giving views of the Danube as it winds towards Budapest.

WESTERN HUNGARY
Good for family holidays and outdoor activities

BEST BASES

Lake Balaton

The southern shore is a tacky series of crowded, unremarkable resorts. Shallow water and no waves mean that children are safer than at the seaside and beginners can try sailing and windsurfing. Equipment hire is cheap. Concern is rising about the cleanliness of the water, though.

The vine-cultivating hills of the northern shore are more secluded and more upmarket. Tennis courts are generally plentiful and cheap.

BEST SIGHTS AND EXCURSIONS

Badacsony is a hilltop town with volcanic soil producing quality vines. It has a lively wine harvest. At Keszthely the baroque Festetics Palace, home to the eponymous Hungarian aristocratic family, was the country's first public forum for literary criticism. A medicinal spa is nearby at Hévíz. North of the lake, Herend makes famous delicate porcelain. The idyllic streets of the Tihány peninsula get overrun with tourists and folk craft sellers, but try to visit the abbey-church with its 900-year-old crypt, and maybe walk inland to see the lakes and geysers.

Sopron

A horseshoe-shaped town with a medieval layout, Roman walls and baroque architecture. Austrians come for dental treatment and cheap shopping. A music and dance festival is held in early summer.

EASTERN AND SOUTHERN HUNGARY
Good for culture, food/wine, outdoor activities and scenic landscape

BEST SIGHTS

Eger

The city's ecclesiastic and secular architecture is fascinating; the castle saw the Hungarians' last stand against the Turks in the sixteenth century. The nearby 'Valley of the Beautiful Women' is home to Bull's Blood red wine.

Pécs

With two mosques and a synagogue, Pécs reflects Hungary's multicultural past. A collection of work by the Hungarian illusionist artist Victor Vasarély and the Zsolnay porcelain exhibit are the best museums.

BEST SCENIC LANDSCAPES

Bükk Hills

These rolling, wooded hills with underground stalactite caves span Hungary's northern border with Slovakia.

Great Plain

This expanse of prairie and lakes is home to rare, aquatic birds and other wildlife, also to the original Hungarian cowboys.

Tokaj and Zemplèn

The unspoilt, wild, wooded hills of the Zemplèn region sit alongside the villages of the tamer Tokaj, where the world-famous dessert wine is made. Wine tastings are held in labyrinthine, mould-covered cellars.

WHEN TO GO

TEMPERATURES HIT extremes in January (-5°C) and August (35°C). Air-conditioning is still uncommon, so Budapest swelters in July and August. Budapest holds a film festival in February and a Spring Festival in March (with national and international contributions). Sopron's festival in early summer features ancient music and dance.

Average daily maximum temperature °C											
London	6	7	10	13	17	20	22	21	19	14	10	7
Budapest	1	4	10	17	22	26	28	27	23	16	8	4
	JAN	FEB	MAR	APR	MAY	JUN	JUL	AUG	SEP	OCT	NOV	DEC
Budapest	13	12	11	11	13	13	10	9	7	10	14	13
London	15	13	11	12	12	11	12	11	13	13	15	15
Average number of rainy days per month											

PACKAGE TRAVEL

CITY BREAKS to Budapest and holidays to Lake Balaton are the main package destinations. City breaks feature hotel or pension accommodation and self-catering apartments. Opera tickets and excursions can be booked in advance by specialist tour operators, as can Spring

Festival packages. Two- or three-centre holidays featuring Budapest with Prague or Vienna are on offer, as are Danube cruises.

Outside Budapest your options are to take a fly-drive tour visiting towns such as Pécs or Sopron, or stay put on the shores of Lake Balaton.

Activity holidays include walking, riding, cycling, spa holidays and dental packages (getting your teeth capped is cheaper in Hungary).

Tour operators

Birdwatching: Limosa, Naturetrek, Ornitholidays, Sunbird **City breaks**: British Airways Holidays, Cresta, Crystal, Inghams, Made to Measure, Moswin, Osprey, Sovereign, Time Off, Thomson, Travellers Czech, Travelscene **Music**: Prospect, Travel for the Arts **Spa**: Hungarian Air Tours, Thermalia **Other activities**: Anglo Dutch (cycling), Arblaster & Clarke (wine), Hungarian Air Tours (riding & dental), Martin Randall (cultural), Ramblers Holidays (walking), Solo's Holidays (singles)

INDEPENDENT TRAVEL

BUDAPEST IS ideal for a weekend city break. Hungary is a budget destination (food, drink, travel and entry to tourist sights are all cheap) so travelling independently is cheap if you want to see all the country.

Travel agents such as IBUSZ, the state tourist agency, Tourinform and Budapest Tourist can help with accommodation and travel. They also offer bus sightseeing trips, wine tastings and grape picking, horse-riding excursions, goulash parties with gypsy music, folk dancing evenings, and boat trips on the Danube. If you are short of time, the organised trips are a reasonably priced way to get a flavour of the country.

Direct flights go to Budapest, or you can fly to Vienna and take the hydrofoil down the Danube to Budapest for a more scenic route. Cheap packages transport you on a gruelling 30-hour bus journey. Budapest is a convenient starting-point for visiting Slovakia to the north and Transylvania, in Romania, to the south-east.

Within Hungary buses and trains provide an extensive and cheap, if not particularly fast, service. Car hire is expensive, but easy if you have a passport and credit card. If you are planning to take the hire car across the border to Slovakia or Austria, mention this in the hire office to get the requisite papers. Most offices are unhappy about you taking their cars into Romania and may charge extra. Hungary's motorway network is still primitive and some country roads are narrow and badly lit. Queues at the Austrian and Romanian borders are usual in summer.

Budapest and most major towns are crawling with taxis, which can be very cheap if you choose carefully and avoid the swanky Mercedes. The public transport system is also cheap and reliable. One recently renovated part of the underground is Europe's oldest after London and is a tourist sight in itself. Heavy traffic, difficult parking and one-way systems mean that it is not usually worth driving in Budapest yourself.

Hotels follow the star grading system and Budapest is well served with top-notch hotels catering mostly to business travellers. Of the top hotels, the art nouveau Gellért Hotel has the most character. Second-grade hotels can be slightly grubby and attract prostitutes. Most are unattractive constructions from the 1960s in dire need of renovation.

Preferable are the privately run pensions – the equivalent of British B&Bs – which are found all over Hungary at various prices and standards. Find out about budget accommodation from IBUSZ, which has offices all over Hungary. Co-optourist handles bookings for private rooms and flats, rentable on a daily, weekly or monthly basis at reasonable rates. During the summer holidays the halls of residence belonging to Budapest's universities serve as cheap youth hostels, with four to a room and shared facilities. Students accost you at the major train stations with fliers to send you in the right direction.

Hungarian campsites are generally well-equipped with a complete range of facilities. Some, particularly around Lake Balaton, provide accommodation in wooden huts for those without a tent.

RED TAPE, HEALTH AND SAFETY

BRITISH PASSPORT-HOLDERS do not require a visa.

Everyone is supposed to carry identification with them at all times. However, pickpocketing is common and you must weigh up the risk of being stopped by the police when you may not have your passport against that of losing it to a pickpocket. If you decide to carry it with you at all times, keep it in a money belt worn *under* your clothes.

Signs and labels are hard to decipher, as Hungarian is un-related to other European languages apart from Finnish. But many young Hungarians speak English. The older generation speaks German.

MORE INFORMATION Hungarian Tourist Office, Embassy of the Republic of Hungary, Commercial Section, 46 Eaton Place, SW1X 8AL, tel 0171-823 1032
Web site: http://www.hungary.com/tourinform/

Danube Travel Ltd, 6 Conduit Street, London W1R 9TG, tel 0171-493 0263

COST OF LIVING £

INDIA

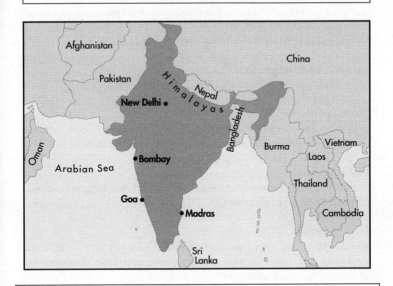

HIGHLIGHTS

Beaches
Goa, Kovalam

Culture
*Delhi,
Rajasthan,
Agra,
Varanasi,
Calcutta*

Local colour
*Delhi,
Rajasthan,
Varanasi,
Ladakh,
Kerala, Mysore*

Nightlife
Bombay, Goa

**Outdoor
activities**
Himalayas

**Romantic
escapism**
*Rajasthan,
Agra*

**Scenic
landscape**
*Rajasthan,
Himalayas,
Kerala*

DELHI
Good for culture and local colour

DELHI IS really two cities – Old Delhi, the capital of Muslim India until the nineteenth century, and New Delhi, the administrative capital created by the British. Old Delhi is crowded, colourful and crazy; the shopping bazaar of Chandni Chowk is the focal point, and represents India at its most frenetic: full of people, rickshaws and cows. New Delhi has wide streets and government buildings.

BEST SIGHTS

Feroz Shah Kotla
A ruined fortress-palace incorporating a 43ft-high pillar inscribed with Ashoka's edicts dating from 1354, this site gives a glimpse of one of Delhi's earliest incarnations as a powerful city.

Gallery of Modern Art
A good collection of works by Indian and colonial artists.

Humayun's Tomb
A precursor to the Taj Mahal and interesting example of early Mughal architecture – domed roof, arched entrances and spacious excess.

India Gate
A 140ft-high stone arch commemorating the 85,000 Indians who died fighting for the British in the First World War.

Jama Masjid
The largest mosque in India, built by Shah Jahan (who also built the Red Fort and Agra's Taj Mahal) offers views over Delhi from the top of the 133-ft southern minaret.

National Museum
Good bronzes, terracotta and wood sculptures, miniatures, mural paintings and tribal costumes. Some exhibits are from the third century BC.

Raj Ghat
Not much to look at, but fascinating to the endless stream of pilgrims, this large field is where Mahatma Gandhi was cremated in 1948. Indira Gandhi and her son Rajiv were also cremated in the area, as were Sanjay Gandhi and Jawaharlal Nehru. You can see memorials to the leaders here.

Rashtrapati Bhavan
Immense palace-like official residence of the President, built in 1929; architecturally a mixture of Mughal and Western styles.

Red Fort
Built by Shah Jahan between 1638 and 1648, this is an impressive Mughal power base, with over a mile of ramparts up to 110ft high. Inside are mosques, palaces, baths and a small archaeological museum.

Qutab Minar
A fine early Afghan work dating from 1193, when the last northern Hindu kingdom fell to the Muslims. A red sandstone and marble 243-ft tower is the centrepiece, along with a mosque and an iron pillar.

NORTHERN INDIA
Good for culture, local colour, romantic escapism and scenic landscape

BEST SIGHTS

Agra
The Taj Mahal is the romantic symbol of India, and rightly so. Between 1631 and 1653 experts from Iran, France and Italy laboured to build a monument in memory of Shah Jahan's dead wife. The result is magical – a floating white building with minarets and *pietra dura* (inlaid semi-precious stones).

The size of the nearby Red Fort bears testimony to Agra's position as capital of the Mughal empire. Set on the bank of the Yamuna river, it contains luxurious living quarters as well as warlike halls for public and private audiences. Fatehpur Sikri, a perfectly preserved example of a Mughal city, is a day-trip from Agra.

Amritsar
The Golden Temple, the holiest shrine for the Sikhs, has a dome said to be gilded with 220kg of gold, and is surrounded by an artificial lake set in a complex constructed almost entirely of white marble. Amritsar itself is not an attractive town.

Jaipur
The walled 'pink city' – pink signifies hospitality in traditional Rajput culture – has wide streets and is a heady brew of exotic shops, constant traffic and colourful Rajasthanis. The palace dates from 1727; it houses a good museum. Johari Bazaar is the centre of the gem trading industry and is a fascinating place. Hawa Mahal, or the Palace of the Winds, built in 1799, is little more than a façade, but it is a beautiful example of Rajput artistry, intricately fashioned in pink sandstone. Jantar Mantar, an enormous observatory, is the largest in India. The sundial has a 99-ft gnomon casting a shadow that moves up to 13ft an hour.

About 7 miles out of Jaipur, Amber is a fortress-palace set high on a hill, and was the ancient capital from 1592 to 1727, with fine views.

Jaisalmer
A magical walled city in the desert, Jaisalmer is essentially a fort, built in 1156 by Rawal Jaisal. Tourism is taking off, but Jaisalmer retains an exotic feel, evocative of camel trains, riches and romance. The old city is filled with temples and *havelis* – sandstone mansions with intricate façades. Camel treks leave from here and you can buy locally made fabrics and wallhangings, embroidery and *appliqué*.

Jodhpur

A classic example of a noisy, dirty and polluted Indian city, Jodhpur nevertheless contains the most impressive of the Rajasthani forts. Enter through a series of gates, the first of which displays cannonball scars; the last, handprints of Maharaja Man Singh's 15 wives, who committed *sati* by throwing themselves on his funeral pyre in 1843. The palace museum is good, as are views from the ramparts over the city.

If you want to splash out, stay at the plush Umaid Bhawan Palace, now a hotel. Built shortly before Independence in 1947, it serves banquet-style meals and is one of India's most atmospheric hotels.

Pushkar

Hindu pilgrims visit this pretty town on the edge of the desert for its calm, its temples and lake with bathing *ghats* (steps down to the river). Pushkar has a Camel Fair in October.

Udaipur

The old city (the 'Venice of the East') is full of whimsical palaces, temples, *havelis* and parks, but the centrepiece is beautiful Lake Pichola, with its magical Lake Palace Hotel. See also the City Palace that towers above the lake, and go to Jagmandir Island for the view of the lake and city. Udaipur is a centre for the performing arts, painting and crafts.

Varanasi

This is the holiest city in India, and also one of the least spoilt, although unbearably hot in the summer. Pilgrims flock to bathe in the River Ganges, and it is every Hindu's dream to be cremated on the burning *ghats* here. The bathing *ghats* are the focal point of the city, bustling with every imaginable activity, from buffalo-washing to sitar concerts.

The Golden Temple, built in 1776, is hidden in the back streets, but the constant stream of pilgrims ringing the bells makes it easy to find. It is small, yet covered with three-quarters of a ton of gold plate. The Durga Temple, also called the Monkey Temple because of its resident simian population, has regular goat sacrifices to appease the goddess Durga.

Six miles outside Varanasi, Sarnath, a good day-trip, is the place where the Buddha first preached after being enlightened in Bodhgaya.

THE HIMALAYAS
Good for outdoor activities and scenic landscape

BEST SIGHTS

Darjeeling

A hill station, Darjeeling is best approached in the toy train. Set amid vast tea plantations, it boasts views of Kanchenjunga and the peaks. The town is full of colourful mountain folk, curio shops and pony-wallahs. It also has excellent walks, tea plantation tours and local Buddhist monasteries.

Dharamsala

This wooded hill resort is the home-in-exile for the Dalai Lama, and as a result has become a captivating Tibetan village, complete with spinning prayer-wheels and strings of colourful flags. Lord Elgin, a Viceroy of India, was buried in 1863 in the Church of St John in the Wilderness.

Ladakh

On the other side of the Himalayas, Ladakh is still unspoilt. The people wear traditional dress, and are superstitious. Leh, the capital, has a palace like a small version of the Potala in Tibet. Try to visit the region in summer, when the monasteries hold their festivals – those at Hemis and Lamayuru are the most flamboyant, but others, especially at Shey and Tikse, are also fascinating.

Manali and the Kulu Valley

Since Kashmir became off-limits to tourists, Manali has boomed as a base for trekking, boat trips along the Beas River, and day-trips to some of the alluring nearby villages. Conditions of travel can be tough. It is possible to take a day-trip to the Rohtang Pass, a spectacular tour through the mountains along one of the highest driveable roads in the world.

Simla

The former 'summer capital' of the British Raj sits high on a ridge in the foothills; cool even in the hot season, it makes a welcome escape from the sweltering plains. The Mall, or main street, is lined with stately mansions and churches. Indians were barred from it until the First World War. There are several magnificent walks locally. The Rashtrapati Niwas, a huge building with beautiful gardens, was the British Viceroy's home.

CENTRAL AND EASTERN INDIA
Good for culture and nightlife

BEST SIGHTS

Ajanta and Ellora

Spectacular, isolated examples of Buddhist, Hindu and Jain cave temples from 200 BC. Ajanta is noted for wall paintings, Ellora for sculptures.

Bombay

The business capital of India is full of swanky limousines of 'Bollywood' stars (from the Indian film industry) sweeping along Colaba Causeway past bullock carts laden with smelly dried fish. The

most important landmark, the Gateway of India, was built to commemorate the visit of George V in 1924. The boat to Elephanta Island
leaves from here to visit the impressive rock-cut temples carved 1,500
years ago. Chowpatty Beach is not for swimming but is a great place
for carnival atmosphere and *bhelpuri* snack stands. The Prince of Wales
Museum, built in Indo-Saracenic style, is interesting inside and out.

Calcutta
Best visited after getting acclimatised to India's extremes, Calcutta is
the old Raj capital and a lively cultural centre, where film, poetry, art,
music, drama and dance events take place every day. The Indian
Museum is one of the biggest and best in all Asia. The Maidan is a
vast expanse of parkland surrounding Fort William and the Victoria
Memorial and recalls the days of the Raj – mounted police patrol,
and you will see cricket fields, gardens and cows. The Memorial is a
large marble museum full of relics of British India's heyday.

The Hooghly river runs near the hub of BBD Bagh (formerly
Dalhousie Square and site of the 'Black Hole of Calcutta') and the
main street, Chowringhee. It is spanned by the famous Howrah
Bridge, the world's busiest. Across the river are the Botanical Gardens,
birthplace of Darjeeling and Assam teas.

Khajuraho
These Indo-Aryan temples are a major site and well worth seeing.
Sculpted 1,000 years ago, they depict vivid images of gods, warriors, ani-
mals and mythological creatures. They are most famous for their erotica.

SOUTHERN INDIA
Good for beaches, local colour, nightlife and scenic landscape

BEST RESORTS
Goa
● For beaches, Goa's the ticket, but do not anticipate crystal-clear water.
● The laid-back Catholic Goanese tolerate almost anything, from sunbathing (impossible elsewhere in India) to motorbike hire and wild
moonlight raves.
● Old Goa was the Portuguese capital. Unique colonial villas and
churches line verdant streets. Fascinating markets at Mapusa and Anjuna.
● Best beaches are at Baga, Vagator and Cavelossim. For total peace (but
basic facilities) head north to Arambol.

Kovalam
● Almost at India's southernmost tip, Kovalam is a tiny relaxing beach
resort worthy of a longer stay.

BEST SIGHTS AND EXCURSIONS

Hampi

The ruined capital of one of India's largest empires sprawls over 13 square miles. Hampi is totally undeveloped but well worth an excursion. The city was founded in 1336, and by the mid-sixteenth century controlled the southern half of India. Today it is a magical place of temples, hidden statues and a bazaar. Beware the vicious mosquitoes.

Kanyakumari

Three bodies of water – the Bay of Bengal, the Indian Ocean and the Arabian Sea – converge at the 'Land's End' of India, Kanyakumari.

Kerala

This magical state of palm trees and sunlit rice paddies full of birds and monkeys is best appreciated by exploring the coastal lagoons. Cochin, a fishing port city of green islands set in lagoons and backwaters, has India's oldest church (the Portuguese explorer Vasco da Gama was once buried here), and Matancherry Palace, which can be visited by ferry.

Madras

Madras has lively street culture; famous for its vegetarian food, it is full of cheap, excellent restaurants. Try *thali* – a complete meal with rice, *dal*, curries and puddings arranged in little dishes on a big circular plate. Madras is the centre for Bharat Natyam, Tamil Nadu state's best-known dance, usually performed by women. Visit Fort St George for its British East India Company memorabilia, and the archaeological section of the Government Museum. Real temple country starts outside Madras; the best temple towns are Madurai, Kanchipuram and Mahabalipuram.

Mysore

An easy-going city with colourful markets, Mysore is a centre of incense manufacture, imparting sensuous pleasure at every turn. The walled Indo-Saracenic Mysore Palace – a confection of brash colours, solid silver doors, stained glass and vast mirrored halls – is hugely over the top, yet elegant and dignified. Chamundi Hill has views over the city and the surrounding villages as well as a seven-storey temple.

WHEN TO GO

OCTOBER TO April is the best time, although it starts getting hot by April. In the north it can be cold at night in January and February. The mountains are best visited after the monsoon in September and October, when the views are good. Ladakh is open for only a few weeks each year in July and August.

Average daily maximum temperature °C

	JAN	FEB	MAR	APR	MAY	JUN	JUL	AUG	SEP	OCT	NOV	DEC
London	6	7	10	13	17	20	22	21	19	14	10	7
Bombay	28	28	30	32	33	32	29	29	29	32	32	31
Bombay	0.5	0.6	0.7	1	2	7	11	10	9	9	4	0.8
London	15	13	11	12	12	11	12	11	13	13	15	15

Average number of rainy days per month

Average daily maximum temperature °C

	JAN	FEB	MAR	APR	MAY	JUN	JUL	AUG	SEP	OCT	NOV	DEC
London	6	7	10	13	17	20	22	21	19	14	10	7
Madras	29	31	33	35	38	38	36	35	34	32	29	29
Madras	0.1	0.1	0.2	2	7	25	27	25	15	10	5	1
London	15	13	11	12	12	11	12	11	13	13	15	15

Average number of rainy days per month

Average daily maximum temperature °C

	JAN	FEB	MAR	APR	MAY	JUN	JUL	AUG	SEP	OCT	NOV	DEC
London	6	7	10	13	17	20	22	21	19	14	10	7
New Delhi	21	24	31	36	41	39	36	34	34	34	29	23
New Delhi	2	2	1	1	2	4	8	8	4	1	<1	1
London	15	13	11	12	12	11	12	11	13	13	15	15

Average number of rainy days per month

PACKAGE TRAVEL

MASS-MARKET TOUR operators such as Thomson, First Choice, Manos, Somak and Inspirations have charter flights direct to Goa (some with extensions to Kerala) for one- or two-week beach holidays.

Several brochures feature tours of the north, typically starting from Delhi and visiting the palaces and fortresses of Rajasthan, Agra, Jaipur, Udaipur, Jodhpur, Varanasi and Khajuraho. Tours are by coach, train or car, and diversions such as visits to the Corbett National Park are on offer. Further north, Darjeeling and its tea plantations are featured on tours of the north-east starting from Calcutta, and walking and adventure holidays utilise the Himalayas. Extensions on offer are to Nepal or to the Andaman Islands in the Bay of Bengal. Southern tours will usually start from Madras or Bombay and include

Bangalore, Mysore and Madras, Kanchipuram and Cochin. Visits to National Parks or a bird sanctuary may be included as well as trips to temples and forts.

Activity holidays include birdwatching, adventure tours, wildlife tours, rail tours and archaeological tours.

Tour operators

General and specialist: Abercrombie & Kent, Airwaves, Asia Experience, Asiaworld Travel, Bales Tours, British Airways Holidays, Cosmos, Cox & Kings, Far East Gateways, First Choice, Hayes & Jarvis, Highlife Holidays, Inspirations, Jasmin, Kuoni, Manos, Mysteries of India, Petitts India, Somak, Sunworld, Thomson, Tradewinds, Trans Indus, Unijet, Voyages Jules Verne **Rail tours**: Butterfields, Coromandel, Explorers Tours **Trekking/walking**: Classic Nepal, Exodus, Himalayan Kingdoms, Ramblers Holidays **Other activities**: Animal Watch (wildlife), British Museum Traveller (archaeology), Cygnus Wildlife (birds), Holts' Tours (battlefields), Encounter Overland (adventure), Explore Worldwide (adventure), Peregrine (horse-riding), Sunbird (birdwatching), Swan Hellenic (cultural tours), Wildlife Worldwide (wildlife)

INDEPENDENT TRAVEL

INDEPENDENT TRAVEL in India is only for the hardy, but worth it. The biggest problem is the bureaucracy and interminable queueing involved in booking transport. You will see India in the raw and you will get frustrated and hot, so if you are keen on getting about and seeing lots of sights in a short time, take a package. But if you go it on your own, give yourself twice as much time as you think you will need, for everything. Take trains rather than buses, bargain with the rickshaw drivers, travel light, stay at good hotels and keep your sense of humour.

India has an extensive domestic flight network. Book from home, but expect possible delays and overbookings. Indian Airlines, the main domestic carrier, has a 21-day flight pass, which must be bought in the UK when you buy your international flight ticket.

The train system, a phenomenon of efficiency in itself, is a great slice of Indian life. The network covers the subcontinent like a web; journeys are slow but give you the chance to feast your senses on what goes on both inside and outside the compartment. Travel in air-conditioned first class for overnight journeys, second class for shorter ones, keep an eagle eye on your luggage, befriend your travelling companions and enjoy.

Trains are bookable in the UK through specialist travel agencies: rail passes from half a day to 90 days are available.

Buses are best avoided in favour of trains, as they tend to be hugely overcrowded. The air-conditioned ones operating in Rajasthan are OK. Buses are the only option in the mountains – sit near the front, but do not go if you have vertigo.

Self-drive is not an option, but it is possible to hire a taxi for a day or even longer. This way you get a rough-and-ready guide to the area as well. Do not be bullied by drivers who offer to go to places not on your itinerary – the chances are that it is a 'brother' with a gem shop. If the meter is not working, bargain hard and agree a rate before you start.

Accommodation comes in all standards, from super-luxury to total fleapit. Choose hotels recommended in guides. In some places you will have to rough it: look for a secure lock, reasonable facilities and a mosquito net. One of the most unpredictable aspects of travel in India is accommodation, even for those on a package holiday. If you prefer international-standard hotels (and there are plenty) stay well on the beaten track. Big hotels are bookable from home. Take the chance to stay in some classy Raj hotels or the wonderful Lake Palace Hotel in Udaipur. Do not think about camping.

RED TAPE, HEALTH AND SAFETY

VISAS ARE required. Application forms are obtainable from the High Commission. For a six-month visa, you need three passport-size photographs. The cost is £19. If you apply in person at the High Commisssion between 9.30am and 1pm Monday to Friday, the visa can be processed on the same day. Postal applications can take up to a month.

Check with your GP about vaccinations and malaria protection. The biggest health problem for visitors to India is 'Delhi belly'. See the tips on page 11 for how to avoid this. For the latest advice on security, contact the Foreign Office Travel Advice Unit (see page 11).

MORE INFORMATION Indian Tourist Office, 7 Cork Street, London W1X 2LN, tel 0171-437 3677, brochure line (01233) 211999, web site: http://www.indiatourism-la.org/welcome.html

High Commission of India, India House, Aldwych, London WC2B 4NA, tel 0171-836 8484

COST OF LIVING £

INDONESIA

HIGHLIGHTS

Culture	*Gili Islands*	**Shopping**	*(Lombok),*
Ubud (Bali),	*(Lombok),*	*Ubud (Bali),*	*Mount Bromo*
Jakarta,	*Mount Bromo*	*Yogyakarta*	*(Java)*
Yogyakarta	*(Java)*	*(Java)*	
(Java)			**Local colour**
	Beaches	**Scenic**	*Ubud (Bali),*
Outdoor	*Gili Islands*	**landscape**	*Mataram*
activities	*(Lombok)*	*Ubud, Lake*	*(Lombok),*
Lovina, Lake		*Batur (Bali),*	*Yogyakarta*
Batur (Bali),		*Gili Islands*	*(Java)*

BALI
Good for culture, local colour, outdoor activities, scenic landscape and shopping

FOR SOME, Bali has become a pastiche of its former glory as the jewel in the Indonesian archipelago. For others, it remains a paradise whose charismatic culture sits relatively easily with mass tourism.

In many ways, both images are accurate. Kuta, Sanur and other towns have been well and truly discovered – the former is now a daunting strip of clubs, restaurants and often fractious tourists. Yet despite the hype, Bali has retained much of its original charm and allure, particularly away from the coast – the northern and central areas are steeped in Balinese culture and offer superb scenery. Those seeking radiant sunsets, temples and terraced rice paddies will certainly not be disappointed.

BEST TOWN
Ubud
Many arriving and wishing to escape the chaotic scenes of swirling hawkers and manic traffic outside Denpasar airport choose a trip to Ubud. Though Sanur and Kuta are closer alternatives, the southern tip of the island has taken the brunt of recent development and Ubud, more sedate and unhurried and away from the coast, is preferable. There are some magnificent restaurants and bars here, framed by temples and gorgeous lotus gardens.

Ubud is the ideal place to stock up on traditional Balinese craftwork and fabrics such as batik, though owing to the unabated flow of tourists prices are not what they were. Shopkeepers vie for your attention and window-shopping here is a full-contact sport. Tarry for a second outside any of the market stalls and the owner will appear from nowhere in a flurry of quotes and offers. Don't take his or her first price too seriously, or feel flattered when offered the 'special morning price'. Find out from other travellers what the going rate is and work around that.

The Monkey Forest Sanctuary is a growing attraction at the bottom of Monkey Forest Road.

BEST RESORTS
Candi Dasa
● A small village on the eastern coast in Amuk Bay which has now mushroomed into a bustling resort.
● It has some of the best diving sites on Bali and excellent snorkelling – but beware the area's strong rips and currents.
● Close by is Tenganan Village. Its people adhere most closely to the island's animistic past which predates its conversion to Hinduism.

Kuta
● At this brash resort located along a once-gorgeous beach, watch Antipodeans on holiday misbehave or party through to dawn. Not for the faint-hearted. You will either love it or loathe it.
● Kuta has now extended and blurred into Legian, its northerly neighbour on the coast.
● The *gangs* (alleyways) host a myriad of *losmen* (small and normally very competitively priced hotels), bars and restaurants.
● It is a good place to change money as the competition for foreign currency normally ensures a very reasonable rate of exchange.
● There is a stunning temple at Pura Tanah Lot, just north of Kuta.

Lovina
● Like Kuta, this conurbation grew out of several villages, this time along the northern coast.
● Snorkel, go dolphin-watching or visit the nearby waterfalls and hot springs.
● Less frenetic than Kuta, it has a reasonable selection of restaurants at which to try the local variation of *gado gado*.

Sanur
● An upmarket and more relaxed version of Kuta.
● Many Europeans choose it as part of a package; several expensive hotels cater for a well-heeled clientele.
● The beach, which is reasonable, is backed by an unending sequence of restaurants from where you can take in the view out towards Lombok.

BEST SIGHTS

Balinese temple dancers
By far the most dramatic spectacle is provided by the Balinese temple dancers. Bali is an island of festivals and many of these are celebrated in and around the temples of Ubud – check with the Indonesian Embassy in London or the tourist desk at Denpasar Airport for further details of events.

Goa Gajah and Yeh Pulu
These ancient sites, both close to Ubud, delight thousands of overseas visitors every year. Goa Gajah, which means Elephant Cave, is especially popular; Yeh Pulu has huge, stunning panels carved out of the rockface. The walk down to Yeh Pulu takes you through terraced rice paddy fields.

BEST SCENIC LANDSCAPE

Lake Batur
Towards the north of the island, the area combines the largest lake in Bali with some magnificent walks up the side of the adjacent and dormant volcano, Gunung Batur. The road up to Lake Batur from the south winds through some of the most arresting scenery on the island.

This is a popular spot to watch the dawn come up and most visitors set off for the rim of the volcano's caldera at around 4am to be at the top by sunrise. The walk starts quite gently through a lowland wood but soon inclines steeply so good walking shoes are essential. The guides who take you to the top are feverishly competitive so ask around for the best price. Breakfast (normally boiled eggs and pancakes) is provided at the summit for an additional supplement. Agree your price with the guides before heading off.

LOMBOK
Good for local colour

LESS DRAMATIC than its neighbour to the west, Lombok can still boast some magnificent scenery of lush paddy fields, coconut groves and towering volcanoes. It is only beginning to be opened up to tourism and there is a wonderful sense of space if you have just arrived from Bali. Lombok can be reached by ferry from Padang Bai on Bali or from a number of places throughout Indonesia by air.

The road north of Mataram is especially dramatic as it winds its way up through mahogany forests before plunging down to the coast opposite the Gili Islands.

Lombok has a very different culture, being essentially Muslim, and whereas temples dot the road in Bali, you will find mosques here.

BEST TOWN
Mataram
This main town on Lombok is essentially a conurbation of four separate towns – Mataram, Ampenan, Sweta and Cakranegara. Mataram is a thriving and relatively unreconstructed Asian town with all the aromas and bustling street life that you would expect, and is a good place to base yourself for exploring the rest of the island.

Worth visiting are the largest market on the island (next to the main bus terminal in Sweta), bursting with exotic fruits and spices, and a good museum in Ampenan. If the traffic gets too much then visit the relaxed environs of the Mayura Water Palace, located in the centre of town.

BEST RESORT
Senggigi
● A developed but still engaging coastal resort just to the north of Mataram, Senggigi is a long way from the excesses of Kuta on Bali.
● Wide range of bars and restaurants along the seafront.
● Enjoy nightlife here or in Mataram – there's not a great deal elsewhere on Lombok.

BEST SCENIC LANDSCAPE
Gunung Rinjani
This magnificent volcano rises up from the lush lowlands of central Lombok. Popular walking trails wind up to the crater rim, the most convenient leaving from the village of Senaru. From the summit you can look down on the stunning expanse of Segara Anak, the lake enclosed within the crater rim.

BEST SIGHT

Narmada

This impressive palace and temple complex just to the east of Mataram was built in the early nineteenth century by the Raja of Mataram as a token of his enduring reverence when he became too infirm to climb the slopes of Gunung Rinjani to make his offerings to the gods.

BEST SHOPPING

Whereas on Bali no one leaves without buying a batik sarong or throw, the expertise on Lombok is in beautiful handwoven cottons, bone whittling, boxes made from palm leaves, bamboo carving and pottery.

Selong

Selong is the bustling capital of East Lombok. Here you can purchase many crafts, though it is cheaper to buy them at source in the villages.

Village shopping

Some of the best villages to visit for craftwork include Kotaraja (pottery), Loyok (basket-weaving), Rungkang (pottery), Banyumulak (pottery) and Pringgasela (*endek* cloth).

GILI ISLANDS

Good for beaches, outdoor activities and scenic landscape

THESE WERE a closely guarded secret among backpackers for years, but are now well and truly 'on the circuit'. These three gorgeous islands off the north-west coast of Lombok are circled by pristine stretches of silicone, beyond which lies some of the best coral around Lombok.

'Gili' simply means 'island', which gives these three a rather enigmatic ring in translation. Each island has its own character. Gili Meno is the quietest, Gili Trawangan the most lively and largest with Gili Air somewhere in between. They all lie within easy reach of each other and can be accessed quickly by boat from Bangsal on Lombok.

JAVA

Good for culture, local colour, outdoor activities, scenic landscape and shopping

THE COMMERCIAL and political hub of Indonesia, this predominantly Muslim island is one of the most populated parts of the world with over 160 million people living within its shores. It boasts a fantastic diversity of scenery, astonishing temples and a wonderfully vibrant people.

BEST CITIES

Jakarta

This is the brash, urban heartland of Indonesia and the traffic and pollution are everything you might expect from a developing city. It takes a little time and patience to begin to appreciate its charms, and many tire of the place and leave before realising that it has much to offer. However, if you keep an open mind, Jakarta can provide a rewarding and diverse insight into Javanese life and culture.

Though Jakarta has none of the aesthetic appeal of Bangkok or the sophisticated *élan* of Hong Kong, it does have a myriad of superb restaurants and clubs. The old Dutch quarter (Kota) and Chinatown are both worth visiting and there are a few excellent museums, including the Indonesian National Museum which is located on one side of the vast Merdeka Square. You may also choose to visit the Taman Ismail Marzuki (cultural centre), or the fascinating Textile Museum close to Tanah Abang railway station.

Yogyakarta

A compact and attractive town east of Java, famous for both its markets and culture.

Much of the activity in the town radiates from Jalan (street) Marlioboro, near the railway station. There are many wonderful and historical buildings, such as the Kraton, and some excellent museums, such as the Museum Sono-Budoyo.

Yogyakarta is probably one of the best places in Indonesia (Solo is another) to buy batik. The two main areas for accommodation are in Sosro and Prawirotaman: Sosro has a unique charm and is favoured by most backpackers; Prawirotaman is more expensive.

BEST SIGHTS

Prambanan and Borobudur

These temple complexes were constructed in the ninth century and are relatively close to Yogyakarta. They are astonishing testimonies to the architectural acumen of the Javanese and constitute two of the most visually compelling religious sites in the region.

Prambanan is a series of Hindu temples – the eight largest and most comprehensively restored stand in the central area.

Borobudur, further from Yogyakarta, is a Buddhist temple that rises up impressively from the surrounding countryside. Nothing else exists on this scale in Indonesia and both complexes are definitely worth a visit.

BEST SCENIC LANDSCAPE

Mount Bromo

This is one of the most theatrical natural wonders on Java, located well to the east of the island. Another magnificent vantage point from which to herald the dawn, this is the most active of the popular volcanoes with intermittent eruptions and lots of steam.

WHEN TO GO

ROUGHLY SPEAKING, the best time to visit Indonesia is around April/May and October when you will probably avoid the humidity and torrential downpours of the wet season as well as the peak holiday weeks. However, strong regional fluctuations affect the start of the monsoon season, so you need to consider this before booking.

At the time of going to press, smog was proving a considerable health hazard to both residents and visitors.

If you are interested in attending some of the larger festivals that occur throughout the year, check the dates with the Indonesian Tourist Office.

	Average daily maximum temperature °C											
London	6	7	10	13	17	20	22	21	19	14	10	7
Jakarta	29	29	30	31	31	31	31	31	31	31	30	29
	JAN	FEB	MAR	APR	MAY	JUN	JUL	AUG	SEP	OCT	NOV	DEC
Jakarta	18	17	15	11	9	7	5	4	5	8	12	14
London	15	13	11	12	12	11	12	11	13	13	15	15
	Average number of rainy days per month											

PACKAGE TRAVEL

TOUR OPERATORS allow you to choose your own itinerary by combining overland cultural tours of Java with beach holidays in Bali or Lombok and cruises of the Spice Islands. Tours of Java may include internal flights to allow more time for sightseeing. A typical ten-day tour starting from Java will take in the sights at Borobudur and Yogyakarta on the south coast, visit the rim of the Mount Bromo volcano at sunrise and include a flight from Surabaya to Bali for a few days' relaxation. Alternatively, choose a beach hotel on the smaller, less developed island of Lombok. Many operators also offer Spice Island cruises out of Bali – these involve three or four nights at sea, and drop in on the islands east of Bali including Lombok, Sabolan, Flores and Komodo. Other options include self-drive tours exploring the interior of Bali. Accommodation is generally in mid-range hotels on tours of Java, and in Bali beach hotels range from simple to deluxe.

> ### Tour operators
>
> **Adventure**: Exodus, Explore Worldwide, Guerba, Travelbag **Birdwatching**: Sunbird **Cultural**: Prospect **Cruising**: Noble Caledonian **General**: Abercrombie & Kent, Asean Explorer, Asiaworld Travel, Bales Tours, British Airways Holidays, Coromandel, East Travel, Elegant Resorts, Far East Dream Holidays, Far East Gateways, Garuda Indonesia Holidays, Hayes & Jarvis, Jetset, Kuoni, Magic of the Orient, Oriental Magic, Saga, Silk Cut Travel, Silverbird, Steppes East, Thomson, Tradewinds, Trailfinders, Travelsphere, Tropical Places, Voyages Jules Verne

INDEPENDENT TRAVEL

ACCOMMODATION IS plentiful, although less so at festival times, and normally includes a complimentary breakfast of banana pancakes and clove tea.

The three main internal airlines are Merpati, Sempati and Garuda's domestic service. On Java the trains and air-conditioned coaches are efficient and connect with the ferries. On Bali private minibuses run the busy routes; *bemos* (the tiny public buses) are very cramped, and only for the patient!

It is important to remember when visiting an Indonesian temple or *pura* that dress must be appropriate. Ceremonial sarongs are often provided but it's useful to have one at hand in case they aren't.

RED TAPE, HEALTH AND SAFETY

FOR BRITISH passport-holders, a 60-day tourist visa is issued upon entry if you have an onward ticket out of Indonesia and at least six months still remaining on your passport. This is not extendable and you must leave and re-enter if you wish to remain longer. It is worth checking your flight routes as there is a risk of disruption over Afghanistan owing to military activity. Contact the Foreign Office Travel Advice Unit for up-to-date information (see page 11).

Three major diseases you could be at risk of catching are malaria, typhoid and viral hepatitis. Polio is also a minor threat. Unless you have come from a country where yellow fever is known to be endemic, you will not need to prove that you have been inoculated against the disease, but it is strongly recommended that you consult your GP or a travel clinic before leaving for the latest health advice.

Outbreaks of pickpocketing on Java have been reported over the years, especially in Yogyakarta – take the usual streetwise precautions (see page 12). Visitors are advised against mountain trekking without a professional guide.

MORE INFORMATION Indonesian Tourist Office, 3 Hanover Street, London W1R 9HH, tel 0171-493 0030, web site: http://www.visit-indonesia.com

COST OF LIVING £

REPUBLIC OF IRELAND

HIGHLIGHTS

Beaches
*West coast,
north-west*

Local colour
*Cobh, Kinsale,
Youghal*

Nightlife
*Dublin,
Galway,
Westport*

Culture
*Dublin,
Kilkenny,
Wexford, Sligo*

History
North-west

**Outdoor
activities**
*Glendalough,
Schull, the*

*Burren, Ben
Bulben, River
Shannon*

**Romantic
escapism**
*South and
south-west*

**Scenic
landscape**
South and

*south-west,
north-west*

**Family
holidays**
*Cobh,
Enniscrone,
Mullaghmore*

Wildlife
*Saltee Islands,
River Shannon*

DUBLIN
Good for culture and nightlife

DUBLIN HAS great charm; it is compact and easily explorable on foot, with fine Georgian squares and stately government buildings. The River Liffey bisects the city: most museums, churches and the best choice of shops, restaurants and hotels are located on the south side of the river.

BEST SIGHTS
Hugh Lane Municipal Gallery of Modern Art
In a fine building in one of Dublin's earliest Georgian squares you can see works of art from the 1880s to modern times, with a concentration of Irish and continental artists, including some Impressionist paintings.

National Gallery of Ireland
Good collection of British and Irish art and a comprehensive programme of visiting exhibitions.

Newman House
This newly restored Georgian town-house built by Richard Castle in the 1730s gives some idea of St Stephen's Green as it was in the eighteenth century. The interior is superb.

Temple Bar
One of the city's oldest parts, rejuvenated as a trendy cultural centre. Cobbled streets are packed with interesting arts centres, theatres, cafés, pubs, live music, street theatre, ethnic restaurants and unusual shops.

Trinity College
The peaceful gardens and cobbled squares of the oldest university in Ireland (founded 1592) are in the centre of the city. You can see the ninth-century *Book of Kells*, visit the magnificent old library and tune into 'The Dublin Experience' – an audio-visual introduction to the city.

St Patrick's and Christchurch Cathedrals
St Patrick's, the Church of Ireland's national cathedral, has many important monuments to influential dignitaries, including the eighteenth-century satirist and former dean, Jonathan Swift. Christchurch, at the other end of the street, is linked to a multimedia experience, 'Dublinia', an evocative account of the city's history.

SOUTH-EAST
Good for culture, outdoor activities and wildlife

IN THE 'Garden of Ireland' (County Wicklow) you can drive from green valleys to the bleak Sally Gap in the Wicklow Mountains within minutes. It is a good area in which to spend a week visiting the best sights, before spending a week by the beach on the west coast.

BEST BASES
Kilkenny
● Best example of an Irish medieval city, with intact cathedral and castle.

● Delightful setting on banks of the River Nore.
● Lots of craft and artists' workshops close to the city, and in addition an important arts festival in August.

Wexford
● Ancient, attractive harbour town, the south-east's commercial centre.
● International opera festival staged in October.

BEST SIGHTS AND EXCURSIONS

Glendalough
One of the most important early Christian sites in Ireland. Splendid setting with a high round tower above the glen and its two small lakes.

National Stud and Japanese Gardens
Formerly owned by Lord Wavertree, the 1,000-acre estate at Tully is now state-run. Visit the museum, then see horses at work in the fields. The superb gardens were created in the early 1900s.

Powerscourt Gardens and Waterfall
Stunningly set in the foothills of the Wicklow Mountains, these Italianate gardens were designed in the 1730s but took over 100 years to complete. Fire gutted the house in 1974. The waterfall, nearly three miles away, is worth visiting for its romantic setting.

Russborough
A very pretty Palladian mansion, designed by Richard Castle (also architect of Powerscourt House) in the mid-eighteenth century. It has a notable art collection.

Saltee Islands
Great and Little Saltee Islands off the east coast are Ireland's largest bird sanctuary.

SOUTH AND SOUTH-WEST
Good for family holidays, local colour, outdoor activities, romantic escapism and scenic landscape

THE GULF Stream hits the coast around Cork, and as you travel westwards towards Kerry the scenery turns almost tropical. Here you will find some good small family resorts, where high rocky shores alternate with long pale sandy beaches (strands). It is also a great area for touring, with lakes and mountains inland and a beautiful coastline enhanced by offshore islands, such as the Blasket Islands (good for beaches and seal-spotting).

BEST RESORTS

Cobh

- Attractive town with huge natural harbour which serves as international port for Cork.
- Stony beach but good swimming and lots of facilities.
- International Sailing Centre offering all kinds of water-based sports, including a regatta weekend in August.
- Fota Wildlife Park and Arboretum a few miles north of Cobh.

Kinsale

- Narrow streets lined with painted houses and interesting shops.
- Charming harbour with plenty of places to stay at.
- Excellent restaurants – fish is a speciality. Renowned countrywide for the quality of its food. Kinsale Gourmet Week is held here in August.

Schull

- Sheltered harbour, with sporting and sailing festivals in July.
- Mount Gabriel (1,339 ft) is worth the climb for memorable views.

Youghal

- Ancient port at the mouth of the River Blackwater.
- Appealing architecture in and around Main Street.
- Lots of traditional music in local bars.

BEST SIGHTS AND EXCURSIONS

Blarney

The home of the infamous Blarney stone, which is said to bestow the gift of eloquence on all who kiss it. Worth it for believers only.

Gallarus Oratory

This remarkable structure is thought to have been built in the eighth or ninth century. It is in the shape of an upturned boat and is the best example of dry-stone masonry in the country.

Garinish Island

Rocky island converted into an outstanding garden by John Allen Bryce at the beginning of the century.

Killarney National Park

Over 40 square miles of lakes, mountains, peat bogs, gardens and woodland, most of which you can drive or walk around.

Ring of Kerry

This is the scenic circuit of the Iveragh peninsula – the standard route consists of a drive of about four hours. The views of Macgillycuddy's Reeks mountains, the valleys, lakes and sea are spectacular, but it is not worth going if it is raining or misty. The road also gets particularly busy in July and August, when crawling along the narrow roads behind gleaming tour buses can get frustrating. The town of Killarney is the best touring base for both the Ring of Kerry and Killarney National Park.

CORK

CORCONIANS CONSIDER their city more important than Dublin and the two compete both commercially and culturally. Cork has an international jazz festival in October, and lots of *craic*, pronounced 'crack' (loosely translated as 'fun'), all year round.

BEST SIGHTS

The Crawford Art Gallery and the Municipal School of Art offer a great variety of sculpture and paintings. St Anne's Shandon, a city landmark with a huge tower of which two sides are red sandstone and the other two grey limestone, provides an excellent panorama of the city.

WEST
Good for beaches, culture, family holidays, nightlife, outdoor activities, romantic escapism and scenic landscape

THE WEST of Ireland is thought by many to be the 'real' Ireland, with some of the country's wildest and most beautiful landscapes. You are more likely to hear Irish spoken here than in any other part of Ireland. It is a good area for beach or walking holidays as well as touring.

BEST BASES
Galway
Galway's fine city walls have been painstakingly restored. Cultural events are frequent; the city boasts a July arts festival, in addition to year-round great music, theatre and exhibitions. A horse-racing festival is held in the last week of July. Try Clarinbridge Oyster Festival (7 miles south of Galway) in September – great 'crack' for the connoisseur.

Rounstone
Connemara's prettiest fishing harbour offers local accommodation – you will find B&Bs and hotels in the village. Two magnificent beaches, Dog's Bay and Gurteen Bay, are sited a mile or so to the north. Try the exceptional fish chowder in O'Dowd's pub.

Westport
This delightful town was designed in the eighteenth century by James Wyatt. It has an interesting variety of shops, and some of the best musical pubs in the west. Eighteenth-century Westport House, designed by Richard Castle and a mile from the centre, is open to visitors.

BEST SIGHTS AND EXCURSIONS

The Burren
This extraordinary multi-fissured limestone plateau in the north-west of County Clare covers over 25 miles east to west and is a delight to potholers and botanists alike, with an intricate underground cave system and alpine and Mediterranean flowers growing side by side.

Ceide Fields
Archaeological site preserved beneath the bog for about 5,000 years, now revealed as the peat is cut away. Superb visitors' centre.

Cliffs of Moher
The five-mile stretch of cliffs reaches 660ft in places. The birdlife is abundant and the views magnificent.

Croagh Patrick
The mountain from where St Patrick is said to have banished all snakes from Ireland is the west's holy symbol. The 2,500-ft climb takes about two hours; the views on a clear day are breathtaking.

Lough Corrib
The largest lake in the Republic is famous for its pike, trout and salmon fishing. Boat trips are available from many locations.

Twelve Pins and Maumturk Mountains
These spectacular mountain ranges dominate the Connemara landscape.

BEST ISLANDS

Aran Islands
Inishmore, Inishmaan and Inisheer: Irish is spoken everywhere. Good for craft, pre-historic monuments, natural history.

Clare Island
Good for ruins and Irish music.

Inishbofin
Historical interest, fascinating ruins and secluded sandy beaches are the main attractions of this island off County Galway.

NORTH-WEST

Good for beaches, culture, family holidays, history, outdoor activities and scenic landscape

THE POET William Butler Yeats and his brother Jack used the landscape of Sligo as the inspiration for their writing and painting. The county is also rich in archaeological remains. Donegal's rugged coastline is studded with fine sandy beaches. It has some of the oldest mountain ranges in the country and a strong Gaelic tradition.

BEST RESORTS

Enniscrone

● Long sandy beach on Killala Bay.
● Hot sea-water baths with seaweed and steam.

Mullaghmore

● Appealing harbour full of boats and a good sandy beach.
● Views across Donegal Bay to the Blue Stack Mountains.

BEST SIGHTS AND EXCURSIONS

Ben Bulben

The unforgettable, brooding profile of this mountain dominates all around it. Plateau-topped and solitary on the north Sligo plains, it is easy to climb. W. B. Yeats is buried, as he requested, 'Under bare Ben Bulben's head/In Drumcliff churchyard'.

Carrowmore

The largest Stone Age cemetery in Ireland, with over 60 passage graves.

Cliffs of Bunglass

The views of the south face of Slieve League dropping 1,980ft into the sea are worth the climb.

Glenveagh National Park

Nearly 10,000 hectares of lakes, woodlands and bog plus a romantic nineteenth-century granite castle and mature exotic gardens.

Knocknarea

See spectacular views from this 1,080-ft mountain. Queen Maeve's cairn, 540ft round and containing a passage grave, lies on the summit.

Sligo

The County Museum and Art Gallery holds a memorial collection of W. B. Yeats' manuscripts and papers, and pictures by Jack B. Yeats.

MIDLANDS
Good for outdoor activities and wildlife

A GENERALLY uninspiring region, except for the area beside the great River Shannon. The longest river in Ireland is navigable from Carrick-on-Shannon in County Roscommon to Killaloe in County Clare. The Shannon-Erne waterway links the Republic to the North. You can hire cruiseboats from many riverside locations; the river widens into loughs at various points along its course. The scenery is beautiful and the birdlife exceptional. Avoid July and August, as locks become congested.

BEST SIGHTS
Clonmacnois
The Republic's most famous monastic site. Founded in the sixth century, it is the burial place of the Kings of Connaught and Tara.

Lough Key Forest Park
An outstanding 350-hectare park near the Shannon. Climb the modern Moylurg Tower for spectacular views over Lough Key and nearby mountains. Boat trips on the lake, gardens and nature trails are on offer.

WHEN TO GO

IN SUMMER the weather is generally a bit wetter and cooler than it is in southern England. Late spring and early summer are often relatively dry.

	Average daily maximum temperature °C											
London	6	7	10	13	17	20	22	21	19	14	10	7
Dublin	8	8	10	13	15	18	20	19	17	14	10	8
	JAN	FEB	MAR	APR	MAY	JUN	JUL	AUG	SEP	OCT	NOV	DEC
Dublin	13	10	10	11	10	11	13	12	12	11	12	14
London	15	13	11	12	12	11	12	11	13	13	15	15
	Average number of rainy days per month											

PACKAGE TRAVEL

MOST TOUR operators offer inclusive holidays to Ireland by ferry and air. As car hire is relatively expensive in the Republic of Ireland

235

you may do better to take your own car, or hire in Northern Ireland, where it is cheaper. Go-as-you-please options, including ferry crossings and pre-paid accommodation – from manor-house hotels to village inns and guesthouses – cater for varying budgets. You can also go on self-drive itineraries of the whole country or an area such as Cork and Kerry, staying in accommodation which you have to have booked in advance.

Self-catering accommodation featured in tour operators' brochures is often in purpose-built modern houses, arranged in small clusters; more individual and picturesque properties are thinner on the ground. Holiday parks are featured by various tour operators and include wet-weather facilities and activities.

City breaks to Dublin by air and ferry are based in a range of accommodation, from five-star hotels to guesthouses. With competitive airfares and budget accommodation or special offers in hotels you may find it cheaper to travel independently.

Specialists provide a wide range of activities, including touring by horse-drawn wagons, golfing, fishing, river cruising, walking and cycling.

Tour operators

City breaks: British Airways Holidays, Cresta, Crystal, Inghams, Osprey, Sovereign, Thomson, Time Off, Travelscene **Coach tours**: Bowens, DA Tours, Excelsior, Shearings, Travelsphere, Wallace Arnold **Specialists**: Aer Lingus Holidays, CIE Tours, Drive Ireland, Irish Ferries, Kerry Holidays, PAB Travel, Ryan Holidays, Stena Line Holidays, Sunward **Walking/cycling**: Bike Tours (cycling), Countrywide (walking), Exodus (walking), Headwater (cycling and walking), Joyce's Hidden Ireland (walking), Kestours (walking), Ramblers Holidays (walking), Sherpa (walking), Waymark (walking) **Other activities**: AA Motoring (motoring), Ace Study Tours, Anglers World (fishing), Blakes (river cruising), Holts' Tours (battle-fields), Kings Angling (fishing), Limosa (birdwatching), Peregrine (horse-riding), Solo's Holidays (singles), Travel for the Arts (music)

INDEPENDENT TRAVEL

AER LINGUS is the national carrier and flies from the UK to Dublin and regional airports all over the Republic. Ryanair, British Midland and Virgin Cityjet also fly from the UK to the Republic. There is not much difference between the SuperApex fares offered by these airlines, but it is worth ringing around for special offers.

All the major car-hire firms are represented at the airport in Dublin centre, the regional cities and some towns, but local firms are cheaper and generally reliable. A UK driving licence is acceptable. Petrol is more expensive than in the UK.

Irish Ferries, Stena Sealink and Swansea Cork ferries run regular services to the UK. Stena operates the new HSS 90-minute ferry from Dun Laoghaire to Holyhead as well as the Sea Cat hydrofoil. Car ferry prices are extremely high; although all companies offer special rates, none is cheap. Even so, for a two-week touring holiday it is less expensive to bring your own car on the ferry than to fly and hire.

Getting to the Republic by bus and ferry is very cheap but time-consuming; train and ferry costs much less than flying. Once in the Republic the train system is run by CIE (Coras Iopair Eireann), which also operates the bus system. It is a bit archaic but good value and you will reach your destination, albeit by a circuitous route. Special travel cards offer the best value.

Accommodation, and plenty of it, is available to suit all pockets. Bookings are necessary in high season, and, if you are touring, the tourist offices offer an excellent booking service. Several organisations produce their own brochures, such as *Hidden Ireland*, featuring a collection of large, privately owned houses. *The Blue Book* is another popular collection, while Bord Faílte (the tourist board) has information on hotels, B&Bs, farmhouses and self-catering.

RED TAPE, HEALTH AND SAFETY

UK PASSPORT-HOLDERS are not even required to show a passport to enter Ireland.

Like many European cities, Dublin has a problem with street crime – take care of valuables and leave nothing on display in parked cars. Be particularly wary in O'Connell Street after dark. For other advice see page 12.

MORE INFORMATION Irish Tourist Board, Ireland House, 150-151 New Bond Street, London W1Y 0AQ, tel 0171-493 3201, web site: http://www.ireland.travel.ie/

COST OF LIVING *£££*

ISRAEL

HIGHLIGHTS

Culture/history
Jerusalem, Holy Land, the coast

Beaches
The coast

Family holidays
The coast

Local colour
Jerusalem

Outdoor activities
The coast

Scenic landscape
Holy Land

JERUSALEM
Good for culture/history and local colour

PRESENT-DAY JERUSALEM continues to be driven by symbolism and dreams. The Old City is a labyrinth of alleyways that creep through the Arab, Christian, Jewish and Armenian quarters. The New City is vast and exhausting and much more European in outlook, apart from Me'a She'arim, the ultra-orthodox Jewish *shtetl*, which embraces the traditions of eighteenth-century Eastern Europe.

OLD CITY

Christian Quarter
The Way of the Cross traces Christ's route to crucifixion, ending at the Church of the Holy Sepulchre. Long queues form outside Christ's tomb here; many visit the alternative Garden Tomb in East Jerusalem.

Jewish Quarter
The Western (Wailing) Wall is the last remnant of Herod the Great's Second Temple and an important political and religious symbol. Underground, the Herodian mansions reveal life in Roman times.

Muslim Quarter

The Dome of the Rock is the city's most impressive sight, its huge golden dome dominating the skyline. At the centre is the rock from which, Muslims believe, Mohammed ascended to heaven.

NEW CITY

Israel Museum

Under the Shrine of the Book the frail leather of the Dead Sea Scrolls is displayed in a subtly lit, almost mystical setting.

Tower of David

This superb museum mixes archaeology, walks round ramparts and a trip into the city's history via dioramas, holograms, models and films.

Vad Yashem

The memorial and research centre for the six million victims of the Nazi Holocaust explains the events in a simple and dignified way.

HOLY LAND
Good for culture/history and scenic landscape

FOR THOUSANDS, a trip to the Holy Land is the affirmation of a life-time's faith: biblical place names that resonate deep in the consciousness.

BEST SIGHTS

Bethlehem

The humble manger has long since been engulfed by the cavernous Church of the Nativity, a fortress-like stone structure. The Grotto of the Nativity lies beneath. Christ's birthplace marked by a silver star.

Dead Sea

Most resort hotels are at En Boqeq, which owes its spa status to thera-peutic Dead Sea minerals. In AD 70, Jewish zealots took refuge in the spectacular rock fortress of Masada during a revolt against Rome: you can visit the remains. The celebrated Dead Sea Scrolls were found in the caves at Qumran: subsequent excavations unearthed several buildings of the Essene community. Just north of the sea, Jericho is the world's oldest continually inhabited community – nearly 10,000 years old.

Nazareth

The Roman Catholic Basilica of the Annunciation, boldly modern in design, obliterates the spot where the Archangel Gabriel appeared to the Virgin Mary. Inside are the Grotto of the Annunciation and the remains of Byzantine and Crusader churches.

Sea of Galilee

Here are some of the Holy Land's loveliest areas. At Tabgha, the Church of the Multiplication of the Loaves and Fishes marks the site of the feeding of the five thousand. The Church of Mensa Christi denotes the spot where Christ supposedly charged Peter with the keys of the kingdom; remains of what is said to be Peter's house are at Capernaum, complete with damaged fresco work.

THE COAST
Good for culture, beaches, family holidays and outdoor activities

BEAUTIFUL BEACHES stretch the length of the Mediterranean coast, while Eilat on the Red Sea has year-round water sports.

BEST RESORTS

Eilat
- Popular resort with every conceivable water sport on offer.
- Beaches not as good as Mediterranean ones, but Eilat is a livelier place.
- Most evening entertainment based in and around hotels.
- Inconvenient for biblical sights: excursions involve an overnight stop.

Netanya
- Best Mediterranean resort: low-key, good for families and the elderly.
- Fine cliff-backed white sand beach, stretching for over five miles.
- Pedestrianised town centre with lively main square.

BEST SIGHTS AND EXCURSIONS

Akko
This Crusader city was once held by Richard the Lionheart. It is worth visiting the splendid eighteenth-century mosque of Ahmed Jezzar, and the now underground Crusader city in the heart of the Arab quarter.

Caesarea
This two-mile site includes a Roman amphitheatre and aqueduct, a Byzantine street and a Crusader city. The restored amphitheatre where Christians and Jews were thrown to the lions is used for concerts.

Tel Aviv (Jaffa)
An ugly modern city with a lively beach, Tel Aviv was built almost overnight – and it shows. The Diaspora Museum has beautiful displays conveying the strong sense of nationhood felt by present-day Israelis. Jaffa's old port offers more local colour, while the cobbled alleyways of the reconstructed Crusader city house an artists' colony of craft shops.

WHEN TO GO

PILGRIMS MAY wish to spend Christmas in Bethlehem or Easter in Jerusalem. Spring is probably the best time for a coach tour, before it becomes too hot. Eilat excels for winter sun, with reliable temperatures. For summer sun, sea and sand, choose the Mediterranean coast.

	JAN	FEB	MAR	APR	MAY	JUN	JUL	AUG	SEP	OCT	NOV	DEC
Average daily maximum temperature °C												
London	6	7	10	13	17	20	22	21	19	14	10	7
Jerusalem	13	13	18	23	27	29	31	31	29	27	21	15
Jerusalem	9	11	3	3	0.6	0.1	0	0	0.1	1	4	7
London	15	13	11	12	12	11	12	11	13	13	15	15
Average number of rainy days per month												

PACKAGE TRAVEL

ALL THE major tour operators feature Israel; only specialists offer a wide variety of holidays. A week-long coach tour may feature the Dead Sea, Masada, Jericho, the Sea of Galilee, Lake Tiberias, Nazareth, Haifa, Caesarea, Bethlehem and Jerusalem, staying in hotels and guesthouses.

Fly-drive packages are available. Some specialists offer accommodation on kibbutzes, either in guesthouses or hotels.

On the Mediterranean Netanya, Herzlia and Caesarea are alternatives to the Red Sea resort of Eilat. Peak season in Eilat is December, and package prices in July and August carry a high-season supplement. Accommodation is mostly in hotels, with some self-catering apartments.

Tour operators

Birdwatching: Abercrombie & Kent, Limosa, Ornitholidays, Sunbird **Diving**: Connections, Regal Holidays, Speedwing **General and specialist**: Airtours, Cosmos, First Choice, Sunworld, Thomson, Unijet **Pilgrimages**: Highway Journeys, Inter-Church Travel, McCabe Travel, Orientours **Walking**: Exodus, Explore Worldwide **Other activities**: British Museum Traveller (archaeology), Club Med (all-inclusive)

INDEPENDENT TRAVEL

SCHEDULED FLIGHTS go to Tel Aviv and charter flights to Eilat. Eilat has internal flights to Tel Aviv and Jerusalem, which can save you time if you want to combine a beach holiday with a bit of sightseeing.

Israel's internal transport system is well developed. Motorways link the main cities, and roads are of a high standard. For car hire, you need a valid UK licence and must be over 21. Road signs are in Hebrew, English and Arabic; driving is on the right. Public transport is efficient and cheap.

The national bus company, Egged, covers most of Israel. You can buy passes for up to a month. Trains are cheaper but less frequent and more limited. Public transport closes down on Friday afternoon and Saturday.

Within towns, taxis have meters; for taxis between towns or villages agree the fare in advance. *Sherut* (shared taxis) also link most places in Israel and, though more expensive than buses, are still reasonable.

Israel offers every kind of accommodation, from deluxe hotels and self-catering apartments to kibbutz guesthouses and campsites. Some Christian pilgrims stay at hospices run by various churches.

RED TAPE, HEALTH AND SAFETY

BRITISH PASSPORT-HOLDERS do not require a visa. The tentative nature of the Middle East peace process means that security is very tight, even before you arrive – extra baggage checks are required when you check in at the airport, so you should allow plenty of time.

If you are having a beach holiday on the Mediterranean coast or in Eilat you are unlikely to see any sign of the troubles. But if you plan to visit the West Bank cities you may find that unrest limits your travels. Bethlehem is the most likely of the biblical sights to be out of bounds. Organised tours may have to drop a destination from the itinerary.

In Jerusalem, the new city is relatively safe, but you are advised not to wander alone in the evenings around East Jerusalem and parts of the Old City. Cars with Israeli numberplates risk stoning in areas of the West Bank, including the Mount of Olives – seek advice if you hire a car. If heading for East Jerusalem at night, you might be refused lifts from Israeli taxis. For the latest information on safety contact the Foreign Office Travel Advice Unit (see page 11).

MORE INFORMATION Israel Government Tourist Office, 180 Oxford Street, London W1N 9DJ, tel 0171-299 1111, web site: http://www.infotour.co.il/

COST OF LIVING *£££*

ITALY

HIGHLIGHTS

Beaches
*Liguria, heel of
Italy, Sardinia*

Culture
*Northern cities,
Venice,
Florence,
Tuscany,
Umbria,
Neapolitan
Riviera, Rome,
heel of Italy,
Sicily*

**Family
holidays**
Liguria

Food/wine
*Northern cities,
Tuscany,
Umbria,
Neapolitan
Riviera*

History
Sardinia

Local colour
Venice

Nightlife
Sicily

**Outdoor
activities**
Tyrol, Lakes

**Romantic
escapism**
*Neapolitan
Riviera*

**Scenic
landscape**
*Tuscany,
Tyrol,
Lakes,
Umbria,
Neapolitan
Riviera,
Sardinia*

NORTHERN CITIES
Good for culture and food/wine

DISCOVERING THE northern Italian cities is like a potted art history lesson, covering everything from the Romans to the Futurists.

BEST CITIES

Bergamo

The medieval alleys and brick herringbone streets of the upper part of this pretty hill town converge on a Venetian-style square. The lavish Colleoni chapel was built to house a fifteenth-century mercenary's tomb.

Bologna

An attractive university town, known for good food. The Basilica of San Petronio dwarfs the cathedral. Santo Stefano is a group of four interlinked churches: one contains the bowl in which Pontius Pilate reputedly washed his hands.

Mantua

At the Palazzo Ducale, portraits by Mantegna of the Renaissance ruling family, the Gonzagas, decorate the Camera degli Sposi. At the other extreme, the Palazzo del Tè displays bawdy scenes by Giulio Romano.

Milan

Industrialised Milan has Italy's only High Gothic cathedral: visit the roof for distant views of the Alps. The Brera Gallery houses north Italian Renaissance paintings, while the Gallery of Modern Art has Italian modernists, French Impressionists and post-Impressionists.

Padua

Pilgrims make for the domed Basilica of Sant' Antonio, patron saint of lost property, to touch his sarcophagus. The other top attraction is Giotto's fresco cycle of the Redemption in the Scrovegni Chapel.

Parma

Parma was heavily bombed in the Second World War. At the Palazzo della Pilotta is the Teatro Farnese, based on Palladio's theatre in Vicenza. The cathedral dome displays a fresco of the Assumption by Correggio.

Ravenna

Brilliant Byzantine mosaics are dotted around town, sumptuous gold backgrounds setting off glowing robes and detailed flowers. To save money, buy a block ticket from the first church you visit.

Verona

The huge irregular Piazza Brà is the focus of Verona, with cafés on one side and a Roman arena at the northern end. Smaller but fringed by fine *palazzi* are Piazza delle Erbe and Piazza dei Signori. The loveliest of the many churches is San Zeno Maggiore, a striped Romanesque basilica.

Vicenza

Palladio's stately *palazzi* fill the town, also boasting his stucco and wood Teatro Olimpico and the symmetrical Villa Rotonda. Several Palladian-style villas surround Vicenza, not all designed by the architect himself.

VENICE
Good for culture and local colour

THE FRAGILE, melancholy, decaying beauty of Venice makes it incomparable. Despite the riches of its museums, churches and palaces, nothing compares with exploring the canals and back streets.

BEST SIGHTS

Accademia

Venice's foremost art gallery spans five centuries, starting with fine Byzantine-style altarpieces. The Renaissance collection includes work by the Bellini family, Carpaccio, Titian, Tintoretto and Veronese.

Basilica of St Mark

Consecrated in 1094, this exotic Byzantine basilica has been much altered. Pay to see gilded horses from the church door (in the Museo Marciano) and a jewelled altarpiece, the Pala d'Oro (by the high altar).

Grand Canal

Venice's main thoroughfare flows past bubble-domed churches and extravagant palaces. The best and cheapest way to see the canal is from the No 1 waterbus: you can seldom walk along it, except around the Rialto Bridge. Try a night trip to see frescoed rooms lit by chandeliers.

Piazza San Marco

The city's most famous piazza, its series of repetitive arcades form a foil to the Gothic Doge's Palace and the basilicas, domes and mosaics.

FLORENCE
Good for culture

MOST OF the city's attractions are historical, and lie inside its galleries and museums; outside, life proceeds at twentieth-century pace.

BEST SIGHTS

Accademia

Queues form to see the original sculpture of David by Michelangelo, but do not overlook the sculptor's four unfinished Slaves.

Bargello

The best Italian collection of Renaissance sculpture has Donatello's David and Brunelleschi and Ghiberti's entries for the baptistery doors.

Cathedral and baptistery

Brunelleschi's masterpiece is built on a vast scale, but the interior is rather plain. The baptistery has stunning mosaics in the dome and copies of Ghiberti's beautiful bronze doors.

Museo dell'Opera del Duomo

The original panels from Ghiberti's baptistery doors are here, as well as two lovely musicians' galleries by Donatello and della Robbia.

Palazzo Pitti

Within the palace are several galleries. The Galleria Palatina includes works by Titian, Raphael and Veronese, while the Museo degli Argenti is a chaotic collection of marble, silver, ivory and porcelain.

Uffizi

The east wing gives a fine introduction to Florentine Renaissance art. Botticelli's *Birth of Venus* and *Primavera* are the main crowd-pullers.

TUSCANY
Good for culture, food/wine and scenic landscape

AN ENGAGING succession of medieval hill towns in a landscape of sunflowers and cool green cypresses sums up, for many, the essence of Italy. Chianti is the most popular area for renting a villa.

Arezzo

The church of San Francesco contains frescos of the True Cross by Piero della Francesca. Visit the house of Renaissance art historian Vasari, who designed the loggia along one side of the Piazza Grande.

Cortona

The massive city walls encircle a hilly mix of old *palazzi* embellished with architraves, scrolls and lions' heads.

Lucca

A handsome provincial capital with two superb Pisan Romanesque churches: San Martino's façade is decorated with fine sculptures, San Michele in Foro is topped with a statue of the Archangel Michael.

Montepulciano
The main street, the Corso, has shops selling *vino nobile*, perfect for quaffing as you toil up to the cathedral on Piazza Grande. Beyond the walls, Antonio da Sangallo's church is a perfect Renaissance temple.

Pienza
The town's central tiny square is the model of a Renaissance city, built by Aeneas Sylvius Piccolomini on his election as Pope Pius II in 1458.

Pisa
The famous leaning tower adjoins a matching cathedral and baptistery, all aligned on the wonderfully traffic-free Campo dei Miracoli.

San Gimignano
Thirteen lofty towers remain out of 76. Climb the tallest, the Museo Civico's. The *collegiata* church has a veritable X-rated *Last Judgement*.

Sansepolcro
Piero della Francesca fans seek his mesmeric painting of a resurrected Christ. To the north-west, La Verna monastery, where St Francis received the stigmata, has fine enamelled terracotta by della Robbia.

Siena
A city of rosy pink alleys, free of traffic. At the central Campo piazza, climb the Museo Civico's tower for superb views. Inside is Simone Martini's famous Maestà. The cathedral has fine inlaid marble floors, sadly usually covered, and a library with frescos by Pintoricchio.

Volterra
Volterra's Roman theatre is well preserved. The Etruscan Museum has many alabaster sarcophagi; the stone is mined here for tourist souvenirs.

TYROL
Good for outdoor activities and scenic landscape

THIS REGION, melding two distinct ethnic traditions – Italian and Tyrolean – into one political entity, has experienced sporadic tensions. Visitors, however, will thrill to the majesty of the saw-toothed Dolomites. The walking season lasts from late June to late September.

BEST BASES
Bressanone
A baroque cathedral dominates the old quarter. The town hosts a festival every second August. Good base for Gardena and Pusteria valleys.

Merano
With its mild climate and spa status, Merano boomed in the nineteenth century. Visit arcaded shopping streets and the castle. Ideal base for the Venosta valley and Monte Giovo Pass.

Molveno
Pretty lakeside village with a pedestrianised centre, small gravel beach and good hotels. Handy for the Brenta Massif and the Rendena valley.

Ortisei
The Gardena valley's main resort with a museum on Ladin culture, derived from a local Roman garrison. Handy for Fassa and Ega valleys.

Solda
A quiet village in the Solda valley; visit a glacier by cable-car. Mountaineer Reinhold Messner has set up an Alpine climbing museum.

BEST SIGHTS AND EXCURSIONS

Bolzano
Stroll from cobbled Piazza Walther through the old town's arcaded streets. The Romanesque-Gothic cathedral has a lovely Gothic pulpit.

Trento
There is a Romanesque cathedral and treasury, a thirteenth-century castle and a lovely central square, with frescoed Renaissance buildings.

BEST SCENIC LANDSCAPES

Ega valley
The road hugs the base of a narrow ravine, opening out to reveal fir-covered hills and the dramatic distant Catinaccio mountains. From the pretty Lake Carezza the road climbs up over the Costalunga Pass.

Gardena valley
Guarded by the dramatic Gardena and Sasso Lungo passes, this crosses the Ladin people's land (street signs become trilingual) to reach the Sella Mountains. Great views of winding Pordoi Pass and Falzarego Pass.

Monte Giovo Pass
See snow-capped Austrian peaks from the top. The descent to the pretty tourist honeypot town of Vipiteno is spectacular.

Rendena and Genova valleys
The Rendena valley is fir-clad; Pinzolo, its most pristine village, is the starting-point for the more spectacular Genova valley, where a dead-end forest road follows the river to Bedole, a lovely picnic spot.

BEST MOUNTAIN TRIPS

Brenta Massif
The cable-car goes up 7,920ft to the barren landscape of the Groste Pass. From here experienced walkers can hike east to Molveno.

Catinaccio
Multi-level walks bisect the splendour of the Catinaccio. The cable-car from Vigo di Fassa goes to the start. At sunset the rocks glow red.

Mount Paganella
Go by cable-car from Andalo to see the Brenta range and Lake Como.

LAKES
Good for outdoor activities and scenic landscape

GO TO the Italian lakes for a lazy, relaxing holiday. Take a boat trip, linger in cafés, stroll by the water and admire the scenery.

Lake Como
● At picturesque, unspoilt Bellagio, the grounds of Villa Serbelloni occupy a rocky outcrop between the two arms of the lake. Visit also the gardens of Villa Melzi.
● At Cadenabbia an avenue of plane trees leads to Tremezzo and Villa Carlotta, with attractive terraced gardens.
● Cernobbio is a relaxed resort near the splendid Villa d'Este, a grand hotel with famous gardens. Treat yourself to tea on the lakeside terrace.
● Como is a busy city with an interesting centre, the highlight of which is the cathedral with its fine Renaissance altar screen.
● Villa Monastero is now a conference centre but the gardens, shaded by an old magnolia tree, are lovely, with avenues of fruit trees.

Lake Garda
● Popular Gardone has a botanical garden and the fascinating Villa Vittoriale, home of the historian, fascist, womaniser and poet Gabriele D'Annunzio.
● Salo's splendid cathedral contains a gilt polyptych; Malcesine sits at the foot of Monte Baldo and is dominated by a castle once home to the Scaligers of Verona. Good views of the lake from Monte Baldo.
● Sirmione also has a Scaliger castle, and Roman poet Catullus' villa.
● Bardolino has an elegant Romanesque church, and famous wine.

Lake Lugano
● Subdued Morcote is below a steep hillside. Lots of fish restaurants.
● In busy Gandria, houses cling to the lakeside. Spectacular views.

● The Sighignola Belvedere, four miles east of Campione, is called the 'balcony of Italy' – on a clear day you can see Mont Blanc.

● There are also super views from Sacro Monte, which has a pilgrimage church dedicated to the Virgin, and from the Campo dei Fiori.

Lake Maggiore

● Stresa is the best base for island-visiting. A cable-car to Mottarone gives fine lake views.

● Boats ply among the Borromean Islands: Isola Bella is the prettiest. Count Charles Borromeo III's palace and gardens are here. Isola Madre has an elegant villa; unspoilt Isola Pescatori has many restaurants.

● Pallanza's quays are flower-decked. Nearby are Villa Taranto's gardens.

● Cannero is a pretty ferry stop where cafés on wooden platforms over-hang the lake. A ruined castle stands on a tiny island to the north.

● Angera's castle has fine frescos depicting life in the Middle Ages.

Lake Orta

● Orta San Giulio is a small resort on a tiny promontory on the east-ern side of the lake. An arched town hall dominates the cobbled square.

● San Giulio Island is a tiny, tranquil place, whose houses cluster tightly around a Benedictine monastery and the twelfth-century basilica.

LIGURIA
Good for beaches and family holidays

THE COASTLINE between Tuscany and France divides into upmar-ket eastern resorts – stopovers on the eighteenth-century Grand Tour – and unpretentious, family-oriented beach resorts in the west.

BEST RESORTS

Alassio

● Lively resort with a variety of large modern hotels and some older, more characterful ones catering for affluent, largely Italian market.

● Best sandy beach in Liguria, almost entirely divided into concessions.

● Good restaurants and late-night shopping around a long, narrow street behind the beach, known to the English as 'the Drain'.

Finale Ligure

● Splendid setting below craggy cliffs and wooded mountains.

● Long sandy beach with more free areas than most neighbours.

● Most hotels, shops and restaurants are in area called Finale Marina.

● Old quarter of Finalborgo is a knot of alleyways around a Gothic church and Renaissance convent.

Laigueglia
● Circled by hills draped in olive groves.
● Peeling network of alleyways in old fishermen's quarter.
● Long, broad sandy beach, much of which is divided into concessions along the length of the resort.

Santa Margherita Ligure
● Well-established, fashionable resort in beautiful Gulf of Tigullio.
● Swanky hotels, shops and restaurants, a harbour full of luxury yachts.
● No beach, though you could take a boat trip to the tiny, photogenic resort of Portofino in neighbouring bay.

BEST SIGHTS AND EXCURSIONS

Cinque Terre

Five unspoilt fishing villages, improbably wedged into fissures or over-hanging rock faces. Accessible by boat, train and to some extent by car; best seen by taking the scenic footpath connecting all five. **Monterosso** is largest and most touristy, with a pebble beach and hotels; **Vernazza** is prettiest – an arcaded lane leads to a seafront piazza with bars and restaurants; **Corniglia** has a stony beach and dull old town; **Manarola** is a delightful huddle of houses hugging the rock face; and **Riomaggiore** is really just one charming street shoe-horned into a ravine.

Genoa

Christopher Columbus's birthplace is still Italy's premier seaport; Genoa has unsightly docks, but the back streets (*carrugi*) of the old quarter house some atmospheric *trattorie*. Take a day-trip to see Genoese and Venetian paintings in the Palazzo Rosso, Antonello da Messina's *Ecce Homo* at the Palazzo Spinola and the Pisan-Romanesque cathedral of San Lorenzo.

UMBRIA
Good for culture, food/wine and scenic landscape

AS IN neighbouring Tuscany, soul-satisfying landscape and medieval hilltop towns are Umbria's main attractions. The main sightseeing cities are in the centre and north, but the best countryside is in the south.

BEST SIGHTS AND EXCURSIONS

Assisi

The Basilica of San Francesco boasts Giotto's wonderful frescos of the saint's life. Few tourists actually reach the town itself. Just out of town, the Porziuncola, the chapel where St Francis founded the Franciscan monastic order, is dwarfed by the seventeenth-century Basilica of Santa Maria erected around it.

Gubbio
A grey, frontier-like town. The Museo Civico contains seven Eugubian Tablets, the only record of the Umbrian language. The city's bishop-saint Ubaldo lies in a pink brick basilica reached by funicular.

Orvieto
High on a volcanic outcrop, Orvieto has a magnificent cathedral, with gruesome frescos by Luca Signorelli. Visit also a 12-sided belltower in the Piazza della Repubblica, and a sixteenth-century well.

Perugia
The city has a cosmopolitan feel, thanks to the Foreigners' University. The pink-and-white cathedral overlooks the Fontana Maggiore, a fountain with mythical scenes. The National Gallery of Umbria has works by locals Perugino and Pintoricchio.

Spoleto
In the Piazza del Duomo is a Romanesque cathedral. Nearby, four-teenth-century Ponte delle Torri was built to replace a Roman aqueduct.

Todi
Piazza del Popolo is a stunning medieval square with a cathedral, the crenellated Palazzo del Popolo and the Gothic Palazzo del Capitano.

BEST SCENIC LANDSCAPE
Nera valley
Towering cliffs stretch to Visso, before a thrilling climb up to the Gualdo Pass, overlooked by the bleak Sibillini Mountains. Nearby, wild horses roam the huge basin of the Piano Grande. The route back is greener.

NEAPOLITAN RIVIERA
Good for culture, food/wine, romantic escapism and scenic landscape

THIS PART of the Italian coastline has stunning scenery, charming cliffside towns and some of the finest archaeological sites to be found anywhere in the world.

BEST BASES
Amalfi
The terraced houses and lemon groves are best admired from the sea. The town's focal point is a small piazza at the foot of the stairway to the cathedral. For a quieter side of town, take one of the little alleyways off the main street to emerge above the belltower.

Positano
There is no real centre to this town of sugar-cube houses, except Santa Maria Church. A one-way street leads to the beach and promenade.

Ravello
The escapist's choice, Ravello sits 200 feet above Amalfi at the end of a series of hairpin bends. Villa Rufolo and Villa Cimbrone have public gardens with wonderful coastal views. The plain cathedral has some fine mosaic pulpits and bronze doors.

Sorrento
Good for public transport and hotels. The attractive old town is lit up in the evening, but beneath the touristy veneer, Italian traditions and lifestyle linger. To escape most of the crowds, visit San Francesco's cloisters or the Marina Grande, a fishing port with a few good restaurants.

BEST SIGHTS AND EXCURSIONS

Capri
Most visitors seek the Blue Grotto – a pricey tourist trap. More interesting is the stylish Villa San Michele in Anacapri, built by the Swedish doctor Axel Munthe. Try a coastal walk from the Tragara terrace for cliff views, or see the ruins of Villa Jovis, one of Emporer Tiberius's haunts.

Herculaneum
Herculaneum was a wealthy suburb destroyed by the AD 79 eruption of Vesuvius. Don't miss the baths, the House of the Deer, and the House of the Neptune Mosaic, with two lovely multicoloured mosaics.

Naples
Brave the chaos and traffic for the National Archaeological Museum. Highlights are mosaics and paintings from Pompeii, and fine sculpture.

Paestum
Three magnificent Doric temples on windswept marshy plains south of Amalfi. The museum displays pottery, friezes and tomb murals.

Pompeii
The layer of pumice stone and ash that buried the city when Vesuvius erupted in AD 79 kept Pompeii – and some of its inhabitants – in an amazing state of preservation. Highlights include the Forum, the Forum Baths, the House of the Vettii, the theatres and the Villa of the Mysteries.

Vesuvius
A zigzag path leads to the top (about half an hour). The crater is a

sheer-walled funnel filled with scree, ash and boulders. From the belvedere at the end of the path you can see Pompeii, on a clear day.

ROME
Good for culture

A CORNERSTONE of Western civilisation and still the focus of the Roman Catholic faith, the Eternal City offers incomparable sightseeing for those fascinated by archaeology, ancient history or Renaissance and baroque art and architecture. But opening hours are maddening, so you will need to plan your time carefully.

BEST SIGHTS

Colosseum
This vast cauldron of brick and stone arches is one of Rome's most recognisable sights. Scene of gladiatorial combat and other 'entertainments' from the year AD 80, it has 76 entrances and was designed to accommodate 50,000 people.

Forum
The east side of the Capitoline Hill overlooks the columns and temples of the Roman Forum. Important buildings include the Curia, where the Senate met; the Temple of Castor and Pollux; the Temple of Vesta, with the House of the Vestal Virgins; and the Temple of Saturn.

St Peter's
The awesomely scaled church is the work of several architects, including Michelangelo, Bramante and Bernini – who designed the sweeping colonnades symbolising the church's embracing arms. Impressive interior highlights are the baroque *baldacchino* (canopy) above St Peter's tomb, and Michelangelo's exquisite Pietà. Splendid views from the roof.

Vatican Museums and Sistine Chapel
The Vatican museums are so vast as to leave you glassy-eyed. Signposted routes lead to the Raphael Rooms and the Sistine Chapel, where you can develop a rubber neck and lockjaw gaping at the stunning frescos.

HEEL OF ITALY
Good for beaches and culture

ITALY'S POOREST regions – Apulia, Calabria and Basilicata – have traditionally been beyond the tourist pale, but more adventurous travellers will find much of interest here. The landscapes vary from the flat and fertile plains of Apulia to the stark mountain scenery of Basilicata. Calabria combines scenic wildness with near-deserted beaches. Lovers of art and architecture will find touring Apulia most rewarding.

BEST RESORTS

Gargano Peninsula
- The spur on Italy's heel has superb coastal scenery and corniche drives.
- Best resorts are Peschici and Vieste, both lively with sandy beaches.
- Best excursion is Monte Sant'Angelo, a pilgrimage town.

Maratea
- Best resort south of Campania, despite a poor beach.
- A deserted medieval quarter overlooks the Gulf of Policast.

Scilla
- Fishing village with a sandy beach and charming residential quarter.
- The rock Scylla (named in Homer's *Odyssey*) dominates the scene.

Tropea
- A decent coarse sand beach helped Tropea to become a lively resort.
- The fishing port and old town are picturesque.

BEST SIGHTS AND EXCURSIONS

Lecce
A small town full of flamboyant baroque churches, carved from soft local limestone that enables exuberant carving. Santa Croce is stunning.

Matera
An extraordinary town. The handsome new town has a fine cathedral; below is a honeycomb of squalid cave dwellings where the population lived until forced out in the 1950s.

Reggio di Calabria
The town boasts the superb National Museum, housing items from the cities of Magna Graecia. Drive to the Aspromonte Mountains for views.

Romanesque churches
'Apulian Romanesque' style is mostly Norman (also Byzantine and Saracenic). Characteristics are a rose window above an elaborate portal. Best seen in cathedrals at Bari (San Nicola), Bitonto, Altamura and Molfetta. Those at Canosa, Barletta, Bisceglie and Trani are also good.

Sila Massif
The plateau is 3,300ft above sea-level, with mountains, forests and lakes. Accommodation is chalet-style.

Trulli

Trulli are whitewashed conical huts, unique to Italy, found between Locorotondo and Martina Franca. See them *en masse* at Alberobello, the *trulli* capital. The caves at Castellana make a worthwhile excursion.

SICILY
Good for culture and nightlife

SUCCESSIVE WAVES of invaders have bequeathed a rich architectural legacy. Classical, Norman and baroque masterpieces litter the entire island. Best bases for a stay-put package holiday are Taormina and Cefalù.

BEST RESORTS

Cefalù
● Delightful fishing port successfully developed as a resort.
● Characterful old town – a grid of narrow streets sloping down from a magnificent Arabo-Norman cathedral – remains unspoilt.
● Golden, sandy beach stretches out west of the town.

Taormina
● Picturesque hill village with beguiling views of Mount Etna.
● Lively town of designer boutiques in medieval *palazzi* and *al fresco* bars lining mini-piazzas.
● Numerous restaurants and discos buzz till the early hours.
● A cable-car takes you to the pebble beach at Mazzaró, though the broad, sandy beach at Giardini-Naxos, half a mile west, is far better.

BEST SIGHTS AND EXCURSIONS

Agrigento
The Valley of the Temples is Sicily's best classical site. Ruins of nine temples from the sixth and fifth centuries BC are visible; the Doric Temple of Concord is the largest and best-preserved. There are also significant remnants of the Temples of Juno, Jupiter and Hercules.

Casale
Ruined Roman villa with mosaics laid by African artists for Emperor Maximian in the third century. Some famous scenes (the 200-ft 'Large Hunt' and the bikini-clad girls) were recently vandalised.

Monreale
The small hill town above Palermo is dominated by the Norman cathedral. The exterior is dull, but the interior is covered by glittering mosaics.

Mount Etna
Europe's largest active volcano dominates Sicily's eastern end and is spectacular during its frequent eruptions. Organised tours to the crater.

Noto
Showpiece Sicilian baroque town, built after the 1693 earthquake. Ornate churches line Corso Vittorio Emanuele. To the south lie the baroque towns of Ragusa and Modica. Inland is a scenic drive to the prehistoric necropolis of Pantalica or the ceramics town of Caltagirone.

Palermo
In one day in this melting-pot of Islamic, Latin and Byzantine cultures you should be able to see the twelfth-century cathedral; the Matorana, an Arabo-Norman church; the National Archaeological Museum; the Cappella Palatina, decorated by Byzantine and Arab craftsmen; and the National Gallery, housing Francesco Laurana's bust of Eleanor of Aragon.

BEST ISLANDS
Most interesting of the islands around Sicily are the Aeolian Islands.

Aeolian Islands
The largest is **Lipari**, a popular resort with a pebble beach and an archaeological museum in the old quarter. Find good hotels and restaurants here. **Stromboli** is volcanic and less developed for tourism with a black sand beach. Boat trips to see the eruptions by night go from Lipari. On **Vulcano**, bathe in sulphurous mud or visit the Great Crater.

SARDINIA
Good for beaches, history and scenic landscape

SARDINIA'S ATTRACTIONS are simple but beguiling: magnificent beaches, glorious coastal scenery and intriguing archaeological sites.

BEST RESORTS
Alghero
● Biggest, cheapest and most satisfying resort, with bustle and charm.
● Old town is maze of vibrant streets opening on to large square.
● Main beach stretches for over three miles.

Baia Sardinia
● Most pleasant resort on north-east coast.
● Small but delightful curving bay of white sand.
● Smart shopping centre of boutiques and cafés, with lively buzz.

Villasimius
● A charming village in the island's most beautiful part, fast develop-ing into a resort.
● Good beach (far from centre) and decent bars and restaurants.

BEST SIGHTS AND EXCURSIONS
Cágliari
The National Archaeological Museum is the city's greatest sight, its highlight being the large collection of bronze nuraghic figures dating from around 1400 to 300 BC.

Sássari
The island's second city also has an excellent archaeological museum, including Punic-era toby jugs and spindly prehistoric bronze statuettes in its collection.

WHEN TO GO

Italians seem to holiday *en masse* in August, deserting the cities in droves to head for the hills, lakes or coast. Prices shoot up, rooms become scarce, and some hotels and restaurants in the cities may close. Short city-breaks are popular all year round, but for self-catering and touring holidays it is better to avoid peak season if you can.

Average daily maximum temperature °C											
London	6	7	10	13	17	20	22	21	19	14	10	7
Rome	6	9	13	17	22	26	28	28	24	20	13	8
	JAN	FEB	MAR	APR	MAY	JUN	JUL	AUG	SEP	OCT	NOV	DEC
Rome	8	5	8	8	7	7	4	5	6	8	11	9
London	15	13	11	12	12	11	12	11	13	13	15	15
Average number of rainy days per month											

Average daily maximum temperature °C											
London	6	7	10	13	17	20	22	21	19	14	10	7
Palermo	16	16	17	20	24	27	30	30	28	25	21	18
	JAN	FEB	MAR	APR	MAY	JUN	JUL	AUG	SEP	OCT	NOV	DEC
Palermo	12	8	8	6	3	2	0	2	4	8	8	10
London	15	13	11	12	12	11	12	11	13	13	15	15
Average number of rainy days per month											

PACKAGE TRAVEL

ALL THE mass-market tour operators offer holidays in Italy, particularly on the Neapolitan Riviera, the Venetian Riviera and the Italian Lakes. Coach tours of the highlights of Italy or of a particular region of Italy such as Sicily or the lakes are also widely available. City breaks are on offer in numerous cities, sometimes with an activity included, such as opera in Milan or Verona. Specialists in self-catering offer a wide variety of accommodation; anything from a modern apartment on the Neapolitan Riviera to a lavish villa in the hills of Tuscany or Umbria.

Tour operators

Battlefields: Holts' Tours, Midas **Birdwatching**: Limosa, Naturetrek **Camping**: Canvas, Eurocamp, Eurosites, Keycamp, Select Sites, Sunsites **City breaks**: Airtours, British Airways Holidays, Cosmos, Cresta, Crystal, Inghams, Italian Escapades, Kirker, Made to Measure, Osprey, Premier, Sovereign, Thomas Cook, Thomson, Time Off, Travelscene **Cultural**: Andante, British Museum Traveller, Martin Randall, Prospect **Specialists**: Abercrombie & Kent, Airtours, Belleair, Bridgewater Travel, Carefree Italy, Citalia, Costa Smeralda, Crystal, CV Travel, Hello Italy, Ilios Island Holidays, Italian Affair, Italiatour, Magic of Italy, Page & Moy, Skybus, Serena, Siesta International, Simply Tuscany & Umbria, Sunvil, Vacanze in Italia, Voyages Ilena **Walking**: Alternative Travel Group, Exodus, Explore Worldwide, Headwater, HF Holidays, Inntravel, Ramblers Holidays, Sherpa, Waymark **Wine**: Arblaster & Clarke, Winetrails **Other activities**: Ace Study Tours, Club Med (all-inclusive), Cox & Kings (flora), Ffestiniog Travel (rail tours), Inter-Church Travel (Christian tours), Highway Journeys (Christian tours), Solo's Holidays (singles), Thermalia (spa)

INDEPENDENT TRAVEL

CHEAP FLIGHTS are not easy to find. There are scheduled flights to most large Italian cities. Charter flights go to Rome, Venice, Milan, Pisa, Naples, Florence, Treviso, Rimini and Catania – also to Bergamo, Turin and Verona in winter. Milan is usually the cheapest charter destination.

Touring independently is not ideal, as car hire and petrol are expensive, and motorway tolls can add up. In addition, local drivers make sure that you never relax at the wheel, particularly in the cities, and parking is often a nightmare. Nevertheless, it is often the only way to see some of the countryside, and it gives you extra flexibility. If you pre-book your car from the UK (usually the cheapest option), check what is included in the price – you often have to pay extra for theft protection when you pick up the car. A British driving licence is acceptable.

The extensive, reasonably reliable and relatively cheap rail network is a good alternative to touring by car, especially if you are visiting the northern cities. You can buy passes that are valid for unlimited rail travel for a certain number of days or a set number of kilometres.

Buses are often quicker than trains, but are usually also more expensive. In cities they usually charge a flat rate, and you must buy tickets before you get on, at tobacconists, news kiosks or at ticket machines. Stamp your ticket in the machine when you board.

Hotels are rated from one to five stars, and bargains are few and far between. Standards in budget *pensioni* vary widely from region to region, and it is pot luck whether you chance on a good place. Italy is best at characterful hotels in converted historic buildings – but you will pay accordingly. Renting a farmhouse or villa is another option, particularly in Tuscany and Umbria. Many agencies and tour operators offer self-catering deals, but the cheapest option is to look at private ads in Sunday papers or magazines like *The Lady*. Remember to get written details of what exactly is included. Most owners require a hefty cash deposit to cover breakages.

RED TAPE, HEALTH AND SAFETY

BRITISH PASSPORT-HOLDERS do not need a visa to visit Italy. Petty theft (pickpocketing and bag-snatching) is common, especially in southern cities like Rome and Naples. Leave valuables in a hotel safe-deposit box and keep your money in a moneybelt worn beneath your clothes rather than in a 'bum bag'. Never leave valuables in a car; even when you are in the vehicle stow your bag under a seat out of sight, as thieves on motorbikes may smash the window and grab your bag from the seat. It is usually safer to park in car parks with attendants.

MORE INFORMATION Italian State Tourist Board, 1 Princes Street, London W1R 8AY, tel 0171–408 1254, brochure line (0891) 600280 (premium rate number), web site: http://www.ipzs.it/enit/

COST OF LIVING £–££

JAPAN

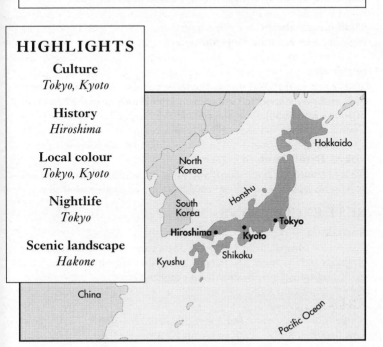

TOKYO
Good for culture, local colour and nightlife

FAST, FRANTIC and crowded, Tokyo still has a lot to offer tourists. Away from the flashing neon, pockets of traditional life thrive all over the city, despite its sprawl of ugly modern buildings, making it a bizarre mix of old meets new and East meets West.

BEST SIGHTS

Asakusa
Senso–ji is Asakusa's main attraction and one of Tokyo's most interesting temples – it has a narrow street of shops within the temple grounds.

Ginza
Ginza is perhaps the most expensive shopping area in the world. Look out for the Sony building on the Sukiyabashi crossing – a vast

building displaying the company's newest and most high-tech products, or watch a traditional Kabuki play at Kabuki-za Theatre.

Meiji-jingu Shrine
Built in memory of the Emperor Meiji.

Shinjuku
Shinjuku train station is one of the busiest in the world. Visit the 45th floor of the Metropolitan Government Offices for one of the best views of Tokyo. The Kabuki-cho, the red light district of Tokyo, is a safe area to walk in and has some excellent restaurants.

Tokyo Disneyland
A great family day out – but if you go at a weekend or on a Japanese holiday be prepared for uncomfortably long queues for almost all rides.

BEST EXCURSIONS
Kamakura
The capital of Japan from 1192 to 1333 is within easy day-trip distance of Tokyo and has many fine temples and shrines. The huge bronze statue of Daibutsu (Great Buddha) was completed in 1252.

Nikko
Nikko also boasts some impressive shrines and temples. The extravagant Tosho-gu Shrine is not to be missed. Also visit Lake Chuzenji with its beautiful scenery and breathtaking Kegon Waterfall.

HAKONE
Good for scenic landscape

THIS MOUNTAINOUS region is especially lovely during the autumn, when the maple leaves turn spectacular colours. If the weather is clement you will also get splendid views of Mount Fuji.

BEST SIGHTS
Hakone Open-Air Art Museum
This impressive museum set in a large area of parkland features work by many Western artists.

Owakudani and Lake Ashi
A cable-car transports you up to steaming volcanic hot springs. Try one of the black, hard-boiled eggs that are cooked in the boiling mud. The cable-car continues up to beautiful Lake Ashi.

KYOTO
Good for culture and local colour

HOME TO the Imperial family from 794 to 1868, Kyoto has too many temples, shrines and gardens to see in just one visit.

BEST SIGHTS
Byodo-in Temple
Byodo-in is pictured on the 10-yen coin.

Kinkaku-ji Temple
Covered in gold-leaf, this is one of the most photographed sights in Japan.

Kiyomizu Temple
This temple's large veranda is built on stilts and juts over the hill.

Ryoan-ji Temple
For a quintessentially Japanese experience head for Ryoan-ji Temple, famous for its traditional Zen garden.

BEST EXCURSIONS
Himeji Castle
The castle was built in 1580 and is one of the finest in Japan.

Nara
Another ancient capital of Japan, Nara has its fair share of temples, shrines and national treasures. Most of the main sights are in Nara Park. The Todai-ji Temple is the largest wooden building in the world and also claims to have one of the largest bronze statues of Buddha.

HIROSHIMA
Good for history

DURING THE Second World War this city was obliterated when the first atom bomb was dropped. The shell-like remains of the Industrial Promotion Hall (now called the Gembaku Domu, or A-bomb Dome) have been left untouched since 8.15am on 6 August 1945.

BEST SIGHTS
Miya-jima
Easily reached from Hiroshima, Miya-jima island is a peaceful place with a 'floating' red torii gate, part of Itsukushima-jinja Shrine, in the bay.

Peace Memorial Park
The central focus of this park is the cenotaph which holds the names of all those killed by the bomb.

The A-bomb Museum
A powerful and moving museum which conveys its message with force.

WHEN TO GO

THE BEST times to visit Japan are spring and autumn. Spring, when the cherry blossom is out, is also the most popular time for Japanese to travel within Japan, so be prepared for large crowds, especially in Tokyo and Kyoto. If possible, avoid 'Golden Week' (end of April to beginning of May), when the entire population of Japan is on holiday. Summer is very hot and humid, and September is the typhoon season.

Average daily maximum temperature °C												
London	6	7	10	13	17	20	22	21	19	14	10	7
Tokyo	8	9	12	17	22	24	28	30	26	21	16	11
	JAN	FEB	MAR	APR	MAY	JUN	JUL	AUG	SEP	OCT	NOV	DEC
Tokyo	5	6	10	10	10	12	10	9	12	11	7	5
London	15	13	11	12	12	11	12	11	13	13	15	15
Average number of rainy days per month												

PACKAGE TRAVEL

JAPAN IS often featured by tour operators as part of a Far Eastern tour, with combinations including Hong Kong, Thailand and Bali. If you want to spend your whole holiday in Japan a popular itinerary includes Tokyo, Kyoto and Nara. Specialist operators offer more extensive options for those who want to see more of the country.

> **Tour operators**
>
> **General**: Asiaworld Travel, Dream Journeys, Far East Gateways, Jasmin Tours, Kuoni, Oriental Magic, Premier Holidays, Virgin Holidays **Specialists**: Creative Tours, Japan Experience, Nippon Travel Agency **Other activities**: British Museum Traveller, Explore Worldwide, Prospect

INDEPENDENT TRAVEL

JAPANESE PEOPLE are generally very friendly towards foreign tourists, keen to practise their English and help you at the same time. The major tourist centres like Tokyo, Kyoto and Nara cater well to visitors: the only time you might encounter problems is if you venture off the beaten track.

The easiest way to get around Japan is by the very efficient and extensive rail network. If you intend to travel any distance in Japan it is worth buying a Japan Rail Pass which allows unlimited travel on the entire Japan Railway (JR) network, including the bullet train (*shinkansen*), JR ferries and JR buses. You must buy a voucher in your home country and validate it once you arrive in Japan. Passes for children aged 6-11 are half-price. In the Hakone region you can buy a Hakone Free Pass, valid for several days: it allows free travel on all forms of transport. Accommodation is not cheap, although a few budget options are available. The Japanese Inn Group is an organisation of *ryokans* (traditional-style inns where you sleep on a futon mattress on the tatami matting floor) and *minshku* (Japanese B&Bs) and is used to foreign guests. Youth hostels are another budget option, as are some of the cheaper business hotels (which have small Western-style rooms). For an unusual experience there are also capsule hotels (which mostly only accept male guests), where you pay for a coffin-sized pod with a TV above you and access to a communal bath, plus bar and restaurant.

RED TAPE, HEALTH AND SAFETY

BRITISH PASSPORT-HOLDERS do not need a visa to visit Japan. Japanese people are famed for their honesty, and there are no particular crime or health problems – just take the usual precautions (see page 12).

MORE INFORMATION Japan National Tourist Organisation, 20 Savile Row, London W1X 1AE, tel 0171-734 9638, web site: http://www.jnoto.go.jp/

COST OF LIVING £££

JORDAN

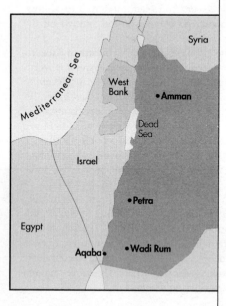

Syria

West Bank

•Amman

Mediterranean Sea

Dead Sea

Israel

•Petra

Egypt

Aqaba•   •Wadi Rum

HIGHLIGHTS

Culture
Amman, Madaba

History
*Desert castles,
Kerak, Jerash,
Petra, Umm Qeis*

Local colour
Wadi Rum

Outdoor activities
Aqaba, Wadi Rum

Romantic escapism
Petra, Wadi Rum

Scenic landscape
*Dead Sea, Petra,
Wadi Rum*

AMMAN
Good for culture, history and scenic landscape

BUILT ON a series of narrow ravines crammed with small white apartment blocks, Amman is a useful base for visiting northern Jordan.

BEST SIGHTS

National Archaeological Museum
Built next to the original citadel, with its ruins of Roman, Byzantine and Islamic buildings, this small but impressive museum has fragments of the Dead Sea Scrolls, plus some fine Roman sculpture.

Roman Theatre
This is the bustling, well-preserved hub of the city. A walk around its nearby streets will reveal a fascinating mix of shops selling Arab bread,

galvanised buckets, or carpets woven with an image of King Hussein. A folklore museum beside the theatre offers insights into the customs and costumes of the Bedouin.

BEST EXCURSIONS

Ajlun
A Saracen fortress built to counter the Crusader threat on the edge of the Jordan plateau. A guide should be available to show you the elaborate battlements and L-shaped hall where Saladin planned his strategy (and jailed the builders to prevent them disclosing defensive secrets).

Dead Sea
The lowest point on earth, the Dead Sea basin radiates furnace-like heat. The high salt content means that floating, rather than swimming, is the only option – but don't shave beforehand, as the salt can be agony if you have any cuts! The Dead Sea Spa Hotel near Suweimeh offers daily rates for bathing.

Desert castles
Out in the barren eastern desert is a scattering of palaces and forts built by the luxury-loving Omayyad caliphs, rulers of the Arab world from AD 661 to 750. They can be covered in a day-trip from Amman.

Furthest east is the squat black fort of Azraq, where Lawrence of Arabia wintered – more interesting for its history than its features. By contrast, the walls of the tiny barrel-vaulted pavilion of Qasr Al-Amra, where the caliphs rested in steam baths after hunting, are covered in lavish frescos. Finally there are the imposing walls and decorative stone windows of Qasr Al-Karaneh. The castle contains almost 100 rooms on two floors, including lofty camel stables.

Jerash
As part of the league of ten free cities known as the Decapolis, Jerash flourished under Roman rule. Well-preserved, it stretches over a vast area. From the magnificent Oval Plaza, you walk along a colonnaded main street lined with temples, a market and a splendid nymphaeum, or public fountain. A ceremonial stairway leads to the Temple of Artemis, which has a pillared sanctuary on top of a stone platform (if you slide your little fingers below the base of a column, you can feel it moving in the wind!). Two restored theatres sit at either end of the site.

Madaba
The Christian roots of this town, which was prosperous in Byzantine times, are much in evidence. St George's church contains a remarkable sixth-century mosaic map of the Near East. For more mosaics, visit the archaeological park in the centre of town, where the remains of a

Byzantine church lie on top of a Roman house. The mosaic floor of the Hippolytus Hall shows mythological figures, while in the Church of the Apostles another huge mosaic is being renovated.

Ten minutes from Madaba, Mount Nebo is the point from which Moses gazed at the Promised Land; a monastery marks the spot where he is said to be buried. Mosaics in the chapel show local wildlife, while nearby is Moses' spring, where fresh water greens the hillside.

Umm Qeis

In a stirring location overlooking the Golan Heights (be prepared for military checkpoints and restrictions) is the former Decapolis city of Gadara. The remains of the Byzantine basilica include a striking mix of black basalt and white limestone columns with a row of vaulted shops beneath, and a basalt theatre. Climb up behind the nymphaeum for a view of the Sea of Galilee, or Lake Tiberias.

KING'S HIGHWAY
Good for history and scenic landscape

THE DESERT Highway is the quickest road to the south, but the scenery is mainly flat and arid. Far more interesting is Route 35, known as the King's Highway since biblical times. This road twists through small, shallow valleys filled with grazing goats and sheep and pockets of fertile farmland.

A string of fortified towns along the way became a significant part of the Crusader empire, preying on caravan trains heading northwards.

BEST CASTLES
Kerak

The most magnificent castle is at Kerak, where dramatic sloping stone escarpments and chunky yellow stone walls are perched on the side of a deep ravine. Many of the sprawling, labyrinthine ruins are virtually subterranean, as the knights and followers wanted to keep cool.

Shobak

On the edge of town is another imposing Crusader fortress, less interesting than Kerak. The guardian will show you around.

AQABA
Good for outdoor activities

JORDAN'S ONLY access point to the sea is not a particularly attractive resort. The town is lively in the evening, but the hotels are showing signs of wear. The beach is only a small strip of sand. The aquarium at the Marine Sciences Centre has an excellent display of local underwater life.

BEST WATER SPORTS

The most worthwhile sight is the wonderful coral reef fringing the coast. The Royal Jordanian Diving Centre offers tuition and easy access to the reef.

PETRA
Good for history, romantic escapism and scenic landscape

FEW ANCIENT wonders can match Petra's magical location: a lost kingdom hidden from sight by arid mountains and reached only through a natural gorge, or *siq*. Forgotten by the West until its rediscovery by the Swiss explorer Jean-Louis Burckhardt in the early nineteenth century, Petra retains its grandeur and romance despite the influx of tourists.

The Nabataeans, a nation of traders at the time of Christ, carved tombs and monuments on an extraordinary scale out of the reddish sandstone. The colours are truly staggering, reflecting every hue of a rosy rainbow.

You need at least two days to make the most of Petra. Be prepared for plenty of walking and climbing – tackle the High Place of Sacrifice and the monastery on separate days, as they are both strenuous climbs. The coolest and least crowded times are early morning and after 4pm. Note that horses are expensive and take you only 300 metres to the entrance of the *siq*; elderly or disabled visitors can hire a carriage to reach the Treasury.

BEST SIGHTS

Treasury
The city's first and most unforgettable monument. The scale and colours are extraordinary – as you move forward, details of the columns, pediments and carved horsemen come into focus. Morning sunshine illuminates the Treasury, so be sure to arrive before 10am.

Viewpoints around Petra
The High Place of Sacrifice is a dramatic table mountain once used for animal sacrifices. Nearby are the reliefs of a Nabataean goddess and a lion and the Garden, Roman Soldier and Renaissance Tombs. In the main valley are the Royal Tombs – the three-storey Palace Tomb, the biggest in Petra, is collapsing to reveal the crazy swirling patterns of the rock beneath. At the end of the Cardo Maximus, the Roman High

Street, is the Qasr El-Bint, a ruined temple with rosette decorations. The façades of the Royal Tombs can be seen from the outcrop of El-Habees at the end of the main valley. The Ed-Deir monastery is an even bigger version of the Treasury, though less intricately carved. The forum museum displays Nabataean pottery and jewellery.

BEST EXCURSIONS
Little Petra
About 20 minutes' drive from Wadi Musa, Siq El-Baared, or Little Petra, is a gorge with some well-preserved tombs and a view across the mountains.

Umm El-Biyarah
This is the highest mountain in Petra, with spectacular views. The path is a little tricky to find (hire a guide).

WADI RUM
Good for local colour, outdoor activities, romantic escapism and scenic landscape

THIS COLOURFUL landscape of sandstone outcrops was the location for the film *Lawrence of Arabia*, and is home to the Bedouin people.

BEST LOCAL COLOUR

The Bedouin are happy to welcome travellers to their encampments, where they inhabit low, open-sided tents of black goat's wool. If you join a group you will probably be treated to communal singing around the fire and a meal of *mensaf* (boiled and roasted goat).

BEST EXCURSIONS

There are plenty of Bedouin around Wadi Rum who can organise a night in the desert, a camel ride, or a four-wheel-drive tour visiting strange rock formations and enigmatic carvings and inscriptions. Some overnight trips are more touristy than others – the tourist office inside Wadi Rum Rest House can give you comprehensive information. Guides can also be found to take you on longer treks and climbs.

WHEN TO GO

MARCH TO May and September to November are the best times to visit, with hot days and cool nights. Aqaba is not warm all year round; Amman and Petra can get very cold in winter. Summer is uncomfortably hot.

Average daily maximum temperature °C

	JAN	FEB	MAR	APR	MAY	JUN	JUL	AUG	SEP	OCT	NOV	DEC
London	6	7	10	13	17	20	22	21	19	14	10	7
Amman	12	13	16	23	28	31	32	32	31	27	21	15
Amman	8	8	4	3	1	0	0	0	0	1	4	5
London	15	13	11	12	12	11	12	11	13	13	15	15

Average number of rainy days per month

PACKAGE TRAVEL

TOUR OPERATORS offer a large range of trips, from cheap over-land jaunts to full-blown archaeological expeditions with lecturers. They all follow a similar route and take around seven to ten days – be sure to choose one that allows enough time at Petra (minimum two days) and Jerash (half a day). Some tours combine Jordan with Israel, Syria or Egypt.

Tours of Jordan follow a predictable route, starting from Amman and stopping off at Jerash, Madaba, the Dead Sea, Mount Nebo, Kerak and Petra, occasionally diverting off the beaten track before finishing in Aqaba on the Red Sea. Some packages focus on Petra, taking you from Amman to Petra and back again – you can book these in the UK and from Israel.

Travel is by coach, minibus or perhaps, on a private tour, by chauffeur-driven car. The more adventurous tour itinerary will include a couple of days in the desert on a camping safari. Other possible extensions include relaxing on the beaches of Sinai and Egypt or a visit to Lebanon.

Activities available include taking part on an archaeological dig and cultural tours, birdwatching and scuba diving.

Tour operators

Adventure: Exodus, Explore Worldwide, Guerba, Top Deck **Birdwatching**: Naturetrek, Sunbird **Cultural**: Andante, British Museum Traveller, Prospect **General**: Abercrombie & Kent, Bales Tours, Cox & Kings, Hayes & Jarvis, Jasmin Tours, Kuoni, Page & Moy, Saga, Titan HiTours, Tradewinds, Travelsphere, Voyages Jules Verne **Scuba diving**: Aquatours, Regal Holidays **Tours from Israel**: Goldenjoy, Israel Travel Service, Pullman Holidays (UK), Superstar Holidays

INDEPENDENT TRAVEL

A PACKAGE holiday will work out cheaper than going independent-ly, as tour operators get better deals on the (expensive) hotel prices, but if you want more freedom, doing it on your own is easy.

The roads are good, so car hire is a feasible option – though stick to taxis in Amman, where the road system is confusing. Alternatively, you can rent a car with a driver at most large hotels in Amman to visit the desert castles, Jerash, Umm Qeis and the Dead Sea. From Amman there are JETT buses to Petra and Aqaba.

RED TAPE, HEALTH AND SAFETY

TO OBTAIN a tourist visa for Jordan, you will need a passport valid for six months, one passport photograph and a completed application form (available from the Jordanian Consulate). A three-month single-entry tourist visa costs £27, a double-entry visa is £48. Courier your application or visit the consulate in person between 9.30am and 1pm, Monday to Friday. Visas take 48 hours to process and can be collected between 1.10 and 2.30pm, Monday to Friday.

Inoculations against hepatitis A, typhoid and polio are recommended. Immunisation against yellow fever is essential if you arrive from an 'infected' country but is not required if you travel direct from the UK.

Jordanians are very friendly, and you are unlikely to be hassled or pressured in shops or markets. When driving, always carry your pass-port, as there are army checkpoints near the border. Female travellers should have no problems as long as they dress conservatively. Both men and women should cover legs and shoulders.

The Foreign Office advises against travel to the West Bank, unless on essential business. For the latest information, contact the Foreign Office Travel Advice Unit (see page 11).

MORE INFORMATION Jordanian Travel Office, 32 Brook Street, London W1Y 1AG, tel 0171-878 6333

No tourist office web site exists, but you can access information about Jordan at: http://www.tourist-offices.org.uk/Jordan/index.html

Jordanian Embassy and Consulate, 6 Upper Phillimore Gardens, London W8 7HB, tel 0171-937 3685, visa information (0891) 171261 (premium rate number)

COST OF LIVING £-££

KENYA

HIGHLIGHTS

**Beaches/
family holidays**
Coast

Local colour
Game parks

Nightlife
Nairobi, coast

**Outdoor activities/
scenic landscape**
Game parks

Romantic escapism
Coast, game parks

Wildlife
Nairobi, game parks

NAIROBI
Good for nightlife and wildlife

THE NATIONAL Museum offers a good introduction to Kenya's fauna. Nairobi National Park, ten minutes from the city centre, has all the plains animals, except elephant, in a remarkably natural environment. Giraffe Manor, Langata, offers close encounters with native wildlife.

The Carnivore (a well-known tourist spot), Bombax Club and many other local clubs feature sizzling live music most nights. You should be prepared to venture into the unknown, hiring a taxi for the whole evening – much of the nightlife takes place on the outskirts of the city.

THE COAST
Good for beaches, family holidays, nightlife and romantic escapism

AS WELL as resorts and beaches, there are superb diving opportunities, and simple snorkelling can be a rewarding experience.

BEST RESORTS AND BEACHES
Several all-inclusive beach resorts offer excellent value for money.
● Turtle Bay at Watamu and Sun 'n' Sand on the north coast are the best for children. Unfortunately these resorts do not give you much of a feel for Kenya.
● Diani Beach is long and fringed with coconut palms.
● Watamu consists of several idyllic bays in the Marine National Park, with limpid water ideal for snorkelling. The coastline can be strewn with seaweed from June to August.

BEST NIGHTLIFE
Diani Beach has some good discos away from the hotels' own (which can be bland). A few minutes north of Mombasa town is Bora Bora, the coast's best nightclub. Malindi has lively nightlife in high season.

BEST FOR ROMANTIC ESCAPISM
Kiwaiyu, Lamu and Msambweni have rustic-style exclusive hotels.

BEST SIGHTS AND EXCURSIONS
The ruins of the mysterious fourteenth-century town of Gedi, near Watamu, include mosques, a palace and stone houses.

BEST LOCAL COLOUR
Lamu island, at the northern end of the coast, is small. The town, Lamu, has to a large extent preserved its medieval town plan. There are no cars on the island: you get about on foot or by *dhow* - (simple, wooden sailing vessel). A fine, often deserted, beach is another attraction.

GAME PARKS
Good for local colour, outdoor activities, romantic escapism, scenic landscape and wildlife

ALTHOUGH KENYA has over 40 parks and reserves only about a dozen are commonly visited. All charge daily fees.

BEST WALKING

All the following are fairly accessible by hired car or public transport and open to walkers (unlike most game parks, which are not, usually because of lions): Mount Kenya National Park (beautiful Afro-alpine vegetation); Hell's Gate (dramatic gorge with plenty of wildlife); Lake Bogoria National Reserve (impressive hot springs and greater kudu antelope); Saiwa Swamp (home of the rare sitatunga antelope).

BEST FOR ROMANTIC ESCAPISM

Upmarket tented safari camps, such as Finch Hattons in Tsavo West, or private safaris, camping wild, can be booked in Maasai Mara and Tsavo East.

BEST LOCAL COLOUR

In the Maasai and Samburu tribal areas traditional costume is worn, with elaborate jewellery and weaponry. Visits to local villages are often arranged while on safari – you pay a fixed fee to the headman and are then free to take photographs. The extreme poverty of the villagers can be disturbing and there is often pressure to buy souvenirs.

BEST WILDLIFE

Overall Maasai Mara, a vast plain of undulating grassland with woodland along the banks of the Mara river (crocodile and hippo), has a huge variety of plains game (elephant, lion, cheetah, antelope and some rhino). The most exciting time to visit is during the annual mass migration of wildebeest, which peaks for three unpredictable weeks some time between August and October. Despite the all-day bumpy, dusty drive or expensive flight from Nairobi, the Mara is very popular; on cheaper safaris you may feel part of a crowd, with other minibuses present. The park can be very muddy during rains, often immediately after Christmas. You can also go on expensive balloon safaris and microlight flights in Maasai Mara.

Samburu, a dry country reserve north of Mount Kenya, is a runner-up, with acacia woodland and superb birdlife near the Ewaso Ngiro river. It has fewer predators than the Mara, but lots of grazing animals.

For birds Kakamega Forest is a patch of equatorial lowland rainforest in western Kenya. Unique bird, monkey, reptile and insect life can be seen on forest walks. This park is not included in ordinary package safaris. Access by hired car or public transport is straightforward, but the park is a day's journey from Nairobi.

For flamingos The endless flocks are usually seen at Lake Nakuru or Lake Bogoria, but the birds are nomadic and very unpredictable. Both parks are less than three hours' drive on good roads from Nairobi.

For views of Kilimanjaro Amboseli is a very busy park of flat plains and swamps, easily reached from Nairobi or the southern coast. It is most famous for its herds of elephant and other plains game, including cheetah and lion, set against the backdrop of Mount Kilimanjaro, over the border in Tanzania. The park is small and there are always other vehicles.

For scenery Tsavo West has hilly, volcanic scenery and a beautiful oasis, Mzima Springs, with hippos and crocodiles. Aberdare is a cool mountain park with rainforest on the lower slopes and moorland on the tops. Observe dramatic waterfalls from many walking routes.

WHEN TO GO

KENYA HAS three seasons: low from Easter to 30 June, mid-season from 1 July to 30 November and high season from 1 December to 31 March. The 'long rains' fall during the low season, when beaches are often wet in the morning. During this 'long rains' safaris can be less rewarding as the animals are dispersed away from rivers and waterholes.

Average daily maximum temperature °C											
London	6	7	10	13	17	20	22	21	19	14	10	7
Mombasa	32	32	33	31	29	29	28	28	29	30	31	32
JAN	FEB	MAR	APR	MAY	JUN	JUL	AUG	SEP	OCT	NOV	DEC
Mombasa	5	4	8	16	18	13	14	15	13	13	11	10
London	15	13	11	12	12	11	12	11	13	13	15	15
Average number of rainy days per month											

Average daily maximum temperature °C											
London	6	7	10	13	17	20	22	21	19	14	10	7
Nairobi	27	28	28	26	25	24	23	23	26	27	25	25
JAN	FEB	MAR	APR	MAY	JUN	JUL	AUG	SEP	OCT	NOV	DEC
Nairobi	5	4	8	16	14	5	4	5	4	7	16	11
London	15	13	11	12	12	11	12	11	13	13	15	15
Average number of rainy days per month											

PACKAGE TRAVEL

THE BASIC choice of package holiday is between beach only and safari-and-beach. If you want for a beach-only option you can still quite easily book a one- to three-night safari. Cheaper packages use charter flights to Mombasa, while the more expensive safari packages tend to use scheduled flights to Nairobi (usually British Airways or Kenya Airways, which is a reliable, generally high-standard airline). If you are going on safari, it is best to schedule your trip for early in your holiday, and relax on the beach afterwards. Some tour operators combine safaris in Kenya with ones in neighbouring Tanzania. Many Kenya specialists are tailor-made safari experts. A few companies offer Kenyan safaris in combination with beach holidays in Zanzibar, Mauritius or even Dubai. If you are going on a Mombasa-based safari-and-beach holiday, you need to bear in mind that after the overnight flight your transfer inland to the national parks will take two to three hours, in high temperatures. Similarly, if you are going directly to a coast hotel, you should find out what the transfer time is. Some journeys take as little as 20 minutes, but the one to Malindi takes about two hours.

Accommodation on the coast varies considerably in quality, from just-about-adequate beach hotels to state-of-the-art palaces. You generally get what you pay for, with food, room size and the variety of facilities on offer being the first casualties of competitive pricing. But further probing of your travel agent or a detailed guide book may reveal good-value hotels that have facilities well above average for the price. Holiday reps tend to have responsibility for several properties and often visit each hotel only once or twice a week. If you have a problem it is often easier to befriend the reception staff, who may go out of their way to transfer you to a more suitable room if one is available.

Accommodation in Nairobi is usually in good-quality town hotels close to the city centre. Most packages that include Nairobi treat it only as a necessary one-night stay.

Accommodation in the game parks is generally in lodges – hotels in the bush designed to provide the best opportunities for relaxation and game viewing. These are built either as conventional hotels, sometimes with the rooms in chalets known as *bandas*, or as comfortable tented lodges, which have 'rooms' made of canvas, with separate,

---

Tour operators

Adventure: Sherpa **Birdwatching**: Limosa, Ornitholidays, Peregrine, Sunbird **General**: Abercrombie & Kent, Airtours, Bales Tours, British Airways Holidays, Cosmos, CV Travel, Elite Vacations, Hayes & Jarvis, Kuoni, Thomson, Tradewinds, Tropical Places, Worldwide Journeys **Specialists**: African Experience, African Safari Club, African Safari Trails, Guerba, Kumuka Expeditions, Somak **Wildlife**: Animal Watch, Wildlife Worldwide thatched, waterproof roofs, mosquito screening and built-in bath-rooms.

Other than safari holidays, activities include birdwatching and adventure holidays. Scuba diving and deep-sea fishing are also available.

INDEPENDENT TRAVEL

CHARTER FLIGHTS to Mombasa are usually available for two- to three-week stays; scheduled flights go to Nairobi.

Independent beach holidays need some research, as there are only a few cheap or reasonably priced hotels on the beach itself. Staying in package-standard hotels on the beach will cost you more than if you were on a package. Inland hotels have a greater range of prices. You can usually find something modest but comfortable quite cheaply.

A British driving licence is sufficient, but car hire is expensive. The commonest hire vehicle is a Suzuki jeep. Check that your vehicle has the necessary windscreen documentation. Driving is on the left. Hiring a car is one way to visit the game parks independently, but buy appro-priate game park maps.

The other way to visit the parks independently is on a locally organ-ised lodge or camping safari, bookable with safari operators in Nairobi or at most coast hotels. Follow word-of-mouth recommendations to get the latest on suitable companies. Try where possible to book directly with the operator, rather than through an agent. One common source of disappointment is to having to spend a long time travelling to the parks, ending up with insufficient time on game drives within them.

If you want to travel around Kenya but do not mind not getting into the parks, the country is well served by buses, which charge very rea-sonable fares. Book seats in advance. For off-the-cuff local travel, you can use *matatus* (shared taxi-minivans), but they are notoriously unsafe.

A single rail route runs from Mombasa to Nairobi, then forks west to Kisumu on Lake Victoria, or north-west to Uganda. If you are head-ing on from Nairobi to the coast, this is the best way to travel. The first-class ticket includes dinner, bed with sheets and blankets, and breakfast. Although most rolling stock is now modern, the journey is a leisurely one, and the service full of charming old-fashioned touches. It is important to book ahead.

Many independent travellers take the opportunity to climb Mount Kenya. Clothing and equipment can be hired in Nairobi or before the ascent. Although any reasonably fit person can reach Point Lenana among the glaciers, you should not rush the climb, as altitude sickness can be very dangerous. Allow at least four days. The view from the top is only occasionally really clear.

RED TAPE, HEALTH AND SAFETY

BRITISH PASSPORT-HOLDERS require a visa. A single-entry visa costs £35 and can be obtained from the Kenya High Commission. Applications are processed within 24 hours of receipt; postal applicants should include an sae.

Consult your GP about the latest recommended vaccinations; anti-malaria tablets are also advisable. Stick to bottled water; in hotels and restaurants the water is boiled first.

Muggings and armed attacks can occur at any time, particularly in Nairobi and Mombasa. Avoid travelling after dark. Do not accept food or drink from strangers. Car-hijackings can also occur – do not attempt to escape from hijackers or resist their demands.

The Foreign Office Travel Advice Unit advises visitors to avoid the North Eastern Province, the Tana River district of Coast Province and the Isiolo and Marsabit district of Eastern Province (apart from the Samburu Game Reserve and, when accompanied by tour operators, the Shaba Game Reserve). Visitors to Lamu Island are advised to travel by air. For further advice, see page 11.

MORE INFORMATION Kenya National Tourist Office, 25 Brooks Mews, London W1Y 1LF, tel 0171-355 3144

No tourist office web site exists, but you can access information about Kenya at: http://www.tourist-offices.org.uk/Kenya/index.html

Kenya High Commission, 45 Portland Place, London W1M 4AS, tel 0171-636 2371

COST OF LIVING £-££

THE MALDIVES

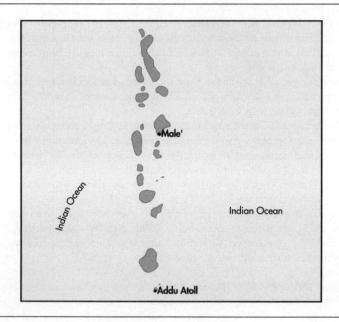

HIGHLIGHTS

Beaches/ scenic landscape	Family holidays	Outdoor activities	Romantic escapism
The resort islands	*Biyadoo, Holiday Island, Kanifinolhu, Laguna Beach*	*Ellaidoo, Bathala, Kuru, Vaadhoo, Biyadoo, Alimatha, Helengeli, Tari Village*	*Banyan Tree, Cocoa Island, Nika, Soneva Fushi*
Culture/ local colour			
Male', Addu Atoll			

THE MALDIVES is a chain of some 26 coral atolls extending 450 miles across the Indian Ocean south-west of Sri Lanka. Each atoll has a ring of reefs, sandbars and islands around a lagoon – officially there are 1,192 islands altogether, none larger than a mile across. About 200 islands have Maldivian communities and another 70 islands have been developed as tourist resorts. Most islands are so tiny you can stroll around them in ten minutes.

MALE'
Good for culture and local colour

THE TINY capital of this Islamic republic is packed with people – some 65,000 permanent residents and as many as 30,000 temporary visitors on a one-square-mile island. The bustling waterfront, winding backstreets and many mosques can be seen in an afternoon's stroll, then you can shop for souvenirs or join the local gentry in a teashop for 'short eats' – little snacks both savoury and sweet.

Much of the action takes place down on the waterfront, where small boats called *dhonis* are the trucks and buses of the Maldives. They shuttle to the airport, which is on a separate island nearly half a mile across the water.

BEST SIGHTS
Grand Friday Mosque
The golden dome of the Grand Friday Mosque shines in the sunlight – it is actually aluminium, but it looks imposing beside the tall white minaret. At around noon on Friday the faithful assemble, quietly coming from every direction, leaving shoes by the thousands around the stairs.

Market
Every evening the fishing fleet comes in and dozens of *dhonis* pull up beside Marine Drive. Elegant silver fish, many more than three feet long, are unloaded by hand and carried across to the market, where the floor is soon tiled with tuna.

THE RESORTS
Good for beaches, family holidays, outdoor activities, romantic escapism and scenic landscape

THE COUNTRY boasts over 70 resorts, each one on its own picture-perfect, palm-fringed island with a pure white beach and a turquoise-blue lagoon. On these resort islands there is no motorised transport.

BEST WATER SPORTS
Diving and snorkelling
The Maldives is famous as a diving destination. Every resort has a diving operation offering courses and trips daily. The whole country consists of coral atolls, and the reefs are carefully preserved. The fish life is amazing – it is like swimming in an aquarium, even with a snorkel just a few feet from the beach.

Experienced divers enjoy the wrecks, the larger marine life (manta rays, turtles, whale sharks, morays and more), and the long drift dives. Some of the best resorts for serious divers are Ellaidoo, Bathala, Kuru, Vaadhoo, Biyadoo, Alimatha and Helengeli.

Surfing

From March to November there is some great surfing in the Maldives, but only a few resorts have accessible 'breaks' (all the surf spots are 'reef breaks', where the waves break over coral reefs). Tari Village is the best resort for surfers, with Lohifushi and Kanifinolhu also possibilities.

BEST FOR FAMILY HOLIDAYS

As a self-contained community, with no traffic and just one resort per island, a Maldives resort can be perfect for families. Try Biyadoo, Club Med, Holiday Island, Kanifinolhu and Laguna Beach.

BEST FOR ROMANTIC ESCAPISM

The most romantic resorts are the small and luxurious getaways such as Banyan Tree, Cocoa Island, Nika and Soneva Fushi.

BEST EXCURSIONS

Safari boats

Increasingly popular 'safari trips' offer one or two weeks' cruising through the atolls on a live-aboard boat. These safari trips are great for getting to the more remote diving sites, visiting uninhabited islands and seeing some different scenery. Make sure you have compatible companions.

ADDU ATOLL
Good for culture and local colour

IN THE far south of the country is Addu Atoll, which was a remote RAF base from 1956 to 1976. The base is now the Ocean Reef Club resort, on the island of Gan, unique because it is linked to neighbouring islands by a causeway. A few trucks and minibuses run along the ten-mile road across the islands and causeways – this is the longest road in the country and quite exceptional.

BEST LOCAL COLOUR

Rent a bicycle from the resort, and pedal across to the adjoining islands of Feydhoo, Maradhoo and Hithadhoo. The villages have straight sandy streets, shady trees, old mosques and coral-stone houses. It is a world of its own – traditional, unhurried and as well-ordered as the tenets of Islam.

WHEN TO GO

DECEMBER TO April is the dry season, though it can rain a little. It is the peak tourist season too, when resorts can be fully booked and prices are higher.

The Christmas to New Year period is the busiest and most expensive time. From May to November the skies can be cloudy, humidity is higher and rainstorms are more likely. There are fewer people and lower prices, though August is more expensive.

	Average daily maximum temperature °C											
London	6	7	10	13	17	20	22	21	19	14	10	7
Minnicoy	29	29	30	31	31	30	29	29	29	29	29	29
	JAN	FEB	MAR	APR	MAY	JUN	JUL	AUG	SEP	OCT	NOV	DEC
Minnicoy	3	1	1	3	9	17	14	12	10	11	8	4
London	15	13	11	12	12	11	12	11	13	13	15	15
	Average number of rainy days per month											

PACKAGE TRAVEL

NEARLY ALL the visitors to the Maldives are on package holidays. Most mainstream tour operators feature the Maldives in their long-haul brochures and there are direct charter and scheduled flights into Male'. Most of the tourist resorts featured are scattered among the three main groups of islands: North Male' Atoll, South Male' Atoll and Ari Atoll to the west. Transfers from the airport are by boat, helicopter or seaplane.

Nearly all of the beach resorts occupy their own tiny island and there is a variety of styles and budgets to choose from – from the exclusive and highly sophisticated to simple, laid-back resorts with few frills. Accommodation is in small huts and can be basic with ceiling fans and unheated water. Packages are on a half-board, full-board or all-inclusive basis. Entertainment is low-key with maybe an occasional barbecue or Maldivian theme evening. Each resort has its own water sports and diving centre and non-motorised water sports tend to be free (depending on the resort).

Scuba diving packages can be pre-booked through a tour operator. You can also take a cruise through the islands or combine the Maldives with destinations such as Sri Lanka (around 400 miles away), Dubai and Singapore.

> **Tour operators**
>
> **General**: Abercrombie & Kent, Airtours, Airwaves, Asiaworld Travel, British Airways Holidays, Coromandel, CV Travel, Elegant Resorts, Elite Vacations, Hayes & Jarvis, ITC, Kuoni, Premier Holidays, Steppes East, Sunset Travel, Sunworld, Thomson, Tradewinds, Trailfinders, Tropical Places, Worldwide Journeys **Multi-activitiy**: Club Med **Scuba diving**: Aquatours, Regal Holidays

INDEPENDENT TRAVEL

IT IS almost impossible to travel independently. If you arrive without a hotel reservation, the immigration authorities will ask you to make arrangements with a tour operator before you leave the airport. Government policy restricts visitors to Male' and resorts in the 'tourism zone'. A permit is required to go outside this zone, for which you need a sponsor from a local island.

RED TAPE, HEALTH AND SAFETY

BRITISH PASSPORT-HOLDERS are given a free 30-day visitor's permit on arrival. Visitors should have a return ticket and US$25 for every day of their intended stay.

The Maldives is remarkably free of health problems and crime, especially the resorts, but inoculations against hepatitis A, typhoid and polio are recommended. If arriving from an 'infected' country, immunisation against yellow fever is essential. Consult your GP or a travel clinic for the latest health advice before departure. Scuba diving presents some risks, and divers should have insurance which covers them for helicopter evacuation and decompression treatment.

No alcohol, pornography, pork, narcotics, spearguns or 'idols of worship' can be brought into the country. Baggage is searched, and any alcohol will be taken and held until departure. Magazines may be regarded as pornographic if they contain advertisements showing women in underwear. Export of turtle shell (sometimes called 'tortoiseshell'), or any turtle shell products, is forbidden.

MORE INFORMATION The Maldives High Commission, 22 Nottingham Place, London W1M 3FB, tel 0171-224 2135, web site: http://www.visitmaldives.com

COST OF LIVING £-££

MALTA

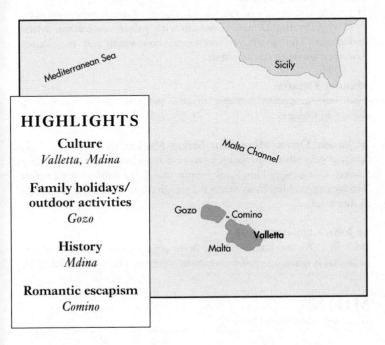

Mediterranean Sea

Sicily

Malta Channel

Gozo

Comino

Valletta

Malta

HIGHLIGHTS

Culture
Valletta, Mdina

**Family holidays/
outdoor activities**
Gozo

History
Mdina

Romantic escapism
Comino

VALLETTA
Good for culture

PLANNED IN 1565 as both a fortress and a city home for the Knights of St John, the capital still has an aristocratic air. It is comparatively small, but inside its bastion walls is a rollercoaster grid of narrow streets and endless stairs. Walk it during the daytime, when it is alive with people.

BEST SIGHTS

Admiralty House/Museum of Fine Arts
Originally a knight's private residence, it was until 1961 the headquarters of the British Mediterranean fleet. There are 30 rooms of exhibits.

Auberge de Provence/Museum of Archaeology
This 1571 hall of residence for the Knights from Provence now

contains most of the prehistoric finds from the islands (under refur-
bishment at the time of going to press).

Grand Master's Palace
The former residence of the Grand Master of the Knights and until
1928 that of the British Governor, the palace houses the Malta
Parliament. The principal staterooms, courtyards and the Palace
Armoury are open to the public.

Manoel Theatre
Tiny but sumptuous baroque theatre: the third-oldest functioning
theatre in Europe.

St James' Ditch/Merchants Street Market
Situated beneath the eponymous bastion is a vibrant Sunday morning
market selling everything from puppies and Tiger Balm to the English
Sunday papers. Merchants Street is a scaled-down daily version and not
as much fun.

St John's Co-cathedral
Built in 1578, this houses Malta's finest art treasures. The floor of the
cathedral is made up of 400 tessellated tombs of pre-eminent Knights.

MDINA
Good for culture and history

PUT THE old capital of Malta at the top of your 'sights to see' list.
Dating from the twelfth century, it has been preserved and is mostly
devoid of tacky modern development. St Paul's Cathedral is the most
skilful piece of Maltese baroque architecture anywhere and is built on
the site where St Paul converted the Roman governor Publius to
Christianity.

GOZO
Good for family holidays and outdoor activities

GOZO IS the least spoilt corner of the archipelago. Malta's smaller
sister island, five miles away, is reached either by a heli-link or a ferry
service. It is greener, more tranquil and yet sophisticated. The diving,
walking and rock-bathing is better than on Malta. If you want a
quiet, family, villa-type holiday bypass Malta altogether and head for
a farmhouse on Gozo. Do not miss a Gozitan summer *festa* (see
'When to go').

BEST SIGHTS

Mgarr harbour

Mgarr harbour has all the hubbub of a local ferry terminus and three excellent waterside restaurants. The best bar on the island, the Gleneagles, is here too.

Sannat

Sannat is good for cliff walking, and on cooler afternoons traditional lace-makers weave in the shade. The excellent Hotel Ta'Cenc is near-by.

Victoria (Rabat)

This is the hub of Gozo's cosmos. The bus terminus, morning market, powerful local wine, patriarchal 'citadel' and dinky museums make it almost a daily 'must'.

Xaghra

This is the tranquil village from which to start and finish scenic walks through what used to be the Grand Master's hunting grounds. The prehistoric 'temples' of Ggantija are easily accessed from here.

COMINO
Good for romantic escapism

FLECKED WITH sparse vegetation and overgrown dry-stone walls, Comino from afar seems barren and unappealing. But it boasts some attractive rocky bays, just one hotel and a smattering of local inhabitants. It is ideal for those who enjoy an away-from-it-all holiday after the day-tripper boats have left in the afternoon.

WHEN TO GO

DUE TO its geographical position Malta enjoys a long season: from April to October. Visit in May to see a surprisingly verdant island and its wild flowers; go in July and August if you do not mind crowds and the aroma of sun oil, and in September and October if you want to see a country gently unwind.

King Carnival, a celebration of decorated floats and open-air dancing, is held during the four days before Ash Wednesday. Holy Week celebrations include Maundy Thursday pilgrimages, Good Friday pageants and Easter Sunday processions. Village *festi*, in honour of the local patron saint, are held nearly every weekend in summer.

	Average daily maximum temperature °C											
London	6	7	10	13	17	20	22	21	19	14	10	7
Valletta	14	15	16	18	22	26	29	29	27	24	20	16
	JAN	FEB	MAR	APR	MAY	JUN	JUL	AUG	SEP	OCT	NOV	DEC
Valletta	12	8	5	2	2	0	0	1	3	6	9	13
London	15	13	11	12	12	11	12	11	13	13	15	15
	Average number of rainy days per month											

PACKAGE TRAVEL

BECAUSE OF their small size the islands can be treated as one industrial-sized resort. Just about everywhere is accessible – even on Gozo. All the hotels are three-star standard or better. It cannot be emphasised enough that long stretches of sandy beaches do not exist in Malta; but the water is more often than not substantially cleaner than on a 'costa'. Many of the principal hotels have large pools and sea access off the rocks, from which the elderly and very young should exercise caution.

Packages to Malta are cheap compared with many other Mediterranean destinations. All major tour operators go there, and most packages offer hotel and self-catering apartments in the main beach resorts. Many tour operators also offer the island of Gozo, alone or as part of a two-centre holiday. Here there are also farmhouses converted into upmarket self-catering or hotel accommodation.

Only a handful of specialist tour operators offers holidays on Comino. Package accommodation is limited to the single hotel around which most of the tourist activities on the island revolve. Specialist activities on the islands include Christian or cultural tours, golf, sailing, scuba diving and walking.

Tour operators

Church tours: Inter-Church Travel, McCabe Travel **Cultural**: Martin Randall, Prospect **General**: Airtours, Aquasun, Belleair, Cadogan, Chevron Air, Cosmos, Crystal, First Choice, Inghams, Sunworld, Thomas Cook, Thomson, Unijet **Golf**: Aquasun, Belleair, Malta Direct **Scuba diving**: Aquasun, Aquatours, Belleair, Gozo Holidays, Malta Direct, Sunspot Tours **Short breaks**: Belleair, Cresta, Inghams, Malta Direct **Walking**: HF Holidays, Ramblers Holidays

---

INDEPENDENT TRAVEL

VERY FEW British tourists visit Malta independently. The odd buc-caneering soul turns up on a cargo vessel from northern Italy but most, due to the sheer economic weight of numbers, book flights and accommodation through an operator.

Air Malta, Air 2000, Britannia and British Airways operate both scheduled and charter flights. Regular ferry services leave from Naples in Southern Italy, and Catania and Syracuse on Sicily.

Malta has the cheapest car-hire rates in Europe. Driving is on the left; a British driving licence is acceptable. Some car-hire firms have a minimum age limit of 25 and a maximum age limit of 70: check when booking. Maltese driving leaves much to be desired. Most of the roads are unlit and outside the main towns there are no pavements. Extreme care should be taken when driving, and pedestrians should always walk facing oncoming traffic.

The main bus terminus is in Valletta, from where buses go to all parts of Malta, though there are also direct point-to-point services. Taxis are all fitted with meters.

The Gozo Channel Company operates a car-passenger ferry service between Malta and Gozo, with about 30 crossings each way daily in summer. In peak season a hydrofoil service links Malta, Gozo and Comino. Air Malta also runs a helicopter service linking Malta and Gozo (stopping at Comino on request).

RED TAPE, HEALTH AND SAFETY

BRITISH PASSPORT-HOLDERS do not require a visa. Tap water is safe to drink, and the crime rate is relatively low – just take the usual precautions (see page 12). Topless bathing is illegal.

MORE INFORMATION Malta National Tourist Office, Malta House, 36-38 Piccadilly, London W1V 0PP, tel 0171-292 4900, web site: http://www.tourism.org.mt

COST OF LIVING *££–£££*

MEXICO

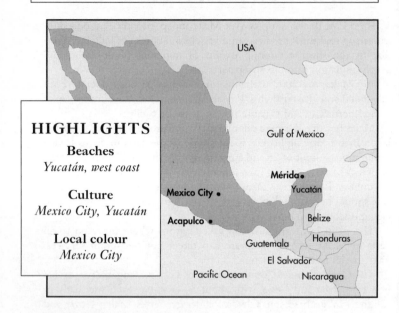

USA

Gulf of Mexico

HIGHLIGHTS

Beaches
Yucatán, west coast

Culture
Mexico City, Yucatán

Local colour
Mexico City

Mérida •
Yucatán

Mexico City •

Acapulco •

Belize

Guatemala

Honduras

El Salvador

Pacific Ocean

Nicaragua

MEXICO CITY
Good for culture and local colour

THIS IS a vast, smoggy, sprawling, poverty-stricken city, but one with some exquisite historical sights and bags of character. You will warm to this place rather than being bowled over by it.

BEST SIGHTS
Museo Nacional de Antropologìa
Astonishing artefacts from every middle-American civilisation are displayed in halls surrounding a central courtyard. The Mayan collection is a must if you plan to go on to the archaeological sights in the Yucatán.

Zócalo
This vast open square in the historic centre of the city is bordered by the sinking baroque cathedral, the Palacio Nacional (coated with Diego Rivera's murals inside) and busy shopping and sightseeing streets.

BEST EXCURSION
Teotihuacán
The Aztec capital is an hour's drive from the city. Two great pyramids

dominate the site – from the summits the ceremonial design of the city unfolds along the mile-and-a-half length of the Avenue of the Dead.

WEST COAST
Good for beaches

MEXICO IS a popular sun-and-sand destination for Americans, who flock to the two biggest resorts on the west coast – Acapulco and Puerto Vallarta (also offered by British tour operators). Both have large beaches and continuous runs of fast-food outlets, malls and high-rise hotels.

YUCATAN PENINSULA
Good for beaches and culture

BEST RESORT

Cancún
● Purpose-built resort; modern US-style hotels line a 15-mile sandbar.
● The turquoise waters of the Caribbean Sea lap one side and an inky-coloured lagoon fringed with mangroves the other.
● Plushest of novelty palaces are at furthest end of the sandbar, with older hotels, malls and water-sports complexes nearer to the mainland.
● Hotel beaches and grounds are very appealing, but food and drink are ferociously expensive; there is very little to do away from the water.
● The Mayan sights, Chichén Itzá and Tulúm, are easy day-trips.

BEST MAYAN SIGHTS

The scrub-like jungle that coats the flat Yucatán peninsula in southern Mexico hides an untold number of mysterious ruins – the remains of the Mayan civilisation that ruled before the Spanish conquest. A few lost cities have been rescued from the undergrowth.

Chichén Itzá
Probably the best-known and most visited Mayan sight. Complexes of temples rise from an expanse of green lawn. Kukulcan's Pyramid is the dominating central structure, overlooking the massed ranks of sculpted columns in the Temple of the Warriors and the vast I-shaped ball court.

Cobá
An out-of-the-way sight, unsung, unexploited and largely unexcavated, where one can recapture the feeling of discovery. Tramp through paths skittering with iguanas to the Nohoch Mull pyramid, for a view across the lurid green Lake Cobá and the surrounding jungle.

Palenque

The best setting of all the sites, with rainforest coating the hills behind the sandy stone of what was once a powerful city. Reliefs of warriors and gods in stucco and stone guard the palaces and temples.

Tulúm

A collection of ruins in a spectacular setting – a white sand beach overlooked by two ruined towers on the cliffs.

Uxmal

The most beautiful of the Mayan cities for the elaborate decoration of the stones smothered with geometric gargoyles, zigzags and diamond lattice work. A string of smaller sites in the vicinity is worth visiting.

WHEN TO GO

THE YUCATAN is always blisteringly hot, and breathlessly humid in the rainy season (May to September). November is a good month to travel, before prices rise for the winter season, when the weather is best.

Average daily maximum temperature °C											
London	6	7	10	13	17	20	22	21	19	14	10	7
Mérida	28	29	31	33	33	33	32	32	32	30	28	28
	JAN	FEB	MAR	APR	MAY	JUN	JUL	AUG	SEP	OCT	NOV	DEC
Mérida	4	4	3	3	6	13	15	13	17	10	6	6
London	15	13	11	12	12	11	12	11	13	13	15	15
Average number of rainy days per month											

PACKAGE TRAVEL

Tour operators

Activities: American Adventures (camping), Animal Watch (whale watching), Trek America (adventure camping) **General**: British Airways Holidays, Cosmos, First Choice, Hayes & Jarvis, Kuoni, Sunworld, Thomas Cook, Thomson, Unijet **Tailor-made tours**: Bales Tours, Cox & Kings, Encounter Overland, Exodus, Explore Worldwide, Journey Latin America, Latin America Travel, Nomadic Thoughts, South American Experience

MAINSTREAM TOUR operators offer beach packages in Acapulco, Puerto Vallarta or Cancún, or combine a tour of the sights of the Yucatán peninsula with a week on a beach. Prices, routes and hotels vary considerably. Some specialists will tailor-make packages for you.

INDEPENDENT TRAVEL

TRAVELLING INDEPENDENTLY in Mexico requires stamina, and it helps if you speak and understand a little Spanish. Reaching the Mayan ruins by public transport is difficult, so car hire is essential despite the expense. There are some excellent new highways, but away from large conurbations road conditions often leave something to be desired.

Scheduled flights go to Mexico City, charter flights to Cancún and Puerto Vallarta. Internal flights can save time and are likely to be more comfortable than a hot bus-ride (the main way to get around). Long-distance buses usually have air-conditioning. These are reasonably comfortable, local rural buses considerably less so. Shared minibuses and taxis may be a better option. Trains are cheaper and even slower than buses, and are recommended only for really long journeys.

In theory, hotels and prices are regulated by the tourism authorities, but due to stupendous inflation, prices have usually increased to more than those advertised. Always ask for a reduction on the quoted price of hotels. Be sure to see the room before agreeing to take it. Air-conditioning costs more. Very few official campsites exist.

RED TAPE, HEALTH AND SAFETY

BRITISH PASSPORT-HOLDERS do not require a visa to enter Mexico. Montezuma's Revenge, or upset stomach, is the commonest health problem – see page 11 for tips on how to avoid it. Air pollution is at its highest in Mexico City between December and May. See your GP or a travel clinic for advice on recommended vaccinations.

In October 1997, Hurricane Pauline blasted the Pacific coast, killing at least 59 people. Some luxury hotels were shut down.

The Foreign Office warns about the risk of armed robbery in urban areas – do not resist, and avoid travel after dark and isolated beaches at all times. For the latest advice contact the Travel Advice Unit (see page 11).

MORE INFORMATION Mexican Ministry of Tourism, 60–61 Trafalgar Square, London WC2N 5DS, tel 0171-734 1058, web site: http://www.mexico/travel.com/

COST OF LIVING £-££

MOROCCO

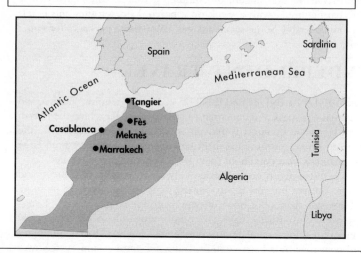

HIGHLIGHTS

Culture
Middle Atlas, High Atlas

Shopping
Fès, Mèknes, Marrakech

Scenic landscape
South Morocco and Sahara

Local colour
Middle Atlas,

Northern Morocco

Outdoor activities
Essaouira, High Atlas,

Northern Morocco

Beaches
Agadir, Asilah, Essaouira

NORTHERN MOROCCO
Good for local colour and outdoor activities

BEST SIGHTS

Rif Mountains

The saw-toothed crags of the Rif are excellent hiking country. The trips focus on the relaxed little town of Chefchaouen, which is hardly more than a village. The cool air and friendly, pester-free ambience is a relief after Tangier.

Tétouan is worth a trip for the Medina and Andalusian heritage: Spanish is still spoken widely. Be prepared for maximum hassle.

Tangier

The word 'cosmopolitan' could have been invented to describe

Tangier. It is a seedy old roué of a town that bears the marks of every race or civilisation that has passed through. Smuggling, drug-running and illegal immigrants to Spain – in fact, money made by whatever dubious means – are Tangier's real trade. The main points of interest centre on the Grand Socco at the entrance to the Medina, and the Petit Socco inside the walls. The fortified Kasbah gives great views over the sweep of the bay. Unfortunately, the touts and hustlers are so tenacious that they spoil many people's visits. Have a drink in the Tanger Inn for a taste of the Tangier that once attracted writers such as Paul Bowles and William Burroughs.

MIDDLE ATLAS
Good for culture, local colour and shopping

IF YOU do nothing else in Morocco, see the imperial cities — Fès, Meknès and Rabat. You can whizz around them quite quickly if time is limited, although two weeks is a realistic timespan. The medinas (or old towns), rather than the modern parts of the cities, are the focus of interest.

Fès
Visiting Fès's medina is perhaps the highlight of any trip to Morocco. It is a step back to another age, into a walled medieval labyrinth, whose colours, smells, noise and bustle are as much a shock to the system as, say, a first visit to India. The down side – and it is a large one – are the armies of touts and would-be guides who can make this wonderful experience hellish.

The best way to take it all in is just to follow your nose through the souks (the henna souk is especially fascinating) and bazaars, ferret around, drink mint tea and not worry too much about getting lost – you will inevitably do so, but there are various walls and landmarks to help out with orientation. Try to visit the tanneries for a fragrant experience of local colour. The mosques and *medersas* (theological colleges) are masterpieces of architecture dating back to the twelfth century. Look for the Medersa bou Inania, Medersa el Attarine and Kairouine mosque. Sadly, the mosques are off-limits to non-Muslims, and the restored Royal Palace, Dar el-Makhzen, is not open to the public.

Meknès
Meknès owes its current position of fame to Sultan Moulay Ismail's barbarous reign in the seventeenth century; he came to power in 1672, a time when Meknès had fallen into obscurity. During his 55-year reign he endowed the town with an enormous palace and 15 miles of walls. As head of the Alawite dynasty he introduced an

unprecedented period of stability to Morocco by butchering all his enemies and any dissenting elements mercilessly. The massive palace complex is the focal point of this city. Exploring Meknès involves less hassle than Fès, although it is certainly not a 'guide-free' zone. The Bab el-Mansour gateway is one of the most magnificent in the country. The usual restrictions on visiting mosques and palaces apply. The more peaceful atmosphere of the souks and bazaars is particularly enjoyable here.

Rabat

Rabat is Morocco's modern capital and seat of government. King Hassan resides here, so the city has a rather orderly feel. It is definitely the most relaxed of the imperial cities. Its main highlights are the Kasbah des Oudaias, Tour Hassan and the Necropolis of Chellah. The medina is fascinating, and the comparative lack of hassle and hustle is quite a relief but somehow less interesting than the spectacular chaos of Fès or Marrakech. Visit the neighbouring town of Salé for its unspoilt and tranquil medina.

ATLANTIC COAST
Good for beaches and outdoor activities

HUNDREDS OF miles of beaches cover the coast between Tangier and Mauritania.

BEST RESORTS AND BEACHES
Agadir
● Morocco's main package destination is clean and modern, but expensive.
● Great sheltered beaches and good restaurants but lacks Moroccan character.

Asilah
● Relaxed and low-key resort town being smartened up for wealthy Moroccan and European holidaymakers.
● Portuguese walls date from the fifteenth century.

Essaouira
● Fortified town with delightful cool blue whitewashed houses and lazy squares.
● Fantastic beaches, world-class windsurfing, no hassle or hard sell.
● Good for thuya wood carvings, thuya being the most common tree in the Essaouira hinterland.

BEST EXCURSION
Taroudannt
The walled city of Taroudannt, 53 miles inland from the coast, is unmissable if you are in the area. It is one of the highlights of Morocco. Hordes of day-trippers from Agadir invade during the day, but it retains a quintessentially south Moroccan character. Browse through the souks or explore the tanneries, kasbah and crumbly ramparts.

HIGH ATLAS
Good for culture, outdoor activities and shopping

BEST SIGHTS
High Atlas
Treks are a viable option for the fit and adventurous. Morocco's highest peak is the 13,745-ft Jebel Toubkal. The views are spectacular, but this is a fairly serious undertaking and a guide is necessary. Less hardy types could opt for a day-trip out from Marrakech to the gorgeous waterfalls of Cascades d'Ouzoud.

Marrakech
Indelibly printed on the 'sixties hippy trail, the ochre ramparts of Marrakech are now Morocco's biggest puller of tourists. The almost permanently snowcapped Atlas Mountains provide an unbeatable and incongruous backdrop to the exotic tumult of the old town. The heart of this quarter is a surprisingly open and vast square, the Djemaa el-Fna, pinpointed by the landmark Koutoubia mosque. Evening is the best time to visit, when snake charmers, jugglers, story tellers, magicians and fakirs put on a Brueghelian show for tourists and locals alike.

Islamic architecture buffs should seek out the Ali ben Youssef mosque and *medersa*, Mouassine mosque and El Badi Palace. Unlike other Moroccan museums, which can be rather disappointing, the Museum of Moroccan Arts is well worth a visit for the spectacular crafts and artefacts housed in the Dar Si Said, a lavishly decorated merchant's town house. Marrakech souks are brilliant as long as you have mastered the art of haggling. If you are unsure of your bargaining skills, beware, as the merchants are mercilessly rapacious.

THE SOUTH AND SAHARA
Good for scenic landscape

IT PAYS to hire a car and tour this region at your own pace to appreciate the awesome natural beauty of the region, with its mountains, valleys, oases and villages untouched by tourism or the twentieth century.

BEST SIGHT

Ouarzazate is worth a stop-off to see the kasbah, although there is a better one in nearby Ait Benhaddou, which has featured in many films, including *Jesus of Nazareth* and *Lawrence of Arabia*.

BEST LANDSCAPE

Dadès Valley

More stunning scenery east of Ouarzazate. Of special interest are the kasbahs around Skoura, and impressive mountains of the Dadès and Todra Gorges. From Erfoud you could extend the tour along the Ziz Valley.

Drâa Valley

This leads south-east from Ouarzazate through a spectacular variety of gorges, kasbahs, date-producing *palmeraies*, to a first glimpse of the Sahara's magnificent dunes. The towns themselves have little of interest, but offer an insight into authentic rural life.

WHEN TO GO

THE MAIN religious holiday period is Ramadan, which usually begins in December or January and lasts for about a month. The faithful are expected to fast during the day, and opening times are disrupted. The end of Ramadan is marked by four or five days of family festivities (rather like Christmas) and can also be an awkward time to travel.

Average daily maximum temperature °C											
London	6	7	10	13	17	20	22	21	19	14	10	7
Agadir	19	21	23	23	24	25	27	27	27	26	24	21
	JAN	FEB	MAR	APR	MAY	JUN	JUL	AUG	SEP	OCT	NOV	DEC
Agadir	6	4	5	3	2	1	0	<1	1	4	5	5
London	15	13	11	12	12	11	12	11	13	13	15	15
Average number of rainy days per month											

Average daily maximum temperature °C											
London	6	7	10	13	17	20	22	21	19	14	10	7
Fès	15	18	20	22	26	31	36	36	32	26	20	16
	JAN	FEB	MAR	APR	MAY	JUN	JUL	AUG	SEP	OCT	NOV	DEC
Fès	12	9	12	9	6	4	1	1	3	7	11	12
London	15	13	11	12	12	11	12	11	13	13	15	15
Average number of rainy days per month											

PACKAGE TRAVEL

MOST TOUR operators offer the beach resort of Agadir or visit Tangier or Marrakech and perhaps offer a southern coach tour. Specialists offer the inland towns of Taroudannt and Fès, Zagora, Ouarzazate, southern tours, Land-Rover safaris and trekking in the High Atlas mountains. City breaks on offer are to Marrakech.

Activities include walking, horse-trekking, birdwatching, natural history tours and camping safaris.

Tour operators

Birdwatching: Naturetrek, Ornithology, Sunbird **Camping safaris**: Acacia, Guerba, Worldwide Journeys **City breaks**: British Airways Holidays, Sovereign, Travelscene **Cultural**: Martin Randall, Prospect **General**: Abercrombie & Kent, Best of Morocco, Cadogan, Cosmos, CV Travel, Goldenjoy, Hayes & Jarvis, Inspirations, Prestige, Steppes East, Thomas Cook **Walking**: Exodus, Explore Worldwide, Headwater, Peregrine, Ramblers Holidays, Sherpa **Other activities**: Andante (archaeology), British Museum Traveller (cultural), Club Med (multi-activity), Cosmos (coach tours), Peregrine (riding), Solo's (singles)

INDEPENDENT TRAVEL

SCHEDULED FLIGHTS run from London to Tangier, Casablanca, Marrakech and Agadir.

High-speed trains operate between Rabat and Casablanca, and Casablanca and Marrakech; slower services link major towns and cities. There are two classes: in hot weather it is worth paying extra to go first-class for the air-conditioning.

Several companies run coach services, which cover most of the country. Although they are fast, they tend to stop at nearly every town, sometimes for as long as half an hour, which adds considerably to the length of the journey. Nevertheless, it is a good way to experience local colour, if you are not in a hurry. Coach travel is usually slightly more expensive than economy class on trains.

Morocco has a well-maintained road system as well as a network of unsurfaced mountain and desert tracks (some of which are passable only in a four-wheel-drive vehicle). Driving regulations are similar to those of France – remember the *priorité à droite*. A British driving licence is normally sufficient, but some smaller hire-car agencies may require an international driving permit. It is best not to drive at night. Look out for animals straying on to the roads, slow-moving horse-drawn carts and local children.

Hotels are classified from one to five stars, and prices are fixed by the Ministry of Tourism. Plenty of unclassified hotels vary their prices according to season and how much they think they can squeeze out of you. Rooms in cheaper hotels tend to be small, if clean and basic, and many do not have hot water – you have to use public baths or showers. More expensive hotels may be renovated older palaces or modern, 'international'-style buildings.

There are quite a few campsites, but all the extra charges for hot water, electricity, cars or motorbikes can add up, and it is often almost as cheap to plump for a hotel.

RED TAPE, HEALTH AND SAFETY

NO VISA is required by British passport-holders. For the latest advice on recommended vaccinations, see your GP or a specialist travel clinic.

Hustlers are a way of life in Morocco. On foot or motorbike, they are very persistent, trying to direct you to hotels or leatherware shops. Sometimes they will say they are guides and offer to show you round the old city. All official guides have a badge and identity card issued by the Ministry of Tourism, and you are advised not to employ anyone who is not qualified.

Contact the Foreign Office Travel Advice Unit (see page 11) for the latest advice on safety and security.

MORE INFORMATION Moroccan National Tourist Office, 205 Regent Street, London W1R 7DE, tel 0171-437 0073

No tourist office web site exists, but you can access information about Morocco at: http://www.tourist-offices.org.uk/Morocco/index.html

COST OF LIVING £

NAMIBIA

HIGHLIGHTS

Local colour	**Wildlife**	**Outdoor activities**	**Scenic landscape**
Bushmanland, Kaokoland and Damaraland, Lüderitz	*Namib-Naukluft National Park, Etosha National Park, Waterberg Plateau, Skeleton Coast*	*Namib-Naukluft National Park, Etosha National Park*	*Namib-Naukluft National Park, Etosha National Park, coast*
History *Lüderitz*			

SOUTHERN AND CENTRAL NAMIBIA
Good for outdoor activities, scenic landscape and wildlife

BEST SIGHTS

Fish River Canyon

The second-largest canyon in the world, yet virtually unknown so you will share the dramatic viewpoints with only a handful of other people, or maybe get the whole place to yourself. A tough five-day hiking trail is provided for those wishing for a more in-depth introduction.

Namib-Naukluft National Park

The Namib Desert stretches the length of Namibia. This national park is the most accessible area for tourists. The giant sand-dunes at Sossusvlei are an absolute must-see, particularly dramatic at sunset or sunrise. Sharply contrasting, the rocky Naukluft Plateau is an oasis for wildlife and an excellent hiking area.

Windhoek

Namibia was briefly a German colony and Windhoek, the capital, retains a Germanic flavour, now interestingly mixed with local African styles. It is not worth setting aside more than a day to take in the atmosphere of this small, pleasant city.

NORTHERN NAMIBIA

Good for local colour, outdoor activities, scenic landscape and wildlife

BEST SIGHTS

Bushmanland

The Bushman people (more correctly called San) are Namibia's original inhabitants, a fascinating race adapted to desert life, now pushed to the country's margins and on the verge of extinction. Their current homeland, a remote, roadless area, is accessible only by organised tour or skilful self-drive.

Etosha National Park

One of the finest wildlife reserves in Africa, occupying semi-desert landscape with a seasonal lake that attracts huge herds of animals. Excellent game-viewing, good accommodation options and straightforward access (by hire car or locally organised tour).

Kaokoland and Damaraland

Kaokoland is the most remote of all Namibia's wild areas – its rugged landscape may be appreciated only by true wilderness fans. The local Himba people are culturally intact, maintaining traditional dress and lifestyle. Damaraland is more accessible, and has the intriguing 'natural gallery' of ancient Bushman rock art at Twyfelfontein.

Waterberg Plateau

A smaller park, often overshadowed by Etosha National Park, but with a contrasting rocky and vegetated landscape. Game-viewing is rewarding but more specialised. Short and long wilderness hiking trails are also available.

THE COAST
Good for history, local colour, scenic landscape and wildlife

ICY OCEAN currents hinder plant-growth on Namibia's coast, so the waves break on the edge of the desert. Some people call it 'the biggest beach in the world' but, with cold winds and frequent mists, don't expect typical seaside resorts. Once again, Namibia's stunning natural landscapes, plus a few eclectic historical pockets, constitute the main attractions.

Lüderitz
This is a small port, out on a limb some 190 miles across the empty desert from the next big town, Keetmanshoop. The historical German–African mix is more evident here, hence the town's nickname: 'Bavaria on the beach'. Nearby is Kolmanskop – a diamond mine ghost town gradually being reclaimed by the dunes.

The Skeleton Coast
A stark, dry region, with harsh temperatures and occasional valley oases which support a surprising range of wildlife, including Namibia's famously hardy desert elephants. The northern part of the Skeleton Coast can be reached only by exclusive fly-in safari, while the southern sections are more accessible to independent tourists.

Swakopmund
This compact holiday and sea-fishing centre for Namibians and South Africans now welcomes the recent influx of other nationalities and is a good place to arrange wildlife safaris or desert tours (by car or camel). Best sights nearby, apart from suburban sand-dunes, include the Cape Cross seal colony – also the site of a fifteenth-century Portuguese landing.

WHEN TO GO

THE BEST time to visit Namibia is between May and August when the weather is relatively cool. From August to November it is hot, and from November to April the weather is hot and humid, although in these less popular periods there is more space in the parks and less need to book ahead for accommodation.

Namibia is very popular among South Africans, and busy in school holiday periods – roughly: most of December and the first half of January; the second half of March and the first half of April; the end of June and the first half of July; the end of September and early October.

	Average daily maximum temperature °C											
London	6	7	10	13	17	20	22	21	19	14	10	7
Windhoek	30	29	27	26	23	20	21	24	27	29	30	30
	JAN	FEB	MAR	APR	MAY	JUN	JUL	AUG	SEP	OCT	NOV	DEC
Windhoek	12	11	10	5	2	0	0	0	1	3	7	7
London	15	13	11	12	12	11	12	11	13	13	15	15
	Average number of rainy days per month											

PACKAGE TRAVEL

SEVERAL UK companies now organise tours to Namibia, some as longer journeys around southern Africa, although Namibia's size means a minimum two weeks are required to do the country justice. Many of the specialist tour operators to Namibia organise individual itineraries based on your requirements and budget. Mainstream tour operators offer a selection of tours of the country by coach, minibus or four-wheel-drive vehicles. Most offer a taste of a safari with visits to national parks and game reserves, while others focus on game viewing.

A two-week highlight tour might include visits to Windhoek, the Namib Desert, the Sossusvlei sand dunes, Swakopmund and the Skeleton Coast, the seal colony at Cape Cross, the Etendeka Mountains and of course a trip into the Etosha National Park. Some include internal flights to avoid long road journeys.

Tour operators

Adventure: Acacia, Encounter Overland, Exodus, Explore Worldwide, Guerba, Kumuka Expeditions, Travelbag **Birdwatching/wildlife**: Naturetrek, Ornitholidays, Sunbird, Wildlife Worldwide **Cultural**: Andante, Prospect **General**: Abercrombie & Kent, Cox & Kings, Cricketer, Kuoni, Somak, South African Airways, Sunset Travel, Sunvil, Thomas Cook, Travelsphere, Worldwide Journeys **Specialists**: Abercrombie & Kent, Africa Exclusive, African Explorations, Africa Travel Centre, Art of Travel, Carrier, Cazenove & Lloyd Safaris, Cox & Kings, Designer Travel, Frontiers, Grenadier Travel, Hartley's Safaris, Okavango Tours & Safaris, Safari Consultants, Safari Drive, SAR Travel, Scott Dunn World, Somak, TCA Holidays, Temple World, Tim Best, Union Castle Travel, Wild Africa Safaris, Worldwide Journeys

---

Upmarket safari specialists can take you off the beaten track in search of better game viewing and to more exclusive lodges and bush-camps. It will probably cost more to stay in tents rather than hotels.

Accommodation is in hotels, guest farms, private lodges, bungalows or luxury permanent tented bush camps and is generally of a good standard.

Self-drive holidays are also on offer – with or without a pre-arranged itinerary but remember, distances are vast.

Activity holidays include safaris, birdwatching and wildlife, horse-riding safaris, cultural tours and adventure trips.

INDEPENDENT TRAVEL

NAMIBIA CONSISTS mainly of desert and semi-desert and is about three times the size of Britain, with one of the lowest population densities in the world. This gives the country a distinctive sense of space.

Access by air from Britain is straightforward; Air Namibia offers direct flights and Windhoek can be reached on several other European and southern African airlines. Public transport is limited; there are buses between the main towns but not into wilderness areas (i.e. to the best sights). Independent travellers usually find their own way between the towns and then arrange tours locally in Windhoek, Swakopmund or Etosha to see the wildlife or natural landscape areas.

Another option is to hire a car. Even main roads in Namibia provide a sense of emptiness and adventure, without the logistical worries involved with driving in some other parts of Africa. Rates for saloon cars (which can be used to reach many areas) are around £50 to £75 per day. Four-wheel-drive (for remote areas) is around double this. If your budget is limited, hiring a car for even a few days means you see much more. If you are planning to hire a car for your whole visit, a fly-drive package is worth considering.

One disadvantage of independent travel here is that much national park accommodation must be booked in advance. Namibia's Teutonic heritage has created an efficient system which limits over-crowding, but assumes all visitors have fixed itineraries. Less rigid travel is not impossible, but may be tricky at busy periods.

RED TAPE, HEALTH AND SAFETY

NAMIBIA GAINED independence from South Africa in 1990 and only since that point has it opened up to tourists from Britain and elsewhere. Visas are not required by British citizens, but do check the current regulations at the Namibia High Commission in London before departure in case procedures change. You can stay in the country for three months but must be able to produce a passport valid for six months and a return ticket.

Hepatitis A, typhoid and polio inoculations are recommended. If entering Namibia from an 'infected' country, you must show proof of immunisation against yellow fever. There is a low malaria risk but prophylaxis is usually recommended – see your GP or a travel clinic.

Health conditions are generally good; you are unlikely to come into contact with many exotic diseases, although the usual commonsense rules concerning food and water apply (see page 11). Sunburn and dehydration are real risks, so be sure to cover up and drink plenty.

In the national parks some animals can be dangerous. Commonsense rules about not approaching the elephants or feeding the lions should be followed.

Namibia is a safe country; the risk of robbery or theft is very low. Avoid the township areas at night. Contact the Foreign Office Travel Advice Unit (see page 11) for up-to-date advice.

MORE INFORMATION Tourist Information, Namibia High Commission, 6 Chandos Street, London W1M 0LQ, tel 0171-636 6244,
web site: http://www.iwwn.com.na/namtour

COST OF LIVING ££

NEPAL

HIGHLIGHTS

Culture/history
Kathmandu and the valley

Local colour
Kathmandu and the valley, Himalayas

Outdoor activities
Pokhara, Himalayas

Romantic escapism
Pokhara

Shopping
Kathmandu and the valley

Scenic landscape
Pokhara, the Terai, Himalayas

Flora/wildlife
The Terai

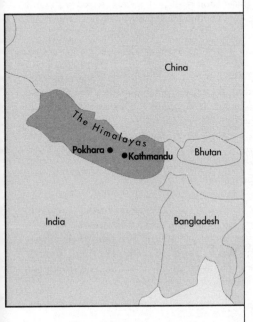

KATHMANDU AND THE VALLEY
Good for culture, history, local colour and shopping

THIRTY YEARS ago, life in Kathmandu and its isolated valley was essentially medieval, revolving around agriculture and spiritual devotion. Now it is one of the most polluted cities in the East, and uncontrolled development and the advent of mass tourism mean the old tranquillity is lost forever. This said, it remains a magical place, crammed with temples, palaces, exotic markets, Tibetan refugees, and an architectural tradition which transports the visitor into another time. Woodcarving, sculpture and religious iconography have been the creative responses to Nepal's spiritual diversity, historical richness and cultural exchange – the legacy of its unique geographical position.

Most of your exploration can be done on foot, soaking up the atmosphere. Take time to scout the backstreets: at every turn you will stumble upon sacred shrines, enchanting courtyards and examples of the cultural melting-pot that is Kathmandu – pagoda-style palaces, Hindu temples, Tibetan *stupas* (onion-shaped domes crested with gold, with Buddha's all-seeing eyes painted on the top) and souvenir shops.

BEST SIGHT

Durbar Square

Old Kathmandu's focal point, bursting with medieval temples, hawkers and holy men. Locals throng the busy vegetable market. You may get a glimpse of the Kumari, a living child-goddess at Kumari Behal. Sit on the steps of the Maju Deval Shiva temple and be entertained by touts and tourists alike. Durbar means 'palace': each town has its own palace and corresponding square.

BEST TEMPLES

Boudanath

This is a vast *stupa* in what is now a dirty but fascinating suburb of Kathmandu. Hundreds of Tibetans come here daily to walk *koras*, or circumambulations, of the immense dome, and to twirl their prayer-wheels and chant mantras. You will also see them performing prostrations on special boards – some do thousands at a time. The setting and atmosphere is other-worldly.

Dashinkali

At this isolated Hindu temple complex, visitors face one of the most confronting, yet fascinating experiences in Nepal. The goddess Kali is destroyer of demons, and to perform her work effectively she demands regular blood sacrifices. On Tuesdays and Saturdays goats, chickens, buffalo and sheep are despatched in a steady stream over her image. This is a religious ceremony, but still, it is not for the faint-hearted.

Pashupatinath

The Hindu place of pilgrimage draws devotees from all over the sub-continent. Wandering *sadhus* (holy men), Tantric iconography, ritual bathers in the holy Bagmati river and cremations on the burning *ghats* are just some of the sights you will see at this temple complex the size of a village.

Swayambunath

A white *stupa*, within walking distance of the centre of Kathmandu. Swathed in colourful prayer-flags and surrounded by clusters of small satellite temples, this is Nepal's most famous Buddhist pilgrimage site.

It is also known as the Monkey Temple, thanks to the amusing, and thieving, simian population.

BEST EXCURSIONS

Bhaktapur

This town retains the strongest feel of the Middle Ages. Many old, architecturally fine buildings have been restored, and the Nyatapola Temple is the tallest in the valley, as well as one of the most elegant of the traditional Nepali temples. Its five ornately carved storeys resemble a medieval wedding cake. In Durbar Square, you can spy on tiny, carved copulating elephants high up in the Shiva-Parvati temple, or on cavorting couples performing Tantric union on the Pashupatinath Temple.

Patan

Patan is adjacent to Kathmandu and can be reached by taxi in 20 minutes. It also has its own Durbar Square which is a veritable forest of wooden pagoda-style temples, all elaborately carved and guarded by stone animals on the first level – lions, snakes and peacocks. From here, avenues extend to the four Ashoka *stupas*, which, legend has it, date back to 500 BC. The Golden Temple is a unique monastery full of Buddha images and frescos and the Kumbeshwar Temple is five storeys of ornate religious statuary.

HIMALAYAS

Good for local colour, outdoor activities and scenic landscape

'THE KINGDOM of the Gods' is blessed with the highest mountain range in the world – Mount Everest soars to 29,030 feet. From the lowlands of the Gangetic Plain, the Himalayas rise in fairy-tale peaks and valleys to the barren Tibetan plateau. Annapurna and Everest dominate, but the trekking possibilities are endless. Climbing among breathtaking panoramas, through remote medieval villages, you experience the people as much as the scenery.

BEST OUTDOOR ACTIVITIES

Trekking can be as arduous as you like, but you need a modicum of fitness. In return you will behold the most inspiring scenery in the world, and encounter people as hospitable as they are hardy. Popular treks are to the Everest Base Camp, around the Annapurna Circuit and the Langtang and Jomsom Treks. Several shorter treks start from Pokhara. Overnight accommodation is basic, usually in simple mountain lodges. For most treks, permits are required. This takes a day at Kathmandu's Immigration Office, or in Pokhara, but to be prudent allow two days just in case.

White-water rafting is a growing activity, with expeditions available for the novice and the expert. For the average newcomer, the Karnali river offers trips where you can float along admiring the scenery and running a few small rapids.

POKHARA
Good for outdoor activities and scenic landscape

IF YOU can, fly to Pokhara through the Himalayas, and sit on the right-hand side of the plane for staggering snow-capped views. Pokhara has the perfect recipe for relaxing: a mild climate, a beautiful setting next to the large, limpid lake known as Phewa Tal, the awe-inspiring backdrop of the Annapurna Range, and plenty of hotels and restaurants. Row out and contemplate the reflection of Machhapuchhare, or Fish Tail Mountain, in the lake. Alternatively, shop at the Tibetan stalls.

THE TERAI
Good for flora, scenic landscape and wildlife

THIS NARROW strip of fertile plain at the foot of the Himalayan range is home to half the human population of Nepal, as well as to elephants, rhinos, Bengal tigers, leopards, sloth bears, crocodiles, dolphins and innumerable species of birdlife. The wildlife is best viewed at the Royal Chitwan National Park, where the animals roam freely through 500 square miles of open grassland, riverine vegetation and hardwood forests. Stay in rustic luxury inside the park for a true safari experience.

The Terai is a tropical zone, very distinct from the temperate and alpine areas of the Himalayas: plant life includes sal forests, tall elephant grasses and acacia and rosewood.

WHEN TO GO

Average daily maximum temperature °C											
London	6	7	10	13	17	20	22	21	19	14	10	7
Kathmandu	18	19	25	28	30	29	29	28	28	27	23	19
	JAN	FEB	MAR	APR	MAY	JUN	JUL	AUG	SEP	OCT	NOV	DEC
Kathmandu	1	5	2	6	10	15	21	20	12	4	1	0
London	15	13	11	12	12	11	12	11	13	13	15	15
Average number of rainy days per month											

FOR PERFECT visibility and a mild temperature, choose October to November. It is too cold in December and January, too hot in May and June, and the rainy season is between July and September.

To see the flowers, especially the rhododendrons, which bloom in the temperate mountain regions and the lower Himalayas, choose February to April, but you can risk the views being obscured by haze.

PACKAGE TRAVEL

SEVERAL TOUR operators offer Nepal as part of a tour of Northern India combining a couple of days' sightseeing with some relatively gentle trekking. Specialists and adventure tour operators tend to focus on trekking and expeditions of varying levels of difficulty although sightseeing and cultural tours, white-water rafting, mountain biking and mountaineering are also on offer.

Two-week sightseeing tours of Nepal typically start from Kathmandu, exploring the sights of Patan, Bhadggaon, Bodath and Pashupatinath before travelling on to Pokhara, They also fit in a couple of days trekking and a visit to the Royal Chitwan National Park to observe the wildlife.

Accommodation is generally in hotels, though when trekking you mostly live under canvas.

Tour operators

Adventure: Dragoman, Encounter Overland, Exodus, Explore Worldwide, Guerba, Travelbag **General**: Abercrombie & Kent, Bales Tours, British Airways Holidays, Coromandel, Cox & Kings, Imaginative Traveller, Kuoni, Steppes East, Travelpack, Travelsphere, Worldwide Journeys **Mountaineering**: Himalayan Kingdoms, KE Adventure, Sherpa **Specialists**: Classic Nepal, Himalayan Kingdoms **Tailor-made specialists**: Mysteries of India, Trans Indus **White-water rafting**: Adrift **Wildlife**: Naturetrek, Wildlife Worldwide

---

INDEPENDENT TRAVEL

YOU CAN now fly direct to Nepal from the UK, and independent travel is a distinct option. If you are not on a package, give yourself plenty of time to get around, but in general, bureaucracy is nowhere near as time-consuming as in India. Travel inside the country is by bus or plane; bus journeys are long and gruelling, but cheap; plane journeys are short, exciting and also relatively cheap. There are plenty of travel agents in Nepal who will arrange tickets. In the Kathmandu valley, travel by taxi is cheap and easy, but make sure you agree a price before you start. Most of your sightseeing can be done on foot. Hotels of all standards in Kathmandu can be booked from the UK, and the city is widely regarded as the culinary capital of the area. Pokhara has no shortage of accommodation, and you will be met by touts at the bus station and airport.

You can make your own arrangements for trekking, applying for the permits when you arrive, or, if you require porters (who can create elaborate camps, as well as cook for you), a local agent will help.

RED TAPE, HEALTH AND SAFETY

VISAS ARE required. To obtain a visa allowing 30 days' stay in Nepal you need your passport, one passport photograph and £20 cash. Apply by mail (courier your application) or in person to the Nepal embassy, open 10am to 12pm, Monday to Friday. Allow 24 hours processing for personal applications, two weeks for postal applications.

Inoculations against hepatitis A, polio and typhoid are recommended. If arriving from an 'infected' country, immunisation against yellow fever is essential. Some areas are affected by malaria – check with your GP or a travel clinic about malaria protection. If you are trekking above 10,000 feet you may experience altitude sickness – see page 10 for precautions. The biggest health problem for visitors to Nepal is diarrhoea – follow the precautions on page 11 to avoid stomach upsets.

Bad driving and poor vehicle maintenance cause many accidents; travel by long-distance bus is a particular cause of concern.

The country has experienced some political unrest, and it is a good idea to avoid street demonstrations. For more information, contact the Foreign Office Travel Advice Unit (see page 11).

MORE INFORMATION Tourist Information, Nepal Embassy, 12A Kensington Palace Gardens, London W8 4QU, tel 0171-229 1594/6231, web site: http://www.south-asia.com/dotn

COST OF LIVING £

THE NETHERLANDS

HIGHLIGHTS

Beaches *Zuid-Holland,* *Wadden Islands*	*The Hague,* *Leiden,* *Het Loo Palace*	**Flora/** **wildlife** *Giethoorn,* *Wadden* *Islands, De*	**Local colour** *Alkmaar,* *Aalsmeer,* *Hoorn,* *Giethoorn,*
Culture *Amsterdam,* *Haarlem,* *Zuiderzee-* *museum, Delft,*	**Nightlife** *Amsterdam,* *Rotterdam*	*Hoge Veluwe* **History** *Amsterdam*	*Het Nederlands* *Openlucht-* *museum*

AMSTERDAM
Good for culture, history and nightlife

BEST SIGHTS

Anne Frank's House
The house where Anne Frank and her family hid from the Nazis before being betrayed is well worth a visit.

Canal trip
A trip in a perspex-roofed boat is by far the best way to see the canal-side architecture and to admire the ranks of bell, neck and step gables.

Rijksmuseum
A pilgrimage to Rembrandt's *Nightwatch* is a must – you can also admire the works of Frans Hals, Ruisdael, Bol and Steen.

Van Gogh Museum

This collection charts the evolution of the tragic artist's work.

NOORD HOLLAND
Good for culture and local colour

LONG SANDY beaches line the west coast; former seaspots on the eastern side have become lakeside towns on the now enclosed Ijsselmeer. The countryside is flat and criss-crossed with canals and polders.

BEST SIGHTS

Alkmaar

This town, enclosed by a canal, is renowned for its weekly cheese market.

Bloemenveiling (flower auction)

Daily flower auctions are held in the early morning in a 156-acre building near Aalsmeer. Visitors can watch the proceedings from footbridges.

Edam

Less touristy than its neighbours Marken and Volendam, this town is home of the famous cheese – red-waxed for export, otherwise yellow.

Haarlem

The museum named after Frans Hals contains a gallery of his portraits of the town's dignitaries and a good general collection of paintings by sixteenth- and seventeenth-century Dutch artists. The Teylers Museum offers an eclectic mixture of art and scientific exhibits.

Hoorn

Hoorn has lots of attractive façades and old Dutch barges, as well as a wide selection of restaurants and cafés.

Zuiderzeemuseum

The indoor section (*Binnenmuseum*) and outdoor section (*Buitenmuseum*) make up the outstanding museum in Enkhuizen showing what life was like on the Zuiderzee before 1932.

ZUID-HOLLAND
Good for beaches, culture and nightlife

BEST SIGHTS

Keukenhof Park

Over 70 acres of gardens where you can wander among daffodils, narcissus and hyacinths in late March/early April, and six million tulips from mid-April until the end of May. Bulbs can be bought there.

Delft
The best-preserved town in the Netherlands is famous for its blue-and-white pottery. It has pretty, shaded canals and a historical centre.

Gouda
The attractive main square (Markt) has a fifteenth-century Gothic Stadhuis (Town hall). St Janskerk has beautiful stained-glass windows.

The Hague (Den Haag)
The Hague, the country's diplomatic centre and seat of government, is a sophisticated city with many parks and gardens, and is close to the sea. The Mauritshuis is one of the finest picture galleries in the world.

Kinderdijk
Nineteen traditional Dutch windmills, built in the 1740s, are spread along the canals, meadows and reedbeds close to the River Leek about nine miles east of Rotterdam.

Leiden
Rembrandt's birthplace is the oldest university town in the country and has a very attractive old town centre dissected by canals, and the oldest botanical gardens in Europe. There are also some excellent museums, particularly noted for antiquities and decorative arts.

Rotterdam
Extensively bombed during the Second World War, Rotterdam lacks the atmosphere of other Dutch cities. Delfshaven, all that is left of old Rotterdam, is a chic, trendy area with galleries, designer shops, restaurants and cafés in the traditional gable-roofed houses lining the waterfront. The fine-art museum of Boymans-van Beuningen is excellent.

THE NORTH
Good for beaches, flora/wildlife and local colour

OF THE three provinces that make up the north of the country, Friesland is the most popular with tourists, although Groningen town attracts quite a number of visitors.

BEST SIGHTS
Barrier Dam (Afsluitdijk)
After devastating floods in 1916 the Zuiderzee was restrained by the

building of a huge dam. This left the Waddenzee beyond the barrier and created an internal freshwater lake, the Ijsselmeer.

Giethoorn
The heart of this fenland area can be reached only by bicycle, boat or on foot. Thatched houses and neat gardens are tended by locals in traditional dress. It is very touristy in summer.

Wadden Islands
The five islands (Schiermonnikoog, Texel, Vlieland, Terschelling and Ameland) off the Netherlands' north-west tip are quiet, with beautiful beaches and lots of flora and fauna; they are popular with the Dutch.

CENTRAL NETHERLANDS
Good for culture and flora/wildlife

BEST SIGHTS
De Hoge Veluwe
This 13,300-acre national park is rich in birdlife and wildlife.

Het Loo Palace
On the edge of the Hoge Veluwe is this magnificent palace built by William III and Mary in 1685.

Rijksmuseum Kroller-Muller
One of the country's most important art collections is housed in this museum in the middle of the Hoge Veluwe.

THE SOUTH
Good for food/wine and local colour

BEST BASE
Maastricht
This sophisticated, cosmopolitan city has plenty of expensive designer shops, good hotels and restaurants. European rather than specifically Dutch in feel, it is an ideal place to spend a couple of days.

BEST SIGHTS
Het Nederlands Openluchtmuseum (Netherlands Open-Air Museum)
Spread over 110 acres, this museum has brought together examples of houses, windmills, barns, cottages and numerous other traditional buildings from all the provinces of the Netherlands. If you have too lit-

tle time to travel around the country you can experience the variety in this microcosm.

Stormvloedkering Oosterschelde (Storm Surge Barrier) and Delta Expo

This exhibition details the extraordinary engineering achievement of the Delta Plan. Drawn up after the disastrous floods in 1953 and later revised, it took over 30 years to complete. Boat trips take you up to the barrier.

WHEN TO GO

GOOD WEATHER cannot be guaranteed, so the cities are all-year destinations. The Wadden Islands are at their best between May and September, but if you want to see the bulbfields visit in April and May.

Average daily maximum temperature °C											
London	6	7	10	13	17	20	22	21	19	14	10	7
Amsterdam	3	4	8	12	16	19	21	20	18	13	8	5
	JAN	FEB	MAR	APR	MAY	JUN	JUL	AUG	SEP	OCT	NOV	DEC
Amsterdam	22	18	17	14	14	13	17	17	17	21	22	23
London	15	13	11	12	12	11	12	11	13	13	15	15
Average number of rainy days per month											

PACKAGE TRAVEL

Tour operators

Camping: Eurocamp, Eurosites, Select Sites **City breaks**: British Airways Holidays, Cresta, Crystal, Inghams, Kirker, Made to Measure, Osprey, Sovereign, Thomson, Time Off, Travelscene **Coach tours**: Armchair, Bowens, Crusader, Leger, Shearings **Cultural**: Ace Study Tours, British Museum Traveller, Martin Randall **Cycling**: Anglo Dutch, Bike Tours **General**: Amsterdam Travel Service, P&O European Ferries (boating), Scandinavian Seaways, Stena Line **Other activities**: Anglers World (fishing), European Waterways (river cruises), Ffestiniog Travel (rail tours), Holts' Tours (battlefields), Limosa (birdwatching), Solo's Holidays (singles), Swan Hellenic (river cruises)

MANY TOUR operators offer city breaks to Amsterdam. Outside Amsterdam, self-catering in holiday villages is popular, either in mobile homes or chalets. Coach tour operators feature short trips to the bulb-fields or visits to the northern countryside in spring.

INDEPENDENT TRAVEL

FLIGHTS TO Amsterdam airport (Schipol) from London and many other UK airports are widely available. Schipol is linked to Amsterdam city centre by a frequent, fast train service.

Car hire is extremely expensive; if you are planning to tour you should bring your own car. The fastest route to the Netherlands by car is via the Dover to Ostend jetfoil or Le Shuttle to Calais. Both routes link in with a good motorway system to the Netherlands. Stena offers excellent deals for a car and four passengers from Harwich to the Hook of Holland, but the journey takes six-and-a-half hours.

The Netherlands is connected to Europe's rail network and has a highly efficient internal rail service. Rover cards (*Dag Karten*) are valid for up to nine days and offer considerable savings. Unless you are plan-ning extensive touring it is advisable to fly and use trains. Parking is expensive, and a car can be a liability in the cities.

The cheapest way to travel around is by buying a *Stippenkaart*, which is valid on all buses, trams and metros countrywide.

All types of accommodation are available, from smart hotels to self-catering apartments, and are generally of a high standard. Hotels are priced according to their facilities; two- and three-star hotels are per-fectly adequate. They are all usually spotless. Tourist offices have compre-hensive lists of what is available and can make bookings for you. Advance booking is essential in summer and always advisable in Amsterdam.

RED TAPE, HEALTH AND SAFETY

BRITISH PASSPORT-HOLDERS do not require a visa. The Netherlands has no particular health or crime problems – just take the usual precautions (see pages 10–12).

MORE INFORMATION Netherlands Board of Tourism, 18 Buckingham Gate (PO Box 523), London SW1E 6NT, tel (0891) 717777 (premium rate number), web site: http://www.nbt.nl/holland

COST OF LIVING ££££

NEW ZEALAND

HIGHLIGHTS

Beaches
*Coromandel Peninsula,
Abel Tasman National
Park*

Culture
North Island

Flora/wildlife
Kaikoura, Dunedin

Food/wine
*Hawkes Bay,
Marlborough*

Outdoor activities
*Coromandel, Tongariro
National Park,
Queenstown*

North Island

Auckland ●

Tasman
Sea

Wellington ●

Nelson ●

● Christchurch

● Queenstown

South Island

Pacific Ocean

NORTH ISLAND
Good for beaches, culture, food/wine and outdoor activities

BEST BASES

Bay of Islands
The attractive, weatherboarded town of Russell is the best base for
exploring this historically important area of wooded hills and small
beaches. Settlers came here for the whaling and the kauri trees,
impressive forest giants which survive now only in isolated pockets.
They grow near Bay of Islands at Puketi Forest, but to see the largest
specimens head for Waipoua on Highway 12, easily combined with a
loop journey back to Auckland.

Coromandel peninsula
A popular spot for weekending Aucklanders, the Coromandel peninsula
is a wild, wooded spit of land with golden beaches and forest walks.
Once the scene of New Zealand's first gold-rush, it now attracts tourist
summer onslaughts. It is a good area for walks and birdwatching.

Napier

This stylish, brightly painted town has a pleasant ocean-front atmosphere. Destroyed by an earthquake in 1931, the town was rebuilt according to the most progressive ideas of the time, entirely in art deco style. The rich wine-producing region around Napier is known as Hawkes Bay; 22 wineries are open to the public. The oldest is the Mission; you can take an organised tour or wander around and chat to the staff. At the end is the sampling table – and a chance to stock up at discount prices for New Zealand's many BYO (bring-your-own) restaurants.

Tongariro National Park

A popular ski resort area in the season, this is also excellent tramping country for experienced hill-walkers, with expansive views of the classic volcanic cone of Ngaurahoe and the active Ruapehu.

Wellington

Windy Wellington, New Zealand's capital, is in a fine waterfront location and has a sophisticated edge over its commercial rival Auckland. Swanky modern buildings stand beside weatherboard houses, and along the quay at Queen's Wharf are some stylish converted warehouse restaurants. For most people, however, the city is primarily a jumping-off point for the South Island.

BEST GEOTHERMAL SIGHTS

Rotorua

The faint whiff of sulphurous gases is ever-present here – the best base for day-trips to geothermal sites and Maori cultural attractions. Most Maori 'experiences' on offer at Rotorua come as packaged and processed as cheese slices, but a few Maori-owned companies do run more authentic visits to traditional *hangi* dinners and dance displays; choose carefully.

Waimangu Valley

You can see all types of geothermal activity and experience them going on under your feet. Scorching streams, bubbling lakes and small geysers culminate in the electric-blue pool at Inferno Crater.

Waiotapu

Further down Highway 5, the landscape is a little less infernal, but pools of boiling mud and the aptly named Champagne Pool make it a worthwhile trip.

Whakarewarewa

Visit the Prince of Wales and Pohutu geysers at the best 'quickie' geothermal sight; exhibitions and shows are to be seen at the Maori Arts and Crafts Institute there.

AUCKLAND

A BUSINESS and commercial centre, New Zealand's largest city has some good sights based on its maritime traditions, but most visitors soon head off for attractions such as the Bay of Islands or Rotorua.

BEST SIGHTS

The Maritime Museum has an interesting waterfront collection of boats, from outrigger canoes to America's Cup winners. Displays include a reconstruction of an immigrant ship plus a computer database with the names of the settlers who passed through Auckland harbour. At the National Museum the fine display of Maori carvings is seen in the context of the South Seas region. The museum is surrounded by attractive parkland. The aquarium at Kelly Tarlton's Antarctic Encounter and Underwater World, reached by a snowcat journey through a penguin colony, is fun for children, but the highlight is the display of Captain Scott's Antarctic base camp. (Scott used New Zealand as his final departure point for Antarctica.)

A short ferry journey across from Auckland quayside, is Devonport, a bright, lively village of restaurants and cafés.

SOUTH ISLAND
Good for beaches, flora, outdoor activities and wildlife

SOUTH ISLAND, with its vast wilderness of forests, lakes and mountains, is perhaps New Zealand's greatest attraction. Visitors come for the wildlife, walks, outdoor sports and simply to enjoy the beauty of the place: towns and settlements are few and far between.

BEST BASES

Christchurch

A very 'English' city with its cathedral square and willow-lined river (complete with punts), Christchurch is a settlement that was planned from England by Anglicans who believed the world was turning evil and wanted to make a fresh start in a New World. You will find plenty of pubs and roast dinners, but there is a selection of international restaurants too.

Just south of Christchurch, the Banks peninsula has some fine harbours built on the craters of extinct volcanoes. Walking is the most popular activity for visitors, and there are pretty villages like Akaroa – an early French settlement – to visit. The superb glaciers and ice walls of Mount Cook National Park can be visited from the west by helicopter, or by driving in from the east to Mount Cook village. Walks with unforgettable views are the main attraction here.

Nelson

Reputedly the sunniest place in New Zealand, Nelson is a pleasant town at the centre of a large fruit- and vine-growing region. It is also close to some of the country's best beaches. Nelson Lakes National Park is 70 miles from the town and a popular walking area in summer, with views of Lake Rotorua. Abel Tasman National Park is a coastal park with some fine remote beaches accessible from the long-distance coastal path. Wine is produced in Marlborough.

Queenstown

During a period of only 20 years (mid-1970s to mid-1990s) bustling, bungee-jump capital Queenstown has developed from a sleepy trading post into tourist and sports centre of the South Island. Thrill-seekers will find everything they ever wanted, from jetboat rides on the Shotover River to whitewater rafting and bungee jumps out of helicopters. Less frenetic are the four-wheel-drive safaris to explore forgotten gold-mining outposts like Skippers Canyon and Macetown. The scenery is stunning, and there is always a chance that you will find a nugget. The former goldrush settlement of Arrowtown still thrives, a pretty street of weatherboard cottages with a good local history museum.

BEST WILDLIFE

Dunedin

A university town with many cafés, restaurants and bars, Dunedin can be a lively place in term-time. The central point is the Octagon, a public 'square' where a statue of Robert Burns stands. The royal albatross colony at the end of the 18-mile-long Otago peninsula is the only easily accessible nesting place in the world for the world's largest seabird. The birds lay their single egg around November, and 11 months later the chick finally flies away. You will get closer by taking the tour on land – coach trips up to the observation centre – but sea tours of the harbour might include views of blue penguins, fur seals and, more rarely, a whale.

Kaikoura

Fenceposts made from the bones of humpback whales betray Kaikoura's past as a whaling station. This small peninsula is located close to a prime feeding area for the whales and now that they are no longer slaughtered the chance of spotting a sperm whale is quite good. Boat trips use echo-sounders to locate the animals before moving closer: if nothing appears then you get your money back. Helicopter trips are slightly more expensive but can often succeed in marginal weather conditions. From October onwards, swimming with the dolphins is also a big attraction.

BEST SCENIC LANDSCAPE

Doubtful Sound

Less popular than Milford, perhaps because the scenery is less stunning, Doubtful Sound is in many ways a more typical fjordland sight, with its vast primeval forests and brooding unvisited side channels. Trips take a full day, starting with a boat journey across Lake Manapouri and then a coach trip up a dirt track to Doubtful and a second boat ride up the fjord. The guides are impressively well-informed, and on your return to Manapouri there is the unusual extra of a journey 700 feet down into a hydroelectric power station hewn from the solid rock.

Franz Josef and Fox Glaciers

These two neighbouring ice tongues curl down from Mount Cook almost to the Tasman Sea. Franz Josef has the more spectacular valley but Fox has fewer visitors. Guided tours will take you up the blue face of the glacier if you are fit and have sufficient nerve. Less energetic are the helicopter flights through the spectacular ice valley up to Mount Cook. Choose a trip that lands on the snowfield below the summit and have a memorable snowball fight.

Milford Sound

According to Rudyard Kipling this is the eighth wonder of the world, and few would dispute his description of this magnificent fjord, its sheer sides streaked with waterfalls and scars left by forest landslips. Mitre Peak dominates the boat journey from Milford to the sea, where you might spot penguins and seals. The drive up from Te Anau is almost as spectacular in itself.

Punakaiki

On the wild west coast, this little oasis of bizarre plants and geological freaks is a great one-night stop-over. The rocks, piled up like pancakes, are blasted with fountains of spume from the sea. Check on the high tide times if you are planning a quick stop.

WHEN TO GO

THE CLIMATE is maritime, so temperatures can fluctuate wildly during any season. Take warm clothes and waterproofs (unless you are there only in the height of summer and not planning to do any serious walking). Be very cautious about exposure to the sun, as its rays can burn quickly in the relatively unpolluted atmosphere – it is advisable to carry (and apply) suncream and sunblock at all times, even on cloudy days.

Because Christmas occurs in summer in New Zealand, most New Zealanders take their annual holiday in either December or, more commonly, January. If you want to beat the crowds remember to book accommodation and activities early.

Average daily maximum temperature °C

	JAN	FEB	MAR	APR	MAY	JUN	JUL	AUG	SEP	OCT	NOV	DEC
London	6	7	10	13	17	20	22	21	19	14	10	7
Auckland	23	23	22	19	17	14	13	14	16	17	19	21
Auckland	10	8	9	10	12	13	13	11	10	10	10	10
London	15	13	11	12	12	11	12	11	13	13	15	15

Average number of rainy days per month

PACKAGE TRAVEL

MOST TOUR operators offer detailed individual itineraries. You can select from car hire, bus and rail passes, accommodation passes, guided walks, self-drive touring itineraries, motor homes, coach tours and two- or three-night tours around popular areas such as the Bay of Islands or Franz Josef and Fox glaciers. Accommodation ranges from guest-houses, farm- or homestays or motels to exclusive lodges in the countryside. Activities include whale-watching, trekking, wine tours and birdwatching.

Tour operators

General and specialist: AAT Kings, Airwaves, AllWays Pacific, Australia Pacific Tours, Australian Affair, Australian Flight Centre, Austravel, Bakers Dolphin, Bridge the World, British Airways Holidays, Cadogan, Jetabout, Jetset, Kuoni, Noble Caledonian, Saga, Trailfinders, Travelbag, Travelmood **Walking**: Explore Worldwide, Ramblers Holidays **Other activities**: Arblaster & Clarke (wine), Caravan Abroad (motor-homes), Limosa (birdwatching), Naturetrek (wildlife), Sunbird (birdwatching), Top Deck (adventure)

INDEPENDENT TRAVEL

IF YOU have time to travel for longer than three weeks, journeying to New Zealand is the perfect opportunity to stop over in some exotic destinations on the way. If you decide to go in one direction without back-tracking, a round-the-world ticket can be a good option and excellent value. There are plenty of discounted fares to New Zealand, particularly outside high season (December to February) – bear in mind that the cheaper ones may include compulsory stop-overs which make your flight longer.

New Zealanders drive on the left-hand side of the road, and it is compulsory to wear seat-belts at all times. The open road speed limit is 60mph (100km/h) and in built-up areas usually 30mph (50km/h). Roads are generally uncluttered, although you can expect some congestion around busy holiday times. Almost all roads are tar-sealed, although some country back roads are not. The few motorways are usually around the major cities. Signposting is good.

You have to be over 21 and hold either a British driver's licence or international driving permit before you can hire a car or camper-van. All major international car hire firms are represented in New Zealand.

If you are a member of the AA in Britain, take your membership card with you, as it has a reciprocal agreement with the AA in New Zealand. This gives you the benefit of free detailed maps, emergency breakdown services and free technical advice about your car.

Hiring a camper-van (or motor-home) is very popular and a great way to tour some of the more remote areas. However, it is not necessarily cheaper than hiring a car and staying in budget accommodation, particularly in high season. Depending on the size of your party you can hire a two-, four- or six-berth van.

Public transport, although extensive, can be slow and expensive. At least one rail journey, however, is recommended: the Geyser Express from Auckland to Rotorua.

There is no shortage of accommodation in all the tourist spots, but try to book in advance during the highest season (mid-December to end January, Labour Weekend and Easter). If you plan to travel extensively, staying in motels is your best bet as most have rooms with two double beds, are priced per room, and are therefore very good value for families.

If you stay in B&Bs, homestays or farmstays you will get to meet more New Zealanders, and these places are worth staying in if you intend to spend a long time in one place – tourist information centres have comprehensive details of those in their area. B&Bs tend to be priced per person and are better value for single travellers. Homestays or farmstays are priced according to the number of people per group.

If you want to book in advance, the New Zealand Tourism Board publishes a *Where to Stay* guide which lists all kinds of accommodation (though it is not entirely comprehensive) along with their official facility and quality rating, called Qualmark, which is gradually being introduced throughout the country.

RED TAPE, HEALTH AND SAFETY

BRITISH PASSPORT-HOLDERS and UK citizens do not need a visa and will be issued a permit upon arrival to stay in the country for up to six months, provided that: your passport is valid for at least three months beyond the date you will be leaving New Zealand; and you hold a fully paid onward or return ticket to a country you have permission to enter.

Remember to keep aside $20 per person for your New Zealand departure tax.

No vaccinations are required before you enter New Zealand. Tap water is safe to drink. If you are planning to take part in any outdoor activities make sure that you take out comprehensive travel insurance. Sandflies, irritating midge-like, blood-sucking insects, are small black flies that live on the ground, so the bites are usually around the ankles. Wear plenty of insect repellent and shoes with thick socks if you are spending any time near water.

MORE INFORMATION The New Zealand Tourism Board, New Zealand House, 80 Haymarket, London SW1Y 4TQ, tel (0839) 300900 (premium rate number), web site: http://www.nztb.govt.nz

COST OF LIVING £

NORWAY

OSLO
Good for culture and family holidays

OSLO FEELS more like a wealthy provincial town than a capital city. Its charms may be low-key, but this spacious, graceful city is filled with excellent museums and enjoys a vibrant outdoor life. Beaches, islands, forests, lakes and hills are only minutes away from the centre.

BEST SIGHTS
Akerhus Castle
Built around 1300, the original castle was modernised by Christian IV in the seventeenth century. The Resistance Museum in the grounds documents Norwegian resistance in the Second World War.

Bygdøy Peninsula
Five museums across the bay include the Kon-Tiki Museum, displaying the balsa raft in which Thor Heyerdahl crossed the Pacific in 1947.

Frogner Park
This houses the marvellous Gustav Vigeland Sculpture Park and Museum, with fantastical works by the renowned Norwegian sculptor.

Munch Museum
An essential stop for most visitors, displaying a wide selection of Munch's diverse work, including his best-known painting, *The Scream*.

National Gallery
The country's finest collection of art includes Greek and Roman sculpture, sixteenth- and seventeenth-century religious painting and more modern works by Monet, Munch and Cézanne.

National Museum of Contemporary Art
This wonderful art nouveau building is as notable as the mainly Scandinavian paintings and sculpture it contains.

SOUTHERN NORWAY
Good for beaches and outdoor activities

BEST SIGHTS
Frederikstad
Located between Oslo and the Swedish border, this remarkably preserved seventeenth-century fortified town is well worth a visit.

Lake Mjøsa
Norway's largest lake lies in gentle landscape. The major winter-sports centre Lillehammer hosted the 1994 Winter Olympics.

Stavanger
Stavanger has an appealing old town and is a good base for hiking in the nearby Rogaland country and for boat trips on the local fjords.

BEST RESORT
● Kristiansand, a major resort on the south coast, has great beaches.
● To the east are attractive, less crowded beaches, islands and resorts like Arendal.

THE WESTERN FJORDS
Good for scenic landscape

THE SPECTACULAR western fjords are most people's idea of Norway, and these dramatically beautiful inlets rarely disappoint.

BEST SIGHTS

Bergen

Norway's second-largest city offers medieval buildings, intriguing museums and lively street life. The Bryggens Museum contains local medieval artefacts and the huge fish market of Torget is unmissable. The highlight of the medieval castle of Bergenhus is the Rosenkrantz Tower; guided tours are available. South of Bergen is the house of Troldhaugen, where the composer Edvard Grieg lived, worked and is buried.

BEST FJORDS

Aurlandsfjord

A spectacular train journey leads to the town of Flåm on this narrow fjord. It is wonderfully peaceful when the tourist hordes are absent.

Geirangerfjord

This tiny, snaking fjord offers some of Norway's most dramatic scenery with precipitous cliffs, plunging waterfalls and dizzying views.

Hardangerfjord

The most accessible fjord from Bergen is near Voss, an excellent winter-sports centre and also the best base for further exploration of the region.

Nordfjord

Despite high mountains falling to the waterside, it is the most accessible of the fjords by car and close to the mighty Jostedalsbreen Glacier.

Romsdalfjord

One of the few fjords accessible by train (at the town of Åndalsnes). The most appealing base in the area is Molde, which hosts an international jazz festival every July.

Sognefjord

This is Norway's deepest, longest and most popular fjord. Balestrand and Sogndal are good bases for exploring. There are fine traditional stave churches in the area.

NORTHERN NORWAY
Good for culture and local colour

BEST SIGHTS

Lofoten & Vesterålen Islands

These dramatic, weather-beaten (yet surprisingly temperate) islands may be on many cruise ships' itineraries, but they have preserved their own identity and distinctive culture. Vestvågøy is the most charming island.

Nordkapp

The North Cape is (arguably) Europe's most northerly point. Looking off this bleak cliff with reindeer-specked tundra behind and bleak mountains to the sides, the visitor truly feels on the edge of the world.

Røros

Once a copper-mining centre, the grass-thatched cottages and restored mine-works of this carefully preserved town are now a UNESCO World Heritage Site.

Tromsø

Despite its isolated and northerly position, this small city is surprisingly lively and interesting, particularly if you are lucky enough to see the fabulous Northern Lights. The Tromsø Museum has a fascinating and varied collection of exhibits, especially the religious art section.

Trondheim

Once the site of the early Norse parliament, Norway's third city is a compact, friendly place with a fine medieval centre. The magnificent cathedral of Nidaros Domkirke, dating from the eleventh century, is the traditional burial-place of Norwegian monarchs. Visit the fine Museum of Applied Art to see a superb collection of clothes, furniture and other applied work from the Renaissance onwards.

WHEN TO GO

GENERALLY SPEAKING, Norway is driest in June and warmest in July. It is usually drier inland than on the coast. Until early June some mountain passes remain blocked by snow – July and August are the best months for driving.

Many museums and galleries have restricted opening hours outside the peak summer months, and some close altogether from September.

	Average daily maximum temperature °C											
London	6	7	10	13	17	20	22	21	19	14	10	7
Oslo	-2	-1	4	10	16	20	22	21	16	9	3	0
	JAN	FEB	MAR	APR	MAY	JUN	JUL	AUG	SEP	OCT	NOV	DEC
Oslo	15	12	9	11	10	13	15	14	14	14	16	17
London	15	13	11	12	12	11	12	11	13	13	15	15
	Average number of rainy days per month											

		JAN	FEB	MAR	APR	MAY	JUN	JUL	AUG	SEP	OCT	NOV	DEC
Average daily maximum temperature °C													
London		6	7	10	13	17	20	22	21	19	14	10	7
Tromsø		-2	-2	0	3	7	12	16	14	10	5	2	0
		JAN	FEB	MAR	APR	MAY	JUN	JUL	AUG	SEP	OCT	NOV	DEC
Tromsø		18	17	19	18	18	18	15	19	21	21	18	19
London		15	13	11	12	12	11	12	11	13	13	15	15
Average number of rainy days per month													

PACKAGE TRAVEL

OPTIONS INCLUDE scenic tours by rail, bus and boat, car tours to pre-booked hotels and coastal tours of spectacular fjord scenery. Rent a country cottage, stay in a chalet in a holiday centre, visit the Arctic Circle, go on a whale safari, or dog sledging, or take a city break. Activity tour operators offer birdwatching, walking, battlefield and study tours.

Tour operators

Birdwatching: Limosa, Ornitholidays, Sunbird **City breaks**: British Airways Holidays, Cresta, Crystal, Inghams, Osprey, Premier, Time Off, Travelscene **Specialists**: Finlandia, Colour Line, Inntravel, SAS Holiday World, Scandinavian Seaways, Scandinavian Travel Service, ScanMeridian, Scantours, Sovereign Scanscape, Specialised Tours, Taber Holidays **Walking**: Explore Worldwide, Headwater Holidays, Ramblers Holidays, Waymark **Other activities**: Ace Study Tours (study tours), Anglers World (fishing), Discover the World (wildlife), Eurocamp (camping), Holts' Tours (battlefields), Solo's (singles), Arctic Experience (whale watching)

INDEPENDENT TRAVEL

DIRECT DAILY flights leave the UK for Oslo, Bergen and Stavanger. Ferries run two or three times a week from Newcastle to Stavanger and Bergen.

Despite the frequently harsh weather in Norway, the bus, rail and ferry systems are remarkably reliable. Train tickets are expensive, although several discounts are available. Buses are considerably better value and reach many destinations not accessible by train. In contrast, tickets for the coastal ferries are pricey. Sometimes internal flight prices compare favourably with train fares, and some companies offer discount airpasses. Ask at the Norwegian Tourist Board office in London.

Car rental is expensive. A standard British driving licence is sufficient documentation. Cycling is popular, and bike rental places abound.

Hotel rooms are very pricey, although you may get summer or weekend discounts. Investigate hotel discount schemes for considerable savings. The Norwegian Tourist Board and Norwegian State Railways Office in London can supply details. Small pensions and inns are the next cheapest option.

Most of the 300 youth hostels in Norway have a few double or family rooms and offer the best value for money in the country. You will almost certainly have to book them in advance.

A huge network of excellent campsites exists in Norway, and campers have the legal right to camp rough in any open area. Most campsites also have *hytter* or cabins, often well equipped and a cost-effective option for groups and families.

Tourist offices can make reservations for hotels and for rooms in private homes, although they may charge a small fee.

RED TAPE, HEALTH AND SAFETY

BRITISH PASSPORT-HOLDERS do not require a visa. Norway has no particular health or crime problems: just take the normal precautions (see pages 10–12).

MORE INFORMATION Norwegian Tourist Board, Charles House, 5 Lower Regent Street, London SW1Y 4LR, tel 0171-839 2650, web site: http://www.tourist.no

COST OF LIVING £££

OMAN

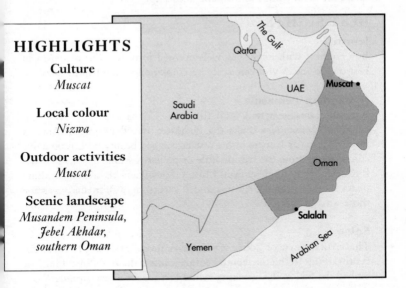

HIGHLIGHTS

Culture
Muscat

Local colour
Nizwa

Outdoor activities
Muscat

Scenic landscape
*Musandem Peninsula,
Jebel Akhdar,
southern Oman*

The Gulf

Qatar

UAE

Muscat •

Saudi
Arabia

Oman

Salalah

Yemen

Arabian Sea

MUSCAT
Good for culture and outdoor activities

THE OMANI capital has a large number of museums. Two that should not be missed are the Sultan's Armed Forces Museum, which offers the best overview of the country's history, and the Natural History Museum which has excellent displays on the country's flora and fauna.

BEST SIGHT
Mutrah Souk
The best traditional souk in the Gulf region. Take some time to wander its alleyways looking at everything from spices to silver-clad daggers.

BEST WATER SPORTS
Al-Bustan Palace Hotel
Getting on to the beach at the Al-Bustan Palace Hotel will set you back a few pounds if you are not staying in the hotel, but it is worth it. The facilities are excellent, and you can rent equipment for a wide variety of water sports.

NORTHERN OMAN
Good for local colour and scenic landscape

BEST SIGHTS

Jabrin

In a country with many old, well-restored fortresses, this is the single best one to see. A visit can easily be combined with a trip to Nizwa.

Musandem Peninsula

A remote area separated from the rest of Oman by the UAE's east coast, the Musandem offers the dedicated traveller some of Arabia's most spectacular scenery. It has a stark, rugged beauty with mountains rising steeply from the sea and little or no flat coastline. The main town is Khasab. Try to fly there from Muscat if possible. This saves time, eliminates the need for a UAE visa and is surprisingly affordable, even for those on a budget.

Sohar

The coastal town of Sohar was Oman's most important port for six centuries (up to the thirteenth century), and is the traditional home of Sinbad the Sailor. Its distinctive white fort merits a diversion.

Sur

It is a four-hour car journey from Muscat to Sur, but the town's two forts and the good beaches available at its main hotel are worth it.

BEST LOCAL COLOUR

Nizwa

The cultural centre of Oman's interior, Nizwa is worth the trip for its well-restored fort and large market area. Adjacent to the market are workshops where you can see daggers and other handicrafts being made. The town also provides a good base for exploring the striking Jebel Akhdar region with its dramatic mountains rising up from the desert, a welcome relief from the flat, rather featureless terrain closer to Muscat. It is advisable to see the area on an organised tour – or hire a four-wheel-drive vehicle.

SOUTHERN OMAN
Good for scenic landscape

BEST CITY

Salalah

The capital of Oman's Dhofar province offers a completely different climate and pace of life from Muscat. The hills above the city are lush and green in the autumn, watered by the rains of the Indian monsoons. Don't miss Job's Tomb, a mosque perched on a hill overlooking the city. The small museum in the city centre has a display on the British explorer and author Wilfred Thesiger, who spent time in Salalah while making some of the journeys recounted in his classic *Arabian Sands*.

Ubar

Avoid this remote site of a 'lost city', thought to have once been a great and rich trading metropolis. It is three hours by car from Salalah and frequently disappoints all but the most dedicated students of archaeology (there is little to see).

BEST BEACHES

Mughsail

There are fine beaches at Mughsail, 17 miles west of Salalah. Salalah's Holiday Inn Hotel offers a good beach club.

BEST EXCURSION

Taqa

Taqa, 14 miles east of Salalah, has an interesting small fort, a cemetery containing the grave of the Sultan of Oman's mother. Just outside the town are several spring-fed oases.

WHEN TO GO

OMAN IS very hot for most of the year. From mid-October to mid-March is the best time to visit. From June to September the Salalah area is soaked by monsoon rains.

Avoid visiting during Ramadan, the Muslim month of fasting. This usually begins in December or January. The faithful are expected to fast during the day, and opening times are disrupted. The end of Ramadan is marked by four or five days of family festivities (rather like Christmas) and can also be an awkward time to travel.

	Average daily maximum temperature °C											
London	6	7	10	13	17	20	22	21	19	14	10	7
Muscat	25	25	28	32	37	38	36	33	34	34	30	20
	JAN	FEB	MAR	APR	MAY	JUN	JUL	AUG	SEP	OCT	NOV	DEC
Muscat	2	1	1	1	0	0	0	0	0	0	1	2
London	15	13	11	12	12	11	12	11	13	13	15	15
	Average number of rainy days per month											

PACKAGE TRAVEL

NOT MANY tour operators feature Oman and those that do tend to be smaller specialist operators. Four-wheel-drive tours of the country generally start from Muscat. These may take in forts, wadis, sand dunes and markets and visit Nizwa, Jabrin, Wahiba Sands, Sur Beach and the old frankincense trading centre at Salalah. They are generally escorted; some operators organise self-drive and chauffeur-driven tours.

Accommodation is generally in upmarket hotels with the opportunity to camp out in the wilderness on some tours. Note that most of the local agents leave brochures in the lobbies of the bigger hotels. But beware – most of their tours presume four or more people, and solo travellers or couples are likely to be charged the full price for four people if they cannot fill the vehicle.

Activity holidays include birdwatching, and tailor-made holidays can be arranged.

Tour operators

Birdwatching: Ornitholidays **General**: Steppes East, Somak, Elite Vacations **Specialists**: Abercrombie & Kent, Coromandel, Cox & Kings, Explore Worldwide, Jasmin Tours, Kuoni, TCA Holidays **Tailor-made specialists**: East Travel, Peltours

---

INDEPENDENT TRAVEL

A DIRECT service is available from the UK to Muscat. Overland, the Omani capital can be reached via a twice-daily air-conditioned coach from Dubai, in the United Arab Emirates. Internal flights link Muscat with other Omani cities, most notably Salalah in the south, and Khasab in the Musandem Peninsula.

An extensive coach network aids internal travel, although aside from the coaches travelling between Muscat and Salalah few are air-conditioned. Prices are very low by UK standards and reservations are rarely necessary except on the Muscat to Salalah route. Shared taxis and minivans go everywhere the coaches go and also travel to many smaller places not served by the coaches. Taxi and minivan fares are only slightly higher than coach fares but are worth the extra flexibility.

Car hire is widely available in Muscat but is often very expensive. Rented cars rarely come with unlimited mileage, and as the distances in Oman are often great the extra charges can soon mount up.

In Muscat and Salalah hotels are available in all price ranges except the very cheapest. Outside of these two cities, however, there is little moderately priced accommodation. If you like Indian food eating cheaply is never a problem.

Entry to most forts and archaeological sites is free, but requires a permit issued by the Ministry of Culture and National Heritage. The ministry's office is in a building attached to the Natural History Museum in Muscat. Permits are issued free of charge in a few minutes.

RED TAPE, HEALTH AND SAFETY

FOR A single-entry, three-week visa you will need a passport valid for three months, a completed application form (available from the embassy; send an sae), proof of funds or current employment, evidence of your travel itinerary and £30 (cash, postal order or cheque). Send your application by registered delivery or apply at the embassy in person between 9.30am and 12.30pm, Monday to Friday. The visa takes one week to process and must be used within one month of issue. It is not renewable or extendable.

Sanitary conditions in Oman are very high. Cities and towns are always extremely clean and orderly, and the tap water is safe to drink. Make sure your hepatitis A, typhoid and polio vaccinations are up to date – check with your GP or a travel clinic. You may wish to consider taking anti-malaria medication, particularly if you plan to travel in the south of the country.

Life in Oman is very safe. Always bear in mind, however, that it is, by Western standards, an extremely conservative country. Shorts and tight or revealing clothing are considered offensive on both men and women and may get you into trouble with the local authorities. Foreign women are not required to cover their heads while travelling in Oman, but it is prudent to dress conservatively (wear loose trousers or a long skirt).

MORE INFORMATION Embassy of Sultanate of Oman, 167 Queensgate, London SW7 5HE, tel 0171-225 0001, visa information (0891) 600567 (premium rate number)

COST OF LIVING £££

PERU

HIGHLIGHTS

Culture
Lima,
Arequipa,
Cusco

Wildlife
Paracas
National
Reserve,
Manu
National Park

Local colour
Sacred Valley

Romantic
escapism/
scenic
landscape
Colca Canyon,
Lake Titicaca,
Machu Picchu,
Huarez

Outdoor
activities
Huarez

Flora
Manu
National Park

Nightlife
Lima, Cusco

Shopping
Cusco

History
Lima, Nasca,
Arequipa,
Cusco,
Sacred Valley,
Machu Picchu,
Trujillo

LIMA
Good for culture, history and nightlife

THIS VAST, sprawling city offers a challenging initiation into Peru's history and culture. At the heart of Lima, around Praça das Armas, the fairly dilapidated colonial centre has preserved much of its charm and atmosphere. In addition to the wealth of fine architecture here, the city boasts a richly decorated cathedral and a good selection of museums.

BEST SIGHTS

Convento de los Descalzos
Guided tours offer an intriguing glimpse of the way Franciscan friars lived when they occupied this beautiful convent during the colonial and early Republican periods.

Miraflores
The bourgeois seaside suburb of Lima is an important social centre with shops, a market, many restaurants, video bars and discos. Further south from here are a number of popular beach resorts.

Museu de la Nación
The large anthropological and archaeological collection includes interesting displays on Peru's many ruined sites.

Museu de Oro
Impressive displays include pre-Columbian gold, ceramics, mummies and Spanish colonial arms. Thousands of well-presented exhibits give a chronological history of Peruvian culture from the second century BC.

PARACAS NATIONAL RESERVE
Good for wildlife

BOAT TRIPS visit islands teeming with noisy sea lions, pelicans, penguins and an abundance of other birdlife. This impressive reserve claims one of the highest concentrations of marine birds in the world.

NASCA
Good for history

CARVED INTO the arid landscape are the mysterious Nasca Lines – some abstract, some forming the outlines of animals – which date from around the first or second century BC. The purpose of the lines, which because of their scale are best appreciated from the air, has been the subject of much speculation. Also in the area are many cemeteries with mummified human remains strewn across the bleak desert landscape.

AREQUIPA
Good for culture and history

A PLEASANT city at the foot of a snow-capped volcano, Arequipa possesses some attractive colonial buildings and has a relaxed atmosphere. It is also home to a number of fine churches, a cathedral and a couple of museums.

BEST SIGHT
Santa Catalina Convent
Almost a miniature town in itself, the convent feels very remote from the lively city beyond the monastery walls. It comprises calm courtyards, flower-filled abbeys and the personal quarters of the 400 or so nuns, whose forebears once lived here in total isolation.

COLCA CANYON
Good for romantic escapism and scenic landscape

A BEAUTIFUL, unspoilt area where you can absorb local life in the primitive Andean villages that dot the terraced mountainsides. You can often spot condors at the deepest point of this dramatic canyon.

LAKE TITICACA
Good for romantic escapism and scenic landscape

A TRANQUIL and idyllic region where weary travellers can recuperate and take in the spectacular views across the still waters of the lake.

BEST ISLANDS
A number of islands are worth visiting, including the floating islands made of piles of reeds and the peaceful Amantani Island.

CUSCO
Good for culture, history, nightlife and shopping

ONCE THE capital of the Inca empire, Cusco is today the heart of tourism in Peru. It is a beautiful city with plenty to offer, including markets and shops selling local crafts, many restaurants and bars catering to Western tastes and a vibrant lifestyle. The city is notable for its numerous colonial churches.

BEST EXCURSION
Many Inca ruins can be found in almost every street in the city centre and on its outskirts. An enjoyable way to visit the ruins around the city is on horseback – you can book an expedition with one of the many tour companies.

THE SACRED VALLEY
Good for history and local colour

MANY FASCINATING villages and ruins interrupt the gentle slopes of this attractive valley.

BEST SIGHTS
Ollantaytambo
The pyramid–like temple fortress of this striking Inca town is a superb example of the sophistication of Inca engineering.

Pisac
There is a notable Inca fortress here.

MACHU PICCHU
Good for history, romantic escapism and scenic landscape

THIS ANCIENT Inca city perched amid its stunning setting of lush, dramatic mountains is truly magical. Shrouded in mystery by the mist and low clouds, the ruined city is at its most enchanting at dawn. It is worth the strenuous four-day hike along the Inca trail to have the place to yourself before the tourists arrive on the train from Cusco.

MANU NATIONAL PARK
Good for flora and wildlife

THIS NATURE reserve is situated in the Amazon basin which provides a third dimension to the Peruvian landscape, otherwise characterised by desert or mountains. Extremely rich in tropical flora and wildlife, the Manu National Park is still relatively unexplored.

Organised tours of the park, mostly by river, usually include basic food and involve fishing, hunting and sleeping in hammocks.

HUAREZ
Good for outdoor activities, romantic escapism and scenic landscape

BEST WALKING
Cordillera Blanca mountains
Huarez is the focal point of the Cordillera Blanca mountain range and is the most popular starting-point for trekking in this spectacular

341

region. Dramatic mountain scenery provides the setting for many excursions in the area.

TRUJILLO
Good for history

INTERRUPTING THE monotonous desert scenery of northern Peru's coastline is the oasis of Trujillo, which has numerous old churches and some picturesque colonial buildings.

BEST EXCURSION
Chan Chán
Most visitors to Trujillo come to explore the nearby ruins of Chan Chán, an extraordinary, vast adobe city which was built by the Chimú kings in the first century AD. Within the 12 square miles of the walls lies an entire city with ruined streets, houses, temples and palaces.

WHEN TO GO

EACH AREA of Peru has its own climate and so *when* you go depends very much upon *where* you go. The dry season falls between April and October and it is best to visit during these months. The most popular period for tourism (around Cusco in particular) is June to August, during which time prices tend to be higher.

	Average daily maximum temperature °C											
London	6	7	10	13	17	20	22	21	19	14	10	7
Lima	28	28	28	27	23	20	19	19	20	22	23	26
	JAN	FEB	MAR	APR	MAY	JUN	JUL	AUG	SEP	OCT	NOV	DEC
Lima	1	0	0	0	1	1	1	2	1	0	0	0
London	15	13	11	12	12	11	12	11	13	13	15	15

Average number of rainy days per month

PACKAGE TRAVEL

MOST SPECIALIST tour operators will create individual itineraries with a diverse choice of escorted tours and excursions. Machu Picchu and Cusco are the highlights of most tours, with Arequipa, the Colca Canyon and Trujillo accompanying sights of interest in the Andes.

You can take a trip into the Amazon jungle from Iquitos or Puerto Maldonado to stay in jungle lodges for a couple of days, viewing the jungle wildlife with guides.

Transport may be by coach, minibus or public transport. The rail journey from Cusco down to Lake Titicaca, which takes you through tremendous Andean scenery and fertile valleys, is often included on many tours. Trips to the Nasca Lines are also popular and some operators offer visits to the Ballesta Guano Islands off the Pacific coast.

Activity holidays include escorted treks along the Inca trail, mountain trekking in the Cordillera Blanca or environmental expeditions. You can also try mountain biking and white-water rafting. Wildlife and ornithological holidays are also available.

Peru can be combined with Bolivia, Ecuador, Chile and other South American countries.

Tour operators

Adventure: Dragoman, Encounter Overland, Exodus, Explore Worldwide, Guerba, Travelbag **Birdwatching**: Animal Watch, Sunbird **Cultural**: British Museum Traveller **General**: Bales Tours, Cox & Kings, Hayes & Jarvis, Kuoni, Worldwide Journeys **Specialists**: Journey Latin America, Passage to South America, Travel South America, Union Castle Travel **Trekking**: KE Adventure

---

INDEPENDENT TRAVEL

INDEPENDENT TRAVEL in Peru is mostly for the adventurous, but with tourism rapidly on the increase it is becoming easier. Standards of travel and accommodation are improving.

Simple accommodation is easy to find on arrival in most places along the traveller trail, but more expensive hotels should be booked in advance. In places such as Cusco, many tourist agencies arrange excursions offering a good compromise between independent and package travel.

It is fairly easy to find transport between the main tourist destinations in Peru, which has over 1,300 miles of railway and a few major roads including the Pan-American Highway, which runs along the whole Peruvian coast. Travelling by train is fun and scenic and preferable to the buses, which can vary greatly and can be exhausting due to poor roads. For those with little time or those wishing to forfeit the experience of overland travel, flights are cheap and easy to reserve.

RED TAPE, HEALTH AND SAFETY

NO VISA is required for Western Europeans, Canadians, Americans, Australians or New Zealanders. A Tourist Card is issued on arrival allowing a visit of up to 90 days.

Inoculations against typhoid, hepatitis and polio are recommended as are malaria tablets if you are visiting the jungle. Visit your GP or a travel clinic for further advice, and follow the precautions on page 11 to prevent stomach upsets. Altitude is often a problem in the Andes and you should allow yourself time to acclimatise – see page 10 for hints on combating altitude sickness. Take warm clothing, as temperatures in the mountains can be bitterly cold at night.

Today terrorism is no longer a threat in the main tourist areas and theft is likely to be the main hindrance. Watch your belongings at all times, especially on buses and trains and in markets. Be warned that the consequences for possession of illegal drugs can be particularly severe.

The Foreign Office advises that travellers register with the British Embassy in Lima on arrival in Peru. For more information, contact the Foreign Office Travel Advice Unit (see page 11).

MORE INFORMATION Tourist Section, Embassy of Peru, 52 Sloane Street, London SW1X 9SP, tel 0171-235 1917/2545, web site: http://www.rcp.net.pe/promperu/TURISMO

COST OF LIVING £

PORTUGAL

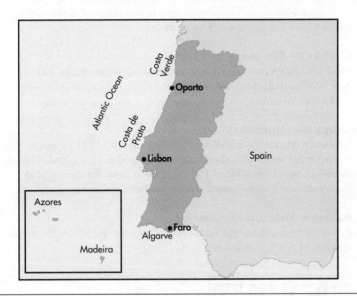

HIGHLIGHTS

Beaches
Algarve

Flora
*Madeira,
Azores*

Nightlife
Algarve

**Family
holidays**
Algarve

**Outdoor
activities**
*Algarve,
Madeira,
Azores*

Local colour
*Costa de Prata,
Oporto,
Costa Verde*

**Scenic
landscape**
*Costa Verde,
Madeira*

Culture
*Lisbon, Costa
de Prata*

Wine
*Oporto,
Madeira*

LISBON
Good for culture

ALTHOUGH IT is not the most exciting European capital, Lisbon has a charming provincial atmosphere and is conveniently small-scale for a city break. The city itself boasts a few great buildings but there is plenty of architectural detail and decoration to admire.

345

BEST SIGHTS

Calouste Gulbenkian Museum
Part of a complex that includes shady grounds, concert halls, an out-door amphitheatre and exhibition spaces, the museum is divided into ancient, non-European and European art.

Castelo de São Jorge
Moorish castle strengthened and embellished by later kings, laid out as park with gardens, peacocks and deer, terraces, pricey café, and rampart walkways.

Jéronimos Monastery
Exuberant Manueline building in western suburb of Belém, one of the few to have survived Lisbon's 1755 earthquake: exotic and nautical themes prevail. Downriver is Torre de Belém from the same period – a former defensive tower softened by fancy balconies and pinnacles.

National Museum of Azulejos
Attractive museum in sixteenth-century convent that charts the devel-opment of *azulejos*, or painted tiles.

THE ALGARVE
Good for beaches, family holidays, nightlife and outdoor activities

IF YOU are looking for a resort-based holiday, with great beaches, a comfortable and convenient hotel, and good facilities, the Algarve is an excellent choice. However, a lot of insensitive development is going on and large numbers of tourists crowd the most popular beaches.

Outside the summer season the Algarve is also anxious to attract the golfer – there is a golf course within 10 minutes of nearly every major resort, and many hotels and villa complexes will also offer you dis-counts on green fees.

BEST SIGHTS

The natural beauty of the Algarve's coastline is the highlight of any trip. Boat trips are offered all along the coast, but the most dramatic coastline is between Albufeira and Carvoeiro. The best views are at Benagil and particularly Algar Seco, where viewing steps and a tunnel have been built into the rock.

Faro is worth a day-trip for its eighteenth-century port buildings around the seafront and the small medieval walled town, or an evening outing to sample the healthy nightlife of the bars and clubs around Conselheiro Bivar and Do Prior.

A 45-minute drive east of Faro, Tavira straddles the River Gilão, with traditional Algarvan houses covered in decorative tiles. West of Faro, Silves was once the splendid Moorish capital of the region, and Cabo do São Vincente, the most westerly point of Europe, is the site of the renowned school of navigation set up by Prince Henry the Navigator in 1418.

BEST RESORTS

Most resorts have huge stretches of top-quality beach. The final choice comes down to whether you want a proper town with busy nightlife or a purpose-built villa/apartment complex with sports facilities.

Albufeira
● Old Moorish town slowly being overwhelmed by tourism, though the fishing tradition remains alive.
● Acres of golden beach below the town.
● Lively place at night, especially the tacky neon stretch of Largo Cais Herculano; for a quieter time, stick to the white-walled alleys and staircases of the town above, with a choice of small quiet restaurants.

Armaçao de Pêra
● Medium-sized resort with balustraded clifftop promenade.
● Stairs down to huge curving beach of good-quality sand.
● Old village and fascinating fishermen's beach filled with brightly painted boats.
● Ugly sprawl of development behind the pretty beachfront.

Carvoeiro
● Steep narrow sandy cove means that the old part of the fishing village has kept its charm and intimate quality.
● Large number of bars and restaurants, several run by British ex-pats.
● Modern development on the two roads leading up the valley away from the sea or on the clifftops above the town.
● First sizeable beach is closer to Ferragudo, a pretty fishing village.

Lagos
● Historic and picturesque fortified port, steep cobbled streets dotted with small churches and intriguing shops.
● Few hotels; nearest beaches at Meia Praia, a 10-minute drive away.

Quinta do Lago
● Attractive, though large, purpose-built resort with beautiful shoreline.
● Mostly low-rise villa complexes dotted between several golf courses.
● Southern half of the resort is preferable, as it is close to the natural

beauty of the Ria Formosa lagoon and the dunes beyond.
● Huge beach of fine sand, stretching into the distance.

Vale do Lobo
● Swanky, purpose-built resort with its own cricket pitch, two golf courses, a large tennis centre, a driving range and aerobics classes.
● Orderly and efficient small development, too orderly for some.
● Long, narrow beach backed by sandstone cliffs.

COSTA DE PRATA
Good for culture and local colour

THIS AREA has some important historical sights and good beaches, but much of it is flat and featureless, interrupted only by the occasional large stretch of pine woods; the coast often suffers from strong winds. The resorts, though scarred by the occasional tower block, often sustain a traditional way of life, but the beaches are not as good as those of the Algarve. Fierce Atlantic rollers also make sections of the coastline hazardous for bathers, though heaven for surfers.

BEST RESORTS
Cascais
● One-time fishing village that made it big, with a reputation for the best seafood on coast.
● Good for stay-put holiday, but the quality of bathing water is dubious.
● Nicest resort beach is Praia da Conceição; biggest and best beach in the area is Praia do Guincho, 4 miles west of town.

Ericeira
● Low-key Portuguese family resort, popular with surfers.
● Large, intermittently rocky beach shared by sun-worshippers and fishermen, who use tractors to haul the boats up the shore.
● Pleasant town built around square lined with plane trees.

BEST SIGHTS
Batalha
The Flamboyant Gothic church of this monastery is notable for its profusion of pinnacles, buttresses and open balustrades.

Coimbra
The riverside home of one of the country's leading universities has a youthful energy that sits well with its mature medieval charm. The university library is very fine, while the Machado de Castro Museum's diverse collection includes a range of sinister hand-shaped reliquaries.

Fátima
A piazza that can hold up to 300,000 pilgrims fronts a neoclassical 1930s basilica commemorating appearances of the Virgin Mary to three local children in 1917. View spectacular pilgrimages on 13 May and 13 October, when all the massive car parks around town are full.

Mafra
The astonishing monastery-palace of Mafra combines Italian neoclassical and German baroque architecture. The tour is recommended.

Sintra
This historic town among wooded hills was for centuries the royal family's summer residence, and has a profusion of palaces. The Royal Palace is most memorable for its domed Hall of Arms. The hill above is crowned by the Pena Palace, an orgy of mock-medieval kitsch.

OPORTO
Good for local colour and food/wine

THREE FINE bridges span the River Douro, linking the port centre of Vila Nova de Gaia with the intriguing, dignified city on its right bank. The narrow alleyways of the Italianate old town lead down to the riverside. Numerous tea houses and grand coffee shops are dotted around the city. The main sights are in the old quarter, including the Church of St Francis, with a staggeringly ornate rococo interior, and the rich art collection of the Soares dos Reis Museum. Not to be missed is a tour of the port wine warehouses across the river. Free guided tours are available at most lodges – you get to sample the wine and see the oak casks with their precious maturing contents.

COSTA VERDE
Good for local colour and scenic landscape

THE COSTA Verde is one of the most rewarding areas of Portugal to tour, offering a combination of mountain scenery, sandy beaches, historic towns and unspoilt villages – all contained within a fairly compact area.

BEST RESORTS
The coast has many long sandy beaches, but the relatively cold water and frequent onshore winds limit their appeal for stay-put sunbathing and swimming holidays.

Ofir

- Some of Costa Verde's best beaches – large expanses of sand with dunes and pine woods behind.
- Several hotels, restaurants and bars, but other tourist facilities limited.

Viana do Castelo

- Attractive setting on wooded estuary of River Lima.
- Busy town with attractive views from Sta Luzia hill.
- Nearest beaches two miles away on other side of river.

BEST SIGHTS

Amarante

This wine-making town lies on the edge of the Serra do Marrão. Its tiers of balconied houses rise steeply up the slopes on either side of the River Tamega, around the sixteenth-century convent of São Gonçalo.

Barcelos

Home of the painted pottery cockerels (now an emblem of Portugal), this is a picturesque riverside town with a popular Thursday market.

Guimarães

The old quarter of the original capital of Portugal contains lovely squares and narrow fifteenth-century streets, while in a park stands the Palace of the Dukes of Bragança, housing a collection of tapestries and furniture.

Peneda-Gerês National Park

Some of Portugal's most dramatic scenery is to be found among these magnificent mountains, forests and artificial lakes. The high peaks of the Serra de Gerês are harsh, with sparse vegetation, but around the lakes the slopes are gentler, and there are opportunities for fishing, swimming and boating. The spa town of Gerês, dotting the tree-covered slopes near the head of Caniçada Lake, is a peaceful place to stay at.

Valença do Minho

The cobbled streets of this fortified hilltop settlement overlooking the river frontier with Spain are crowded with souvenir shops, but it still has considerable charm and character.

MADEIRA

Good for flora, food/wine, outdoor activities and scenic landscape

THE ISLAND lies in the Atlantic, on the same latitude as Morocco. A holiday here may involve strolling in formal gardens and mosaic paved shopping streets, visits to a wine lodge to learn how the various Madeira wines are made, or expeditions into the hinterland, perhaps following the *levadas* (irrigation channels) that criss-cross the island.

BEST BASE

Funchal

Most people choose to stay in Funchal, a large, bustling town with several museums, a good market, plenty of shops, a casino, and a pleasant if touristy port area and old town to explore. The São Francisco Wine Lodge offers tours on the making of Madeira wine, plus generous tastings; the Museum of Sacred Art contains fine pieces and Flemish art while the Quinta das Cruzes Museum offers glimpses of leading Madeiran families' lifestyles in the eighteenth and nineteenth centuries. The Botanic Gardens give an excellent introduction to Madeira's sub-tropical flora.

BEST EXCURSIONS

Curral das Freiras

A tiny mountain village, founded by nuns as a refuge against pirates.

Porto Moniz and Paúl da Serra

The thrilling corniche road along the northern coast to Porto Moniz features rock tunnels and cascades of water tumbling down cliff faces.

THE AZORES
Good for flora and outdoor activities

OTHER THAN sailors, walkers and plant-lovers are the commonest visitors, coming for the attractive and not too strenuous coastal and hill walks and the enormous variety of trees, flowers and grasses.

BEST ISLANDS

Faial
● The most touristy island, much frequented by yachts.
● Prettiest main town Horta has good restaurants and local shopping.
● Excellent walks around the central volcanic cauldron.
● Most deserted beach is at Faja da Praia do Norte in the north-west.

Flores
● Remote, particularly attractive to botanists and walkers.
● Seven lakes in rugged interior and waterfalls that drop into the sea.

Graciosa
● Remote, sleepy, away-from-it-all island.

● Handsome town of Santa Cruz with wide square.
●Volcanic crater with lake of sulphurous water inside huge grotto.

Pico

● Mostly visited as day-trip from Faial.
● Best volcanic landscape, with the highest peak: for good climbers.
●Whaling museum at Lajes.

Santa Maria

● Tiny, bypassed by most tourists – you can tour the whole island by car in half a day.
●Two first-class beaches of golden sand: Praia attracts more sunbathers, while São Lourenço Bay has a prettier setting.
● Most attractive part is in the east, around Pico Alto.

São Jorge

● Lovely, wild rugged landscape, with central plateau punctuated by volcanic cones, and almost vertical shore cliffs.
● Superb coastal hill walks, the best being on the north coast.
● Only beach is at Faja do João Dias, an hour's walk from the road.

São Miguel

● Largest and one of the busiest islands.
● Several black sand beaches; the best are on the enclosed bay near Porto Formoso on the north coast, and near Ribeira Quente and Vila Franca do Campo on the south.
● Natural sights include the Terra Nostra forest park in the east and the lakes in the crater of Sete Cidades in the west.

Terceira

● Busy, the most densely populated island, with villages and towns forming an almost continuous ring round its shores.
● Fine volcanic landscape in the middle, with sulphurous fumaroles and the cave of Alvar do Carvão, but otherwise the least appealing.
● The only beach is at Vila Praia da Vitoria.

WHEN TO GO

THE MOST colourful time to go to Lisbon is at Carnaval, which takes place around Shrove Tuesday, and in June, when three major saints' days (St Anthony, St John, and St Peter) are celebrated with processions, concerts, fireworks and street parties.

On the Algarve and the Atlantic coast, it is cheaper and less crowded in June and September. From October till April the weather is good for walking. For golfers, October and May are good times to choose. The Algarve features as a winter destination in brochures, and resort hotels stay open throughout the year.

Madeira's major event is an annual flower festival in late April, when colourful floats traverse Funchal. There's also a September wine festival.

The islands of the Azores are among the few places left near Europe where you can still happily go in July and August – there are no great crowds, and the weather is pleasantly warm, not sweltering. But count on a few rainy days and book your hotels in advance.

	Average daily maximum temperature °C											
London	6	7	10	13	17	20	22	21	19	14	10	7
Lisbon	14	15	17	20	21	25	27	28	26	22	17	15
	JAN	FEB	MAR	APR	MAY	JUN	JUL	AUG	SEP	OCT	NOV	DEC
Lisbon	15	12	14	10	10	5	2	2	6	9	13	15
London	15	13	11	12	12	11	12	11	13	13	15	15
	Average number of rainy days per month											

PACKAGE TRAVEL

MANY BRITISH tour operators offer two-, three-, or four-night packages to Lisbon, but you may find going independently slightly cheaper. A few city-break specialists also offer packages to Oporto.

All the mass-market tour operators feature package holidays in hotels in the Algarve. Prices can be expensive compared with other Mediterranean resorts, but they drop outside July and August. Restaurant food is generally inexpensive, so you may want to book only B&B. As with hotels, villa accommodation can be pricey, particularly at the 'exclusive' purpose-built resorts, but the mid-range self-catering villas and apartments are good value.

In northern Portugal specialist operators feature holidays in *pousadas* – state-run hotels, often in converted historical buildings. You can use one as a base for day-trips, or combine several on a touring holiday.

Most package holidays to Madeira are based in Funchal – some hotels are more than half an hour's walk from the hub of things, although the bus service is good and taxis reasonably cheap. Specialist operators offer wider coverage of the islands, including the government-run *pousadas* in the interior. For beach-bums, some operators offer two-centre holidays based on a week in Funchal and a week on Porto Santo.

Specialist tour operators offer stay-put hotel packages or tailor-made island-hopping trips to the Azores. If you are staying put, choose an island in the middle group, from where you can easily visit others on boat trips. Specialist activities on offer include walking, wine-tasting, flora and birdwatching, as well as pilgrimages to Fátima.

Tour operators

City breaks: Kirker, Time Off, Travelscene **General**: Abreu, Airtours, Allegro, Alternative Travel Group, Cadogan, Caravela, Cosmos, Crystal, First Choice, Inghams, Mundi Colour, Sunvil, Sunworld, Thomas Cook, Thomson, Unicorn Holidays, Unijet **Specialists**: Destination Portugal, North Portugal Travel, Portugal Travel, Portugala, Portuguese Travel Centre **Villa specialists**: CV Travel, European Villas, Individual Travellers Spain & Portugal, Meon, Something Special, Travel Club of Upminster, Villa Club, Vintage Travel **Other activities**: Arblaster & Clarke (wine), Exodus, Explore Worldwide, Holts' Tours (battlefields), Limosa (birdwatching), Longshot Golf, Lotus Supertravel Golf, Martin Randall (cultural)

INDEPENDENT TRAVEL

YOU WILL not save money by going independently to the seaside, but it is worth considering if you are going to tour – though check the fly-drive deals first. British Airways flies direct to Lisbon and Porto from Heathrow and from Manchester to Faro in summer. TAP Air Portugal flies to Lisbon, Porto and Faro from Heathrow, and from Manchester to Lisbon. Cheaper charter flights are also available to Lisbon all year round (more so in summer) from Gatwick, Luton and Manchester, but most are based on one- or two-week holidays. Charter flights are available from most regional airports to Faro on the Algarve.

Car hire is relatively cheap. By law, motorists must carry some form of identification with a photo or face an on-the-spot fine. For most British holidaymakers this means carrying a passport (photocopies are not valid). Make sure you also have your driving licence and the hire-car contract (or logbook for private cars). Front seat-belt use is compulsory.

A rail network connects Lisbon with the main northern towns and the Algarve. The Portuguese railway company CP sells a *Bilhete Turistico* rail pass, valid for first-class travel on all trains except Lisbon-Madrid. Long-distance buses, usually quicker than trains, also link the main centres, but are more expensive. Services tend to be less frequent at weekends. Buses are the main form of local transport; rail services also run between Lisbon and Cascais, and along the Algarve coast.

There are direct scheduled and charter flights from London to Funchal. Car hire and petrol on Madeira are expensive, but if you want the freedom to explore, hiring is worthwhile. Madeira's roads are steep, twisting and bumpy: you are rarely out of second gear. Taxis are plentiful, and available for half- or whole-day charters at rates set down by the Funchal tourist office. Coach tours are another popular and good-value way of seeing the island, and often include lunch.

You can visit the Azores independently by flying to Lisbon and then on to São Miguel or Terceira. But leave your itinerary flexible – local planes and boats are simpler to book on the spot. The local airline, SATA, connects all islands except Corvo on small, reliable planes (weather permitting). It is easy to make bookings on the spot. Ferries ply between all the islands and are cheaper but take longer. They are most useful on the short distances between islands in the middle group. Taxis are commonly used for getting around all the islands.

Hotels are officially graded from one to five stars; there is a separate one- to four-star system for simpler *pensões* and *residencials*. *Pousadas* are state-owned inns, often in scenic or historic locations, offering reliable standards of comfort. *Estalagens,* classified as three or four stars, are similar to *pousadas* but privately owned, and standards are more variable.

The *Turismo de Habitação* scheme offers bed and breakfast in privately owned accommodation ranging from simple farmhouses to palatial seventeenth-century mansions.

Campsites are generally very simple and cheap, except for a few well-equipped sites on the Algarve. They are graded on a four-point scale.

RED TAPE, HEALTH AND SAFETY

BRITISH PASSPORT-HOLDERS do not need a visa to visit Portugal.

Tap water in most parts of the country is safe to drink, but check with the locals in the area you are staying in. The usual problems with petty theft occur – see page 12.

MORE INFORMATION Portuguese Tourism Office, 22–25A Sackville Street, London W1X 2LY, tel 0171-494 1441, web site: http://www.portugal.org

COST OF LIVING £££

RUSSIA

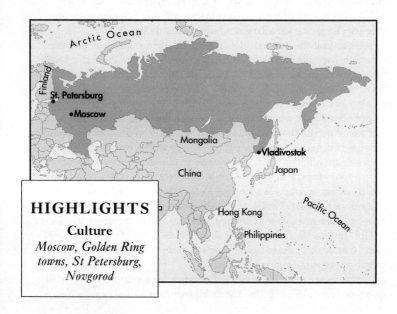

Arctic Ocean

Finland

St. Petersburg

•Moscow

Mongolia

China

•Vladivostok

Japan

Hong Kong

Pacific Ocean

Philippines

HIGHLIGHTS

Culture
*Moscow, Golden Ring
towns, St Petersburg,
Novgorod*

MOSCOW
Good for culture

THE CITY is very much in the vanguard of the new Russia: new energy, new business, new money, new crime. The latest grandiose gesture is
the vast new cathedral, complete with gold onion domes, built by the
river in record time. Moscow is not exactly beautiful, but it is a fascinating (and very expensive) place, with plenty to do in a week. It is best
to combine guided tours with striking out on your own.

BEST SIGHTS

Opening times vary greatly; some sights are available only on guided
tours. Long queues can build up on Sundays for the big museums –
go early in the morning.

Kremlin

Inside the swallow-tailed red walls, the complex of stuccoed palaces
and domed cathedrals takes at least a day to explore. By far the most
beautiful part of it is the Cathedral Square: there is a church here for
every major event in the lifespan of a tsar.

Leo Tolstoy House Museum
An evocative literary museum, giving a rare glimpse into the great writer's daily life.

The Metro
Moscow's underground system is one of its greatest works of art – cathedral-like halls, marble columns, murals and statuary. Of the many stations worth seeing, Ploshchad Revolyutsii, Komsomolskaya and Arbatskaya are especially interesting.

Novodevichy Convent
The restored convent is a peaceful place of red and white buildings within fortified walls. In the adjoining cemetery you can pay tribute to Russian greats including Gogol, Chekhov and Prokofiev.

Pushkin Fine Arts Museum
The museum houses ancient and European art, notably a splendid collection of French Impressionist and post-Impressionist paintings.

Red Square and St Basil's Cathedral
The vast cobbled square is dominated by GUM, a palatial indoor shopping centre now housing smart Western designer chains at exorbitant prices, and by St Basil's Cathedral, Moscow's most exotic and photographed building (the interior is less remarkable). Lenin's embalmed body still lies in the Mausoleum beneath the Kremlin walls.

Tretyakov Gallery
The greatest collection of Russian art resides in a restored building with good facilities. The medieval icons are particularly fine.

GOLDEN RING
Good for culture

THE 'GOLDEN ring' of medieval Russian towns around Moscow contains a panoply of early Russian art and architecture: churches, monasteries and kremlins (fortresses). All can be visited on day-trips or overnight stays from Moscow, by public transport or guided tours.

BEST SIGHTS
Little Suzdal is the most picturesque and the most visited. Also very worthwhile is Sergiev-Posad (formerly Zagorsk), with its fortified complex of the Trinity Monastery of St Sergei, one of Russia's most important religious landmarks, associated with the great Andrei Rublev. Other towns in the golden ring include Vladimir, Yaroslavl and Rostov-Veliky.

ST PETERSBURG
Good for culture

AN ASTONISHINGLY beautiful city, of almost perfect symmetry and dazzling vistas, St Petersburg was purpose-built in the eighteenth century as a 'new town', mainly by Europeans, on Peter the Great's orders. The result is a striking combination of Italianate architecture and northern light (in summer the nights are as light as day). As one of Europe's greatest treasure-troves of art, it deserves up to a week of your time.

BEST SIGHTS
Alexander Nevsky Monastery
In one of the two walled cemeteries here you can pay your respects to Tchaikovsky, Mussorgsky, Rimsky-Korsakov and Dostoyevsky.

Dvortsovaya Ploshchad and Nevsky Prospekt
The Palace Square is a vast theatrical space enclosed by the stuccoed Winter Palace and the classical curve of the Staff Headquarters. Nevsky Prospekt, the city's main avenue, leads off from here, crossed by canals, flanked by classical, baroque and art-nouveau façades and seething with people and street traders for its entire six-mile length.

The Hermitage
You could spend the whole week in this, one of the world's greatest museums, purpose-built to house the royal art collections in some 400 halls which contain two million works of art from all periods of history. The opulent interiors match the richness of the collection.

Literary museums
Lovers of Russian literature should visit the Pushkin Flat Museum and the Dostoyevsky House; in the latter you can see the study where he wrote *The Brothers Karamazov*.

Peter and Paul Fortress
This is a mini eighteenth-century town built as a bastion against the Swedes on the right bank of the Neva. Peter the Great's grave is here, in a church with a thin gold spire.

Royal palaces
Three imperial palace complexes outside St Petersburg can be visited on day-trips. Petrodvorets and Catherine's Palace at Pushkin are baroque echoes of the Winter Palace in St Petersburg in appearance; Pavlovsk is a classical building whose gardens were inspired by those of Versailles in France.

NOVGOROD
Good for culture

NOVGOROD IS one of Russia's oldest towns (founded by Vikings), south of, and easily visited from, St Petersburg – an overnight stop is best. It bristles with blue and gold domes of monasteries and churches.

WHEN TO GO

VISIT IN summer, when temperatures are pleasantly warm; the Moscow winter is grim and long. St Petersburg, further north but with a milder climate than Moscow, is particularly beautiful during the 'white nights' in June (there is also a festival of that name) or during the winter, covered in snow (the buildings are well-heated).

	Average daily maximum temperature °C											
London	6	7	10	13	17	20	22	21	19	14	10	7
Moscow	-9	-6	0	10	19	21	23	22	16	9	2	-5
	JAN	FEB	MAR	APR	MAY	JUN	JUL	AUG	SEP	OCT	NOV	DEC
Moscow	18	15	15	13	13	12	15	14	13	15	15	23
London	15	13	11	12	12	11	12	11	13	13	15	15
	Average number of rainy days per month											

PACKAGE TRAVEL

INTOURIST, ONCE the state-run tour operator for Russia, is still the largest tour operator to Russia from the UK. The choice of packages to Russia is still somewhat restricted. Most operators offer city breaks in

---

Tour operators

Cultural: British Museum Traveller, Martin Randall, Prospect **River cruises**: Swan Hellenic, Titan HiTours **Specialists**: Finlandia, Intourist, Pan Tours, Peltours, Regent Holidays, Steppes East **Walking**: Exodus, Explore Worldwide **Other activities**: Ace Study Tours, Highway Journeys (church tours), Holts' Tours (battlefields), Ornitholidays (birdwatching), Solo's Holidays (singles)

---

either Moscow or St Petersburg, or a two-centre holiday in both cities with transfers by air or rail. Other options include the Trans-Siberian and Trans-Manchurian Railways, which run between Moscow, Vladivostok and China (where destinations include Beijing and Guangzhou), or activity holidays based on walking, birdwatching or river cruises.

INDEPENDENT TRAVEL

UNLESS YOU are a well-versed traveller and know some Russian (and the Cyrillic alphabet), it is not worth going to Russia independently. You will not save money by taking a package, but you will save yourself a lot of hassle. Once there you can strike out on your own by using the cheap and generally excellent public transport or joining the readily available organised tours. The best policy is to use a combination of both and explore on your own once you feel more confident.

Aeroflot, an airline which has always had a poor reputation, has now been broken up into several smaller airlines, leading to further doubts about safety. As a result, domestic flights are probably best avoided. Trains are more reliable, and cheap, though they are slow. The ultimate rail journey is on the Trans-Siberian Railway from Moscow to Vladivostok, a unique six-day experience.

Although car hire is now easily available, the traffic in the cities is nightmarish, the standard of driving abysmal and the roads outside the cities mainly in very bad condition, with signposting rather poor and in Cyrillic only.

There is a dearth of moderately priced, reasonable-standard hotels. For most tourists the choice is between the featureless square blocks inherited from the Soviet era and the new generation of luxury hotels that are affordable only by business travellers. As a guide, a three-star hotel will usually be a 1960s/'70s tower block with several restaurants and a bar or a nightclub. Always check the menus and prices in hotel restaurants before you order – some have the attitude that foreigners are there to be fleeced. When booking a package, check the location of your hotel – if it is way out of the centre, make sure it is near a metro station. Specialist agencies can arrange B&B accommodation in private households (mainly in blocks of flats), and both Moscow and St Petersburg now have youth hostel accommodation.

RED TAPE, HEALTH AND SAFETY

IT IS best to let your travel agent or tour operator get your visa for you; essentially, the more you pay the quicker it will arrive (it can cost

anything from £10 to £60).Three passport photographs are required
and visas applied for in person may take two weeks to issue.Your application may be rejected arbitrarily if you want to travel independently,
outside an escorted tour.

Although reports of crime are exaggerated in the Western press, you
should take the same precautions as you would in any big city - do not
carry valuables and cameras ostentatiously and do not leave them lying
around in your hotel. For the latest advice, contact the Foreign Office
Travel Advice Unit (see page 11).

MORE INFORMATION There is no tourist board in the UK for
Russia. The largest operator is Intourist, Intourist House, 219 Marsh
Wall, London E14 9PD, tel 0171-538 8600, visa information (0891)
171271 (premium rate number)

COST OF LIVING £££

THE SEYCHELLES

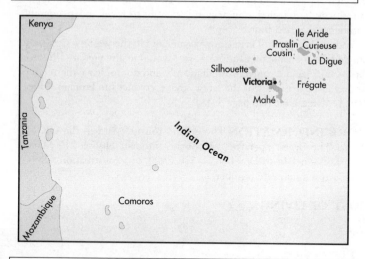

HIGHLIGHTS

Beaches
Mahé,
Praslin,
La Digue,
Frégate

Food/wine
Mahé,
Praslin

Flora
Praslin

**Local
colour/
shopping**
Mahé

**Outdoor
activities**
Mahé,
Praslin,
La Digue

**Romantic
escapism**
Frégate

**Scenic
landscape**
La Digue

Wildlife
La Digue,
Bird Island

THE SEYCHELLES is a group of 115 named islands in the western Indian Ocean off the coast of east Africa, north of Madagascar. They retain a French identity.

MAHE
Good for beaches, local colour, outdoor activities and shopping

MAHE, DOMINATED by the green hump of Morne Seychellois, is the hub of the islands, and the one with most to offer tourists. You can choose from 68 beaches, learn to dive, visit a tea plantation, or the casinos. The Creole fish curries are excellent.

Victoria

As capitals go, Victoria is definitely in the modest league. It is about the size of an average English market town, and you can wander round it on foot. The centre of town is the silver clock-tower, erected in 1903 as a tribute to Queen Victoria and a replica of one which stands on Vauxhall Bridge Road in London.

BEST LOCAL COLOUR

Sir Selwyn Clarke Market

The best place to catch some local colour in Victoria, where massive fish are gutted for waiting housewives. Other market stalls sell colourful arrays of spices as well as tiny bottles of vanilla essence and fiery chutneys.

BEST BEACHES AND WATER SPORTS

Anse Intendance

This beautiful beach is particularly good for snorkelling; beware of the currents.

Anse aux Pins

Located on the east coast, this beach offers the chance to see the local fishermen selling off their catches during the day and repairing their wicker creels.

Anse Takamaka

A lovely beach in the south-west of the island with fine snorkelling. Care is required owing to hazardous currents.

PRASLIN

Good for beaches, flora and outdoor activities

PRASLIN SEEMS simple and undeveloped after Mahé. You can hire a car or bicycle to get around. Most hotels are close to the beaches.

BEST EXCURSION

Vallée de Mai forest

When General Gordon of Khartoum discovered this eerie forest, he believed he had found the Garden of Eden. The unique tropical habitat includes coco de mer trees, whose thick stems shoot 80 feet into the air while their palms fan out like parasols, shutting out the light.

BEST BEACHES AND WATER SPORTS

Praslin offers numerous diving and water sports opportunities. There are a couple of straggling settlements at Baie Ste-Anne near Anse

Volbert in the north and at Grand Anse in the south; Anse Lazio is pleasant.

LA DIGUE
Good for beaches, outdoor activities, scenic landscape and wildlife

LA DIGUE, half-an-hour from Praslin by boat, is the most photogenic island, and the best partner for Mahé if you visit only two islands.

BEST BEACH
Anse la Source à Jean
An idyllic beach lapped by turquoise waters and backed by huge rocks like giant elephants' feet. You can make your way to the beach by ox-cart.

BEST WILDLIFE

The black paradise flycatcher, one of the world's most threatened birds, can be glimpsed on La Digue at the nature reserve.

BIRD ISLAND
Good for wildlife

BIRD ISLAND – only four metres above sea-level – is flat with open vistas. Most of the island (you can walk around it in a couple of hours) is protected by coral reef, but there are gaps, and swimming on the west side of the island is sometimes very rough. Take plastic sandals to protect your feet from coral and sharp pebbles while swimming.

BEST WILDLIFE

Most visitors come to watch birds. Beginners are given an observation check list to help them get started. On the observation platform watching the roosting of the sooty terns – a spectacular piece of theatre, set against the backdrop of a tropical sunset – you may feel overwhelmed by the sheer volume of birds which descend.

FREGATE
Good for beaches and romantic escapism

FREGATE IS a truly special island. You can see the golden beaches as the plane approaches.

BEST BEACH

Anse Victoria

The beach is about 25 minutes' walk through dense vegetation from the bungalows. Brave the final, steep descent: it is worth it. Beware of the strong current.

OTHER ISLANDS
Good for beaches, flora, outdoor activities and wildlife

Aride

The most important nature reserve of the granitic islands, lying five miles north of Praslin. It is owned by the Royal Society for Nature Conservation and is partially surrounded by coral reef, making it equally popular with bird-watchers and divers. Wright's gardenia blooms here.

Cousin

From Praslin you can take a trip to Cousin, a bird sanctuary open to the public three days a week. The warden will introduce you to white tern, black noddies, brush warblers and white-tailed tropic birds. Be sure to bring insect repellent.

Curieuse

This island can be twinned with Cousin on the day-trip from Praslin. On a walk through the dense vegetation you can identify cinnamon, lime, coco de mer, takamaka, papaya and almond trees and bushes. If you are lucky you might see a hawksbill turtle as you creep across the narrow turtle causeway.

Denis

Among the islands Denis is the fisherman's friend. If big-game fishing doesn't appeal, you can spend your time on astonishingly white beaches which encircle an enormous, tranquil lagoon. Day-trippers are not allowed.

Desroches

Desroches, a platform reef, is the largest of the Amirantes group of islands, and lies 142 miles south-west of Mahé. Its remoteness gives it a special appeal, as do its excellent water-sports facilities. The island's only hotel is the comfortable Desroches Island Lodge.

Silhouette

Silhouette is a large, forested, lumpy granite island rather less developed than the others, though the single hotel is smarter than you might expect. Cinnamon and coconut plantations flourish beneath the slopes of Mount Dauban, where rainforest and pitcher plants survive. The difficult landing deters day-trippers.

WHEN TO GO

THE WEATHER is generally humid and warm, and the year is divided into two monsoon seasons. The heaviest rain sets in during the north-west monsoon season, between November and February, with the number of rainy days peaking in December and January. The south-east monsoon between May and September is considered the dry monsoon but sudden torrential downpours are common. The temperature is fairly even all year.

For those interested in diving, underwater visibility is best when the sea is at its calmest in the interval between the two monsoons in March to May and September to November.

Average daily maximum temperature °C											
London	6	7	10	13	17	20	22	21	19	14	10	7
Victoria	31	31	32	33	32	30	29	29	29	31	31	31
	JAN	FEB	MAR	APR	MAY	JUN	JUL	AUG	SEP	OCT	NOV	DEC
(Mahé)	21	17	14	18	14	15	14	14	15	13	17	21
London	15	13	11	12	12	11	12	11	13	13	15	15

PACKAGE TRAVEL

ONLY EIGHT islands are widely used by UK tour operators, and about a dozen others can be visited easily. Mahé is the most developed and varied island if you want to stay put and has the most accommodation to choose from.

Island-hopping involving stays on a combination of islands is a reasonably flexible option – a choice of Mahé, La Digue, Frégate and Bird Island offers variety with a blend of water sports and unforgettable birdlife, while Silhouette, Desroches and La Digue are good for getting away from it all.

Package accommodation tends to be in large, modern, usually low-rise hotels of a good standard. Accommodation in smaller hotels and guesthouses is also available. Self-catering is on offer on Mahé, although as the cost of living is high this may not be much of a saving on hotel package prices. Activity holidays on offer include birdwatching and scuba diving, or you can take a cruise around the islands.

> **Tour operators**
>
> **Birdwatching**: Naturetrek, Ornitholidays **General**: Airwaves,
> British Airways Holidays, Cosmos, Elite Vacations, Hayes & Jarvis,
> ITC, Kuoni, Silk Cut Travel, Somak, Sunset Travel, Trailfinders,
> Tropical Places, Union Castle Travel, Worldwide Journeys **Scuba
> diving**: Aquatours

INDEPENDENT TRAVEL

THERE ARE no UK charter flights to the Seychelles. Scheduled
flight fares are available, but it may be worth contacting a consolidator.

Mahé is the hub of the transport network and all inter-island flights
are channelled through it. Around 25 return flights link Mahé and Praslin
during the day; connections to the other islands are not as regular.

Car hire is available only on Mahé and Praslin. Driving is on the
left. Bicycles are for hire on Praslin and La Digue.

Diving schools around the islands offer lessons; enthusiasts can take
the top-of-the-range Divemaster course. Snorkelling equipment is
available for hire or free of charge at many hotels. Mahé and Praslin are
particularly good for snorkelling and water sports.

RED TAPE, HEALTH AND SAFETY

BRITISH PASSPORT-HOLDERS do not require a visa. A visitor's permit is issued on arrival provided you have a valid passport, return ticket,
pre-booked accommodation and sufficient funds to cover your stay.

Vaccinations for polio, hepatitis A and typhoid are usually recommended – consult your GP or a travel clinic for the latest advice.

The Seychelles retain a French identity and except for red pillar-boxes
and a requirement to drive on the left, little remains of 160 years of British
rule. Take precautions against stomach upsets (see page 11). Swimmers
and divers should beware dangerous currents, particularly on Mahé. Wear
plastic shoes at all times when swimming to avoid painful stings from sea
urchins and cuts from coral, many species of which are poisonous.

Contact the Foreign Office Travel Advice Unit for up-to-date
information on crime and safety matters (see page 11).

MORE INFORMATION Seychelles Tourist Office, 2nd Floor,
Eros House, 111 Baker Street, London W1M 1FE, tel 0171-224 1670,
web site: http://www.seychelles.demon.co.uk

COST OF LIVING *££–£££*

SINGAPORE

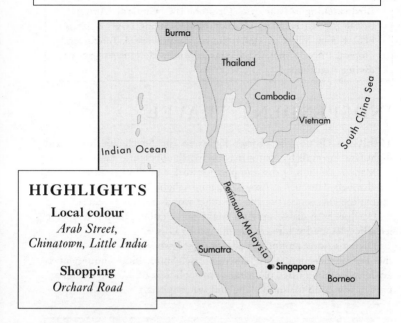

HIGHLIGHTS

Local colour
*Arab Street,
Chinatown, Little India*

Shopping
Orchard Road

ALTHOUGH THE popular image is of a modern, soulless, business city, best known for its shopping, Singapore provides an ideal, easily digestible 'taster' of the cultures and food of South East Asia. Vast shopping malls aside, there are plenty of other reasons to visit the main island of Singapore and perhaps one or two of the 60 smaller islands within its territorial waters.

For those who do come to exercise their credit cards, shops are generally open 10-12 hours a day, seven days a week. In Singapore's air-conditioned malls (mostly located on the Orchard Road) many shops have fixed prices, but haggling is sometimes accepted in districts such as Chinatown.

BEST SIGHTS

Arab Street

The Muslim centre of Singapore is the place to go shopping for batik and sarongs, leatherware and rattanwork, and visit the gold-domed Sultan Mosque.

Chinatown

Over the past few years many of the old colonial shopfronts and alleyways have been restored and gentrified, and smart shops and restaurants have appeared, but you can still get a glimpse of the old ways in the temples and markets as you hunt down some traditional Chinese arts and crafts.

Gardens and zoo
Singapore's climate and fertile land provide ample opportunity for enjoying green spaces. The Mandai Orchid Gardens and the Singapore Botanic Gardens are both excellent places in which to see the orchids for which Singapore is so renowned. The zoo tries to reproduce natural conditions for as many captive species as possible, and has replaced the bars of several animal enclosures with moats.

Little India
Singapore has a vibrant Indian community. In the area of Little India, around Serangoon Road, you can savour the heady aromas of the spice shops, hear Indian music and eat an Indian meal, served on a banana leaf, with your fingers.

Raffles Hotel
Although expensive to stay at, Raffles is still worth a visit, if only for a Singapore Sling in the Long Bar and to imagine life in the colonial days of old. The hotel now sets its sights firmly on the tourist market – both those who stay there and those wishful thinkers who just want to look around and perhaps buy something from the rank of souvenir shops within the hotel grounds. There is also a small museum tucked away on the third floor.

Sentosa Island
This huge family-fun park (crowded with local people at weekends) has something for everyone: a very impressive aquarium (including a 'touch pool' for braver souls), Fantasy Island – a large water theme park – several good museums, a man-made beach, and even a musical fountain which plays music and flashes its coloured lights at night as jets of water shoot skywards.

WHEN TO GO

LOCATED CLOSE to the equator, Singapore is hot and humid all year round and at its wettest from November to January (although the difference between this season and other months of the year is not so dramatic that you should completely rule this period out). Its mix of cultures means that Singapore has a particularly good range of colourful Chinese, Muslim and Hindu events and festivals.

	Average daily maximum temperature °C											
London	6	7	10	13	17	20	22	21	19	14	10	7
Singapore	30	31	31	31	32	31	31	31	31	31	31	31
	JAN	FEB	MAR	APR	MAY	JUN	JUL	AUG	SEP	OCT	NOV	DEC
Singapore	17	11	14	15	15	13	13	14	14	16	18	19
London	15	13	11	12	12	11	12	11	13	13	15	15
	Average number of rainy days per month											

PACKAGE TRAVEL

CITY BREAKS in Singapore are on offer, but the destination is used more often as a starting point for a tour of the Far East. Brochures offer a choice of hotels and pre-purchased excursions. Multi-centre holidays with any combination of other Far East destinations such as Bangkok, Bali, Indonesia and Hong Kong can be arranged.

The train journey on the Eastern and Oriental Express between Singapore and Bangkok is also offered by several tour operators; various cruises start from Singapore.

Tour operators

General: Airwaves, Asian Affair, Asiaworld Travel, Bales Tours, British Airways Holidays, Far East Dream Journeys, Far East Gateways, Hayes & Jarvis, Jetabout, Kuoni, Magic of the Orient, Oriental Magic, Pearl of the Orient, Premier Holidays, Rainbow Holidays, Simply Tropix, Sunset Travel, Tradewinds, Trailfinders, Travelbag, Tropical Places, Virgin Holidays **Other activities**: Holts' Tours (battlefields)

INDEPENDENT TRAVEL

FREQUENT DIRECT flights go to Singapore, but it is also an ideal stop-over point on a long-haul flight to Australia or New Zealand. Changi International Airport is so well equipped that it is almost worth stopping there just to experience the fitness centre, business centre, free film shows and shops and restaurants.

Getting around in Singapore is not a problem as both the bus service and MRT (underground train) services are frequent, reliable and extensive. Taxis are metered – and clean, as drivers can be fined for driving a dirty cab. Trishaws are now used mainly as a tourist attraction; if you want to experience a ride, make sure you agree the fare beforehand.

The main tourist enclave of smart hotels is around Orchard Road. It is best to book in advance and ask for a discount, as cheaper rates are not usually available to people who walk in off the street. The main budget accommodation area is in cheap Chinese hotels around Bencoolen Street and Beach Road. Rooms may be small, and usually have a fan, with shared toilet and shower.

RED TAPE, HEALTH AND SAFETY

UK PASSPORT-HOLDERS do not require a visa; a 14-day stay permit is usually issued on arrival.

No vaccinations are required, and Singapore is not a malarial area. Most visitors to the country comment on how very clean it is, which is perhaps not surprising when you consider that there are hefty fines if you get caught littering the streets (fines are also levied on those caught eating, drinking or smoking on MRT trains or even not flushing the public toilet). Tap water is safe to drink, and food from hawkers' stalls is generally fine. Dehydration is the main problem, due to the heat and humidity – make sure that you drink plenty of fluids.

The crime rate is low due to the harsh punishments meted out to offenders.

MORE INFORMATION Singapore Tourism Board, 1st Floor, Carrington House, 126-130 Regent Street, London W1R 5FE, tel 0171-437 0033, web site: http://www.travel.com.sg/sog

COST OF LIVING £-££

SOUTH AFRICA

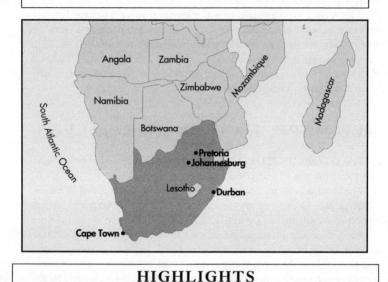

HIGHLIGHTS

Beaches
Western Cape

Outdoor activities
Western Cape

History
Pretoria, Johannesburg

Family holidays
Western Cape

Food/wine
Western Cape

Wildlife
Western Cape, Kruger National Park

Culture
Cape Town, Western Cape, Johannesburg

Scenic landscape
Cape Town, Western Cape, Garden Route

Nightlife
Cape Town

Shopping
Cape Town, Western Cape, Johannesburg

CAPE TOWN
Good for culture, nightlife, shopping and scenic landscape

SOUTH AFRICA'S oldest city nestles in a bowl against the dramatic backdrop of majestic Table Mountain. One of the finest views of the city is from the sea, so be sure to take a boat-trip around Table Bay. Inequality of wealth and strong racial tensions still pervade, but sightseeing is generally hassle-free provided you avoid the established no-go areas such as the Moslem Quarter, which should be visited only as part of a guided tour.

BEST SIGHTS

Castle of Good Hope

South Africa's oldest occupied building, completed in 1676, today houses a small museum of period furniture and paintings. There are also guided tours around the preserved dungeon cells.

Public Gardens

The gardens offer some respite from the throb of traffic, together with an opportunity to view some of Cape Town's finest historic buildings, including the handsome Houses of Parliament (tours available), the National Gallery, with its notable collection of modern South African works, and the South African Museum.

Robben Island

Sailing boats regularly ply the waters between the waterfront harbour and Robben Island, to offer a glimpse of Nelson Mandela's prison (for much of his 27-year incarceration).

Table Mountain

No visit to Cape Town is complete without a trip to the top of its most famous landmark. Most visitors take the five-minute cable-car ride to the top – to avoid queuing, book in advance through the information office in Adderley Street or in the Victoria & Alfred Waterfront visitors information centre. You can also reach the summit on foot by taking one of the many way-marked paths, with differing levels of difficulty; some are suitable only for highly experienced hikers.

Victoria and Alfred Waterfront

Cape Town has an excellent collection of bars and restaurants, but many of those in the city centre can be rather gritty, if not a little sleazy. The redevelopment of the V&A Waterfront has established a lively collection of restaurants, bistros, and bars alongside the busy harbour front.

WESTERN CAPE

Good for beaches, family holidays, flora, food/wine, outdoor activities, shopping, scenic landscape and wildlife

ALTHOUGH IT retains a vibrancy and strong character, the Western Cape has a Mediterranean climate, as well as beach resorts with British names and distinctly Californian atmospheres.

BEST VINEYARDS

Stellenbosch

The heart of South Africa's wine industry is about an hour's drive from

Cape Town, concentrated around the towns of Stellenbosch, Paarl and Franschhoek. Of these, the most historic is Stellenbosch, established towards the end of the seventeenth century in the Eerste River valley. The university town has a striking collection of buildings in Cape Dutch style: of particular note are those found in the village museum, a collection of restored historic houses furnished in period style, including Schreuder House, dating from 1709, and believed to be South Africa's oldest surviving town-house.

Wine enthusiasts will find no shortage of vineyards and estates radiating from the town centre, and linked by well-signed touring routes. Perhaps the pick of the crop are Rust-en-Vrede, a small and rather private estate with a chocolate-box setting and superb red wines, and Delheim, an altogether more touristy experience, with informative and amusing guided tours.

BEST SCENIC LANDSCAPE

Cape Peninsula

The Cape Peninsula's dramatic coastline, long white sandy beaches and imposing mountains provide some of the region's most striking scenery. Keen walkers can attempt the ascent of Chapman's Peak (exertion moderate) for fine views of the peninsula, or the network of trails that criss-crosses the extensive Cape of Good Hope Nature Reserve.

Most visitors to the Cape of Good Hope Nature Reserve make straight for Cape Point. A steep headland rears above the huge car park, with a trail leading up to the promontory.

There is no commercial hullabaloo at the Cape of Good Hope proper – just a rocky coastline and white sand beach buffeted by spume-spraying breakers, plus another walk to the top of the headland.

BEST BEACHES

The western Cape's long sandy beaches provide the perfect setting for exhilarating walks, but not all are suitable for bathers and sun-worshippers, particularly those on the exposed Atlantic coast, which are prone to strong, sand-lifting winds. The western waters are also significantly colder than those on the eastern coast.

Bloubergstrand
● Long sandy beach with terrific views across Table Bay towards Cape Town and across to Robben Island.

Boulders
● Lovely beach set in sheltered cove, good for families.
● Home to hundreds of jackass penguins.

● On the Western Cape's exposed Atlantic coast, so can be chilly and windswept.
● Popular for windsurfing and boardsailing.

Camps Bay
● Good for young trendies: distinctly Californian feel with volleyball on the beach, beauty competitions etc.
● A lovely long beach, backed by a palm-lined promenade and the coast road.
● Extremely exposed to the elements. Water is cold and invigorating.
● Excellent cafés and restaurants.

Clifton
● Popular with young trendies, hence crowded at weekends and in high season – limited parking.
● Four fantastic beaches sheltered from the winds.
● Superb views of the Twelve Apostles, an extension of the Table Mountain range.

Fish Hoek
● Good for families and mature visitors.
● Low-key town with wide sandy beach and a pleasant promenade right on the sea.
● East coast location brings warm waters and less exposure to wind.
● Attracts an older crowd.

Hout Bay
● Good for families, with wide sandy beach backed by low-rise buildings and many good eateries.
● Characterful fishing town with a working harbour.
● In a stunning setting perched between the Sentinel and Chapman's Peak.

Llandudno
● Good for surfers.
● Picturesque village set into cliff, with wide sandy bay, weathered boulders to clamber over and rock pools to explore.
● Limited parking and facilities.

Noordhoek
● Beautiful long sandy beach beneath Chapman's Peak – useful for walkers.
● Cold water and very exposed.
● Popular with horse-riders and dog-walkers.

Sea Point
● Lively resort with English feel, close to Cape Town, popular with younger set and gay crowd.
● Long but rather scrappy beach backed by major road.

THE GARDEN ROUTE
Good for scenic landscape

SOUTH AFRICA'S most scenic coastal terrace stretches from Mossel Bay in the west to the Tsitsikamma area in the east. The attractive shoreline borders the Indian Ocean, and lovely bays and high cliffs have a striking hinterland of imposing mountains, spectacular passes and waterfalls.

BEST BASES
Kynsna
As well as a scenic lagoon and lush, indigenous forest, there is a little museum complex and an eclectic range of arty-crafty shops.

Victoria Bay
Relaxing, laid-back resort with lovely little cove beach flanked by rocky foreshore and rows of Edwardian houses with verandas.

BEST SIGHTS AND EXCURSIONS
Addo National Elephant Park
The rangers at the gate will tell you where the latest sightings have been, and as you nose your car through the park you may see various antelopes, gazelles and vervet monkeys – even black rhino.

Mossel Bay
As well as a fine, crab-strewn beach, the resort has an interesting cluster of museums, a homage to its role as a water station for the Portuguese navigator Bartholomew Dias.

Nature's Valley
A gorgeous blend of ocean, lagoon and milkwood brush, the serene reflections of the wooded mountains in the Groot River, and birds of prey that swoop low over the Bloukrans Pass.

Oudtshoorn
An excellent set of amusements for children includes ostrich farms where you can ride one of the birds, the Cango Caves with their stalactites and stalagmites, and the Cango Crocodile Ranch.

JOHANNESBURG
Good for culture, history and shopping

SOUTH AFRICA'S largest city appears to have little to recommend it to holidaymakers; seldom attractive, notoriously crime-ridden, this congested urban sprawl – known to the Zulus as Egoli, or 'City of Gold' – has lost its glitter in recent years. As a result, perhaps the majority of Johannesburg's visitors prefer to head for established tourist centres such as the Sun City complex, the National Parks or Cape Town.

Certainly, little remains of pioneer Johannesburg, and monuments to the heady gold-digging days have been swallowed up by tower blocks. Crime figures, too, are for once not exaggerated and it pays to be cautious when sightseeing; take guided tours where possible. However, Johannesburg is also a cultural melting-pot, where the Rainbow Nation's many influences converge (not always harmoniously) to create a vibrancy and character less evident in other South African cities. The city boasts museums, galleries, renowned theatrical performances and excellent shopping – all of which are worth a day or two of your time.

Be sure to see the city centre's impressive skyscrapers before heading for Gold Reef City for a reconstruction of Johannesburg's gold-digging days. Touristy it may be, but it is worth bumping around in a horse-drawn carriage and descending an old mineshaft for a glimpse of the workings of South Africa's most lucrative industry. For a more emotive experience, a tour of Soweto, to the south-west of the city, reveals some of the harshness and inequalities of the nation's more recent history and highlights many of the problems faced by the 'New South Africa' in the aftermath of the apartheid era.

PRETORIA
Good for history

JUST 35 miles north of Johannesburg, Pretoria has an altogether different character. Famed for its beautiful jacaranda trees (a riot of colour in spring), charming parkland areas and cluster of handsome and historic buildings, South Africa's administrative centre is instantly more appealing and visitor-friendly than its near neighbour. Be sure to take in the striking Union Buildings, built in 1913 and designed in neoclassical style by the British architect Herbert Baker. And for lovers of more recent man-made attractions, Pretoria is within striking distance of Sun City, a purpose-built holiday resort, offering a wealth of luxurious hotels, casinos and leisure activities, guaranteed to keep even the most active visitor amused.

KRUGER NATIONAL PARK
Good for wildlife

NO VISIT to South Africa would be complete without seeing some of its striking wildlife. Whatever your base, you are likely to be within driving distance of a conservation area (for example, Pilanesberg near Sun City is a small but fascinating game reserve), but for the ultimate wildlife experience, head for the Kruger National Park in Mpumalanga. Named after Paul Kruger, president of the first Republic of South Africa, this vast reserve covers almost 8,000 square miles and is well-stocked with game, including the all-important 'big five' of elephant, buffalo, rhino, lion and leopard, alongside zebra, giraffe, hippo and wild dog. Accommodation in park lodges is comfortable, but book in advance, as Kruger is one of South Africa's premier tourist spots and always busy.

WHEN TO GO

THE WESTERN Cape has a Mediterranean climate with long hot summer days and wet, cool winters. Even in summer the region is prone to strong gale-force winds that can last for several days. The best times to visit are undoubtedly in spring (September/October) and autumn (March/April), when you can count on pleasantly warm temperatures with perhaps a few rainy days.

Average daily maximum temperature °C

	JAN	FEB	MAR	APR	MAY	JUN	JUL	AUG	SEP	OCT	NOV	DEC
London	6	7	10	13	17	20	22	21	19	14	10	7
Johannesburg	25	25	24	21	19	16	17	19	23	24	24	25
Johannesburg	15	11	10	10	5	2	1	2	3	10	15	15
London	15	13	11	12	12	11	12	11	13	13	15	15

Average number of rainy days per month

Average daily maximum temperature °C

	JAN	FEB	MAR	APR	MAY	JUN	JUL	AUG	SEP	OCT	NOV	DEC
London	6	7	10	13	17	20	22	21	19	14	10	7
Cape Town	26	26	25	23	20	18	17	18	19	21	24	25
Cape Town	5	5	5	9	13	12	12	13	10	9	5	5
London	15	13	11	12	12	11	12	11	13	13	15	15

Average number of rainy days per month

PACKAGE TRAVEL

INCREASING NUMBERS of tour operators list South Africa in their brochures, offering a variety of accommodation and tours and a good deal of flexibility. Several tailor-made tour operators specialise in Africa and organise tours and safaris (see below), such as deluxe train journeys, tours of the Garden Route and the winelands, city breaks in Johannesburg and Cape Town, game reserves, safaris and escorted tours. Accommodation standards are high, ranging from upmarket excellent-value B&Bs and luxurious country houses and lodges to deluxe camping safaris in the Kruger National Park.

Activity holidays include battlefield tours, wildlife tours, wine or rail tours, birdwatching and safaris.

Tour operators

Adventure: Acacia, Kumuka Expeditions **Battlefields**: Holts' Tours, Midas **Birdwatching**: Ornitholidays, Peregrine, Sunbird **General and specialist**: Abercrombie & Kent, African Experience, African Journeys, African Safari Trails, Airtours, Airwaves, Beachcomber Tours, Bluebird Express, British Airways Holidays, Cosmos, Designer Travel, Elite Vacations, Finman Travel, SAR Travel, Somak, South African Affair, South African Airways, Thomas Cook, Tradewinds **Tailor-made specialists**: Act, Bundu Safaris, Cape Tours, Cazenove & Lloyd Safaris, Conservation Corporation Africa, Grenadier Travel, Musgrove World Travel, Okavango Tours & Safaris, Safari Consultants, Spearhead Travel, TCA Holidays, Union Castle Travel, Wild Africa Safaris **Wildlife**: Animal Watch, Discover the World, Naturetrek, Wildlife Worldwide **Other activities**: Cox & Kings (flora), Exodus Worldwide (walking), Explore (walking), Ffestiniog Travel (rail tours), Solo's Holidays (singles), Winetrails (wine)

INDEPENDENT TRAVEL

SCHEDULED AND charter flights connect London to Johannesburg and Cape Town.

Getting around is best by car, although the peninsula does have a good network of local trains. Car hire is very expensive, so the cheapest way to travel is to take a fly-drive package. Driving is on the left.

Trains are few and far between, but a good coach network connects all the major centres. Flying is an excellent way to cover long distances and can be inexpensive if you purchase a South African Airways 'Africa Explorer' pass, even if you're not flying out on SAA. For a relaxed tour, the Outeniqua Choo-tjoe is a narrow-gauge steam train that links George with the popular resort of Knysna, running through woodland, along the coast, and across the Kaaimans River Bridge. Coach excursions to Cape Point and winelands are very expensive.

Accommodation is excellent, with a good range of cheaper and characterful B&Bs. Availability should not be too much of a problem in spring and autumn, but as South Africa is increasing in popularity it may be advisable to book at least a few days ahead.

RED TAPE, HEALTH AND SAFETY

VISAS ARE not required for British passport-holders. Both the Cape peninsula and the Garden Route are free of malaria, and no other immunisations are required, but check with a doctor about other regions – especially rainy areas such as Mpumalanga, where malaria precautions are necessary.

Leaflets giving advice on safety and security are displayed in the airport and the Waterfront Tourist Information Centre in Cape Town. The level of violent crime is increasing, particularly in Johannesburg but also in other major cities. Avoid isolated areas, and do not carry expensive jewellery or lots of cash. The Foreign Office Travel Advice Unit advises avoiding townships and surrounding areas. For the latest information contact the Foreign Office Travel Advice Unit (see page 11).

MORE INFORMATION South African Tourism Board, 5 Alt Grove, London SW19 4DZ, tel 0181-944 8080, brochure line (0541) 550044 (premium rate number)

No tourist office web site exists, but you can access information about South Africa at:
http://www.tourist-offices.org.uk/South_Africa/index.html

COST OF LIVING £

SPAIN

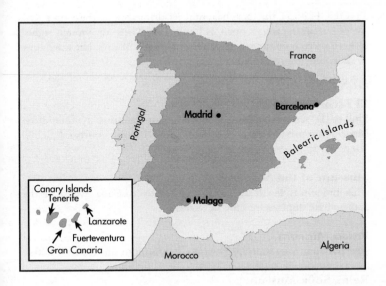

HIGHLIGHTS

Beaches
*Andalucía,
Catalonia,
northern Spain,
Balearics,
Canaries*

**Flora/
wildlife**
Andalucía

**Family
holidays**
*Andalucía,
Balearics,
Canaries*

Food/wine
*Barcelona,
Catalonia,
northern Spain,
Levante*

Local colour
*Aragón,
Andalucía,
Extremadura,
northern Spain*

Nightlife
*Madrid,
Andalucía,
Barcelona,
Catalonia,*

*Balearics,
Canaries*

**Outdoor
activities**
*Andalucía,
Catalonia*

Culture
*Madrid,
Castile,
Aragón,
Andalucía,
Barcelona,
Catalonia*

**Romantic
escapism**
*Andalucía,
Extremadura*

**Scenic
landscape**
*Aragón,
Catalonia,
Extremadura,
northern Spain,
Canaries*

Shopping
Barcelona

MADRID
Good for culture and nightlife

THOUGH NOT the most beautiful, Madrid is one of the most exciting of European capitals, open 24 hours a day. There are enough 'sights'
to keep culture vultures occupied for a couple of days, but leave time
to shop and absorb the vibrant street life.

BEST SIGHTS

El Escorial
Phillip II's sixteenth-century palace, about an hour by train from
Madrid, is a megalomaniacal sort of place: 16 inner courtyards, 2,500
windows, 15 miles of passageways.

Museum of the Americas
This museum is worth the metro ride out to Moncloa, even if all the
audio-visual displays are only in Spanish.

Prado Museum
The museum has about 9,000 works and room to show only 1,500.

Reina Sofía Museum
This superb collection of twentieth-century art includes Picasso's
masterpiece *Guernica*.

Thyssen-Bornemisza Museum
One of the most famous private art collections in the world.

CASTILE
Good for culture

VISITORS KEEN on Spanish art, architecture and history will enjoy
exploring the great central tableland around Madrid known as Old and
New Castile (Castilla-y-León and Castilla-La Mancha). Despite the
capital's radiating influence, Castile still has a rural, provincial air. The
continental climate in this high plateau is extreme; choose spring or
autumn for comfortable travelling.

BEST CITIES

Burgos
The spires of an outstanding Gothic cathedral dominate this provincial
capital, where El Cid's ghost hovers. Just outside its well-preserved old
quarter lie three exceptional monasteries.

León
The oldest glasswork of León's splendid cathedral is 700 years old, but its famous pilgrim *parador*, the Hostal de San Marcos, and the twelfth-century frescos are equally memorable.

Salamanca
Spain's most famous university city offers a showcase of Renaissance architecture, and a magnificent Plaza Mayor.

Segovia
This delightful town's prize monument is its Roman aqueduct. Also visit the fairy-tale folly castle and a cluster of Romanesque churches.

Toledo
Toledo is one of Spain's greatest tourist attractions. The old town, dramatically poised above the Tagus gorge, is stacked with art and architecture from many periods.

Valladolid
Valladolid's main attraction for visitors is its architecture. The Collegio de San Gregorio houses a stunning collection of sculpture by many of Spain's best Renaissance artists.

ARAGON
Good for local colour and scenic landscape

THE VARIETY of scenery in this little-known and depopulated region is astonishing. Best are the high peaks of the Pyrenees, spectacularly encapsulated in the Ordesa National Park. Aragón's largest cities, though not beautiful, contain a remarkable heritage of Moorish monuments. In unspoilt rural areas it is still possible to see ancient ways of life, including some of Spain's strangest *fiestas*.

BEST SIGHTS
Ordesa National Park
This is one of Spain's oldest national parks. Snow makes the park accessible only in summer without specialist climbing gear, and most of it can be visited only on foot.

Teruel
Teruel offers a striking assembly of Mudejar towers in ornate brickwork and one of Aragón's best provincial museums. The cathedral displays dazzling craftsmanship.

Zaragoza

Zaragoza fared badly in both the Peninsular and the Civil Wars, and today forms a dusty sprawl of brick along the Ebro. The most impressive buildings are the multi-domed basilica of Nuestra Señora del Pilar, and the Catedral de la Seo.

ANDALUCIA
Good for beaches, culture, family holidays, flora, local colour, nightlife, outdoor activities, romantic escapism and wildlife

FLAMENCO DANCERS, acoustic guitars and matadors originate from here. Andalucía also offers excellent-value sun and sand packages for all ages.

BEST CITIES

Cadiz

Cadiz is smaller and less grand than the 'big three' capitals but its stretch of fine, golden sand is attractive and remarkably clean for a city beach, and the old fishermen's quarters round the port are quaintly atmospheric. The Museum of Fine Art and Archaeology is worth a visit.

Córdoba

Córdoba is the smallest of Andalucía's three great cities but perhaps the most enjoyable to explore. The compact old town is packed with tiny alleyways of whitewashed houses. The Jewish quarter is home to a delicately ornamented synagogue, one of only three remaining in Spain.

Unmissable is the Mezquita, the greatest mosque in the Western world. The Alcázar de los Reyes Cristianos, once the residence of Fernando and Isabella, the city's Christian 'liberators', has Roman mosaics and beautifully kept geometrical gardens. Visit the Torre de la Calahorra for its panorama of the Roman bridge, water wheel and old town.

Granada

The 'modern' city is pleasant enough, but most visitors come to see the world-famous Alhambra palace, the most perfect example of Moorish architecture in Europe. Highlights are the Patio of the Lions and the luxuriant gardens, which provide a grand approach to the Generalife, the rulers' summer palace. Opposite the Alhambra hill, the Moorish quarter (Albaicín), affords fine views.

The stark Renaissance cathedral is disappointingly conventional, but the adjacent Gothic Capilla Real (Royal Chapel) – mausoleum of Fernando and Isabella – is more flamboyant. On the outskirts of town, La Cartuja is an outrageously lavish Carthusian monastery.

Seville

Andalucía's capital lacks a world-ranking sight to match the Alhambra or Mezquita, but the wealth of sights packed into its narrow streets and the easy-going street life give it a beguiling quality. The most beautiful part of the enormous Gothic cathedral is the Giralda, a gloriously golden twelfth-century minaret, with a magnificent panorama from the summit.

The Alcázar is a tranquil royal palace. Visit the Museum of Fine Art in the delightfully restored Convento de la Merced. Highlights of the María Luisa Park are the Plaza de España, the Popular Arts Museum and the Archaeological Museum. One of Europe's most important wildlife habitats is Doñana National Park; it is best visited in the wet winter and spring months.

BEST RESORTS

Andalucía's four *costas* each have a distinctive character. If you choose your resort and accommodation carefully you will find the ambience of the Costa del Sol more cosmopolitan than you might expect, restaurants and bars for all tastes, and prices kept low by fierce competition. East of the Costa del Sol (Costa Tropical and Costa de Almeria) beaches are wider and less crowded, although the sand is coarse and grey. The best beaches of all are on Andalucía's Atlantic Coast, the Costa de la Luz, though strong winds often gust in from the ocean.

Conil de la Frontera (Costa de la Luz)
● Vast, desert-like beach, more sheltered than others, stretching for four miles to Cape Trafalgar, and backed by a few largish hotels.
● Smaller pensions, low-key bars and craft shops in village centre, and excellent fish restaurants along seafront.
● Popular with Spaniards and Germans.

Mojacar (Costa de Almeria)
● Arty Moorish village of white sugar-cube houses and steep, narrow streets, set amid rugged hills three miles above greyish beach, backed by low-rise apartment and hotel buildings.
● Plenty of trendy bars in old town; more traditional resort-style family fun down below along seafront – and several loud open-air discos.
● Feels rather isolated: a long way from Andalucía's top sights.

Nerja (Costa del Sol)
● Prettiest of Costa del Sol resorts, ringed by mountains.
● Whitewashed houses clustered round aprons of sand, with palm-fringed promenade jutting into sea.
● Generally low-rise development.

● Very good children's facilities and low-key nightlife.
● Good walks in and around the town.

San José (Costa de Almeria)
● Large and growing fast, with low-rise apartment complexes and slick marina, though maintains a sleepy ambience.
● Excellent fish restaurants overlooking grey sand-shingle beach.
● Many isolated beaches, including Monsul and Los Genoveses, two of Andalucía's best, nearby, plus birdwatching opportunities and walks.

Torremolinos (Costa del Sol)
● Brash and irredeemably ugly, with densely packed tower blocks, but constantly lively and certainly never dull.
● Wide range of restaurants to suit all tastes and budgets, golf courses nearby, good water sports, Aquapark and Tivoli World, a child-centred amusement park for family fun.

BEST SIGHTS AND EXCURSIONS

Almerian desert
Go to one of the daily shows at one of three movie sets in this rugged desert landscape; hundreds of films were shot here, including *The Good, the Bad and the Ugly*. From the appealing small town of Sorbas the local tourist office arranges caving excursions into contorted volcanic caverns. Nearby Nijar is also worth visiting for its distinctive ceramics.

Alpujarras
A chain of white mountain villages spread out between the sea and the Sierra Nevada. In many, donkeys file through narrow streets, and labourers tend fertile orchards of vines, oranges, bananas and olives. The most developed villages are Capileira, Bubión and Pampaneira. Trevélez, the highest village in Spain, also makes a good base. Throughout the region, there are good walks along (mostly) well maintained paths, plus opportunities for horse-riding and cycling.

Carmona
Half an hour's drive from Seville, this walled, hilltop town is visible for miles. The historic quarter is small but well-preserved.

Jaén and Renaissance towns
The provincial capital of Jaén is dull, but the surrounding landscape is dramatic; a staggeringly beautiful sierra of jagged rocks in shades of blood-red and vermilion. Cazorla is the main town: an animated place with a superbly located *parador*. Further north, Ubeda and Baeza have ornate palaces and churches sculpted in golden stone.

Jerez de la Frontera

The main reason for visiting is a trip to a sherry *bodega*, best arranged through the tourist office. Also unmissable is the Royal Andalucían School of Equestrian Art. The town has a bizarre hybrid Gothic-Renaissance cathedral and a Moorish alcázar.

Ronda and the Pueblos Blancos ('white towns')

A few miles inland, against a backdrop of pine-clad mountains, olive groves and rocky crags, the *pueblos blancos* make a pleasant break from the seaside crowds. Ronda, in a wonderful location atop a deep chasm, is the biggest and most visited, with attractive seventeenth-century mansions and a famous bull ring. Vejer de la Frontera is one of the most unspoilt; Arcos de la Frontera is more developed but has a church and fine *parador*. Others worth seeking out include El Bosque, Grazalema, Zahara de la Sierra, Setenil, Ojén, Casares, Coín and Mijas; the latter two are distinctly on the tourist trail but none the less pretty.

BARCELONA
Good for culture, food/wine, nightlife and shopping

BARCELONA'S WATERFRONT was given a major facelift in honour of the 1992 Olympics. The old medieval alleyways cluster round the immense Gothic cathedral, through the regular grid pattern of wide streets, known as the Eixample, to the leafier suburbs. Elegant turn-of-the-century cafés, lively *cava* bars, and waterfront tapas bars provide endless opportunities for sampling local food and drink.

BEST SIGHTS

Aquarium
Newest of the top sights on the restored waterfront. State-of-the-art displays, and moving walkways to view the streamlined sharks.

Marès Museum
Wonderfully eclectic display of medieval sculpture.

Miró Foundation
Bright and attractive with changing exhibitions of varied media.

Modernist architecture
The rich concentration of Modernist buildings on plush Eixample boulevard includes Gaudí's La Pedrera (which can be visited) and Casa Batlló. His unfinished church, La Sagrada Familia, is well worth visiting. Take the lift up the spire to appreciate it better.

National Museum of Catalán Art
Collection of Romanesque art in the National Palace on Montjuïc.

Picasso Museum
Chronological display of the master's work.

The Ramblas
Irresistible ribbon of flower and bird stalls, plus lively street theatre.

CATALONIA
Good for beaches, culture, food/wine, nightlife, outdoor activities and scenic landscape

THIS SMALL triangle of land bound by the Pyrenees to the north, the Mediterranean to the east, and Aragón and Valencia to the west, may be on the Iberian fringe geographically and culturally (Catalán is the strongest of Spain's regional languages), but has made a central contribution to Spain's economic miracle.

BEST CITY

Tarragona
Though the modern city is provincial and dull compared with Barcelona, Tarragona's history dates from the sixth century BC. Visit the Archaeological Museum, the cliff-top amphitheatre, stumpy remnants of the Roman forum, the Paleo-Christian necropolis further west, and the Tarragona History Museum. The cathedral is the largest in Catalonia, and the old quarter is also worth exploring.

BEST RESORTS

North of Barcelona, the Costa Brava, or more specifically the unattractive and overdeveloped resort of Lloret del Mar, is considered the birthplace of package tourism, but away from the main resorts the coast remains wild and rugged, with fine golden sand and sparklingly clear water. To the south, the Costa Dorada is less scenic but is a good base for visiting Port Aventura, Spain's answer to Disneyland.

Aiguablava (Costa Brava)
● Good for secluded villas. There are just two hotels.
● Series of tiny inlets with golden sand and turquoise water, backed by thick pine groves and craggy cliffs.
● More life and facilities at nearby Tamarui (a larger but unspoilt resort).

Cadaqués (Costa Brava)
● Cluster of whitewashed, cubic houses in secluded bay.

- Stamping ground for the avant-garde, thanks to nearby former residence of Salvador Dalí; galleries and artists' workshops abound.
- Laid-back ambience, with pavement cafés and rakish jazz clubs.
- Not for beach lovers – the strip of sand is narrow and grey.

Calella de Palafrugell/Llafranc (Costa Brava)
- Twin resorts linked by a coastal path; Llafranc is smaller but more conventionally resort-like; Calella is more of a fishing village, though larger.
- Scenic location backed by hills, and wide, sandy beaches.
- Plenty of seafront cafés and fish restaurants, particularly in Calella.

Cambrils (Costa Dorada)
- Best base for visiting Port Aventura, with good family facilities.
- Developed, with large package hotels, but retains fishing village feel.
- Huge saddle of fine sand backed by pleasant promenade lined with restaurants and pavement cafés.

Sitges (Costa Dorada)
- Mobbed by Barcelonan summer refugees, popular with the gay community, and never dull, with a plethora of bars, restaurants and discos.
- Sophisticated and stylish despite the development, with many fine buildings in narrow back streets.
- Long golden beach; young and lively in the centre; quieter and more family oriented on outskirts.
- Three excellent museums; the Romantic Museum, with collection of dolls and musical instruments, should not be missed.

Tossa de Mar (Costa Brava)
- Developed but mostly low-rise resort, backed by mountains.
- Two decent beaches of slightly gritty sand, with pleasant promenades.
- Walled twelfth-century old town on crest of western headland.
- Range of bars and restaurants: both traditional Spanish and British.

BEST SIGHTS AND EXCURSIONS

Aiguestortes National Park
Visit this national park, with its forested tracks, rocky crags, valleys and streams. Follow the walk to the deep green waters of Sant Maurici lake.

Figueres
Visit the eclectic Salvador Dalí Theatre-Museum.

Girona
Girona's tall Gothic cathedral stands out atop the concentric rings of old houses and labyrinth of steep narrow streets. The Romanesque cloister and rich treasury are also worth a visit.

Montserrat
The monastery building at Montserrat is bland but its setting is spectacular. Visit the three museums or take the funicular to the mountaintop hermitages.

Port Aventura
Spain's answer to Disney mirrors its rival's layout of themed lands and combination of live shows and rides. Tame rides exist for small children.

Pyrenean foothills
A trail of outstanding Romanesque churches and exhibits include the Episcopal museum at Vic; the cloister and twelfth-century portal at Ripoll; a cathedral, cloister and museum at La Seu d'Urgell. Also explore the tiny Romanesque churches at Sant Joan de les Abadesses, Camprodon, Baguerge, Tredòs, Gessa and Salardù.

Santa Maria de Poblet
Santa Maria de Poblet is home to Catalonia's best-known Cistercian monastery. Highlights include the delicate cloister and the Royal Pantheon. Six miles south, at Montblanc, a museum traces the history of the monastery and local trade.

Vilafranca del Penedès and the wine region
For an introduction to Catalonia's best wines, visit the museum at Vilafranca. For wine-tasting, head out to Pacs del Penedès and the Torres *bodega*. Close by, Sant Sadurní d'Anoia is the *cava* capital.

EXTREMADURA
Good for local colour, romantic escapism and scenic landscape

EXTREMADURA IS one of Spain's poorest, least developed areas. Tourism is filtering into the area, particularly in the historic towns and cities, but elsewhere visitors will find little English spoken. The best scenery is in the north, but most of the interesting towns are in the south.

BEST SIGHTS
Cáceres
The modern development is unattractive, but the vast, arcaded plaza, palaces and churches propel you back in time. Three palaces, two churches and the remains of a Moorish bath are worth a visit.

Guadalupe
The winding mountain road makes a visit to the wonderful monastery at Guadalupe feel like a pilgrimage.

Mérida
Although the modern city is disappointing, Mérida was once the cultural centre of Roman Spain. The ruins most worth seeing are close together, near the 60-arch bridge spanning the Guadiana.

Plasencia
Plasencia has quaint alleyways and a part Gothic, part Romanesque cathedral.

Trujillo
The main square is lined with extravagant palaces, but the Méson la Troya, a wonderfully eclectic and inexpensive restaurant is just as much of a crowd-puller.

Zafra and southern towns
Southern Extremaduran towns and villages have an Andalucían flavour, with whitewashed houses lining narrow streets. Zafra has a fine sixteenth-century church. The pinnacles and spires of Jerez de los Caballeros are visible for miles around.

BEST TOURING
Hervás and the Jerte valley
The Jerte valley is full of cherry orchards and olive groves, whilst Hervás, close by, has an unusually well-preserved Jewish quarter.

La Vera
Fruit trees, vines and olive groves abound in the land around the villages of La Vera. Garganta la Olla and Jarandilla de la Vera are the most picturesque places.

NORTHERN SPAIN
Good for beaches, food/wine, local colour and scenic landscape

THE WEATHER is less predictable than in the south but the beaches are not scarred by tower blocks, and the few 'developed' resorts retain a quirky individuality. Inland, the Picos de Europa mountain range offers excellent outdoor pursuits, and there are numerous churches, museums and villages to explore.

Throughout the Basque country and Navarra, you will hear the arcane Basque language (spoken by a minority) and follow Basque road signs. In rural Galicia, Gallego, similar to Portuguese, is the main tongue, and the culture has Celtic roots; bagpipes (*gaitas*) are as much a part of local celebrations here as in Scotland.

BEST RESORTS

Baiona
● Ranged round a gently curving bay within a small fjord.
● Gleaming cafés on the waterfront, traditional tapas bars in the old town, fancy *solanas* (enclosed balconies), and wrought iron balconies.
● Best resort in Galicia, popular with Spaniards; foreigners tend to stay at the secluded castle-*parador* on a pine-clad promontory.
● Best beaches just outside town, or a ferry ride to the Islas Cíes.

Comillas
● Former summer residence of Alfonso XII: an air of regal refinement lingers in faded mansions and cobbled streets of old town.
● Flamboyant folly designed by Gaudí – now an exclusive restaurant.
● Messy modern seaside resort, packed with Spaniards in summer.
● Lively, with plenty of eating possibilities, and fine, wide strip of sand.

Fuenterrabía (Hondarrabia)
● Fishing village with a large, creamy sand beach in sheltered bay.
● Walled medieval quarter on hilltop, with narrow, cobbled streets, and sixteenth-century castle (now a *parador*) with stunning sea views.
● Lively and distinctly French ambience.
● Excellent restaurants.

Laxe
● Traditional fishing village where you can still see people mending nets and bringing in the catch.
● Slowly growing as a resort, with paved promenade planted with baby palm trees, and long sheltered beach.
● Pleasant old town of stone and whitewashed houses.
● Limited accommodation.

Luarca
● Civilised and relaxed former fishing village; the harbour is over-looked by elegant houses and fishermen's cottages.
● Two beaches of hard-packed sand, backed by slate cliffs, and lined with old-fashioned changing cabins.
● Good selection of bars and fish restaurants round harbour.

Muros
● Most developed fishing village, with bars, disco and artificial beach.
● Smartly renovated main plaza overlooks the fjord; rustic back streets.
● Plenty of unpretentious fish restaurants.
● Best beach (Playa de San Francisco) is situated about three miles out of town.

San Sebastián (Donostia)
● Slightly faded but still chic.
● Beautiful scallop-shaped bay with two sandy beaches, closed in by wooded promontories and backed by frilly pavilions.
● Easy-going ambience ideal for both families and couples.
● Picturesque harbour, with arcaded fishermen's cottages, and many restaurants serving delicious local specialities.

Santander
● Vestiges of *belle époque* panache and exuberant, but fading, grand hotels.
● Fine golden beach.
● Colourful fish market, much-restored Gothic cathedral, and Museo de Bellas Artes.

San Vicente de la Barquera
● Costa Verde's most relaxed resort, popular with Spanish families.
● Pavement cafés and seafood restaurants in arcaded main street, pizzerias and lively bars by waterfront.
● Sleepy, walled old town with thirteenth-century church.
● Exposed but large sandy beach across estuary and arched bridge.

Viveiro
● Old town of narrow streets and flaking ochre plazas rises up on one side of the *ría*, around a splendid Gothic church.
● Best nearby beach, Playa de Area, across the *ría*, backed by grassy dunes and sheltered by two promontories.
● Plenty of bars, restaurants and cafés for all tastes.

BEST INLAND BASES

Leyre
Above the Yesa reservoir in the craggy Pyrenean foothills, is an eleventh-century monastery; part of it now houses a restaurant and hotel. Stay for compline, when the brothers sing Gregorian chant in candlelit, incense-laden gloom.

Olite and the Pilgrim route
A tourist honeypot, thanks to its Disneyesque castle, Olite is a good base for exploring the Pilgrim route. Nearby is a fine Cistercian church, the Monasterio de la Oliva, and many smaller villages.

Pamplona (Iruñea)
Famed for July's frenetic San Fermin festival, when bulls are let loose in the street, Navarra's provincial capital has faded *belle époque* buildings and a wonderful café round the main square, an atmospheric old town, with Gothic cathedral and a good museum.

Santiago de Compostela

Santiago, home to St James the Apostle's remains, is the focus of one of the most important medieval pilgrimages. Tourists flock to view the city's architecture of golden-grey, mineral-flecked granite. The cathedral is the centrepiece. The Museo do Poblo Gallego is a former convent.

Santillana del Mar

The medieval ruralism of this misleadingly named inland village is best enjoyed after the coach parties have gone. A fine Romanesque church and an outstanding museum of religious art are the main sights.

BEST SIGHTS AND EXCURSIONS

Altamira caves

If you can, visit Spain's most important prehistoric cave paintings (only 25 people a day). Bookings are made more than six months in advance; if you are lucky, and you arrive early, you may inherit a cancellation.

Betanzos

Three medieval churches add focus to a wander through the back streets of this market town; the fourteenth-century San Francisco is the best.

Bilbao

The revamped old quarter, or Casco Viejo, is full of smart shops, restaurants and tapas bars. Art lovers should visit the Museo de Bellas Artes and the stunning Guggenheim Museum near the River Nervion.

Celanova

A small and not particularly interesting modern town hides a fascinating monastery with a florid baroque façade and vaulted cloister.

Guernica

Thanks to the Luftwaffe's bombs the town is mostly drab and modern.

Haro and the Rioja vineyards

You will see plenty of *degustación* signs, and the state-owned co-operative in Haro, a cheerful small town, is a good place to see the traditional processes. The Palacio Winery outside Laguardia is also worth a visit.

Islas Cíes

Of the three islands reached by ferry from Vigo, one is an out-of-bounds bird sanctuary. The others are linked by a tremendous white sand bar. Swimming is sheltered and Praia de Figueiras is very beautiful.

La Guardia

A rather tacky fishing village worth visiting to see Monte Santa Tecla, a superbly preserved Celtic *citanía* (fortified hill settlement), with scores of circular stone huts, two rebuilt, and extensive coastal views.

Lugo
The surrounding Roman city walls, made of local slate, are 50 feet high, over 20ft thick, and defended by 85 towers, with ten gates.

Mondoñedo
The central point is the plaza, sloping from a row of arcaded houses to the golden façade of the eighteenth-century cathedral.

Oviedo
Asturias's industrial capital is worth visiting only if you have an interest in pre-Romanesque churches. The Archaeological Museum's collection ranges from prehistoric flints to more contemporary folk art.

Pontevedra
A lively, atmospheric market city on the river estuary. Highlights are the Museo Provincial and the Santa María Mayor church.

Tui
The cathedral of Galicía's main frontier town is an austere Romanesque-Gothic structure. The interior is more elaborate.

BEST SCENIC LANDSCAPES
Picos de Europa
Some of the walking routes can be quite strenuous, though the attractive file through the Cares Gorge is suitable for all (and very popular). Potes is the main centre for arranging jeep and horseback safaris, Carmona is one of the loveliest of the villages, while the most popular excursion is the cable-car ascent at Fuente Dé. Covadonga, a kitsch Catholic shrine, is fun. Higher up the hill, two deep azure lakes are popular lunch spots.

Sils Gorge
Inland, Galicía's most memorable drive follows a gorge of cascading rock, with lush woods and tiny terraced plots of maize and vines. Sited on a spur above the gorge, the former monastery at San Esteban de Ribas de Sil has a rather dull church, but three lovely cloisters.

THE LEVANTE
Good for food/wine

THE COASTAL regions of Valencia and Murcia, known collectively as the Levante (the East) are justifiably less visited than their neighbours. But to dismiss the area altogether is unfair; the climate is warm and sunny year-round, the three main cities are appealing, and even the most developed resorts are fun, with plenty of British camaraderie.

BEST RESORTS

The best resorts are clustered around the peninsula separating the Costa del Azahar in the north from the Costa Blanca in the south.

Benidorm (Costa Blanca)
● Much maligned, indisputably kitschy, with high-rise architecture that is more city- than resort-like, but effervescent, fun and friendly.
● Broad, palm-lined boulevards and a tiny, pretty old quarter, though overrun with 'British' bars.
● International crowd from across northern Europe and plenty of Spanish visitors ensure wide choice of bars and cuisines.
● Two decent sandy beaches: Playa de Poniente, backed by hills and promenade, is more attractive than Levante.
● Good for long stays out of season, but best avoided in high summer.

Jávea (Costa Blanca)
● Best of the low-key resorts for a stay-put holiday, nestling in a dip below the pine-clad San Antonio headland.
● Mostly apartment and villa accommodation, the most appealing of which is scattered on the hillsides outside town.
● Year-round resort, popular with retired British, with sandy beach.

Peñiscola (Costa del Azahar)
● Best resort on the flat, featureless coastal plain south of Valencia, with lovely old town built on a rugged crag and capped by a castle.
● Atmospheric narrow streets, particularly at night, when castle is floodlit, but tortuous in high season when packed.
● Excellent fresh fish, lively fishing port and a daily fish auction.
● Not recommended for long stays; though long and sandy, the beach lacks shade and is backed by main road.

BEST CITIES

Alicante
Many unjustifiably dismiss Alicante as a cheap charter-flight destination, but those who stay a night or two will discover the perfect place for strolling and lingering at pavement cafés. In the old Santa Cruz quarter, the patchwork of tiny houses may be decked with geraniums, or decaying, with peeling façades and graffiti.

Castillo de Santa Bárbara affords extensive views over town and sea, while the Museo de Arte Siglo 20 (Museum of Twentieth-Century

Art) has an unexpectedly impressive and comprehensive collection – definitely worth a visit.

Four miles north is San Juan, with a long sandy beach and palm-planted promenade; it surpasses the main town beach for sun-bathing and swimming. Frequent ferries ply visitors to the little off-shore island of Tabarca, a small fishing settlement with a few bars/restaurants, and good beaches.

Murcia

Murcia is not the most enticing of capitals but retains an elegant, if small, old town, and makes a pleasant overnight stop. The pedestrianised centre, with pavement cafés, is particularly lively in the evenings.

The Casino, a florid late nineteenth-century structure now used for exhibitions and concerts, and the cathedral, whose magnificently theatrical baroque façade hides a plainer Gothic interior and two elaborate chapels, are worth a visit. The small museum displays melodramatic works by the eighteenth-century Murcian sculptor Francisco Salzillo.

Valencia

Spain's third-largest city is a curious hotch-potch, but has some atmospheric corners and impressive buildings, sunny plazas with trendy cafés. Evening entertainment is good – as is shopping. The cathedral, which fronts on to Valencia's prettiest square, Plaza de la Virgen, is best known for housing the so-called Holy Grail, brought to Spain in the fourth century. The Miguelete tower is fun to climb.

Visit the Colegio de Patriarca (Patriarch Collegiate Church) on a Friday morning, when there is a dramatic service, complete with incense; it has a small museum. The 5,000 ceramics in the Museo Nacional de Cerámica date from Iberian times to the twentieth century – a must for lovers of Spanish *azulejos* (ceramic tiles).

BEST INLAND SIGHTS

With flat, featureless plains, this is not an ideal area for scenic touring, but pleasant excursions can be made from the main resorts and cities.

Guadalest

Explore the mountains inland from Benidorm, part wild, part terraced with olive, almond and citrus groves; visit the pretty waterfalls at Algar and a couple of caves, the best is at Canolobre. The medieval village of Guadalest, ingeniously clamped to a rock, is topped by a ruined castle.

Morella

Fortified Morella has the appearance of a stylised medieval painting and is unmissable. Main sights are the fourteenth-century Gothic Basilica of Santa María la Mayor, thirteenth-century Monastery of San Francisco and the castle ramparts, from which the views are phenomenal.

BALEARIC ISLANDS
Good for beaches, family holidays and nightlife

THE BALEARICS offer a variety of options, from family beach holidays to luxurious isolation, quiet villas and non-stop nightlife.

IBIZA

IBIZA TOWN itself is the main focus of the island's nightlife.

BEST RESORTS
● Portinatx has three beaches linked by a path across low headlands. Good mix of ages, bars for old and young, enjoyable atmosphere. The drawback is that the beaches are crowded.
● Santa Eulalia del Rio is centred on a small crescent of beach, backed by a neat promenade. If the beach gets too crowded, you can take ferries to nearby coves.

MAJORCA

THE LARGEST and most scenically varied of the islands, Majorca probably has a sun-and-sand resort to suit every taste as well as more than enough sights to satisfy seasoned travellers.

BEST RESORTS
● Magaluf is the place to stay for great nightlife and excellent beaches. Torrenova and Cala Viñas are the quietest places to stay.
● Palma Nova is similar to Magaluf but slightly less frenetic at night.
● Plenty of space on the beach at Sant Ponsa but central area is built-up with hotels and anonymous eateries.
● San Vicente is on a more exposed part of the north coast; many of the villas and hotels are set right back and fringed with pines.
● Nearby Puerto Pollensa is low-key, with a long narrow beach of fine sand and some good hotels and restaurants, far removed from the noisy excess found elsewhere on the island.
● Cala Ratjada, on the east coast, comes the closest to being an authentic resort town. Lively at night, with a variety of clubs and bars.

● Canyamel and Cala Santanyi are small, attractive resorts with excellent beaches and a relaxed atmosphere.

● Purpose-built Cala d'Or spreads itself around a series of coves and tiny beaches. The pedestrianised centre, close to the smart marina, contains a good mix of bars and restaurants – stay in the central area, around Cala d'Or or Cala Gran, if you want to explore this part of the island.

BEST INLAND BASES

The Tramuntana Mountains rear out of the sea on Majorca's western coast, a jumble of gnarled peaks and sheer cliffs. For touring or escaping the coastal crowds make your base here. Banyalbufar, a simple village of tidy cobbled streets, is surprisingly lively in the evening. Deià is a popular refuge for artists and writers, including the late Robert Graves, and has a couple of very smart hotels.

BEST SIGHTS AND EXCURSIONS

Visit sophisticated, self-assured Palma for the cathedral, Almudaina Palace and Museum of Majorca. Art galleries and exhibitions are plentiful.

Valldemossa owes its fame to the long stay of the composer Frederick Chopin and his lover George Sand, who lodged in the Carthusian monastery. The cells they lived in have become a museum dedicated to Chopin's life and work; views from the terrace are fabulous.

Sa Calobra, or 'the snake', is an improbably twisting road that plunges from beneath the peak of Puig Mayor down to the sea. A less tortuous way to get here is by boat from Puerto de Soller.

Cuevas de Artá and Cuevas de Campanet are the best of Majorca's four sets of heavily promoted limestone caves (all are similar).

MINORCA

MINORCA'S PURPOSE-built resorts are designed for sedate convenience, ideal for holidaymakers who want sun and sand on their doorstep, a safe and friendly atmosphere and organised events.

BEST RESORTS

● Son Bou's mix of well-finished apartments and hotels is partly spoiled by two outdated high-rise buildings on the fringes. The beach, separated from the resort by dunes and reed beds, is huge, with fine white sand.

● Santa Galdana feels like a real village, with bars and restaurants on the edge of a bay enclosed within steep cliffs and an attractive river inlet where boats congregate.

● Remote beaches include Cala Turqueta which, despite being reached by a dirt track, attracts lots of visitors in season. Cala Mitjana at Santa Galdana is another pretty but busy beach.

BEST SIGHTS AND EXCURSIONS

Minorca's capital Mahón has charming architecture. The town museum, in an old Carmelite cloister, gives a flavour of the British occupation. Ciudadela is older and smaller and reflects much better its Moorish and Spanish heritage, with honey-hued medieval buildings and shady alleys.

In megalithic times hundreds of huge circular buildings, *talayots*, were erected on the island. The most atmospheric remains include Torralba d'en Salort, an extensive settlement with a huge T-shaped stone, and Navetas d'es Tudons, shaped like a small sawn-off pyramid.

CANARY ISLANDS
Good for beaches, family holidays, nightlife and scenic landscape

SEVEN VOLCANIC islands make up the Canary archipelago. Tourism offers a more stable income than the traditional cash-crops of bananas and tomatoes, and the Spanish life-style is diluted by millions of foreign visitors. Head for the eastern islands of Lanzarote or Fuerteventura, or the southern resorts of Tenerife and Gran Canaria for a sun tan. Collectively, the islands offer an astonishing range of natural scenery: lava deserts, cactus canyons, primeval forests and fever-chart mountains. In parts of the larger islands, unchecked development has drowned the coast in concrete. Most accommodation is purpose-built.

TENERIFE

THE LARGEST and most varied of the Canaries is good for island-hopping: Tenerife acts as the main route hub for the other islands. The beaches consist mainly of black volcanic sand.

BEST RESORT

● Puerto de la Cruz, though not a beach resort (there are only black sand strands pounded by choppy seas on its fringes), is by far the best of the island's main resorts. It has retained an old town of style and character among the ghastly high-rises that provide you with your first impression.

BEST SIGHTS AND EXCURSIONS

Santa Cruz de Tenerife, the island's capital, is relaxing, with a shady boulevard, archaeological museum and fortress. Beyond the town lies Las Teresitas, a man-made beach of golden sand – best on the island. The old university town of La Laguna has more colour, with cobbled streets and pretty squares dominated by old churches, not least the peach-coloured cathedral. The summit of Mount Teide in Las Cañadas National Park is a spectacular region of rough-edged craters, lava flows and weird rocks, and is the island's most popular excursion.

LANZAROTE

A FAVOURITE among the Canary Islands, Lanzarote is more sensitively developed than the other large islands; its reputation as an upmarket destination is due to the mainly low-rise self-catering accommodation.

BEST RESORTS

● Playa Blanca is an isolated resort with a low-key, family atmosphere and plenty of self-catering accommodation. It is close to the very good cliff-backed cove beaches of Papagayo, popular with naturists, though difficult to get to.

● Puerto del Carmen, by far the biggest resort, is a low-rise development based on a long, often wide, decent beach behind which numerous bars and restaurants run; excellent fish bars are to be found by the harbour.

BEST SIGHTS AND EXCURSIONS

Lanzarote's volcanic landscapes are amazing. The Timanfaya National Park is a lunar landscape of twisted rocks and lava. A circular tour by bus starts at the visitor centre. Also visit Cueva de los Verdes, a lava cave formed by a great tube of molten material solidifying into an underground tunnel; Jameos del Agua, a restaurant and nightclub in several landscaped caves; and Los Hervideros – the sea rushes in and out of underground lava caves, spouting out of blowholes.

GRAN CANARIA

THIS THIRD-LARGEST island has the highest population, and its bustling capital, Las Palmas, has a sense of history and shabby, sometimes seedy, cosmopolitanism that is lacking anywhere else in the islands.

BEST RESORTS

● San Agustín, part of the giant sprawl or resort conurbation straddling a series of sandy beaches, remains more sedate than its neighbours Playa del Inglés and Maspalomas. Development is along the dark sand of the gently shelving Playa de las Burras.

● Puerto de Mogán, a smart little low-rise development, is based around a marina crammed with cabin cruisers. A wide choice of bars and restaurants compensates somewhat for a small, scruffy beach.

BEST SIGHTS AND EXCURSIONS

Coach parties descend on the pretty village of Cruz de Tejeda. Other options include the shrine of Teror, where votive offerings are left for the Virgin of the Pine Trees, and the spectacular road west to the market town of San Nicolás de Tolentino.

Regular buses take you to the island's two main family-oriented attractions: the landscaped grounds and performing parrots of Palmitos Park and the Wild West show of Sioux City.

FUERTEVENTURA

THIS BLEAK, sparsely populated island is new to the tourist trade. Its biggest assets are its enormous beaches, lonely and desolate in places but good for windsurfers and anyone who yearns to live like Robinson Crusoe.

BEST RESORTS

● Caleta de Fustes is a tasteful, low-key development of apartments built around a pleasant, sheltered bay of white sand.
● The beaches shelve gently, making it ideal for children, and there is a smart marina.
● Costa Calma is the island's smartest development, catering almost exclusively for the large German market.
● Its accommodation is mostly low-rise, and it has a laid-back feel at night.

BEST SIGHTS AND EXCURSIONS

The best of the island lies within a triangle bounded by Pajara and Tuineje, with the windmill at Llanos at its peak. Between the old capital of Betancuria and Antigua you travel over steep roads, with a volcanic valley unfolding below.

GOMERA

EASILY ACCESSIBLE by ferry from Tenerife, Gomera makes a popular day-trip. With an attractive *parador* and a well-equipped resort hotel, it has the best-quality accommodation of the smaller islands, but comparatively little choice.

The buckled terrain of the interior (partly a national park) is beautiful and full of botanical interest – marvellous for walkers, but slow and potentially hazardous for drivers. A lack of sand and cooler, damper weather than the main islands make it unsuitable for beach-lovers.

LA PALMA

THE WORLD'S steepest island rises dramatically around a vast volcano crater. Lush vegetation cloaks the island with forests, flowers, vines and subtropical crops. The capital of Santa Cruz de la Palma is one of the Canaries' most elegant and pleasing towns. Less tourist-oriented than most of the other islands, it offers a genuinely peaceful hideaway and spectacular touring, but few good beaches.

EL HIERRO

LITTLE TOURIST development has taken place on this, the smallest of the Canary Islands. A pine-covered ridge follows the curve of its boomerang shape, half of the rim of a volcanic crater, whose mirror image is submerged beneath the sea.

WHEN TO GO

THE CANARY Islands are the best choice for a winter break: even in the depths of winter you can expect better weather than during an English summer. The islands' south coasts are drier than the northern ones. Southern Spain and the Balearics are much cooler than the

	Average daily maximum temperature °C											
London	6	7	10	13	17	20	22	21	19	14	10	7
Madrid	9	11	15	18	21	27	31	30	25	19	13	9
	JAN	FEB	MAR	APR	MAY	JUN	JUL	AUG	SEP	OCT	NOV	DEC
Madrid	8	7	10	9	10	5	2	3	6	8	9	10
London	15	13	11	12	12	11	12	11	13	13	15	15
	Average number of rainy days per month											

	Average daily maximum temperature °C											
London	6	7	10	13	17	20	22	21	19	14	10	7
Malaga	17	17	18	21	23	27	29	30	27	23	20	17
	JAN	FEB	MAR	APR	MAY	JUN	JUL	AUG	SEP	OCT	NOV	DEC
Malaga	7	6	8	6	4	1	<1	1	2	6	7	8
London	15	13	11	12	12	11	12	11	13	13	15	15
	Average number of rainy days per month											

Canaries in winter, but they still get a fair amount of sunshine and many hotels stay open. Some tour operators offer special long-stay holidays of several months for pensioners.

Summer weather is warm and dry almost everywhere, but if you are going slightly out of season (e.g. April or October) you will be better off further south rather than on the Costa Brava or Dorada.

PACKAGE TRAVEL

MOST TOUR operators offer classic stay-put sun-and-sea holidays to one of the *costas* or Spanish islands, but the choice of holidays is vast and covers all tastes and pockets, from independent car touring and staying in *paradores* to golfing, wildlife and rambling.

If you are looking for a good-value, stay-put package, shop around. Several tour operators may offer packages to the same resort and the same hotels, with big price differences.

Tour operators

Battlefield: Holts' Tours, Midas **City breaks**: British Airways Holidays, Cresta, Inghams, Kirker, Made to Measure, Osprey, Sovereign, Time Off, Travelscene **Cultural**: Ace Study Tours, Andalucian Safaris, Andante, British Museum Traveller, Inscape, Martin Randall, Prospect **General and specialist**: Airtours, Bonaventure, Cadogan Travel, Castaways, Club Cantabrica, Cosmos, Cresta, Crystal, EHS Travel, First Choice, Globespan, Inghams, Inntravel, Inspirations, Longmere International, Magic of Spain, Mundi-color, Page & Moy, Panorama, Shearings, Siesta International, Sovereign, Spanish Harbour Holidays, Sunworld, Thomas Cook, Thomson, Travel Club of Upminster, Unicorn Holidays, Unijet **Horse-riding/walking**: Alternative Travel Group, Andalucian Safaris, Exodus, Explore Worldwide, Headwater, HF Holidays, Inntravel, Peregrine, Ramblers Holidays, Waymark **Villa specialists**: AA Motoring, Carefree Spain, Casas Cantabricas, Continental Villas, CV Travel, Individual Travellers Spain & Portugal, Lanzarote Leisure, Meon, Palmer & Parker, Spanish Affair **Wildlife/birdwatching**: David Sayers, Discover the World, Limosa, Naturetrek, Sunbird, Wildlife Worldwide **Wine tours**: Arblaster & Clarke, Winetrails **Other activities**: Anglers World, Bike Tours, Club Med (all-inclusive), Cox & Kings (flora), Eurocamp, Golf Holidays International, Insight Holidays (coach tours), Longshot Golf, Minorca Sailing Holidays, Pax Travel (religious), Sherpa, Solo's Holidays (singles)

INDEPENDENT TRAVEL

YOU ARE unlikely to be able to match the deals on offer to the coastal resorts, and most accommodation is block-booked in any case. For inland Spain, however, you may save money, particularly if you take your own car and stay in *hostales* (guesthouses). These offer fewer facilities but may have more character than hotels – there are plenty of them inland. The state-run *paradores* are a good option for those with more money – they offer comfortable rooms in an assortment of often unforgettable buildings, including converted castles, palaces and convents (other guests are more likely to be American than Spanish).

Cheap seat-only charters are plentiful, and cities that are served only by expensive scheduled flights from London can often be accessed from a nearby charter airport – fly to Gerona for Barcelona, for example, or to Malaga for Seville. Iberia's Moneysaver fares allow you to fly into one airport and depart from another.

Ferries cross from Plymouth to Santander and Portsmouth to Bilbao – special deals are often available. If you are taking your car over, a 'bail bond' from your insurer is recommended to prevent your car being impounded in the event of an accident.

British licences are accepted for car hire (minimum age 18); those with old green licences may need an international driving permit. Rates are lower in resorts, and it is cheaper to pre-book. Alternatively, the rail network covers the mainland comprehensively. Tourist passes allowing unlimited travel for fixed periods are available in the UK.

RED TAPE, HEALTH AND SAFETY

BRITISH PASSPORT-HOLDERS do not need a visa to visit Spain. Since 1994 ETA (the Basque separatist movement) has been setting off small bombs in tourist resorts, with the aim of disrupting the tourist industry. Many people, including British holiday-makers, were injured when a bomb went off at Rens airport in July 1996. Travellers should remain alert and report any suspicious bags or objects to the police. For the latest advice contact the Foreign Office Travel Advice Unit (see page 11). Pickpocketing and bag-snatching are common in cities – see page 12 for advice on taking care of your possessions.

MORE INFORMATION Spanish Tourist Office, 23 Manchester Square, London W1M 5AP, tel 0171-486 8077, web site: http://www.spaintour.com

COST OF LIVING £-££

405

SRI LANKA

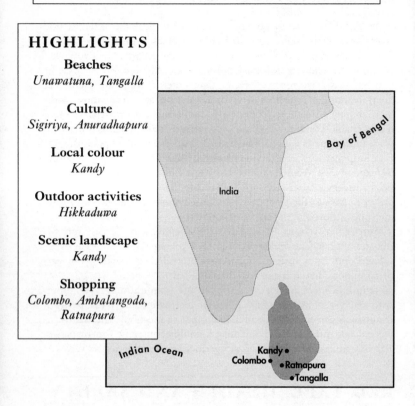

SRI LANKA, so legend has it, is the country where serendipity was invented. Although the island has been established as a tourist destination for some time, it is still charmingly unspoilt, and off-the-beaten-track exploration is so easy that it really is possible to make wonderful discoveries (deserted beaches, intriguing temples) completely by accident. The local cooking is superb – particularly on the coast where fish-based curries are, naturally enough, a speciality – and the Sri Lankan people are warm, friendly and generous.

The Sinhalese, who make up around 70 per cent of the population, are mainly Buddhist, and Buddhism has a distinctive influence, architecturally and culturally, over the whole island. Other influences stem from Sri Lanka's minority communities, including the Tamils, who represent around 15 per cent of the population and live mainly in the north; and from the island's colonial past.

The capital, Colombo, has little to interest most visitors, who are better advised to divide their time between the tropical beaches of the south and west, and the fascinating cultural sites of the interior.

THE COAST
Good for beaches, outdoor activities and shopping

THE COASTLINE that stretches southwards from Colombo boasts mile after mile of unspoilt, uncrowded, palm-fringed sand. All the best beach resorts are here. As a rule of thumb, the further you go from Colombo, the more basic the facilities.

BEST RESORTS
Bentota and Beruwela
● These twin centres are Sri Lanka's main package resorts.
● Facilities include well-equipped hotels and fine beaches which are good for water sports.

Hikkaduwa
● The small town of Hikkaduwa, further down the coast, has a relaxed atmosphere. It is tourist-oriented but still unspoilt.
● It attracts a balanced mix of package holidaymakers and independent travellers.
● You can explore the coral-rich sea with a snorkel or in a glass-bottomed boat, and scuba divers can visit shipwrecks.
● The southern beaches are popular with surfers.

Unawatuna and Tangalla
● Further south are Unawatuna and Tangalla, both low-key, relatively remote resorts, with superb, curving beaches.

BEST LOCAL COLOUR
Ambalangoda
Ambalangoda, a small coastal town famous for its traditional, lurid wooden masks worn in dance-dramas, devil-dances and processions, has a small, informative museum and workshops with masks for sale.

THE INTERIOR
Good for culture, local colour, scenic landscape and shopping

BEST SIGHTS AND EXCURSIONS
Adam's Peak
Adam's Peak is a short journey from Nuwara Eliya. At its summit is a

huge 'footprint' which Buddhists claim to be that of the Buddha; Hindus ascribe it to Lord Shiva; Christians say it is the mark of St Thomas of India; and Muslims believe it to be the first terrestrial footprint of Adam after he was cast out of heaven.

During the pilgrimage season (December to April) a great number of visitors make the climb to the hilltop temple. The mountain is beautiful at dawn.

Anuradhapura

Sri Lanka's most sacred early capital is still an important pilgrimage site. The town was the seat of the Sinhalese kings from the fourth century BC to the tenth century AD, and a number of important *dagobas* (Buddhist shrines) and royal palaces were founded here.

The town's spiritual focus is the Sri Maha Bodhi, or sacred bo tree. This, the oldest historically documented tree in the world, grew from a cutting taken from the tree under which the Buddha is said to have attained enlightenment. It has been a site of worship for 23 centuries.

Kandy

Kandy is famous for the Temple of the Tooth, an important pilgrimage site housing a sacred relic of the Buddha, and for the Perahera, Sri Lanka's most lavish festival, with spectacular processions of elephants, musicians and dancers (held over two weeks in early July).

It is also an excellent base for further exploration of the central highlands and tea estates.

Nuwara Eliya

This hill station is surrounded by scenic countryside.

Pinawela elephant orphanage

A must for elephant enthusiasts: the animals are extremely well-kept and visitors can accompany the herd to a nearby river at bathing time when levels are low enough.

Ratnapura

The capital of Sri Lanka's thriving gem trade offers excellent shopping opportunities. Gems mined in the region include sapphires, rubies, aquamarines, zircons, cat's eyes, quartz and amethysts plus Sri Lanka's 'signature' gemstone, the feldspar or moonstone. Gems, uncut, cut, and made into jewellery, are sold all over Sri Lanka but Ratnapura has a particularly high concentration of dealers. You can also visit the mines.

Sigiriya

Part military stronghold and part elaborate status symbol, Sigiriya was built in the fifth century by Kasyapa, illegitimate son of King

Dhatusena of Anuradhapura, on top of the 656-feet-high Lion Rock. Kasyapa murdered his father and, fearing reprisals, created the lavishly decorated citadel: fragments of magnificent frescos depicting nymphs remain. Kasyapa also installed superb water gardens.

WHEN TO GO

THE MAIN tourist season runs from December to March, when it is mainly dry in the most-visited areas of the island (the west and south coasts). The dry season on the east coast (much of which is currently inaccessible) is from May to September.

During the monsoon (May to September in the centre, south and west; October to December in the centre, north and east) conditions can be severe – the rain varies from light and refreshing to prolonged and drenching – but it doesn't rain all the time, and you can still swim from the reef-protected beaches.

	Average daily maximum temperature °C											
London	6	7	10	13	17	20	22	21	19	14	10	7
Colombo	30	31	31	31	31	29	29	29	29	29	29	29
	JAN	FEB	MAR	APR	MAY	JUN	JUL	AUG	SEP	OCT	NOV	DEC
Colombo	7	6	8	14	19	18	12	11	13	19	16	10
London	15	13	11	12	12	11	12	11	13	13	15	15
	Average number of rainy days per month											

PACKAGE TRAVEL

THE MAIN package holiday choices to Sri Lanka are classical tours visiting historical and colonial sights throughout the centre and south, and a selection of beach hotels along the south-west coast.

Tours that take in the highlights of the country generally run for seven to nine days; transport is by coach or private chauffeur-driven car. A typical itinerary will start at Colombo and take in Anuradhapura, Sigiriya, Polonnaruna, Kandy, Nuwara Eliya, Ratnapura and the Yala National Park. Beach hotels are offered on a half-board, full-board or all-inclusive basis and can be added on to the end of a tour. Alternatively, you can combine Sri Lanka with the Maldives, India, Bangkok or Singapore.

Activity holidays on offer include cultural tours, adventure tours, birdwatching or cycling.

INDEPENDENT TRAVEL

THANKS TO its extensive network of public transport, much of Sri
Lanka is easily accessible to the independent traveller.

From Colombo, the old-fashioned but reasonably efficient railway
runs south to Matara, stopping at the major coastal resorts of Mount
Lavinia, Beruwela, Bentota, Hikkaduwa, Galle and Unawatuna on the
way. It is a slow but interesting journey, with the track running right
along the beach at times. Heading into the central highlands, regular
trains serve Kandy and Anuradhapura (the journey to Kandy is particularly scenic), and it is possible to reach Adam's Peak, the Pinawela
elephant orphanage and Sigiriya by using a combination of trains and
buses.

Travelling by bus is a cheap way to get from town to town, although
the buses can be crowded. Every town has a bus station but buses will
stop *en route* if you indicate. Privately owned minibuses run along
commuter routes: these are air-conditioned, fast, and have higher fares.
The best choice for a short journey is to take one of the ubiquitous
tuk-tuks (motorised rickshaws); make sure you agree the fare in
advance.

Bicycle hire is cheap in busy centres such as Hikkaduwa and
Polonnaruwa, where you can hire a gearless bone-shaker by the hour
or by the day.

Well-visited centres such as Kandy, Anuradhapura and Hikkaduwa
have an abundance of simple, inexpensive guesthouses. Some operate
like small hotels, whereas others are family-run and will provide a
room plus as many (generally excellent) meals a day as you wish in a
homely atmosphere. In less-visited towns you may find it necessary to
ask someone to direct you to a guesthouse since they are not always
clearly marked.

RED TAPE, HEALTH AND SAFETY

BRITISH PASSPORT-HOLDERS do not require a visa to enter Sri Lanka for a stay of 30 days or less. A three-month visa is available from the Sri Lanka High Commission for £32.

Since malaria is a danger in some parts of the island (particularly the hill country) it is advisable to take a course of anti-malaria drugs and take all possible measures to avoid being bitten. Not all hotels and guesthouses automatically provide mosquito nets, so it is a good idea to take your own. Immunisation against polio, tetanus and typhoid is also recommended.

In general, standards of hygiene in Sri Lanka are high and visitors who follow a few basic rules should enjoy a completely healthy stay (see the precautions on pages 10–12).

Although the vast majority of Sri Lankans are genuinely friendly and welcoming towards tourists, it is best to be wise to the fact that touting and hustling do occur: representatives on organised tours get commission on goods purchased by tourist groups, and the more devious touts will go to great lengths to disguise their interest in you as friendship, when their sole purpose is to lead you to a guesthouse, taxi stand or gem shop for a commission. These activities are widespread and can be a considerable nuisance. Although crime is not a cause for great concern, it is a good idea to take the usual precautions against petty theft, particularly in the capital (see page 12). Until a lasting peace settlement brings an end to the long-running Sinhalese-Tamil troubles, the north of the island (the area east of Polonnaruwa and north of Anuradhapura, including Wilpattu National Park and Trincomalee) is out of bounds to travellers. The Foreign Office advises minimising time spent in Colombo as bomb attacks are possible – for more information, contact the Foreign Office Travel Advice Unit (see page 11).

However, the rest of the country is, at the time of writing, safe to visit, and by sticking to the south, west and centre (an area which, in any case, includes some excellent coastal resorts and most of the best cultural sites) tourists are very unlikely to be affected by the unrest.

MORE INFORMATION Sri Lanka Tourist Board, 22 Regent Street, London SW1Y 4QD, tel 0171-930 2627, web site: http://www.lanka.net/ctb

Sri Lanka High Commission, Consular Section, 13 Hyde Park Gardens, London W2 2LU, tel 0171-706 4808 (*send an sae for visa application*)

COST OF LIVING £–££

SWEDEN

HIGHLIGHTS

Beaches
*Northern and southern
Sweden, islands*

Culture
*Stockholm, Gothenburg,
southern Sweden*

Family holidays
Stockholm, Gothenburg

Nightlife
Gothenburg, islands

Outdoor activities
*Båstad, Ystad, Lake
Vättern, Härjedalan*

Scenic landscape
Lakes, Arctic Circle

STOCKHOLM
Good for culture and family holidays

STOCKHOLM IS Scandinavia's most beautiful city. The compact Swedish capital is spread across a series of islands and offers wonderful waterfront views, superb pastel-shaded buildings and a bewildering collection of museums.

BEST SIGHTS

Gamla Stan
Elegant seventeenth- and eighteenth-century houses crowd the islands that make up the old town. This was the original heart of the city, and Gamla Stan's narrow alleys and maze-like streets are now the centre of the modern city's tourist industry.

Kungliga Slottet
The Royal Palace is a triumphant mid-eighteenth-century construc-

tion; although low-key on the outside it has a lavishly decorated rococo and baroque interior. The treasury and armoury should not be missed.

Medeltidsmuseum
The history of Stockholm is brought to life with reconstructed houses, archaeological finds and thorough explanations (in English).

Moderna Museet
A fine modern art museum which displays work by most major twentieth-century artists, including Dali, Picasso, Warhol and Bacon.

National Art Museum
A huge, eclectic and fascinating collection of pure and applied art, ranging from ancient tapestries and art-nouveau coffee pots to Russian icons and some important works by Rembrandt.

Skansen
Huge open-air museum which contains around 150 reconstructed buildings, from windmills to tiny Lapp Saame houses.

Storkyrkan
For centuries the kings and queens of Sweden have been married and crowned in the 'Great Church', notable for its splendid interior, flamboyant royal pews and immense altarpiece.

Vasa Museum
Stockholm's finest museum is devoted to the mighty 204-ft-long warship *Vasa*, which sank in 1628 on its maiden voyage and was preserved in mud for 300 years. The ship is almost complete and is now the centre of an excellent exhibition.

BEST EXCURSIONS

Drottningholm
This marvellous royal palace in a beautiful leafy setting is commonly known as the Swedish Versailles. Rococo decoration fills the interior, and the famous theatre is still in use.

Gripsholm
Dating originally from the fourteenth century, Gripsholm is everyone's idea of what a castle should be – turrets and battlements, great halls and dungeons. The guided tours are recommended.

Millesgården
The outdoor museum of the work of the great Swedish sculptor Carl Milles is a spectacular collection of monumental classical figures.

Uppsala
This ancient university city contains a castle, sixth-century burial mounds and the largest cathedral in Scandinavia.

GOTHENBURG
Good for culture, family holidays and nightlife

SCANDINAVIA'S LARGEST port is also one of Sweden's liveliest and most enchanting cities, with broad avenues, extensive parks and plenty of bars and restaurants.

BEST SIGHTS
Art Museum
The museum has a vast and varied collection; it is strongest on the Impressionists but also includes work by modern Scandinavian artists.

Liseberg
This is the city's major amusement park – and answer to Copenhagen's Tivoli – with rides, restaurants, cafés, bars and pleasant strolling in the huge gardens.

Maritima Centrum
There are boats of all sizes and shapes to scramble over at this outdoor maritime museum.

SOUTHERN SWEDEN
Good for beaches, culture and outdoor activities

BEST SIGHTS
Båstad
The Swedish answer to Wimbledon, this delightful town hosts the Swedish Open but is also notable for its beaches and the rugged Bjäre peninsula nearby, which offers fine walking and swimming.

Bohuslän
This coastline north of Gothenburg up to the Norwegian border is a popular holiday destination, with picturesque fishing villages, fjords and islands. Strömstad is the main resort.

Halland
South of Gothenburg, the Halland coastline is almost one long beach. Varberg has a thirteenth-century castle and 'Bocksten Man' – a grisly

fourteenth-century murder victim preserved in a bog. Other towns worth visiting in the region are Falkenberg and Halmstad.

Kalmar
This historic east-coast town has a spectacular castle on an island and a superb exhibition dedicated to the seventeenth-century warship Kronan.

Kristiansand
This entrancing town was created by the Danish king Christian IV in the early seventeenth century, when southern Sweden was part of Denmark. Elegant buildings, swish shops and agreeable cafés abound.

Lund
The historic university town flaunts its exquisite medieval centre and stunning twelfth-century Romanesque cathedral considered by many to be the finest medieval building in Scandinavia. The church has scarcely changed since it was consecrated in 1145 and contains an intriguing astronomical clock and atmospheric crypt.

Malmö
A short journey across the water from Copenhagen, Malmö is a neat and handsome city, with canals, parks and a historic centre. Lilla Torget, the most picturesque square in the city, is surrounded by half-timbered buildings. In the Malmöhus, an impressive red castle, is a series of excellent museums of art, city history and militaria.

Skåne and Blekinge coasts
The coasts of these two southern Swedish provinces are speckled with fishing villages and good beaches. There is a notable Viking site at Ales Stennar, and the country's finest Bronze Age burial ground, Kungagraven, is near Simrishamn.

Ystad
An attractive town at the southern tip of Sweden, Ystad has neat medieval buildings and good hiking possibilities nearby.

SWEDISH ISLANDS
Good for beaches and nightlife

Gotland
Gotland has acquired a reputation for frenetic, youthful fun in summer, when beaches and bars are packed. It also enjoys a remarkably mild climate and a huge concentration of medieval country churches.

Visby, Gotland's capital, was one of the major cities of medieval Europe, its wealth demonstrated by the magnificent thirteenth-century wall enclosing the town, many churches and splendid buildings.

Öland
A popular Baltic holiday island, Öland has gentle green countryside, promising beaches, windmills, castles and burial mounds. The main town is Borgholm.

CENTRAL LAKE REGION
Good for outdoor activities and scenic landscape

BEST SIGHTS

Dalarna
North of the great lakes, this beautiful region around Lake Siljan is renowned for its gentle, lush countryside, folk traditions and handicrafts. The town of Mora was home to the painter Anders Zorn, whose works, home and studio can be visited. The Grönlitt bear park provides a rare opportunity to watch brown bears in their natural environment.

'The Glass Kingdom'
Between Kalmar and Växjö lie many of Sweden's best-known glassworks. The Kosta Boda factory and shop in Kosta are worth a visit.

Karlsborg
Work on this monumental fortress started in 1818 but stopped in 1909 when it was realised that the castle would be obsolete before it was ever finished, due to altered defence theories and weapons technology.

Lake Vättern
The best bases from which to enjoy the natural attractions of long Lake Vättern are the towns of Gränna, Vadstena and Motala. Ferries run from Gränna to the fascinating island of Visingö.

Linköping
This living and working nineteenth-century town is home to one of Sweden's most notable cathedrals and an entrancing open-air museum.

Mariestad
This compact lakeside town has a fine medieval quarter. Cruises on huge Lake Vänern and the Göta Canal are available from here.

Norrköping
Norrköping is a good base from which to see the ancient rock carvings

of Himmelstalund, the magnificent eighteenth-century Löfstad Manor, and the popular Kolmården Djurpark – a huge complex of safari park, zoo and dolphinarium which is a great favourite with children.

NORTH SWEDEN
Good for beaches, outdoor activities and scenic landscape

BEST SIGHTS

Bothnian coast
North of Stockholm the coast stretches up towards Finland, offering low-key attractions: empty beaches, fine walking and pleasant towns. Among the most interesting stop-overs are Skellefteå, Hudiksvall, Umeå, Gävle, Luleå and Skuleskogen National Park.

Härjedalan country
There is excellent hiking country north of Dalarna: the town of Sveg makes a good base. Åsarna, near the pretty village of Klövsjö, offers fine skiing.

Östersund
Located by the Storsjön lake, this sizeable town has huge open-air museums, at which the Swedes excel. West from here, jagged mountains and fast-flowing rivers lead towards the Norwegian border and Sweden's highest-profile ski resort, Åre.

The far north
The chief attractions of northern Sweden are natural. A series of national parks within the Arctic Circle provide spectacular hiking in settings of soaring mountains, endless forests, icy rivers and herds of reindeer. Muddus is the most accessible and beginner-friendly park, while the most popular trail is the 310-mile-long Kungsleden (Royal Route) from Abisko. Be warned that exploration is feasible only in July and August – when the mosquitoes are at their worst. The major towns of Jokkmokk, Gällivare and Kiruna offer insights into the importance of mining in the region and also the native Same culture.

WHEN TO GO

TEMPERATURES IN high summer are about the same in southern Sweden as in southern England, but Sweden gets more sunshine. Summer days are noticeably longer than in southern England (and winter days shorter). Midsummer is celebrated in many parts of the country, while Stockholm becomes deserted.

	Average daily maximum temperature °C											
London	6	7	10	13	17	20	22	21	19	14	10	7
Stockholm	-1	-1	3	8	14	19	22	20	15	9	5	2
	JAN	FEB	MAR	APR	MAY	JUN	JUL	AUG	SEP	OCT	NOV	DEC
Stockholm	16	14	10	11	11	13	13	14	14	15	16	17
London	15	13	11	12	12	11	12	11	13	13	15	15
	Average number of rainy days per month											

PACKAGE TRAVEL

PACKAGE TRAVEL can include scenic tours by rail, bus and boat, touring by car to pre-selected hotels, renting a country cottage, staying in a chalet in a holiday centre, canal cruises, cruises to islands in the Baltic Sea, staying on a working farm or simply taking a city break. On offer from activity tour operators are walking, battlefield and study tours and birdwatching.

Tour operators

Birdwatching: Limosa, Ornitholidays, Sunbird **City breaks**: British Airways Holidays, Cresta, Crystal, Inghams, Osprey, Premier Holidays, Time Off, Travelscene **Walking**: Explore, Headwater, Ramblers Holidays, Waymark **Specialists**: Colour Line, Finlandia, Inntravel, SAS Holiday World, Scandinavian Seaways, Scandinavian Travel Service, ScanMeridian, Scantours, Sovereign Scanscape, Specialised Tours, Taber **Other activities**: Ace Study Tours, Anglers World, Discover the World (wildlife), Eurocamp (camping), Holts' Tours (battlefields), Solo's Holidays (singles)

INDEPENDENT TRAVEL

BY FAR the easiest way to reach Sweden is to fly – there are several flights a day from the UK to Stockholm and Gothenburg. Ferries from Newcastle and Harwich to Gothenburg are usually cheaper but take at least 24 hours.

In Sweden, the public transport system is as efficient as it is everywhere else in Scandinavia. Almost all cities operate excellent discount card schemes which usually cover free local transport and entry to sights plus a range of other bargains. Train travel is often scenic but generally expensive – it can actually be cheaper to use SAS's internal flights, for which several discounts are available. The cheapest travel option is long-distance bus. Car hire is expensive. A full British driving licence is sufficient documentation.

Given that Sweden is generally a costly country to visit, it is a surprise to find so much good-value accommodation available. Hotels offer a wide range of discounts – particularly in the summer – including a variety of hotel passes, which must be bought in advance. In Stockholm, Gothenburg and Malmö discount cards are available which include a room, local transport and admission to sights for one price.

A cheaper option is a private room or bed and breakfast, often on a farm. Local tourist boards can supply details.

The best-value accommodation is undoubtedly in youth hostels. These are almost always of a very high standard, family-oriented with private rooms and found all over the country. Because of their popularity, advance booking is advisable.

The quality of campsites is also very high, and many have cabins with their own cooking facilities – ideal for groups. As in Norway, the right to camp rough is enshrined in law.

RED TAPE, HEALTH AND SAFETY

BRITISH PASSPORT-HOLDERS do not require a visa. There are no particular health or crime problems in Sweden; just take the usual precautions (see pages 10–12).

MORE INFORMATION Swedish Travel and Tourism Council, 11 Montagu Place, London W1H 2AL, tel 0171-724 5869
Web site: http//www.swetourism.se

COST OF LIVING £££

SWITZERLAND

HIGHLIGHTS

**Family
holidays**
Lake Lucerne

Food/wine
Rhône Valley

Culture
Geneva, Basle

Local colour
*Bern, Zurich,
Ticino,
Rhône Valley*

Flora
*Bernese
Oberland*

**Scenic
landscape**
Bernese

*Oberland,
Graubünden*

**Outdoor
activities**
*Bernese
Oberland*

BERN
Good for local colour

SWITZERLAND'S CAPITAL maintains a small-town atmosphere, particularly in the old town, which nestles in a curl of the Aare river. The covered arcades and historic fountain squares are best explored on foot.

BEST SIGHTS

Cathedral
The Münster has the tallest spire in the country. Treasures include sculpted figures, stained-glass and Renaissance carved choir stalls.

Zytgloggeturm
During the four minutes before each hour, this marvellous clock tower offers a mechanised display of jesters, bears and Father Time himself. Alhough the clock is over 450 years old, its precision is impeccable. Guided tours are available through the tourist office.

BERNESE OBERLAND
Good for flora, outdoor activities and scenic landscape

THE GREAT peaks of the Eiger, Jungfrau and Schilthorn have made this area famous. Access to these forbidding crags is astonishingly good: railways and cable-cars reach remote points. The cost, however, can be prohibitive on prestige lines like the Jungfraujoch. Enjoy the scenery for free by using the many footpaths on the lower hillsides and meadows.

BEST BASES
Grindelwald
Even the large numbers of tourist chalet-style hotels cannot detract from the beauty of this broad U-shaped valley in the shadow of some huge peaks. The further you go up the road, the quieter it becomes.

Mürren
Built on a ledge opposite the Jungfrau range, Mürren has excellent views. In summer the walks are excellent – even the Schilthorn if you are strong enough and the weather good. Go early while any snow patches are firm.

Wengen
Slightly more developed than Mürren across the valley, Wengen is handy for its rail link over the hill to Grindelwald, and is car-free.

BEST SIGHTS AND EXCURSIONS
Alpine meadows
The Grindelwald is noted for its marked footpaths through flower-decked meadows; the species vary with altitude. The first cable-car from Grindelwald village up to Bort station or higher is an ideal starting point. June to July is probably the best time for flowers.

Jungfrau Railway
Expensive but exceptional: the route up through the rock of the Eiger to the highest railway station in the world is an engineering marvel. The views across the snowfields and peaks are magnificent on a clear day.

Oberer Glacier
At the head of Grindelwald valley, a short walk from the road brings you to the steps leading up to the glacier face, from which you can walk on to the ice. The tunnel is about 660ft long with a small grotto at the end, eerily lit by filtered light.

LAKE LUCERNE
Good for family holidays

LUCERNE HAS everything visitors crave from Switzerland: a medieval town to explore, a beautiful lake to cruise, a dizzying rack railway to an impressive peak and, of course, the associations with the William Tell legend. Lucerne and its lake (actually four lakes all linked together) is an excellent base and well placed for trips up to the Oberland, Engadine or Zurich.

BEST SIGHTS
Kapellbrücke Bridge
Destroyed by fire in 1993, but since restored, the thirteenth-century bridge is the focal point of the town, with many waterside restaurants and cafés looking across to its famous octagonal water tower. Stroll downriver to the Spreuer Bridge to see an original, undamaged crossing. Built in 1408, its roof is covered in 67 macabre paintings on the theme of death.

Lake cruises
One of the prettiest Swiss lakes, Lucerne has some quiet lakeside villages where you can stay. From Vitznau the oldest mountain railway in Europe sets off for Mount Rigi (5,940ft).

Mount Pilatus
Views of the lake are magnificent, and the rack-railway ascent can be built into a day-long round-trip, with a steamer to Alpnachstad and the cable-car down.

Transport Museum
The museum is well worth a visit. It is a pleasant half-hour walk along the lake from the Kapellbrücke, or take the steamer to Vehrkershaus pier.

ZURICH
Good for local colour

FAMOUS AS a great financial hub, Switzerland's largest city is also a graceful, ancient place, sufficiently interesting for a short stay. The old town, on the banks of the Limmat river, can be seen on riverside walks or cruises. Zürich is well-placed for trips out to sights like St Gallen, with its superb eighteenth-century cathedral and rococo library.

BEST SIGHTS

Grossmünster
Dating from the eleventh century, the fine minster is emblem of the city. Across the Limmat is Zürich's other cathedral, the Fraumünster.

Landesmuseum
The Swiss National Museum contains displays on Swiss life, culture, art and history.

Weinplatz
This charming sixteenth-century square of Gothic buildings is the site of the city's oldest market. Catch a river excursion here or stroll down the river along the Wühre passageway.

GRAUBUNDEN
Good for scenic landscape

A REGION that prides itself on being quite distinct from the rest of Switzerland with its own language, Romansch, Graubünden also boasts some of Europe's finest ski resorts, at St Moritz, Davos and Klosters.

BEST SIGHTS

Engadine
The Upper Engadine is well known to skiers but also has some good walks linked by cable-cars and postbuses. The best villages are down the valley from Zernez, also the gateway to the National Park. Charming Guarda is the most famous and has plenty of accommodation. Ftan and Ardez are less geared to tourism and have a more authentic bucolic atmosphere. At Tarasp a castle stands on a rock above a charming village.

Rail journeys
From Italy the finest route is via the Bernina Pass. If the weather is good, choose an open-top truck for unrestricted views. From St Moritz the Glacier Express heads down to Chur, then up the Rhine valley to Andermatt through some of Switzerland's best scenery. Book your seat, as this is a very popular journey.

TICINO
Good for local colour

THE ITALIAN-speaking area of Switzerland is often passed over by tourists heading for the cheaper lake regions of northern Italy – a shame, because there are some lovely lakeside villages.

BEST BASE

Lugano

A handsome town of piazzas and promenades, Lugano is preferable to its neighbour Locarno. It is also close to some pretty waterfront villages like Gandria and Morcote and hill villages like Ciona and Carona.

RHONE VALLEY
Good for food/wine and local colour

FROM ITS upper reaches around Gletsch all the way to Geneva, the burgeoning Rhône river is an important communications thoroughfare. The valley itself contains many interesting towns, castles and vineyards, while the side valleys can be very beautiful – though some are marred by hydro-electric projects.

BEST SIGHTS

Château Chillon

This partly thirteenth-century castle is a 20-minute lakeside walk from Montreux. The building itself is the main attraction, and the suggested walking tour is highly recommended.

Montreux

During the TV and jazz festivals the lakeside town is packed with visitors, but usually it is just a quiet, middle-class town of elegant residences with pleasant walks and vineyards along Lake Geneva.

Val d'Hérens

Val d'Hérens is not as pretty as some villages but its traditional way of life is still fairly intact.

Zermatt

Dominated by the Matterhorn, the large resort town retains some charm. Walks and rides are all top rate, but villages like Zmutt are accessible only by bicycle or on foot.

GENEVA
Good for culture

COSMOPOLITAN AND modern, Geneva is home to dozens of wealthy residents and international organisations – as reflected in its range of restaurants, galleries and museums. Some complain that its atmosphere is sterile, but the city certainly warrants a short stay.

BEST SIGHTS

Botanic Gardens
Exotic plants and animals are found in these splendid gardens. The greenhouses are closed on Fridays.

Museum of Art and History
In the old town, this collection is strong on archaeology and painting.

Museum of the International Red Cross and Red Crescent
Compelling displays document the many atrocities perpetrated since the organisation was founded in 1863, and trace its emergent role.

BASLE
Good for culture

A prosperous centre of the pharmaceutical industry, Basle has retained its attractive old town and boasts some excellent museums.

BEST SIGHTS

Barfüsserplatz
The square is the centre of old town life and contains a fourteenth-century Franciscan church house, now a museum of the medieval city.

Münster
The façade of this twin-towered cathedral features many sculptural treasures. Inside is the tomb of Erasmus, the Renaissance scholar.

Museum of Fine Arts
One of the most important art collections in Europe includes works by Picasso, Hans Holbein the Younger, Rodin and Konrad Witz.

WHEN TO GO

	Average daily maximum temperature °C											
London	6	7	10	13	17	20	22	21	19	14	10	7
Geneva	3	6	10	15	19	23	25	24	20	14	8	4
	JAN	FEB	MAR	APR	MAY	JUN	JUL	AUG	SEP	OCT	NOV	DEC
Geneva	11	9	9	9	11	11	9	11	10	10	11	10
London	15	13	11	12	12	11	12	11	13	13	15	15
	Average number of rainy days per month											

THE MAIN Alpine passes are open only from May to September. But around the lakes, the season is longer – especially in the south, where Lugano enjoys relatively warm weather from April to October, though it can be wet. Most Alpine flowers are at their best in June or early July.

PACKAGE TRAVEL

BROCHURES FEATURE hotel and self-catering apartments in a wide choice of resorts in the Bernese Oberland, the Valais and the Lake Geneva region. Multi-centre holidays are also available and include travel by rail between bases. Rail tours, either independent or escorted, are also featured, often with guided walks from selected resorts as part of the package. Rhine cruises beginning or ending in Basle are also on offer. Excursions can be pre-booked. City breaks are available to Bern, Lausanne, Geneva, Lucerne, Zürich and Interlaken, Basle and Lugano. Activity holidays include camping, Rhine cruises, walking, rail tours and wine tours.

Tour operators

Camping: Canvas Holidays, Eurocamp, Select Sites **City breaks**: British Airways Holidays, Cresta, Inghams, Time Off, Travelscene **Cultural**: Martin Randall, Prospect **General and specialist**: Crystal, Inghams, Kuoni, Lakes & Mountains, Osprey, Sovereign, Swiss Travel Service, Thomson **Rail tours**: Ffestiniog Travel, Page & Moy **Walking**: Exodus, Explore Worldwide, HF Holidays, Inntravel, Ramblers Holidays, Sherpa, Waymark **Other activities**: Classic Tours, DER, Moswin, Naturetrek (wildlife), Premier Holidays, Reliance, Solo's Holidays (singles), Ultima, Winetrails (wine)

INDEPENDENT TRAVEL

ARRANGING YOUR own holiday probably will not save you money unless you take your own car and stay in campsites. You can fly direct to Geneva from London and Manchester and to Zürich from London.

The Swiss public transport system is renowned for its punctuality; it is also very well co-ordinated, with trains timed to connect with one another at major junctions, with steamers on lakes, and with buses departing from station forecourts. All sizeable places are served by rail, as branch lines have been kept open, and yellow postbuses run along virtually every public road in the Alps. Bicycles can be hired at most railway stations, though you need to be fit to get the most from them!

If you plan to use public transport, get the Swiss Card, the best of several transport discount cards. It gives unlimited travel on all trains, alpine buses and boats, and on the transport systems in 36 cities too.

Car hire is very expensive, but is cheaper if you book in advance. Fly-drive deals are better value. Roads are generally well maintained and signposted. The largest towns are linked by a fast motorway network, which makes getting round the non-Alpine part of Switzerland very easy indeed. To use the motorways you have to buy a pass, which is valid for one year. There are road tunnels beneath three of the main Alpine passes (Great St Bernard, St Gotthard and San Bernardino), but elsewhere in the Alps driving can be slow and hard work. Few of the higher passes are open before May/June.

Standards of accommodation are high, so you can safely opt for the cheaper and simpler B&Bs and guesthouses. Local tourist offices hold comprehensive lists and can book for you. Many railway stations have maps with pictures of hotels you can book on the spot on a freephone.

Switzerland has a huge amount of self-catering accommodation, especially in popular ski resorts; it is generally cheaper to rent in summer than in winter. Much of this accommodation consists of apartments in large modern chalets, though traditional one- and two-family chalets still exist.

The campsite network is highly developed: most sites are inspected and approved by the Swiss Camping and Caravanning Federation. Sites in the more popular areas can be a bit cramped and regimented, though facilities are generally excellent. It is advisable to book well ahead if you plan to camp in a popular area in summer.

RED TAPE, HEALTH AND SAFETY

BRITISH PASSPORT-HOLDERS do not require a visa. There are no particular health or crime problems in Switzerland – just take the usual precautions (see pages 10–12).

MORE INFORMATION Switzerland Tourism, Swiss Centre, Swiss Court, London W1V 8EE, tel 0171-734 1921, web site: http://www.switzerlandtourism.ch/uk/welcome.html

COST OF LIVING £££

THAILAND

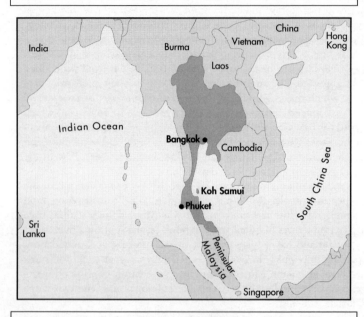

HIGHLIGHTS

Beaches/ romantic escapism
Coast

Food/wine
Bangkok, coast, northern Thailand

History
Bangkok, central and northern Thailand

Scenic landscape
Northern Thailand

Culture
Bangkok, central and northern Thailand

Outdoor activities
Coast, northern Thailand

Local colour
Bangkok, northern Thailand

Shopping
Bangkok, Chiang Mai

BANGKOK
Good for culture, food/wine, history, local colour and shopping

SPRAWLING AND steamy, full of gridlocked traffic, Bangkok is not a beautiful city, but its street life, markets and temples (*wats*) provide a sensory experience that you should not miss.

BEST SIGHTS

Canal tour

To discover how life is lived along the network of urban canals in Thonburi, bargain with the boatmen and take a longtail speedboat from Tha Chang pier near the Grand Palace.

Grand Palace and Temple of the Emerald Buddha

Wat Phra Kaeo, which houses Thailand's most sacred Buddha image, is the first stop on the tourist trail. Golds and metallic blues and reds cover every surface of the roof and walls, while the Emerald Buddha (actually jadeite) is a tiny figurine placed high above the crowds.

Vimanmek Palace

This large, solid teak mansion with royal relics and 81 rooms is worth visiting for its beauty and the peaceful surroundings.

Wat Arun

The Temple of Dawn, across the river from Wat Po, is a Khmer-style temple; when it is open climb up the central tower for good views.

Wat Po

This large temple complex houses a huge reclining 150-feet-long Buddha image. Hundreds more Buddha images inhabit the courtyards.

Wat Traimitr

The Golden Buddha, a five-and-a-half-ton, solid gold, thirteenth-century statue, sits in this small but touristy temple.

BEST EXCURSIONS

Ayutthaya

This was Thailand's capital until 1767, when the Burmese invaded and destroyed it. The ruins, rising from among modern houses and banana plantations, are very atmospheric.

Bridge over the River Kwai

The infamous Death Railway, where many British, Australian and Asian prisoners of war died during the Second World War, is about 80 miles west of Bangkok. The day-trip includes visits to the cemeteries and war museum and a journey along a stretch of the railway.

Damnoen Saduak Floating Market

This early-morning floating market 68 miles from Bangkok is less touristy than the one in the city centre.

COAST AND ISLANDS
Good for beaches, food/wine, romantic escapism and outdoor activities

SINCE THAILAND'S growth in popularity as a package destination, resort development has been inevitable. Some resorts have been spoilt; others are a step behind, with good facilities but still enough room to breathe. For those who like the simple life, there are beaches and islands more or less untouched by tourism.

PHUKET

EASE OF access combined with wonderful beaches have made Thailand's largest island a prime spot for rapid development, but it has not been spoilt entirely. Patong has all the life; hotels in other parts of the island run shuttle services into this resort and Phuket Town.

BEST BEACHES

South of Patong, Kata Yai and Kata Noi beaches are beautiful, with palms and an offshore island. At Nai Han the beach shelves steeply but is extremely attractive, although it is quite isolated. North of Patong, Bang Tao is a long, straight beach with shade and upmarket development. Pansea and Laem Sing are two small coves tucked under steep hillsides.

BEST EXCURSIONS

Two small islands, Phi Phi Don and Phi Phi Le, come very close to picture-book tropical paradises: they offer fine white sand and excellent snorkelling (they are very crowded in high season). Day-trips by boat from Phuket include lunch, snorkelling and a trip in a glass-bottomed boat – or you can stay overnight in bungalow hotels.

At Phang-Nga Bay, sheer-sided limestone peaks jutting from the water have been eroded into fantastic shapes. You can reach some of the islands in the bay, such as James Bond Island, where tourists mingle with souvenir sellers, on trips from Phuket by bus and ferry or longtail boat.

KOH SAMUI

KOH SAMUI has a laid-back feel. The beaches are perfect, and no building is allowed to rise higher than the coconut palms. The chief town of Na Thon is a relaxed fishing port and the central base for the shared taxis that circle the island – good beaches are some distance away.

BEST BEACHES

The north-east peninsula of the island shelters some very pretty sand coves, like Choeng Mon beach, which are good for peace and quiet. Chaweng beach, a wonderful four-mile stretch of sand, is the best (and most popular) beach on the island. Lamai is similar to Chaweng, although smaller and less beautiful.

BEST EXCURSIONS

Over 40 small islands scattered in the sea west of Koh Samui make up Ang Thong National Marine Park and hide caves eroded out of the soft limestone rock and perfect little beaches. Day-trips run from Na Thon, and you can arrange to go snorkelling or diving.

CENTRAL THAILAND
Good for culture and history

IN THE fertile basin of the Chao Phraya river are ruins of Thai civilisations which are much older than those in Bangkok.

BEST SIGHTS

Lopburi

Easily reached on the railway line running from Bangkok to northern Thailand, this historical town is known as much for its hundreds of monkeys scampering around and stealing food as for its thousand-year-old Khmer ruins.

Sukhothai

Unification of Thailand took place here in the thirteenth century after the Khmer empire waned. Now most of the royal city is preserved as a historical park – a bewildering complex of temple ruins among shady trees and lakes. Wat Mahathat, the king's temple, is the most impressive of the ruins.

NORTHERN THAILAND
Good for culture, food/wine, history, local colour, outdoor activities, scenic landscape and shopping

AROUND THE cities of the mountainous north a palpable air of the exotic creeps in, with the misty hills of Laos rising above the Mekong river, and hill-tribe women selling handicrafts.

BEST BASES

Chiang Mai

With scores of beautiful old temples inside the ancient walled city, Chiang Mai is the most popular destination in Thailand for visitors interested in culture and history.

The main centre from which to explore the north has developed rapidly over recent years. Its night market is one of the best places to buy local embroidered bags and belts as well as fake designer goods, but be prepared to bargain hard. In the factories and workshops east of town you can see painted umbrellas, teak furniture, silverware, silk and pottery being made. As an alternative to shopping, the elephant training centre offers rides through the jungle.

Chiang Rai

If Chiang Mai is too city-like for you, Chiang Rai, about 60 miles further north, is well positioned by the River Kok and within close range of the Golden Triangle, the Burmese border and hill-tribe villages.

BEST SIGHTS AND EXCURSIONS

Doi Tung

This mountain rises abruptly from the plains close to the border town of Mae Sai. Taxis run up to the peak, where there is a small temple surrounded by bells. The views are tremendous.

Golden Triangle

Close to Chiang Saen in the tourist village of Sop Ruak stands an archway emblazoned with 'Golden Triangle'. This is the spot where Thailand, Laos and Burma meet, and the village caters for people who just want to stand and be photographed there. There is also a small but interesting opium museum.

Hill tribes and trekking

Northern Thailand's mountains are inhabited by various tribes, each with its own distinctive language, customs, costume and jewellery. Trekking into the mountains to visit the tribes is big tourist business, and however far you walk you are unlikely to find a village that does not have regular visits from tourists. Those close to roads or rivers have become unintentional folk museums, and arguments rage about whether tourism benefits or damages the hill people.

The treks on offer vary in length and may include elephant rides or raft journeys as well as overnight stops in tribal guesthouses. Ask other travellers for recommendations before choosing a trekking company. Ask at the tourist offices; they should have lists of registered guides.

WHEN TO GO

THAILAND IS hot and humid all year round, and wet when the monsoons arrive. The north-east monsoon drenches east-coast beaches between November and January, while the west is affected from May to November. Central and northern Thailand are at their driest and coolest from November to February (April and May are sweltering). Thailand's high season is at the same time as the British winter; the cheapest holiday deals are at other times of the year.

	Average daily maximum temperature °C											
London	6	7	10	13	17	20	22	21	19	14	10	7
Bangkok	32	33	34	35	34	33	32	32	32	31	31	31
	JAN	FEB	MAR	APR	MAY	JUN	JUL	AUG	SEP	OCT	NOV	DEC
Bangkok	1	1	3	3	9	10	13	13	15	14	5	1
London	15	13	11	12	12	11	12	11	13	13	15	15
	Average number of rainy days per month											

PACKAGE TRAVEL

ALL THE major tour operators feature Thailand for long-haul sun and sand holidays with a touch of the exotic. The islands of Phuket, Koh Phi Phi and Koh Samui, the mainland resort of Pattaya, the smaller resorts of Hua Hin and Cha Am and the coast around Krabi are all included in brochures. Pattaya is the most spoilt resort – and a haven for sex tourists. Accommodation is mostly in international-style hotels

Tour operators

Birdwatching: Ornitholidays, Sunbird **General**: Abercrombie & Kent, Airwaves, Asian Affair, Asiaworld Travel, Bales Tours, British Airways Holidays, Cosmos, Elegant Resorts, Far East Dream Journeys, Far East Gateways, First Choice, Hayes & Jarvis, Jetabout, Jetset, Kuoni, Magic of the Orient, Oriental Magic, Premier Holidays, Saga, Simply Tropix, Thomas Cook, Thomson, Tradewinds, Travelbag, Tropical Places, Worldwide Journeys **Walking**: Exodus, Explore Worldwide **Other activities**: Airtours, Animal Watch (wildlife), Club Med (all-inclusive), Explorers Tours (rail tours), Solo's Holidays (singles) for one or two weeks. While many tourists visit only Bangkok and the beach resorts, plenty take tours to the north, visiting palaces and temples on the way to Chiang Mai and Chiang Rai – bases from which to take trips to the hill-tribe villages or to the Golden Triangle.

Other packaged excursions are three- or four-day tours to the River Kwai, cruises on the Chao Phraya river from Bangkok and day excursions from Bangkok to the floating market and Ayutthaya.

INDEPENDENT TRAVEL

DIRECT SCHEDULED flights, as well as charter flights, run daily to Bangkok from London.

Independent travel using local transport is not difficult, but the heat, the language difficulties and the pace of cross-country travel will slow you down. If your time is limited, fly if possible – internal flights are reasonable. Long-distance buses come both with and without air-conditioning. Leg room is not generous, but the system is efficient. Trains are comfortable if you avoid third class, and usually have air-conditioned carriages. If you want to avoid the crush at the ticket kiosks, book in advance through a Bangkok travel agent, particularly for a sleeper or air-conditioned seat.

There is no shortage of transport for short journeys; the only problem is knowing what to pay. Outside Bangkok, conventional taxis are replaced by *songthaews* – pick-ups with bench seats. These sometimes ply regular routes but will act as taxis if empty. *Tuk-tuks* – motorised three-wheelers – seat two in discomfort, as do trishaws, which use pedal power alone. On water, longtail speedboats are powered by car engines, a propeller on a shaft acting as rudder and driving force – these are fast and very noisy. Chartering a whole boat is expensive, but you can share or join a river tour. Car hire is not recommended since alternative forms of transport are generally cheaper, quicker and more efficient. Hiring a car with a chauffeur can be a good deal and some of the drivers are excellent guides.

Thailand's package and business hotels are several steps ahead of their European counterparts. Low labour costs ensure plentiful staff, and service is immaculate. Facilities are generally good, too. The beach resorts and northern towns have a wide choice of accommodation, while Bangkok seems to spawn a new hotel every week. Always ask for discounts, or book from the UK via a tour operator for the best deals. Small hotels and guesthouses are found in all the popular towns and resorts, ranging from dingy doss-houses to cosy rooms in old teak houses. Prices are generally a half to a third less than those of the package hotels. Right at the budget end are rooms separated by flimsy plywood partitions, with space simply for a bed and a bag – and maybe a fan if you are lucky.

RED TAPE, HEALTH AND SAFETY

TOURIST VISAS are required for stays of longer than 30 days. If you need to stay longer you will require either a 60-day tourist visa or a 90-day non-immigrant visa. For more information contact the Thai Embassy.

Protection against hepatitis A, typhoid and malaria is recommended (though in many areas anti-malaria protection is not considered necessary). Check with your doctor or a travel clinic for the latest advice.

Thailand's crackdown on opium has sanitised much of what used to be quite dangerous country in the north and west. But insurgent groups in Burma and the presence of bandits make it unwise to stray too far on your own in remote areas. Check with police.

Thai touts work by friendliness, not aggression. Be firm when saying no to being taken to the local handicraft shop, and beware of anyone who tries to interest you in buying gemstones. For the latest safety advice, contact the Foreign Office Travel Advice Unit (see page 11).

MORE INFORMATION Tourism Authority of Thailand, 49 Albemarle Street, London W1X 3FE, tel 0171-499 7679, brochure line (0839) 300800 (premium rate number)
Web site: http://www.tourismthailand.org/

The Royal Thai Embassy, 30 Queens Gate, London SW7 5JB, tel (0891) 600150 (premium rate number)

COST OF LIVING £

435

TUNISIA

HIGHLIGHTS

Beaches
*Tunis and the north,
central and
southern Tunisia*

**Culture/
family holidays**
*Tunis and the north,
central Tunisia*

Outdoor activities
Tunis and the north

Local colour
*Central and
southern Tunisia*

Scenic landscape
Southern Tunisia

TUNIS AND THE NORTH
Good for beaches, culture, family holidays and outdoor activities

BEST RESORTS

Hammamet
● The broad sweep of Hammamet's bay is the premier package holiday destination in Tunisia.

● Good-value, low-rise hotels here come as a surprise to many people who might expect a North African destination to be less sophisticated.

● The development stretches for miles on either side of the town centre, and provides accommodation for those who want a beach holiday and minimal interaction with local people and culture.

Tabarka
● Close to the border with Algeria in the north-western corner of

436

Tunisia, Tabarka is a fast-growing resort with a relaxed and friendly charm.

● Forests of cork oaks give the area an almost Provençal feel, while the town itself focuses around a lovely little bay with a Genoese fort.

● Golf facilities are nearby, and diving sites around areas of increasingly rare Mediterranean coral.

BEST SIGHTS AND EXCURSIONS

Cap Bon Peninsula

The 'garden of Tunisia' produces a cornucopia of fresh produce. It merits a trip for the undeveloped beaches around the charismatic fishing town of Kelibia, and the Carthaginian ruins of Kerkouane.

Dougga

If you want to visit one of Tunisia's excellent Roman sites, Dougga is perhaps the most interesting. The Tebersouk Mountains provide an impressive backdrop as you explore the extensive ruins. Other Roman sites in the north worth a visit are Bulla Regia and Thuburbo Majus.

TUNIS

FOR A capital city, Tunis is very relaxed and feels as if it belongs on the other side of the Mediterranean, thanks to a legacy of French buildings and pavement cafés. It is cosmopolitan and liberal by Islamic standards, and presents no real culture shock for first-timers. However, it is not all that exciting either.

BEST SIGHTS

The *medina* is as hassle-free as you are likely to find, providing a laid-back introduction to haggling in the *souks* around the Great Mosque, which dates from the ninth century. The Bardo Museum is the best in the country and an essential port of call for the superb collection of Roman mosaics taken from sites like Dougga and Thuburbo Majus, and Carthaginian relics.

BEST EXCURSIONS

Carthage is a suburb of Tunis's urban sprawl. You should not expect too much, as the Romans totally levelled the original Phoenician city, and the various sites are very spread out and not particularly well kept. It is worth a wander for a few hours. Sidi bou Said is an engaging little village of whitewashed houses with blue doors perched on cliffs north of Tunis. The peaceful and romantic atmosphere is rather fragile and depends on the number of tour groups visiting at the time.

CENTRAL TUNISIA
Good for beaches, culture, family holidays and local colour

BEST RESORTS

Monastir

● Nine miles south of Sousse, Monastir is a centre for package tourism.

● The heavily restored eighth-century Ribat has been the setting for several films, including *Life of Christ* and *Life of Brian*.

● It also has a Great Mosque and a chic marina area where you can enjoy a drink or a meal.

Sousse

● Most visitors to Sousse go for the package hotels lining the strip of beach between the centre and the characterless development of Port el Kantaoui to the north, which is totally un-Tunisian.

● Sousse proper has a couple of interesting items in the *medina*, such as the ninth-century Ribat and Great Mosque.

● The *medina* is good for browsing in the bazaars, although it is geared very much towards the tourist trade and prices are accordingly high. Toy stuffed camels are a speciality.

BEST SIGHTS AND EXCURSIONS

El Djem

The impressive Roman amphitheatre that rises out of the dry and dusty olive-growing plains at El Djem is a sight to behold. Nothing detracts from this awesome monument to the civilisation that once flourished here. The museum has stunning mosaics, and classical concerts are held during the July and August music festival.

Kairouan

Kairouan is the fourth holiest city in Islam after Mecca, Medina and Jerusalem, and is culturally significant as it is the most ancient seat of Islam in the Maghreb. The Great Mosque dates from the seventh century and has many fascinating features. Other important monuments are the Aghlabid Basins, and the Zawiyyas of Sidi Sahab and Sidi Abid el-Ghariani. Kairouan is also an important centre of carpet production and a good place to buy local *kilims* or *mergoums*.

Sfax

The main reason for visiting Sfax is to see an authentic working *medina*. The *souks* provide the opportunity to enjoy a relaxed browse without being made to feel like a tourist. The Dar Jellouli Museum, housed in a beautifully ornate seventeenth-century mansion, boasts a fine collection of arts and crafts from the era of the *beys* (a *bey* was governor of a province in the Ottoman Empire). The Kerkennah Islands off the coast offer unspoilt tranquillity, and the chance to wind down completely.

SOUTHERN TUNISIA
Good for beaches, local colour and scenic landscape

THE SOUTH of Tunisia is in many ways the most fascinating area, and for the adventurous it offers the most rewarding sights and experiences. However, remember that you are on the doorstep of the Sahara, so it can get extremely hot in summer.

BEST BASES
Matmata
The Berber people live underground here because of the searing heat. It is a lunar, almost surreal, landscape of craters and TV aerials seemingly sticking out of the ground. The craters are in fact circular wells from which the dug-out rooms radiate in these underground dwellings. It is a prime tourist attraction, and you can stay in an underground hotel – an unusual experience. The nearby village of Haddej has similar attractions but without the crowds. You can also make a side trip to Toujane along a very rough road with stunning views.

Tozeur
In Tozeur, you really feel as though you are in the desert. Four-wheel-drive tours can be taken from here, and there are plenty of palmy oases and dunes to be seen, as well as the magnificent mountain oases of Chebika, Mides and Tamerza. The town itself sits on the edge of a large oasis (*palmeraie*), which you can visit on foot or by rather rickety horse-drawn carriage (*calèche*). The Dar Cherait museum is excellent. It is worth taking a detour to Nefta to wander round its old town and *palmeraie*.

BEST RESORT
Djerba
● Just offshore, in the Gulf of Gabès, the island of Djerba is a well-developed package destination with good beaches.
● It claims to be the 'Land of the Lotus Eaters' in Homer's *Odyssey*.
● The people of Djerba are distinctly more friendly than those on the mainland, and it is an extremely relaxed place for a family holiday.
● The village of Guellala is known for its pottery.

BEST SCENIC LANDSCAPE
Berber settlements
South of Matmata are the *ksour*, fortified Berber settlements built from multi-storey arched granaries called *ghorfa*. Ksar Ouled Soultane has the

best-preserved structures, but Chenini is perhaps the highlight of the *ksour* area. The whole setting is superb, with houses carved out of the cliffside and a ruined *ksar* perched above on the ridge.

Chott el jerid
The *chott* is a massive salt lake covering 2,000 square miles. The principal interest is the range of colours that form on its normally dry surface because of the chemicals in the muddy soup beneath the hard crust. Mirages and surreal optical effects are frequently seen on sunny days. A raised causeway allows visitors to cross the *chott*.

Douz
The Great Dune of Douz is the ideal location for posing as Lawrence of Arabia and looking out over the mighty *erg* (the shifting sand dunes) that stretch to the horizon and beyond. Camel rides, or, for a touch of adventure, camel safaris, allow you to spend a night or two out under the stars in the immense Sahara.

Seldja Gorge
You can take a scenic train ride along this spectacular gorge from Metlaoui to Redeyef. The nineteenth-century 'Red Lizard' train was once the Bey of Tunis's private train and has been refurbished for tourists.

WHEN TO GO

BASICALLY, THE further south you go, the hotter it gets. Northern Tunisia has a typical Mediterranean climate, with hot summers and mild, wet winters. By contrast, parts of the Sahara in the south may not have rain for years. The major religious holiday period is Ramadan, which lasts for about a month. The faithful are expected to fast during the day, and opening times tend to be disrupted. The end of Ramadan is marked by two days' holiday for the whole country (rather like Christmas) and can also be an awkward time to travel.

Average daily maximum temperature °C											
London	6	7	10	13	17	20	22	21	19	14	10	7
Tunis	15	16	18	21	25	29	32	32	30	25	21	16
	JAN	FEB	MAR	APR	MAY	JUN	JUL	AUG	SEP	OCT	NOV	DEC
Tunis	13	11	11	8	5	2	1	3	5	9	9	11
London	15	13	11	12	12	11	12	11	13	13	15	15
Average number of rainy days per month											

PACKAGE TRAVEL

MASS-MARKET TOUR operators feature the coastal resorts of Hammamet, Port El Kantaoui, Sousse and Monastir. Specialists also feature Djerba in the south and have escorted tours inland into the Sahara. Fly-drive and two-centre holidays are also available, with a week on the coast combined with a week in Djerba or touring. Activity holidays include golf, archaeology and cultural tours.

Tour operators

Cultural: Martin Randall, Prospect **General and specialist**: Airtours, Aspects of Tunisia, Cosmos, First Choice, Panorama, Sunworld, Thomas Cook, Thomson **Other activities**: Acacia (adventure), Andante (archaeology), Club Med (multi-activity), Explore Worldwide (walking), Longshot Golf (golf)

INDEPENDENT TRAVEL

THE CHEAPEST fares are for charter flights, which go to Monastir and Tunis. Scheduled flights go to Tozeur, and internal flights from Tunis to Djerba, Tozeur and Sfax.

For long-distance travel the best way of getting around is by bus. The air-conditioned buses, operated by the national bus company, SNTRI, provide good coverage of the main towns and cities, but book in advance. Regional bus companies serve smaller areas; these tend to be slower and are not air-conditioned. Trains are modern and efficient, but the rail network is limited. It is worth paying a bit extra for more comfort in first-class.

Shared long-distance taxis (*louages*) take five passengers and leave when full. Determine the fare before you get in; all drivers are required to carry a list of tariffs set by the government.

Car hire is expensive; it is probably best if you book through your travel agent or tour operator before you arrive. Most rental companies set a minimum age of 21 for drivers. A British driving licence is suffi-cient; usually it must have been valid for at least a year. Roads are excel-lent; some in the south are unsurfaced but can be negotiated with care.

Most hotels are inspected and classified under the government rat-ing system, and are required to display the tariff in reception. In pop-ular package destinations you will come across five-star luxury resorts with all facilities – such places are usually cheaper if they are booked through a tour operator – but in other towns and *medinas* there are plenty of cheap one-star and unclassified hotels (you will often be expected to use public bath-houses). There are a few campsites but they are very basic. You can camp on beaches or in parks, too, as long as you check with the owner first.

RED TAPE, HEALTH AND SAFETY

BRITISH PASSPORT-HOLDERS do not require a visa for a stay of up to three months.

Polio, typhoid and tetanus vaccinations are usually recommended – consult your GP or a travel clinic for the latest advice, and see tips on page 11 about avoiding stomach upsets.

For the latest advice on safety and security, contact the Foreign Office Travel Advice Unit (see page 11).

MORE INFORMATION Tunisian National Tourist Office, 77A Wigmore Street, London W1H 9LJ, tel 0171-224 5561, web site: http://www.tourismtunisia.com

COST OF LIVING £

TURKEY

HIGHLIGHTS

Outdoor activities *Cappadocia*	**Family holidays** *Mediterranean coast*	*Mediterranean coast*	**Culture** *Istanbul, Aegean coast,*
Scenic landscape *Cappadocia*	**Local colour** *Istanbul,*	**Nightlife** *Aegean coast, Mediterranean coast*	*Mediterranean coast, Nemrut Dagi, Konya*

ISTANBUL
Good for culture and local colour

ONE OF the world's great romantic cities, Istanbul straddles the European and Asian shores of the Bosphorus. Most of the best-known sights are grouped together in the Sultanahmet district in the European side, while banks, businesses and nightlife are concentrated in more modern Taksim, across the Golden Horn.

BEST SIGHTS

Aya Sofya
Emperor Justinian's great sixth-century church, seized and turned into a mosque by the Ottoman conquerors in 1453, is now a museum. The impressive Byzantine mosaics and vast interior space are likely to be shrouded in scaffolding for some years.

Blue Mosque

Named for its exuberant blue tiles, the seventeenth-century Blue Mosque stands opposite Aya Sofya, its dome and minarets mirroring those of the older church. Sound and light performances take place in summer.

Chora Church

The gorgeous fourteenth-century mosaic- and fresco-filled church has been restored and turned into a museum.

Covered Bazaar/Egyptian Bazaar

The sprawling, sometimes busy Covered Bazaar is the place to buy leather jackets, T-shirts, etc., while the aromatic Egyptian Bazaar serves up spices and herbs, dates and Turkish delight.

Dolmabahce Palace

Mustafa Kemal Atatürk died in this vast Victorian palace in 1938 – the clocks are still set at the time of his death. Visits are by guided tour only, and the palace is often very crowded in summer.

Topkapi Palace

This sprawling complex of kiosks and courtyards overlooks the Bosphorus, and is where the Ottoman Sultans and their myriad concubines lived from 1453 to 1839. Highlights include the Harem, Imperial Treasury and Suite of the Felicitous Cloak displaying relics of the Prophet Mohammed. Topkapi crawls with coach parties and is best visited out of season.

Turkish and Islamic Arts Museum

A stunning collection of ceramics, carpets, calligraphy and other artefacts is displayed in a sixteenth-century palace off historic Hippodrome. The ethnography section has showcases of nomadic *kilims* and tents.

Yerebatan Sarneci

This is an atmospheric underground cistern, a sea of Byzantine columns rising from the water. You can tread the boardwalk while wild Wagnerian music plays.

AEGEAN COAST
Good for culture and nightlife

THE AEGEAN boasts several large, brash resorts suitable, particularly, for young people in search of lively nightlife. Within easy reach of several spectacular archaeological sites, these resorts make attractive bases for sightseers provided the hotels are chosen with care. The coves and inlets of this coast are extremely beautiful, and boat trips are a highlight of any visit. You can also take day-trips to several Greek islands, although political differences between Greece and Turkey ensure that these are relatively pricey and enmeshed in bureaucracy.

BEST RESORTS

Although there are beaches within easy reach of the big resorts, they are relatively small and scrubby so it is wise to select a hotel with its own pool. The closer you are to a town centre, the more chance there is of being disturbed by the nightlife. However, the quieter hotels on the outlying beaches can seem very characterless.

Assos

● Tiny gem of a fishing harbour with half a dozen simple hotels and restaurants.

● Ruins of Behramkale on hill above; good beach 2½ miles to east.

● Perfect for getting away from it all; tricky to get to and therefore quiet.

Ayvalik

● Medium-sized resort set around pretty harbour ringed with fish restaurants.

● Best beaches 5 miles to the south.

● Boat trips to Lesbos (pricey) and Alibey Island for fish dinners.

● Good base for excursions to Bergama and Troy (a long haul).

Bodrum

● Large, attractive resort encircling yachting harbour, with excellent Castle of St Peter/Museum of Underwater Archaeology to the south.

● Few remains of Mausoleum of Halicarnassus, one of the Seven Wonders of the Ancient World.

● Well-known for Halikarnas outdoor disco and similar venues churning out deafening sounds until the early hours. Nearby Gumbet has similarly loud and popular disco scene.

● Boat trips to Kos and Rhodes and to ruins at Knidos.

● Relatively secluded beaches on adjoining Bodrum peninsula.

Kusadasi

● Large, brash, un-Turkish resort town sprawling out from marina, popular with visiting cruise ships.

● Most quieter package holiday hotels overlook reasonable small beaches north and south of town.

● Well positioned for archaeological sightseeing and tours inland to Pammukale. Boat trips to Samos.

● Bar Street's pubby, chauvinistic nightlife will repel as many as it attracts.

BEST SIGHTS AND EXCURSIONS

Bergama

Less visited than Ephesus, ancient Pergamon offers several disparate attractions – an acropolis with ruined theatre and assorted temples, an *asclepion* (or medical centre), and a fine archaeological museum – scattered around a sleepy, traditionally Turkish town.

Ephesus

Too popular for its own good, this spectacular archaeological site is complete with Roman theatre, library, houses, brothel and public toilets. It is a popular stopping spot for Mediterranean cruises and day-trips out of Aegean resorts. Visit out of season if possible.

Pamukkale

White-calcium travertine pools of warm, mineral-rich water fall down the hillside, well inland from the coastal resorts. Hotels above the travertines currently boast mineral-water pools but are scheduled for closure. Meanwhile, you can swim amid Roman columns at Pamukkale Motel. Nearby are the extensive ruins of Roman Hierapolis.

MEDITERRANEAN TURKEY
Good for culture, family holidays, local colour and nightlife

BACKED BY the Taurus Mountains, Turkey's Mediterranean coast is squeezed into a narrow strip of shoreline, making it hard for resorts to spread far; consequently, several small, picturesque resorts just about cling on to 'fishing-village' status. The coastline is perfect for exploring in *gulets* – wooden yachts that put in at the many secluded bays.

BEST RESORTS

To the west, the best beaches are not actually in the resorts, although they are easily accessible by public transport. Further east, however, resort beaches improve considerably, and are therefore some of the best places for families with children.

Antalya

● Sizeable town with resort areas strung out along indifferent pebble beaches to east and west.

● Thoroughly inviting centre with restored wooden houses above attractive harbour.

● Fine archaeological museum, interesting mosques and Roman ruins.

● Good base for trips to ruins at Perge, Aspendos, Side, Termessos, Olimpos and Phaselis.

Dalyan

● Small village resort, site of a struggle to protect the loggerhead turtles nesting on nearby Istuzu beach.

● Low-key development with many small, attractive restaurants.

● Regular boat trips through reedbeds to sandy Istuzu beach, mud baths and ruins of Kaunos.

Datça

● Small resort on edge of remote fishing village.

● Nightlife centre and marina, plus single street of restaurants.

● Beautiful location, with views across to Greek island of Symi.

● Attractive sandy beach to west of resort.

Içmeler

● Big, modern, purpose-built resort with good standard of hotels, but lacks Turkish character of other resorts.

● Set in attractive sheltered bay within easy reach of Marmaris by boat or road.

● Wide but pebbly beach.

Kalkan

● Smallish resort with pleasant, traditional-style pensions around the harbour. Stylish, upmarket hotels on hills overlooking harbour.

● Nightlife and relatively expensive restaurants catering for yachting clientele.

● Ruins at Xanthos, Letoon and at excellent Patara beach nearby.

● Lengthy airport transfers.

Kas

● Small but growing resort with livelier nightlife than neighbouring Kalkan and wide choice of restaurants. Pick hotel on west side for quieter nights.

● Boat trips to Greek island of Kastellorizo and to idyllic Kekova and Kale. Excursions to Saklikent Gorge, Xanthos, Pinara, Patara and Myra.

● Lengthy airport transfers.

● No sizeable beach nearby.

Olüdeniz

● Wide strip of sandy beach and picture-postcard lagoon make Olüdeniz thoroughly attractive.

● Hastily built resort and village, lacking traditional Turkish culture.

● Hotels straggle back from beach along unpaved, featureless roads. To

protect lagoon from further development, many hotels are actually in Hisaronu, an uninviting inland 'holding tank' for holidaymakers.
● Doubts about quality of bathing water in lagoon.

BEST SIGHTS

Aspendos
The finest of Turkey's many ruined Roman theatres has been restored extensively to make it easier for visitors to imagine it as it was in its glory days.

Olimpos
In the spectacular Bey Mountains National Park, Olimpos was the home of the fiery Chimaera of classical mythology. The Chimaera still manifests itself in a series of mysterious and evocative tongues of fire jumping from the rock. You can also visit the ruins of ancient Olimpos, which line a shady valley.

Termessos
Spectacular and unusual sight reached by 30-minute drive into mountains from Antalya. Sit in the silent theatre and look straight down into plunging valleys on either side.

Xanthos
A UNESCO World Heritage Site, Xanthos is dominated by a Roman theatre and Lycian pillar tombs whose sculptures now reside in the British Museum. Walk round the hill behind the car park to find less-visited rock-cut Lycian tombs.

CAPPADOCIA
Good for outdoor activities and scenic landscape

FOR SCENERY-LOVERS, Cappadocia makes a great touring base. The landscape is a constantly changing panorama of cones and caves created by volcanic eruptions and the corrosive action of wind and rain on soft tufa. Humans have made an impact on it by scooping out the soil to create houses, churches, monasteries, and complete underground cities.

BEST SIGHTS

Goreme
Goreme is in a National Park, with some of the best cone-churches preserved in an open-air museum. Unfortunately the small churches are ill-suited to the coach parties that mob them; visit out of season or try to get there early.

Zelve valley
Villagers lived in the caves and cones of Zelve valley until the 1950s. Their homes now form another marginally less-visited open-air museum. Uchisar and Ortahisar boast fortresses carved out of the *tufa*, ideal perches for watching the sunrises and sunsets over the valleys.

The largest and most popular underground cities at Kaymakli and Derinkuyu can be visited on a multitude of excursions. However, both get very crowded and are certainly not suitable for anyone who is claustrophobic.

NEMRUT DAGI
Good for culture

NEAR ADIYAMAN in Central Anatolia, Nemrut Mountain is surmounted by colossal heads and other statuary fallen from the stupendous tomb of the Commagene king Antiocus I Epiphanes (64-38 BC). Popular at sunrise and sunset (but less crowded at other times), Nemrut Dagi makes a good excursion from Cappadocia, although even in July and August it is cold in the mornings. In winter, snow renders it off-limits to all but the most determined.

KONYA
Good for culture

FOR THOSE interested in Turkish culture, an excursion inland to Konya, erstwhile capital of the medieval Seljuk Sultanate of Rum, is recommended. A large, intensely conservative town, Konya can be busy and hot in summer, but the turquoise-domed shrine of the Mevlana (founder of the Whirling Dervishes) is one of Turkey's finest sights.

WHEN TO GO

	Average daily maximum temperature °C											
London	6	7	10	13	17	20	22	21	19	14	10	7
Istanbul	8	9	11	16	21	25	28	28	24	20	15	11
	JAN	FEB	MAR	APR	MAY	JUN	JUL	AUG	SEP	OCT	NOV	DEC
Istanbul	18	14	14	9	8	6	4	4	7	11	14	18
London	15	13	11	12	12	11	12	11	13	13	15	15
	Average number of rainy days per month											

SEVERAL RELIGIOUS festivals take place throughout the year. The most important is Ramadan, which ends with three-day family festivities and parties. It is extremely difficult to travel during this period.

PACKAGE TRAVEL

TURKEY IS becoming an increasingly popular package destination for those seeking a sun-and-sand holiday. Prices are relatively low, partly because the standard of accommodation in three-star hotels and below can be poorer than in other Mediterranean resorts. Cheap restaurants abound, so B&B is a good option. Two-centre holidays are also available, usually combining Istanbul with a resort on the Aegean or Mediterranean coast. City-break specialists offer Istanbul.

One of the easiest and best ways to explore the attractive coastline and visit more than one resort is to hire a berth on a *gulet*, or wooden sailing boat. Many tour operators offer two-week cruises round different parts of the coast, or one week on a *gulet* and one week in a hotel.

Self-catering complexes of villas and apartments are found mainly around the Bodrum and Marmaris peninsulas, but standards of maintenance are not as high as, for example, in the Algarve.

Tour operators

Archaeology: Andante, Martin Randall **Birdwatching**: Blue Moon Travel, Limosa, Sunbird **City breaks**: British Airways Holidays, Cresta, Inghams, Made to Measure, Sovereign, Time Off, Travelscene **Coach tours**: Archers, Balkan Holidays **General and specialist**: Alternative Travel Group, Anatolian Sky Holidays, Celebrity Holidays, Concept Express Ltd, Cosmos, Crystal, Discovery, First Choice, Ilios, Inghams, Inspirations, Island Holidays, Manos, Metak, President Holidays, Regent Holidays, Savile Row Tours, Simply Turkey, Sovereign, Sunquest, Sunworld, Thomas Cook, Thomson, Unijet **Walking**: Exodus, Explore Worldwide, Headwater, Ramblers Holidays, Waymark **Other activities**: Blue Horizon (paragliding), Club Med (multi-activity), Peregrine (horse-riding)

INDEPENDENT TRAVEL

SCHEDULED FLIGHTS go from London to Istanbul, Izmir and Antalya. Charter flights operate in summer to Antalya, Dalaman and Izmir.

The rail network is rather limited and slow, though trains are often cheaper than buses for getting around. First-class carriages have air-conditioning in summer; second-class do not. Long-distance buses are more popular than trains, and often several companies cover the same routes, so you have a wider, if confusing, choice.

There are lots of taxis and *dolmuses* – cars or minibuses that run along set routes, picking up and dropping off passengers along the way (you stick your hand out, and if there is room, they will stop; passengers usually make room). They cover routes both within towns and between towns and villages. Fares are cheap. Taxis in cities all have meters; in the country, agree a fare before you set off.

Car hire is expensive: it is cheaper to book from the UK or take a fly-drive package. It is wise to take an international driving permit with you. Driving is on the right, but on dual carriageways or multi-lane highways Turkish drivers will overtake in any lane. Roads are usually well surfaced and maintained, but can be narrow. Watch out for pedestrians, livestock and trucks travelling at frightening speeds.

The best-value accommodation is in *pansiyons*, which usually have friendly proprietors and simple but clean rooms. Prices are often set by the tourist authorities, which rate hotels on a scale of one to five stars.

RED TAPE, HEALTH AND SAFETY

VISITORS TO Turkey must obtain a visa (£10) on arrival, at Turkish passport control.

Upset stomachs are the most common health problem in Turkey (see page 11 for tips on how best to avoid this). Bottled water is widely available, and it is best to drink this rather than tap water. Immunisations against typhoid and tetanus are usually recommended, but check with your GP or a travel clinic.

There have been several terrorist attacks and kidnappings of Western tourists by the Kurdistan Workers Party (PKK) in south-east Turkey and around Mount Ararat. The Foreign Office advises people not to go there except for essential business. Even in more popular package holiday areas in western Turkey there have been bomb attacks by the PKK, and visitors are advised to remain vigilant. For the latest advice contact the Foreign Office Travel Advice Unit (see page 11).

MORE INFORMATION Turkish Tourist and Information Office, First Floor, 170-173 Piccadilly, London W1V 9DD, tel 0171-629 7771, visa information 0171-589 0360, brochure line (0891) 887755 (premium rate number), web site: http://www.turkishtourism.demon.co.uk

COST OF LIVING £

UNITED ARAB EMIRATES

HIGHLIGHTS

Culture
Dubai, Sharjah, northern and eastern UAE

Nightlife
Dubai

Local colour
Ras Al-Khaimah, Al-Ain, northern and eastern UAE

Scenic landscape
Northern and eastern UAE, Liwa Oasis

Shopping
Dubai

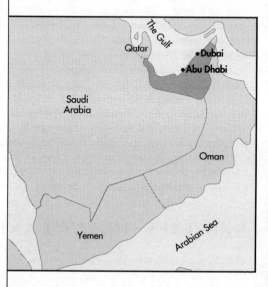

THE UAE is a federation of seven sovereign Emirates of which the best known are Abu Dhabi (the largest of the seven, and the capital of the federation) and Dubai. The others are Sharjah, Ras Al-Khaimah, Ajman, Umm Al-Qaiwain and Fujairah. Each Emirate takes the name of its main city.

DUBAI
Good for culture, nightlife and shopping

THERE IS more to the UAE's best-known city than its famous airport duty-free shop. Dubai is the most vibrant place in the Gulf – well worth the effort either as a stop-over or as a base for exploring the Emirates in greater depth. Though still a very conservative place by

Western standards, it is also the most relaxed city in Arabia, and an excellent introduction to the region for first-time visitors.

BEST SIGHTS

The Creek
The waterway at Dubai's heart offers some of the best views of the city. Water taxis, known locally as *abras*, criss-cross it night and day and are the ideal way to get from one side to the other (rides cost only a few pence – someone will collect the money once you're underway). You can hire one for a 45-minute tour of the Creek. If you do only one thing during a Dubai stop-over, do this.

Dubai Museum
Located in a converted fort near the Bur Dubai souk (market) and the Ruler's Office (palace), the museum offers a good introduction to both the city's history and the region's way of life. The museum is much bigger than it looks, as most of the exhibit halls are underground.

Gold Souk
Even if you are only looking, the largest gold market in the Middle East has to be seen to be believed. Prices are keen – always bargain.

BEST EXCURSIONS

Al-Ain
The Buraimi oasis, about 90 minutes from Dubai by road, is shared by the UAE and Oman. Visitors can cross freely between the two countries without passports or visas. Al-Ain (the UAE side) has a small camel market (try to visit early in the morning) and extraordinary greenery. Buraimi (the Omani side) boasts a small, very traditional souk and the restored Al-Khandaq fort.

Sharjah
About 20 minutes by car from downtown Dubai, Sharjah offers a slower, more traditional way of life. Prices are far keener for oriental rugs in its modern central souk than in Dubai's high-priced boutiques. The archaeological museum on Cultural Square and the restored traditional souk area are both worth a visit.

NORTHERN AND EASTERN UAE
Good for culture, local colour and scenic landscape

BEST TOWNS

Badiyah
This east coast village is the site of the oldest mosque in the country –

a small white-washed structure along the road that runs from Fujairah to Dibba.

Fujairah
The largest city on the east coast of the UAE, Fujairah has a small museum and is an ideal base for exploring the scenic landscapes of the east coast. Nearby Bithna has several interesting archaeological sites. The Fujairah Hilton has good beach club facilities.

Ras Al-Khaimah
The northernmost of the seven Emirates that make up the UAE offers camel racing, a hot spring and a more traditional side of life that is hard to find in Dubai. This is a city of small shops and coffee houses. The fort/palace where Ras Al-Khaimah's rulers lived until the early 1960s is now a museum.

LIWA OASIS
Good for scenic landscape

THIS OASIS deep in the country's interior offers the best desert landscape. A four-wheel-drive vehicle is necessary for the best views, though some spectacular scenery can also be seen from the few paved roads running through the area, particularly the stretch between the villages of Mizaira'a and Hamim.

WHEN TO GO

GO BETWEEN November and February. The temperature during the summer months (roughly mid-April to early October) is oppressively hot with very high humidity. December can sometimes be cold and rainy, but is usually pleasantly warm. Avoid travel during the Muslim holy month of Ramadan, which usually begins in December or January. The end of Ramadan can be an awkward time to travel.

	Average daily maximum temperature °C											
London	6	7	10	13	17	20	22	21	19	14	10	7
Sharjah	23	24	27	30	34	36	38	39	37	33	31	26
	JAN	FEB	MAR	APR	MAY	JUN	JUL	AUG	SEP	OCT	NOV	DEC
Sharjah	2	2	1	0	0	0	0	0	0	0	0	2
London	15	13	11	12	12	11	12	11	13	13	15	15
	Average number of rainy days per month											

PACKAGE TRAVEL

A NUMBER of package holidays to the UAE can be booked from the UK. These are usually based at beach resort hotels in and around Dubai (note – these are often far from the city centre) and may include several excursions. Stays at city hotels in Abu Dhabi also feature in the brochures of some tour operators. Only a few specialist tour operators offer tours of the UAE; packages are generally tailor-made. Tours can easily combine the UAE with the Sultanate of Oman and various other destinations.

Excursions to places like Sharjah, Al-Ain and the east coast can be booked through a number of local agents, as can desert safaris using four-wheel drives, camels or some combination of the two. Birdwatching is the main activity holiday on offer.

Tour operators

Birdwatching: Limosa, Naturetrek, Ornitholidays **General**: Abercrombie & Kent, East Travel, Elite Vacations, Jasmin Tours, Somak **Specialists**: TCA Holidays

---

INDEPENDENT TRAVEL

THERE IS a daily service to both Dubai and Abu Dhabi from the UK. There are also international flights into Sharjah but none from the UK. You will probably land in Sharjah if you travel on a charter flight. A small number of flights are also available to Ras Al-Khaimah, Al-Ain and Fujairah, mainly from India, Pakistan, Egypt and Jordan. There are no internal flights.

No trains run in the UAE and there is no coach service between the Emirates, though coaches do run within both the Abu Dhabi and Dubai Emirates. For most travel between cities you will either need to hire a car or take a service taxi. These travel between cities for very low per-person fares. They leave when the car is full (usually seven passengers). Car hire rates are cheapest in Dubai, where it pays to shop around. The standard of the roads is excellent everywhere throughout the country.

Expensive hotels and hotel/resorts are easy to find in all seven Emirates. Budget accommodation is plentiful in Dubai (which also has an excellent youth hostel) but harder to find elsewhere. Abu Dhabi and Al-Ain in particular are both quite expensive.

RED TAPE, HEALTH AND SAFETY

BRITISH PASSPORT-HOLDERS do not require a visa to enter the UAE. Thirty days' stay will be granted on entry.

No specific vaccinations are necessary to enter the UAE. Except at the very bottom end of the hotel/restaurant scale, sanitary standards are very high, particularly in the main cities. You may want to stick to bottled water, less for health reasons than because the tap water is often heavily chlorinated and tastes awful.

The crime rate is very low and safety, even at night, is not a major concern – though the wild habits of some drivers often can be!

Though liberal and open compared to other Gulf countries, the UAE is still a very conservative place by Western standards. Despite the heat, shorts and short dresses are frowned upon anywhere except at the beach. In rural areas they may get you into trouble with the local authorities. Women should not wear tight or revealing clothing (including sleeveless tops). It is not necessary for foreign women to cover their heads or to wear the all-covering cloaks worn by local women, but it is prudent to dress conservatively in baggy trousers or long skirts.

MORE INFORMATION Dubai Tourist Office, 1st Floor, 125 Pall Mall, London SW1Y 5EA, tel 0171-839 0580, brochure line 0171-839 0581

COST OF LIVING *££–£££*

USA

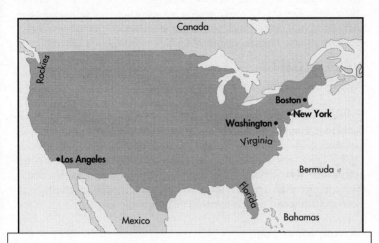

HIGHLIGHTS

Beaches
Virginia,
Florida,
Carolinas,
California

Culture
Washington
DC, Virginia,
Deep South

History
Washington

DC, Virginia,
New York

Family
holidays
Florida,
California

Food/wine
New York,
New England,
Deep South,
California

Nightlife
New York,
Florida,
Deep South,
California

Outdoor
activities
Florida,
Carolinas,
Rockies,
California

Scenic
landscape
New England,
Carolinas,
Deep South,
Rockies,
Desert States

Shopping
New York

WASHINGTON DC
Good for culture and history

VIRGINIA AND Washington DC have always been at the heart of American history – home to the first European settlers and to American presidents. The heart of the city is the Mall – a mile-long boulevard that leads from the Potomac River past monuments to the nation's founders and on to the Capitol where the Senate and House

457

of Representatives are housed in a white colonnaded wedding cake of a building. The neo-classical buildings that line the Mall are the nation's cultural repository as well as the nerve centre of government.

At night head to Georgetown for a wide choice of restaurants and nightlife. There is a canal path and quiet streets to explore, with restored historic houses, including J.F. Kennedy's former home.

BEST SIGHTS

Arlington National Cemetery
The final resting place of President J.F. Kennedy, his wife Jackie and his brother Bobby. This vast cemetery was started on land confiscated from Robert E. Lee, the leader of the Confederate army, whose house you can tour.

Jefferson Memorial
This circular marble edifice houses a bronze of Jefferson, third president and author of the Declaration of Independence.

Lincoln Memorial
A brooding statue of Abraham Lincoln resides in a colonnaded memorial with the words of the Gettysburg address carved on the walls.

National Air and Space Museum
The world's most famous flying machines, from the Wright Brothers' plane through Lindbergh's *Spirit of St Louis* to *Apollo 11*, are unmissable.

National Archives
A patient queue of visitors waits to catch a glimpse of the Declaration of Independence, the Constitution and the Bill of Rights.

National Museum of American History
Visiting here is like rummaging through America's attic. A bewildering collection of exhibits includes the original star-spangled banner.

National Gallery of Art
Includes contemporary art and several rooms on European culture.

The US Capitol
Both the Senatorial and Congressional debating chambers are open when the house is not sitting.

The US Holocaust Memorial Museum
New and so popular that tickets are timed (and distributed at 10am daily). This is the story of the millions of Jews systematically killed by the Nazis in the Second World War. Moving survivors' stories are told.

Vietnam Veterans' Memorial
The names of over 58,000 men and women killed or missing in America's longest conflict are chiselled into a wall of black granite.

Washington Monument
A conspicuous slender marble obelisk over 550ft high. Queues for the lift up to the viewing chamber tend to be shorter at night.

White House
The home of the most powerful man in the world receives a constant stream of visitors. Exhibits show the changes made by successive occupants. Arrive at 7.30am for a chance of tickets that day.

VIRGINIA
Good for beaches, culture and history

VIRGINIA WAS one of the first parts of America to be settled by European colonists, and after Independence became one of the founding states of the USA. During the bloody Civil War, Virginia was on the losing Confederate side.

BEST SIGHTS
Historic Triangle
Three unmissable sites. Jamestown was the first English settlement in America. An excellent museum describes colonial life. At Yorktown's Victory Center there is a re-created army encampment, and an excellent film about the War of Independence. A battlefield driving tour takes you past areas where some of the worst fighting took place. Williamsburg, the former capital, has been lovingly restored to its eighteenth-century glory.

Monticello
The design of Thomas Jefferson's home exhibits his quirky genius.

Mount Vernon
George Washington's modest hilltop house has splendid views across the Potomac.

BEST CIVIL WAR SIGHTS
Appomattox Court House
See reconstructions at the scene of the Confederates' surrender under General Lee.

Fredericksberg
A pleasant town to stroll round as it escaped development. Grand

Kenmore is linked to George Washington's family. Driving and walk-ing tours of the battlefields start from the visitors' centre.

Manassas (Bull Run)
Before Manassas, both sides thought the war would be over quickly. Washington society watched the battle in which 3,500 men died.

Petersburg
A park marks siegelines at this site of strategic Federal/Confederate battles.

Richmond
Richmond has plenty of Civil War sights and a restored tobacco ware-house area near the river. The Museum of the Confederacy gives unbeatable Civil War coverage. The restored White House of the Confederacy was home to Jefferson Davis, the Confederate president who designed the Virginia State Capitol. You can also visit the Old House of Delegates. The Richmond battlefield tour is over 100 miles long. Two sites worth visiting are Chimborazo Hospital, which describes the capital's fall, and Cold Harbour, where a route follows trenches.

BEST PLANTATIONS
Carter's Grove
Red-brick Georgian mansion provides insights into the slave system and the 1930s colonial revival.

Shirley Plantation
Beautiful Queen Anne plantation house that escaped Civil War looting.

Stratford Hall
The imposing family home of the Lees.

BEST BEACHES
Chesapeake
On the Chesapeake peninsula, try Chincoteague Island, whose main town is a prime example of smalltown America. Drive through Chincoteague Wildlife Refuge, home to wild ponies, and on to Assateague Island for a spectacular undeveloped beach.

NEW YORK
Good for culture, food/wine, nightlife and shopping

THE BIG Apple's reputation for energy and excitement is justified: you will feel something of it, even if you are there for only a few days.

But if you are expecting a sophisticated, hi-tech city, you are in for a bit of a culture shock, with slums, ghettos and no-go areas, and massive public monuments surrounded by squalor.

BEST SIGHTS
Circle Line tour
A three-hour boat trip round Manhattan – go only if the weather is good enough for you to sit on the promenade deck. Pithy commentary.

Frick Collection
Frick, a wealthy iron and steel magnate, built this palatial residence on Fifth Avenue to hang his collection of European art in.

Metropolitan Museum of Art
The layout of this huge collection is confusing – take a free tour round the highlights for an introduction. Note the excellent collection of Impressionists and post-Impressionists, and fascinating American wing.

Museum of Modern Art
Everyone from Rousseau to Kandinsky and Klee is represented here. There is a particularly fine gathering of Ernst and Magritte, and some wonderful work by Matisse as well as a couple of Monet's huge waterlily canvases.

Skyscrapers
The twin skyscrapers of the World Trade Center dominate Manhattan's skyline. Take an elevator to the viewing platform at the top of one of the towers to get a great view (if the weather is clear). The Empire State Building also offers stupendous views, and, unlike the World Trade Center, you can look down on the street almost 1,000 feet below.

Statue of Liberty
To land on the island you need to catch the ferry from Battery Park. You can climb up to the crown of the huge bronze lady, or just go to the top of the pedestal. Queues are likely to be long.

FLORIDA
Good for beaches, family holidays, nightlife, outdoor activities and wildlife

BEST CITIES
Miami
This sprawling, effervescent metropolis with a Hispanic flavour has a dazzling skyline, miles of sandy beaches and superb nightlife.

South Beach has the world's greatest concentration of art deco architecture, and Florida's trendiest, wildest nightlife. Coral Gables is a leafy Spanish-cum-Italian-style suburb built in the 1920s. Vizcaya is a twentieth-century replica of a sixteenth-century Italian estate.

Orlando

The theme-park capital of the world is far more enjoyable outside public and school holidays. It is unbearably hot in summer.

If money is no object, stay within Walt Disney World, otherwise around rather tawdry International Drive. Avoid Kissimmee.

BEST THEME PARKS

Walt Disney World, the world's largest entertainment complex, includes three theme parks (four from 1998). The Magic Kingdom is the essential Disney experience divided into seven themed 'lands'. Epcot is the most adult-oriented park, split into a worthy showcase of countries' architecture, culture and food, and science and technology exhibits. Disney-MGM Studios has excellent rides and shows based on film classics, and absorbing behind-the-scenes tours of the studios.

Universal Studios offers a theme park to rival Disney, with replicas of Hollywood, New York and San Francisco streets.

Sea World puts on exhilarating shows featuring performing killer whales and dolphins, plus polar bears and penguins displayed in imaginatively re-created habitats.

BEST NIGHTLIFE

Disney's relentlessly upbeat Pleasure Island is the best place for dancing. In downtown Orlando, Church Street Station, on a western theme, is more sophisticated and adult.

EAST COAST OF FLORIDA

VIRTUALLY ONE long, magnificent beach strung out on barrier islands, the coast is most interesting amid the yachts, mansions and country clubs of the posh Gold Coast, and least developed along the Treasure Coast.

BEST RESORTS

● Fort Lauderdale is a large family resort linked to a booming city by 300 miles of artificial waterways.
● Vero Beach is a small, peaceful enclave.
● Amelia Island has exclusive hotels, beautiful beaches and a pretty little Victorian town.

BEST SIGHTS

Palm Beach is well endowed with the glorious Spanish-style mansions of the rich and famous. Highlights are Worth Avenue, Florida's smartest shopping street, and the Flagler Museum. Historic St Augustine is the oldest city in the US (founded in 1565).

The Kennedy Space Center offers films and tours to Shuttle launch pads, and displays old rockets. Alongside lies the Canaveral National Seashore, Florida's largest undeveloped barrier beach, and the marshy, bird-rich vastness of Merritt Island National Wildlife Refuge.

GULF COAST

A succession of glittering white sand beaches, cultural towns and slow-paced resorts, plus sensational sunsets.

BEST RESORTS

● Naples is a sophisticated town with dozens of golf courses, splendid beaches and trendy shopping.
● St Petersburg's excellent beaches line an over-developed 25-mile stretch of barrier islands.
● Sanibel and Captiva are exclusive verdant offshore islands with stunning beaches.
● Sarasota is a chic, arty town with fabulous barrier-island beaches.

BEST SIGHTS

The Salvador Dali Museum in St Petersburg contains the world's largest collection of the Spanish surrealist's works. The Ringling House and Museums in Sarasota house dazzling collections.

Tampa is a big, modern metropolis, most atmospheric in the Cuban district of Ybor City. Busch Gardens is the top attraction, a theme and safari park.

THE KEYS AND EVERGLADES

THE KEYS are a 100-mile-long chain of islands; there is a dearth of good beaches but an amazing coral reef offshore. The Everglades are an enormous swamp full of wildlife such as alligators and wading birds.

BEST SIGHTS AND EXCURSIONS

Key West is a bohemian, gay-oriented resort with laid-back nightlife, pretty 'conch houses' and literary connections: Hemingway lived here. John Pennekamp Coral Reef State Park is the best place from which to see the Keys' coral, with water sports and boat trips available.

Explore the Everglades National Park on walking trails or canoe and boat trips from Flamingo. Mosquitoes are fewer and wildlife more plentiful in winter.

NEW ENGLAND
Good for food/wine and scenic landscape

IT IS almost axiomatic to say visit in the fall, when the autumn foliage turns on its pyrotechnical displays. But the six states have plenty to offer earlier in the year too. This is ideal touring territory, allowing you to combine coastal scenery such as the windswept dunes of Cape Cod or the rocky Maine coastline, with tree-shrouded mountains and immaculate villages of white weatherboarded houses.

BEST SIGHTS

Boston
Sophisticated, unintimidating city, focus of the first revolt against eighteenth-century British rule. Follow the self-guided Freedom Trail for the historic background and lunch at Quincy Market. The New England Aquarium (whale-watching trips run from outside the aquarium), the Museum of Fine Arts and the unusual ISG Museum are excellent.

Hancock Shaker Village
This former Shaker community is now a living museum.

Mystic Seaport
A nineteenth-century whaling ship and a whaling museum can be seen at this recreated waterfront community.

Nantucket
A flat, scrub and cranberry bog-covered island, appealing for its seclusion and the attractive main harbour town rather than for its landscape.

Newport
This was the playground of the rich and famous during America's 'gilded age'. The Breakers and Marble House are the finest of nine lavish mansions open to the public. The Astors' palace, Beechwood, is also fun.

Old Sturbridge
An idealised 1830s village brought to life as a living museum.

Provincetown
This is an easy-going, culturally lively town at the tip of Cape Cod and a good place from which to take a whale-watching trip.

BEST SCENIC LANDSCAPES
Boothbay Harbour and Acadia National Park
Popular areas of Maine's spectacular, rugged coastline.

Kancamagus Highway
The road from Conway to Lincoln through the White Mountains in New Hampshire provides spectacular viewing of the foliage in the fall. Plenty of easy walking trails are located off the road, including one to the Sabbaday Falls.

THE CAROLINAS
Good for beaches, outdoor activities and scenic landscape

THE APPALACHIAN Mountains and the 500 miles of Atlantic coastline are worth exploring. Unfortunately they are at opposite ends of the states, with hundreds of miles of less fascinating country in between, so you should concentrate on one or the other, unless you have at least three weeks and do not mind long drives.

BEST INLAND SIGHTS
The Blue Ridge Parkway (BRP) is a leisurely 469-mile drive, starting in the Shenandoah National Park in Virginia and crossing the Blue Ridge Mountains, the Craggies, Pisgahs and Balsams in North Carolina. Local sights include the Linville Falls, Chimney Rock or Biltmore. Hiking is popular. The spectacular Great Smoky Mountains National Park, traversed by the BRP, is the most visited in America and particularly busy in high summer and at weekends.

Asheville
An unexpectedly cosmopolitan mountain town with an eclectic mix of buildings downtown.

Biltmore
Elaborate reconstruction of a French renaissance château built by George Vanderbilt. Napoleon's chess set and Richelieu's tapestries are on view. Slickly presented but expensive.

Chimney Rock
A monumental 258-ft column of rock with a lift inside. Lots of boardwalks and trails to follow.

Linville Falls
Well-signed and maintained woodland trails around a sheer-sided gorge where white water gushes from a chimney of quartzite.

Old Salem

The village was originally established by Moravian Protestants in the mid-eighteenth century. Wander for free or pay to hear costumed staff explain the humble life-style inside the shops and school houses.

BEST COASTAL RESORTS AND SIGHTS

An exotic brew of salt marshes, endless dunes topped with wild sea oats, inlets and islands blanketed with green rushes. Most beaches are terrific, but the resorts tend to be uninspiring. Book accommodation in any resorts and major towns along the coast well in advance.

Charleston

Charleston's gaslit cobbled streets are a feast of history and architecture. Grand *antebellum* mansions line the Battery, and rejuvenated warehouses buzz with activity. The Calhoun Mansion is a quirky merchant's house. Middleton Place, Magnolia Plantation and Swamp Garden are the best former cotton plantations, and Patriots Point naval museum is superb.

Myrtle Beach

American Blackpool without the tower, built along a 60-mile stretch of glorious beach. North Myrtle Beach, with its fishing piers, is quieter.

Outer Banks

A 43-mile series of narrow sandbanks off the coast. Ocracoke is the best place to stay.

Savannah

Oaks draped with Spanish moss fill the historic town centre, with its orderly squares, fountains and elegant mansions.

USS North Carolina

Battleship that saw service in all the major naval battles in the Pacific. Virtually the whole ship is accessible on a self-guided tour.

DEEP SOUTH
Good for culture, food/wine, nightlife and scenic landscape

THE GRACIOUS plantation lands of Scarlett O'Hara were also musically fertile – blues, jazz and rock 'n' roll were born in the American South. Much of the wealth, supported by slavery, was curtailed by the Civil War, known locally as the War Between the States.

BEST SIGHTS

Atlanta

This modern city that played host to the 1996 Olympics has come a long way since *Gone with the Wind* – though fans of the film should head for the Road to Tara Museum. Best sight is the Atlanta History Center, where costumed guides escort you round a nineteenth-century plantation house; you can also visit the tomb of Martin Luther King and see his birth house or tour the CNN studios.

Cajun country

The original Acadians ('Cajun' is a corruption of Acadian) were driven out of Canada by the British in the eighteenth century and settled among the bayous and swamps of southern Louisiana, bringing with them French language and customs. Lafayette is the centre of Acadiana, and you can visit a couple of recreated Acadian villages: Vermilionville and the Acadian Village.

A swamp tour is highly recommended. Small boats zigzag along bayous, home to alligators and coypus.

Memphis

Memphis's most famous sight is the much-visited Graceland, Elvis Presley's home, 12 miles south-east. You can also tour Sun Studio, scene of Elvis's first break. Jazz and blues thrive on Beale Street. The Civil Rights Museum commemorates the shooting of Martin Luther King here in 1968; the Mississippi River Museum traces the waterway's history.

Nashville

If you are not a fan of country music check out the full-scale reconstruction of the Parthenon in Centennial Park. Downtown, the Tennessee State Museum gives an insight into slavery.

The main country music sights are centred around Opryland, a theme park/hotel/cable TV network spawned from the original 'Grand Ole Opry' radio programme in 1925, and Music Row, a terrace of gift shops and 'museums' of stars such as Hank Williams Jr and Barbara Mandrell.

Natchez

Unscathed by the war, downtown Natchez is a grid of gracious buildings. Houses open all year include Stanton Hall and Longwood.

New Orleans

The lively French Quarter owes more to the Spanish in architectural terms. Here you can browse in shops selling jewellery or Mardi Gras costumes, sup on Cajun cuisine and party round the clock (for tradi-

tional New Orleans jazz try to squeeze into Preservation Hall). The
Louisiana State Museum contains Louis Armstrong's cornet, while the
Aquarium of the Americas has superb displays. Alternatively, try a
Cajun cookery class or a guided cemetery walk.

Vicksburg
Vicksburg, on a bluff above the Mississippi, was the site of a decisive
Civil War battle; its story is told in the National Military Park, where
you can drive round a battle trail. McRaven House is a good *antebellum* house.

THE ROCKIES
Good for outdoor activities and scenic landscape

THE ROCKIES run through five states: Montana, Idaho, Wyoming,
Utah and Colorado. This backbone of North America is littered with
old mining towns deserted during the boom and slump of the
goldrush years, but it is the awe-inspiring landscape that draws the
tourists.

BEST NATIONAL PARKS
Arches
This is a barren red sandstone desert landscape punctuated by rock
arches, cliffs and precariously perched boulders. Sunset or sunrise,
when the sandstone seems to ignite, are the best times to visit.

Canyonlands
The Green and Colorado rivers have each carved a two-tier canyon on
an extraordinary scale. If you are short of time, drive down the Island in
the Sky section to GrandView Point for breathtaking views. If you have
more time, visit the rock spires of the Needles area. The Maze remains
one of the most remote parts of the USA, accessible only by jeep, involving a 150-mile detour from Moab.

Glacier
The most northerly and remote of the parks attracts more walkers and
fewer cars. The Going to the Sun Road passes beneath the Garden
Wall, a glacial ridge ground away by ice to a blunt edge.

Grand Teton
The most beautiful mountain range in the Rockies, the Tetons rise to
just under 14,000 feet, mirrored in a string of forest-fringed lakes.
Boats shuttle visitors across Jenny Lake to Hidden Falls. Colter Bay
Visitor Center has a fine exhibition of Indian art and artefacts.

Mesa Verde
The park contains the most interesting of the ruins of the Anasazi civilisation (AD 500-1300). Three stone *pueblo* dwellings can be visited: Spruce Tree House, near the museum, Cliff Palace and Balcony House.

Yellowstone
Yellowstone is an extraordinary geological stew of over 10,000 thermal features. Old Faithful, the most reliable if not the most spectacular geyser in the park, reaches 100 feet. For a good variety of geysers, hot springs and pools take the Upper Geyser Basin Trail. The Fountain Paint Pot spouts globules of hot mud. Swim in lukewarm rapids at Firehole River.

BEST SIGHTS

Aspen
A town of clapboard houses and a winter ski resort, which is deserted in summer. A fantastic drive over Independence Pass then turns into the broad Arkansas river valley. West and east, Leadville and Redstone are two mining villages cheap to stay in and worth exploring.

Denver
Gateway to the Rockies, Denver has a high-rise downtown and soulless centre. Excellent museums include the Natural History Museum, Denver Art Museum (one of the most important collections of American Indian art in the USA) and the Colorado Museum of Western Art, an evocation of the Wild West on canvas.

San Juan Mountains
Walkers, trout anglers and ghost-town explorers visit this alpine southwestern corner of the Rockies in summer. Stay at the restored nineteenth-century mining towns of Ouray, Telluride or Durango.

DESERT STATES
Good for scenic landscape

THIS IS cowboys and Indians country, but it is the landscape – vast canyons and fiery pinnacles – that stays in the memory.

BEST NATIONAL PARKS AND MONUMENTS

Bryce Canyon
Not really a canyon at all, rather a steep series of 14 natural amphitheatres notable for the hoodoos – thin pinnacles of rock formed by a constant cycle of freezing and thawing.

Chaco Culture National Historic Park
A display describes building techniques of *pueblo* dwellers at this huge site between the tenth and twelfth centuries. The outstanding ruin is Pueblo Bonito, where up to 1,200 people lived in 800 rooms.

Edge of the Cedars State Park
Informative displays of Indian artefacts with the chance to descend into the underground ceremonial hall, or *kiva*.

El Morro
The visitor centre explains how the cultures of the American Indians, the sixteenth-century Spanish conquerors and their English successors have interacted.

Grand Canyon
A mile-deep, 277-mile-long, 10-mile-wide fissure carved by the Colorado river through the rising Colorado plateau. Visit the South Rim or journey to the canyon floor, and wonder at the scale and the constantly changing hues of light on rock.

Montezuma Castle
Astonishing twelfth-century palace constructed high above a creek by the Sinagua people.

Monument Valley Navajo Tribal Park
Tribal members compete to take visitors by jeep, coach or horseback around the astonishing table of weird rock formations. An enjoyable trail takes you past fabulous monoliths such as the Three Sisters.

Walnut Canyon
Sinagua Indians settled here in 1056, using the overhangs and rock walls bound with mud to create rooms. Follow the interpretive trail, and see ancient fingerprints.

Wupatki
An excellent interpretive trail crosses this red sandstone monument.

Zion
Sheer walls of sandstone flank the Virgin river. The visitor centre has information on short but spectacular trails like Weeping Rock or Emerald Pool that take you to hanging gardens and cascading waterfalls.

BEST SIGHTS
Hoover Dam
More than 720ft high, this is one of America's modern engineering

wonders, begun in 1931. Its reservoir, Lake Mead, can hold nearly 9.2 trillion gallons. Take a guided tour, or stand at the top and look down.

Las Vegas

Las Vegas is famous for its casinos. The hotels lining 'the Strip' are like miniature theme parks in themselves. The gambling paraphernalia remains the same, but background themes vary: ancient Rome, even Arthurian England. To lure visitors away from the big hotels, downtown Vegas offers the Freemont Experience – a free nightly laser show.

Santa Fe

Vibrant cultural centre offering a winning blend of colonial and Indian history. An excellent set of museums includes the Museum of Fine Arts, headlined by Georgia O'Keeffe's collection; and the Institute of American Indian Arts; the Museum of Indian Arts and Culture.

St George

Southern Utah's largest town, settled in the 1860s by Mormons. A hi-tech visitor centre beside the temple explains the basis of the religion.

Taos

A glorious combination of ski resort, artists' colony and historical centre, Taos in New Mexico has a stunning setting at the foot of the Sangre de Cristo mountain. You can also see 55 Indians who remain in their ancestral adobe houses on the Taos *pueblo* (founded nearly 1,000 years ago).

Tombstone

Famous for the 30 seconds of gunfire at the OK Corral in 1881. The 'Historama' features historical tableaux, while the courthouse has a thought-provoking display on the gunfight and a reconstructed gallows.

CALIFORNIA
Good for beaches, family holidays, food/wine, nightlife and outdoor activities

CALIFORNIA IS almost twice the size of mainland Britain. City sight-seeing, combined with sampling the wild national parks and a few days lazing on the beach, would make for a varied and enjoyable holiday.

BEST CITIES

Los Angeles

LA is hot, polluted, difficult to get around and expensive. Two days here is plenty. You can tour the nearby Hollywood and Beverly Hills retreats of the super-rich, but little tinseltown glamour remains. Universal

Studios combines a theme park with a tour of the backlot. Disneyland is over an hour's drive from downtown LA in Anaheim.

San Diego
This growing city has great beaches, a charming old town, sophisticated shopping, worthwhile museums and child-friendly attractions including Seaworld and world-leading San Diego Zoo in the beautiful 1,400-acre Balboa Park, which has several museums and art galleries.

San Francisco
The state's prettiest city is a series of connecting villages, each with its own cultural identity, like Chinatown, Japantown and North Beach Italians. Take the cable-car from Union Square to Fisherman's Wharf for views of pastel Victorian houses or walk across the Golden Gate Bridge, symbol of the city since 1937. Nightlife is camp and outrageous, with lots of Las Vegas-style revues featuring female impersonators.

BEST BEACHES
California's vast stretches of golden sand are surfing, not swimming, beaches, and you will need to keep a constant eye on children. Many city beaches have a distinct culture, as cyclists compete with rollerbladers.

Carmel Beach
This large cove of white sand backed by cypress-covered cliffs is ideal for sunbathing, but strong currents make it dangerous for swimmers.

Mission Beach, San Diego
Ideal for surfing, snorkelling, scuba-diving and fishing.

Muscle Beach
Bodybuilders congregate here to pump iron and strut around.

Pacific Coast Highway
This 400-mile road takes you through some of California's most spectacular coastal scenery, including Big Sur, a dramatic 75-mile stretch of cliffs. Good overnight stops: Santa Barbara, a Spanish-influenced town with several museums, galleries and antique shops; Morro Bay, a small fishing port and boating harbour with fish restaurants; and the Monterey peninsula resorts of Carmel, Monterey and Pacific Grove.

Santa Cruz Beach
Backed by the famous Boardwalk, whose jolly, funfair atmosphere spills over on to the sands. Great for surfing.

Santa Monica Beach
Just beyond LA's metropolitan sprawl is a long expanse of fine, golden sand patrolled by jeep-propelled lifeguards *à la Baywatch*.

Venice Beach, Los Angeles
This is where hip LA goes to hang out – cool dudes, long-limbed bronzed babes, basketball enthusiasts, and many others.

BEST SIGHTS
Malibu, a seashore sanctuary for the seriously rich, houses the J. Paul Getty Museum with its controversial collection of Greek and Roman art and famous paintings, including Van Gogh's *Irises*.

San Simeon was the extravagant personal fiefdom of newspaper magnate William Randolph Hearst. Thousands of European art treasures were incorporated into the design to produce a place of regal sumptuousness and spellbinding vulgarity. Book a tour in advance.

BEST NATIONAL PARKS
Death Valley
The landscape is unforgettable: white salt twisted by evaporation into pinnacles at the Devil's Golf Course; giant ripples of mud at Zabriskie Point; the amazing colours of Artist's Drive. Visit between November and April: in summer, Death Valley has the highest average temperatures on earth.

Joshua Tree
Gnarled trees where Mojave and Colorado deserts meet, thought by Mormons to resemble Joshua's arms leading them to the Promised Land.

Yosemite
The glacier-carved canyon of Yosemite Valley is readily accessible by road. Its stunning scenery of meadows, sheer granite walls and pine and cedar forests can be easily explored along marked trails. More adventurous hikers aim for Hetch Hetchy or Tioga Pass. The best views of the valley are from Glacier Point, an hour's drive away. Do not miss the giant redwoods at Mariposa Grove.

BEST VINEYARDS
The Napa Valley produces California's best-known wines, the cooler southern area being particularly suitable for chardonnay and pinot noir varieties, while the north produces excellent cabernet sauvignon. The less well-known Sonoma is the best place to get to know California's native grape variety – Zinfandel.

WHEN TO GO

HUGE VARIATIONS in weather occur from season to season and from one part of the USA to another. In general, summer is not a good time to visit Florida: the air is hot and sticky, and rainfall is heavy. But winter and spring are pleasantly mild. In New York, spring and autumn are generally agreeable, though the weather can change dramatically from day to day.

For touring in the west, the summer months are best: many national parks in the northern Rockies are not open properly until June. On the coast, July and August are the worst months for fog (around San Francisco) and smog (around LA). Southern California has pleasantly mild winters.

Average daily maximum temperature °C

	JAN	FEB	MAR	APR	MAY	JUN	JUL	AUG	SEP	OCT	NOV	DEC
London	6	7	10	13	17	20	22	21	19	14	10	7
New York	4	4	9	15	21	26	28	27	24	18	12	6

	JAN	FEB	MAR	APR	MAY	JUN	JUL	AUG	SEP	OCT	NOV	DEC
New York	11	10	12	11	12	10	10	10	8	8	9	10
London	15	13	11	12	12	11	12	11	13	13	15	15

Average number of rainy days per month

Average daily maximum temperature °C

	JAN	FEB	MAR	APR	MAY	JUN	JUL	AUG	SEP	OCT	NOV	DEC
London	6	7	10	13	17	20	22	21	19	14	10	7
San Francisco	13	15	16	18	19	21	22	22	23	21	18	14

	JAN	FEB	MAR	APR	MAY	JUN	JUL	AUG	SEP	OCT	NOV	DEC
San Francisco	11	10	9	6	3	1	<1	<1	1	4	7	10
London	15	13	11	12	12	11	12	11	13	13	15	15

Average number of rainy days per month

Average daily maximum temperature °C

	JAN	FEB	MAR	APR	MAY	JUN	JUL	AUG	SEP	OCT	NOV	DEC
London	6	7	10	13	17	20	22	21	19	14	10	7
Miami	24	25	27	28	30	31	32	32	31	29	27	25

	JAN	FEB	MAR	APR	MAY	JUN	JUL	AUG	SEP	OCT	NOV	DEC
Miami	6	6	6	8	10	13	17	16	19	15	9	7
London	15	13	11	12	12	11	12	11	13	13	15	15

Average number of rainy days per month

PACKAGE TRAVEL

OTHER THAN in Orlando or New York, single-centre holidays are rare and limiting. A fly-drive package gives you more flexibility, or you can book twin- or multi-centre packages, or ready-made self-drive tours with pre-booked accommodation. Most tour operators specialising in the US offer a wide range of options, from tailor-made tours to airpasses, so it is easy to get the kind of deal you want.

Treat packages that offer 'free' car-hire with a pinch of salt – you will inevitably have to pay a whole range of extras when you arrive, including collision damage waiver (known as loss damage waiver in the US), top-up liability insurance (see below), airport fee, handling charge, state and local taxes, which could come to as much as £250. It may be cheaper for you to book from a company that includes all these charges up front.

If you are planning to tour over quite a distance, check that the hire company will let you take the car out of the state, and which other states you can visit: some companies have limited coverage.

Most major tour operators offer holiday programmes to the USA, many in dedicated brochures. Florida, California and New England are

---

Tour operators

Battlefields: Holts' Tours, Midas **Birdwatching**: Cygnus Wildlife, Limosa, Ornitholidays, Sunbird **City breaks**: British Airways Holidays, Cresta, Crystal, Inghams, Osprey, Premier, Sovereign, Thomson, Time Off, Travelscene **Cultural**: Explorers, Ffestiniog Travel, Martin Randall, Railtours, Travel for the Arts, **General and specialist**: Airtours, American Adventure, American Connections, APT International, Archers, Bridgewater Travel, British Airways Holidays, Cosmos, Crystal, Delta Airlines, Florida Vacations, Funway, Getaway Vacations, Hamilton Travel, Hawaiian Dream, Inghams, Jetabout, Jetlife, Jetsave, Jetset, Just America, Key to America, Kuoni, NAR, North American Travel Service, Premier Holidays, Saga, Sunworld, Thomas Cook, Titan HiTours, Tradewinds, Trailfinders, Travelbag, Travelpack, Travelsphere, Unijet, Up and Away, US Airtours, Virgin Holidays **Rail tours**: Explorers Tours, Ffestiniog Travel **Walking**: Explore Worldwide, Ramblers Holidays **Wine**: Arblaster & Clarke, Winetrails **Other activities**: Ace Study Tours (study tours), American Round-Up (ranch), Caravan Abroad (motorhomes), Clipper Voyages (river cruising), Discover the World (wildlife), Inter-Church Travel (Christian), Peregrine (horse-riding), Ranch America (ranch), Solo's Holidays (singles) all popular package destinations. Holidays include fly-drive, coach tours, rail tours and cruising, and accommodation is self-catering and in hotels and motorhomes. City breaks are on offer to East Coast destinations including New York, Boston, Washington DC and Chicago. Activity holidays include ranch holidays, covered wagon trails, walking, birdwatching, wine tours, river cruising and rail tours.

INDEPENDENT TRAVEL

FIERCE COMPETITION among airlines on the transatlantic routes means there is plenty of scope for finding special deals and cheap fares. If you are planning to travel extensively within the US, it may be worth buying an airpass. Airpasses are offered by several airlines, and their conditions vary, but most have to be bought in the UK before you go. Check the flight network of each airline: some airlines have a good range of long-distance flights, including coast to coast, while others concentrate mainly on short hops, which may require you to change.

Distances are huge, and the natives rarely walk anywhere, so unless you are just staying in a particular city, hiring a car is by far the best way of getting around. Both cars and petrol are comparatively cheap. Another possibility is the 'drive-away': if you are heading in the same direction as a car that needs to be delivered, you are given insurance, a delivery date and address and the keys, and off you go. This is not always as liberating as it sounds, as delivery dates can be quite tight – so no heading off to the east coast via Alaska – but it is different.

Rail travel is a much less flexible option; if you are not driving it is better to use the Greyhound bus network. In cities, public trans-port is better and often, like San Francisco trams, part of the travel experience.

On the outskirts of every town is a 'strip' of hotels and motels. The motel is part of the experience of touring America, and rooms are more or less standard. Bed and breakfast does exist in America, but it is more upmarket and expensive than in the UK. In cities like Washington book-ing through agencies may save you money on the rack rate.

RED TAPE, HEALTH AND SAFETY

THE VISA waiver programme allows British passport-holders to stay for up to 90 days without a visa if they have an onward ticket.

There are no major health risks, but it is vital that you have adequate travel insurance to cover medical emergencies and public liability. Ironically, virtually all insurance policies exclude third-party liability dur-ing the 'use or possession of any mechanically propelled vehicle' – e.g., a hire car, so it would be wise to take out optional supplementary liability cover.

Periodically reports emerge of tourists being shot/mugged/attacked, notably in Florida in recent years. The usual rules about streetwise behaviour apply (see page 12). If you are unsure about how to get to your hotel from the airport, take a taxi or courtesy bus and ask the car hire company to drop off your car at the hotel the next day, when you have had a chance to recover from the flight and are feeling more alert. The latest advice is available from the Foreign Office Travel Advice Unit (see page 11).

The United States Travel and Tourism Administration has closed down its UK office, but many individual states have offices in the UK from which you can order tourist information. Contact numbers for some of the main destinations are listed below.

MORE INFORMATION Arizona (01426) 946334; California (0891) 200278; Delaware 0171-470 8802; Florida (0891) 600555; Georgia 0121-445 4554; Kentucky 0171-470 8804; Louisiana 0181-760 0377; Memphis (01462) 440787; Mississippi (01462) 440787; Nevada (0990) 238832; New Jersey 0171-404 3703; New Mexico (0839) 300700; North Carolina (0990) 333123; Pennsylvania (0839) 300701; South Carolina 0181-688 1141; Tennessee (01462) 440784; Virginia 0181-651 4743; Washington DC 0181-392 9187; Washington State 0171-978 5233

COST OF LIVING £-££

VIETNAM

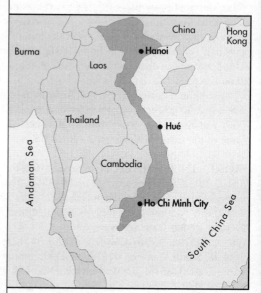

HO CHI MINH CITY AND THE MEKONG DELTA
Good for culture, local colour, nightlife and scenic landscape

HO CHI Minh City, still widely known as Saigon, is the usual jumping–off point for travel in Vietnam and provides a head-spinning introduction to a country in the throes of furious economic change. It makes a good base for exploring the Mekong Delta's quilted ricelands, nearby war relics and the fanciful Cao Dai religious centre.

Vietnam's largest city and commercial capital retains a surprising flavour of its French colonial past, from elegant villas to coffee and croissants. After hours, choose from some of Vietnam's finest restaurants, hottest clubs and hippest bars.

BEST SIGHTS

Cholon
Visit compelling incense-filled Chinese temples and teeming streets.

War Crimes Museum
This gives a grisly and somewhat one-sided view of what locals call 'The American War'.

BEST EXCURSIONS

Boat trips
An excursion on the Mekong Delta's skein of waterways repays the effort – especially if it includes the floating markets in the city of Can Tho, which sell fruit, vegetables and local commodities. Samples of goods are displayed on the boats suspended from bamboo poles. If time is short, the town of My Tho provides an excellent taster of river life.

Cu Chi
Here you can squeeze through tunnels dug by Viet Cong soldiers right under an American army base.

Tay Ninh
The flamboyant Cao Dai cathedral, dominated by the Divine Eye, takes everyone by surprise – time your visit to coincide with one of the four daily services. The cathedral is headquarters of the Cao Dai religion.

BEST NIGHTLIFE
Venues range from spit-and-sawdust *bia hoi* (draft beer) bars to increasingly sophisticated clubs and discos. One of the trendiest is Q Bar, favoured by visiting American film stars. The best known bar is probably Apocalypse Now, which harks back to the GI bars of the 1960s.

CENTRAL PROVINCES
Good for culture, history and scenic landscape

HUE'S TEMPLES and royal palaces are the highlights of central Vietnam, closely followed by Hoi An's traditional merchants' houses. North of Hué, war sights litter the Demilitarised Zone where Vietnam divided for two decades after 1954. The main road north, Highway 1, offers dramatic views of forested mountains fringed with sugar-white sands, but beware, not all beaches are safe for swimming.

BEST SIGHTS

Demilitarised Zone
The bleak battlefields of the DMZ are a poignant memorial to the

thousands who died here in the 1960s and 1970s. There is nothing particular to see, but it is hard not to respond to the sense of enormous desolation. Names such as The Rockpile and Hamburger Hill resound from countless Vietnam War movies.

Hoi An
This pint-size town remains a captivating place despite being firmly on the tourist trail. Once a thriving port, its narrow streets are lined with ancient wooden buildings (some dating from the late sixteenth century) interspersed with eye-catching Chinese Assembly Halls, built by refugee merchants. Nearby, seventh-century Cham temples moulder under luxuriant vegetation at My Son.

Hué
A slow-moving, cultured city on the Perfume River, Hué should not be missed. Ravaged by war and a notoriously wet climate, it is being painstakingly restored to its former glory. Known as the Imperial City after being chosen as the new capital by Emperor Gia Long, who unified Vietnam in 1802, Hué was the country's cultural centre in the nineteenth century and remained the official capital until 1945. The emperors' lavish mausoleums rest in landscaped gardens on the outskirts; they can be reached by river boat.

HANOI AND THE NORTH
Good for culture, local colour, outdoor activities and scenic landscape

HANOI, VIETNAM'S capital, is layered in history. It is a small, rather reserved city where life proceeds at a gentler pace than in the south. From here most visitors take a trip to Ha Long Bay, Vietnam's premier natural attraction. The northern mountains are home to a patchwork of ethnic minorities and provide excellent opportunities for trekking.

BEST SIGHTS
Ha Long Bay
Thousands of limestone islands, some pitted with caves, speckle Ha Long Bay's expansive emerald waters, four hours by road from Hanoi. A full day's boat tour is recommended to see the best of the bay, but note that during winter months (November to March) spells of cold, drizzly weather can dampen its beauty.

Hanoi
Central Hanoi is an attractive scene of lakes, shaded boulevards and tasteful, French-built mansions, contrasting sharply with the neigh-

bouring Old Quarter's intoxicating tangle of market streets. In Ho Chi Minh's Mausoleum the man himself, lying embalmed in a cold, dark hall, still draws pilgrims from around the world. The eleventh-century Temple of Literature dates back to Hanoi's earliest days and represents Vietnam's foremost Confucian sanctuary.

Northern mountains
A wild, fairly inaccessible region containing Vietnam's highest peaks. Apart from the scenery, the prime attraction is the variety of minority peoples, many still following a traditional way of life. A burgeoning trekking industry focuses around Sa Pa village, which also hosts a colourful weekend market.

WHEN TO GO

THE SOUTHERN region has a tropical climate, while the north is sub-tropical. The rainy season is from May to August in the north, but lasts from May to November in the south of the country. The temperature averages 25°C all year round in the south, while the north has two distinct seasons. The best time to travel in Vietnam is between January and April.

Average daily maximum temperature °C											
London 6	7	10	13	17	20	22	21	19	14	10	7
Hanoi 20	21	23	28	32	33	33	32	31	29	26	22
JAN	FEB	MAR	APR	MAY	JUN	JUL	AUG	SEP	OCT	NOV	DEC
Hanoi 7	13	15	14	15	14	15	16	14	9	7	7
London 15	13	11	12	12	11	12	11	13	13	15	15
Average number of rainy days per month											

PACKAGE TRAVEL

HOLIDAY OPTIONS in Vietnam are somewhat limited. In addition to the Vietnam-based tours available, some long-haul operators offer hotels in Hanoi or Ho Chi Minh City as a stopover.

Seven-day tours visiting North and South Vietnam are typical of what is on offer. These use internal flights visiting Hanoi, Da Nang, Hué, Hoi An and Ho Chi Minh City. City tours and excursions to nearby sights are included and a cruise on the Perfume River may be part of the tour. Longer tours may include a trip to the central highlands and the town of Dalat, or a visit to Na Trang for a cruise through the islands and time spent relaxing on the beach. Travel is usually by minibus or coach and some operators include the Reunification Express train journey from Hué to Hanoi in their packages.

Although changing fast, the tourism infrastructure is still relatively undeveloped so accommodation standards are variable.

INDEPENDENT TRAVEL

AS YET there are no direct flights from Britain to Vietnam, so you will probably be routed through a regional centre such as Singapore or Bangkok. Most airlines offer tickets flying into Ho Chi Minh City and out of Hanoi, or vice versa.

Local buses and trains can be fun but are slow and uncomfortable: it is worth paying extra for 'soft-class' train tickets (you get a padded seat). For night journeys there are also hard and soft berths. Increasingly visitors opt for internal flights or tourist buses plying the main routes.

Though self-drive is not available, hiring a vehicle plus driver is not exorbitant and allows greater freedom. You can organise this through a UK travel agent, or a local operator in Vietnam – in which case, allow time to find a reputable agent and ensure the itinerary and costs are agreed in writing.

The local infrastructure is rudimentary and hotels fairly basic, although standards are improving rapidly, especially in the main cities and tourist centres. New hotels open by the week, from private 'mini-hotels' to swish international resorts. As a rule, the newest offer superior standards of comfort and cleanliness. Local tourist offices are not always helpful, so it can be prudent to book accommodation through a UK agent or invest in a reliable, up-to-date guidebook.

Tour operators

Adventure: Explore Worldwide, Guerba, Travelbag **Cycling**: Exodus **General**: Airwaves, Asean Explorer, Asiaworld Travel, British Airways Holidays, East Travel, Far East Dream Journeys, Far East Gateways, Hayes & Jarvis, Kuoni, Magic of the Orient, Oriental Magic, Regent Holidays, Silverbird, Steppes East, Tradewinds, Travel Indochina

---

RED TAPE, HEALTH AND SAFETY

ALL FOREIGN nationals need a visa to enter Vietnam, available from the Vietnamese Embassy or a specialist visa agent (see page 17). The tourist visa costs £40 and the maximum time you can apply for is 30 days. Two passport photographs are required. Processing normally takes a week to ten days, but it is wise to allow longer in case of delays.

If you take simple, commonsense precautions you should not fall ill in Vietnam. Follow the precautions on page 11 and consult your GP or a travel clinic in plenty of time about vaccinations; typhoid and hepatitis A are usually recommended. Make sure your tetanus and polio boosters are up to date. Dengue fever is present in the south and Japanese encephalitis affects parts of the north – regular use of mosquito repellents is recommended. Anti-malaria medication varies according to your length of stay and whether you travel in the cities or off the beaten track – the disease is a problem in the countryside.

Take care on the roads, as poor driving and vehicle maintenance can cause accidents.

MORE INFORMATION Tourist Information Department, Embassy of Vietnam, 12–14 Victoria Road, London W8 5RD, tel 0171-937 1912 (*Press 1 when you hear message in Vietnamese, then ext. 203*), visa information (0891) 171228 (premium rate number)

COST OF LIVING £

ZANZIBAR

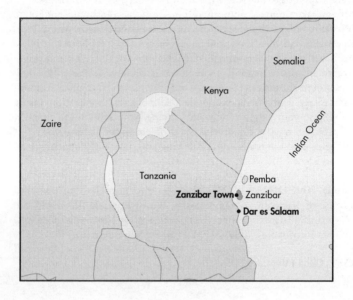

HIGHLIGHTS

Beaches
*Zanzibar
Island*

**Culture/
history**
*Zanzibar
Town*

**Local
colour**
*Zanzibar
Town,
Zanzibar
Island,
Pemba Island*

**Outdoor
activities**
*Zanzibar
Island,
Pemba Island*

Shopping
*Zanzibar
Town*

Wildlife
*Zanzibar
Island*

ZANZIBAR TOWN
Good for culture, history, local colour and shopping

ZANZIBAR TOWN is the capital of Zanzibar. For hundreds of years
it was one of the most important commercial centres in Africa and the
Indian Ocean, with a thriving trade in slaves, ivory and spices – most
notably cloves. Today the town is a touch down-at-heel, but it is still
flourishing with a large and vibrant community.

BEST SIGHTS

Stone Town

Of most interest to tourists is the Stone Town, 'the old quarter': a maze of narrow streets and alleys, edged on two sides by the Indian Ocean. Until the mid-nineteenth century Zanzibar was a sultanate ruled from Oman, before coming under British colonial influence from the 1880s until 1963. Many grand buildings from these times remain – an intriguing mix of Arab, Indian, African and European styles – although the dirt and decay surrounding the fine examples can spoil a few exotic illusions. The best way (often the only way) to explore the Stone Town is on foot – the streets are too narrow for cars.

BEST SHOPPING

Browsers can spend many happy hours at the main market on the edge of the Stone Town, where fruit, spices, fish and meat are stacked in large heaps and sold by the handful, tin-full or truck-full.

Bargain-hunters will enjoy the souvenir shops dotted around the Stone Town. They sell jewellery and carvings from all over Africa, local cloth, spices, colonial antiques and contemporary art. Look out for the indigenous *tinga-tinga* paintings (a brightly coloured, highly stylised, almost pointillist style). There is even a more recent Zanzibari speciality – banana-flavoured bubble bath.

ZANZIBAR ISLAND
Good for beaches, local colour, outdoor activities and wildlife

---

THE ISLAND, forming with Pemba the majority of the state of Zanzibar, is sometimes known as Unjuga.

BEST BEACHES

As befits an Indian Ocean island, Zanzibar's beaches come close to idyllic, although washed-up seaweed covers the sand on some days. The best beaches are on the north and east coasts. Snorkelling or diving on the coral reefs are popular. Fishing, sailing and other water sports are available. Facilities are still relatively low-key, but cater for all budgets. There are simple guesthouses for shoestring travellers, while those with healthier wallets can choose from a range of quiet and exclusive hideaways.

BEST WILDLIFE

Jozani Forest

The forest in the central part of Zanzibar Island is home to a rare species of colobus monkey, plus several other types of primate. You can observe the monkeys from nature trails through the dense vegetation.

Kizimkazi

At Kizimkazi on the southern tip of Zanzibar Island, pods (groups) of bottlenose and humpback dolphin are common. Turtles and other marine animals can also frequently be seen. Boat trips are available; with care and patience it is possible to swim near the dolphins.

PEMBA ISLAND
Good for local colour and outdoor activities

PEMBA IS undeveloped for tourism. There is little in the way of sights and just a handful of hotels, but there are some spectacular beaches. Offshore, the game fishing and diving are reckoned to be world-class.

WHEN TO GO

ZANZIBAR HAS two main dry seasons: December to February and June to October, and these are the best times to visit. Outside these periods it rains for a few hours each day, but the wet weather means fewer visitors, more space and better prices. Even in the dry season, the Indian Ocean makes rain possible at any time. Some diving centres only open from August to December when water conditions are best.

	Average daily maximum temperature °C											
London	6	7	10	13	17	20	22	21	19	14	10	7
Kisauni	34	34	34	33	31	30	30	30	31	32	32	33
	JAN	FEB	MAR	APR	MAY	JUN	JUL	AUG	SEP	OCT	NOV	DEC
Kisauni	8	6	12	19	15	6	5	5	6	7	10	11
London	15	13	11	12	12	11	12	11	13	13	15	15
	Average number of rainy days per month											

PACKAGE TRAVEL

MANY HOLIDAY companies include Zanzibar in their brochures, but most simply offer short 'add-ons' to wider tours of Tanzania or Kenya. If you want more than a few days, only a few specialists have the first-hand knowledge and experience to provide a full, good-quality Zanzibar package.

Zanzibar is relatively new to tourism, so don't automatically expect the 'usual' hotel facilities. Most mid-range places are comfortable and attractive (many are in restored historic buildings) but do not provide televisions, phones and fridges in each room. This is all part of the charm. Even some very exclusive places shun electricity and offer 'barefoot luxury'. However, a few fully-equipped four-star hotels are available, if this is what you want. To avoid surprises, when booking your holiday, check what sort of hotel you're getting.

Tour operators

Adventure: Encounter Overland, Explore Worldwide, Guerba, Travelbag **General**: Abercrombie & Kent, British Airways Holidays, Hayes & Jarvis, Kuoni, Somak, Voyages Jules Verne **Tailor-made specialists**: Africa Archipelago, Africa Exclusive, African Explorations, Art of Travel, Cazenove & Lloyd Safaris, Designer Travel, Frontiers, Grenadier Travel, Hartley's Safaris, Safari Consultants, Safari Drive, SAR Travel, Tim Best, Union Castle Travel, Wild Africa Safaris **Wildlife**: Animal Watch, Sunbird

---

INDEPENDENT TRAVEL

FLIGHTS TO Zanzibar from the UK are available on Gulf Air and Kenya Airways.

Many people visit as part of wider travels in East Africa, but access is still easy. Zanzibar is linked to the mainland by regular flights and fast boat services. Zanzibar Island is fairly small, mostly rural (and mostly flat) so getting around by bus, hire car, moped or bike is easy. Tours, especially to the spice plantations, can also be arranged with companies in Zanzibar Town.

RED TAPE, HEALTH AND SAFETY

ZANZIBAR IS an independent state within the United Republic of Tanzania. Passports are needed, even if you come from another part of Tanzania. Visas for Tanzania (including Zanzibar) are required by most nationalities; application forms are available from the Tanzanian High Commission in London. When you apply, your passport should be valid for six months. You need two passport-sized photographs and £38 in cash. You can visit the High Commission in person between 10am and 12.30pm, Monday to Friday – allow 24 hours for processing. If applying by post, send your application by registered delivery and enclose an sae.

A certificate to prove that you have been inoculated for yellow fever also needs to be shown on arrival in Zanzibar, even if you come from another part of Tanzania.Your doctor or travel clinic will advise on yellow fever and other jabs required. The Foreign Office strongly recommends inoculation against rabies. As a meningitis risk exists in Zanzibar, if you experience symptoms that include severe headache, high temperature, dislike of bright light and a rash that does not fade when pressure is applied, consult a doctor immediately.

Precautions against malaria are important. Take anti-malaria pills, use repellent and wear sufficient clothes in the evening. Most hotels provide mosquito nets, although in cheaper places these may be missing or have big holes. If this is your budget level take a needle and thread or, better still, your own portable net.

Zanzibar is a Muslim country and the people are traditionally conservative. Nudity and topless bathing are forbidden, and scanty clothing anywhere away from the beach is frowned upon.

Buying turtle-shell (sometimes called 'tortoiseshell') products is illegal, as turtles are a protected species.

Robberies (occasionally with violence) are not unknown in the Stone Town and on some beach areas. Use commonsense to keep safe: avoid quiet areas at night, especially if walking alone, and keep valuables (including cameras) out of sight wherever possible.

MORE INFORMATION Tanzania Trade Centre, 78–80 Borough High Street, London SE1 1LL, tel 0171-407 0566
Web site: http://www.zanzibar.net

Tanzanian High Commission, 43 Hertford Street, London W1Y 8DB, tel 0171-499 8951

COST OF LIVING £

ZIMBABWE

Mozambique

Angola Zambia

Victoria
Falls ●Harare

Namibia ●Bulawayo

Botswana

Indian Ocean

Lesotho

South Africa

HIGHLIGHTS

Culture
Harare,
Great Zimbabwe,
Bulawayo

**Family holidays/
wildlife**
Victoria Falls

History
Great Zimbabwe,
Bulawayo

Local colour
Harare, Bulawayo

Outdoor activities
Harare, Victoria Falls

Scenic landscape
Victoria Falls,
Great Zimbabwe,
Bulawayo

HARARE
Good for culture, local colour and outdoor activities

SURPRISINGLY SEDATE for an African city, Harare melds a post-
Second World War provincial British feel with African flamboyance.
There is nothing here you'll kick yourself for missing, but a few
features are worth a look.

BEST SIGHTS

Botanical Gardens
These are full of gloriously oversized tropical vegetation.

Mbare Market
Mbare Market is worth experiencing as Zimbabwe's largest and most
vibrant open-air shopping precinct.

National Gallery
The National Gallery offers a pleasant diversion, especially if you are interested in the local stone-sculpture movement.

BEST EXCURSIONS

Canoeing on the Lower Zambezi
Most canoe safaris – a Zimbabwean highlight – set out from Harare, transferring participants to the remote north of the country by air. Guided trips follow the course of the Lower Zambezi, the best of them passing through game-rich country.

Tengenenge
A two-hour drive north of Harare, Tengenenge is the largest sculptors' community in Africa, numbering among its residents several internationally recognised artists who carve in serpentine.

VICTORIA FALLS
Good for family holidays, outdoor activities, scenic landscape and wildlife

APART FROM the obvious attraction of the Falls themselves – one of the world's most epic geological formations – the town is the adventure capital of Africa, offering a huge range of adrenaline-pumping activities. For families, diversions include a crocodile farm, snake park and 'traditional village'.

BEST SIGHTS

Cruises
Scheduled cruises ply the Zambezi above the Falls, offering 'sundowners' and sightings of hippos and crocodiles accompanied by the truly unforgettable sounds of the impending African night.

Victoria Falls National Park
A paved walkway passes along the mile-long edge of the chasm opposite the crashing drop of the world's most voluminous waterfall. The path meanders through the tropical rainforest that thrives on the spray thrown up by the Falls, as they plunge on to the rocks 300 feet below.

BEST OUTDOOR ACTIVITIES

An exciting one-day white-water rafting trip that runs 18 rapids below the Victoria Falls now overshadows even the Falls themselves as the town's principal attraction.

Less macho and less adrenaline-steeped than rafting, kayaking isn't without its thrills as you negotiate small rapids, hippos and crocodiles.

Meanwhile a bungee jump plunges you 360 feet suspended by only an elastic band (a very strong one!) from the Victoria Falls railway bridge.

BEST WILDLIFE

Hwange National Park

Zimbabwe's flagship game reserve is a two-and-a-half hour drive south from Victoria Falls, has substantial populations of lions, elephants, buffalo and scores of other species as well as being the most accessible of all the country's national parks for self-drive safaris.

Private safari lodges

Although Zimbabwe's game density cannot match east Africa's, the standard of its game guides is excellent. The easiest way to benefit from these highly trained professionals is at one of the dozens of private safari lodges concentrated in and around Hwange National Park.

Zambezi National Park

Just four miles from the centre of town, this game reserve on the banks of the Zambezi river has a satisfyingly broad cross-section of African mammals.

GREAT ZIMBABWE
Good for culture, history and scenic landscape

GREAT ZIMBABWE is a rare phenomenon for sub-Saharan Africa – a permanent structure that has stood for nearly a thousand years. It consists of several square miles of walling that was once the heart of a town that held 10,000 people. The site's beauty lies in the grandeur of the walls with their stonework patterns, and its integration into the hilly landscape. Though they resemble fortifications, the walls were just a display of royal power, creating passages and enclosures that preserved privacy in a grandiose adaptation of the traditional African homestead.

BULAWAYO
Good for culture, history, local colour and scenic landscape

MANY PEOPLE find Zimbabwe's second city, Bulawayo, more appealing than the capital because so many of its colonial-era buildings have been left intact, giving it a charmingly sepia-toned ambience.

Unless you are flying around the country, it also makes a better base than Harare for exploring, because the main roads to Victoria Falls, Hwange National Park and Great Zimbabwe radiate from here.

BEST EXCURSIONS
Khami ruins
Hundreds of stone structures pepper the Zimbabwean landscape and of these, Khami, 14 miles west of Bulawayo, is second in size and significance only to Great Zimbabwe. Khami belongs to a separate polity that arose after the collapse of the Great Zimbabwe culture, around the fifteenth century. Although less impressive than Great Zimbabwe, Khami represents a more highly developed system of architecture and urban layout which drew its inspiration from Great Zimbabwe.

Matobo National Park
Thirty miles south of Bulawayo, the Matobo National Park is packed with Dali-esque landscapes of solid granite whaleback hills. The park protects the world's most dense concentration of ancient rock paintings, some estimated to be 20,000 years old.

It is also the last resting place of Cecil John Rhodes, the British empire-builder who died in 1902. Rhodes made his fortune from the South African gold and diamond mines, became prime minister of the Cape Province and in his private capacity as director of the British South Africa Company annexed Zimbabwe, which was known as Rhodesia in his honour until its independence in 1980.

WHEN TO GO

ZIMBABWE IS blessed with a near-perfect sunny climate throughout the year and can be visited at any time. Seasons are the reverse of Britain's, with the hottest period occurring during October and November, before the onset of the rains which bring short dramatic afternoon thunderstorms. The winter months from May to September, when barely a cloud passes overhead, are best for game viewing as animals congregate around a few scarce water sources and are easier to spot through the sparse vegetation. After the January to April rains, the landscape is lush and the animals are at their prime, although more difficult to see.

Average daily maximum temperature °C											
London	6	7	10	13	17	20	22	21	19	14	10	7
Harare	26	26	26	26	23	21	21	23	26	28	27	26
	JAN	FEB	MAR	APR	MAY	JUN	JUL	AUG	SEP	OCT	NOV	DEC
Harare	18	15	13	5	2	1	1	1	1	4	11	16
London	15	13	11	12	12	11	12	11	13	13	15	15
Average number of rainy days per month											

PACKAGE TRAVEL

PACKAGES OFFER a wide range of options and are generally very flexible. General tour operators provide a good selection of holidays and will put together various tours, activities and excursions to make up a package that suits your requirements. Many tailor-made specialists at the upper end of the market will create an individual tour. Short tours of around a week invariably include internal flights and a stay in Victoria Falls, also taking in the Hwange National Park or Lake Kariba. Longer trips might include the Matobo Hills and the de luxe train service between Bulawayo and Victoria Falls, as well as canoe trips or white-water rafting on the Zambezi and all manner of safaris.

Accommodation ranges from hotels to safari lodges, bungalows to tented bushcamps. Generally, the smaller the outfit the more exclusive your accommodation will be, but read accommodation descriptions carefully to ensure the safari lodge you are expecting is not just a hotel.

Most tour operators offer activities such as canoeing, white-water rafting and wildlife tours. Two-centre holidays with neighbouring South Africa and Mauritius are widely available.

Tour operators

Adventure: Acacia, Encounter Overland, Exodus, Explore Worldwide, Guerba, Kumuka Expeditions **Golf:** Zimgolf **General**: Abercrombie & Kent, Airwaves, Bales Tours, British Airways Holidays, Cosmos, Cox & Kings, Cricketer, Hayes & Jarvis, Kuoni, Okavango Tours & Safaris, Somak, Sunset Travel, Temple World, TCA Holidays, Thomas Cook, Trailfinders, Travel 2, Worldwide Journeys **Horse-riding safaris**: Campfire Adventures **Tailor-made specialists**: Africa Archipelago, Africa Exclusive, Art of Travel, Carrier International, Cathrine Crocker, Cazenove & Lloyd Safaris, Designer Travel, Frontiers, Green Services Travel, Grenadier Travel, Hartley's Safaris, High Class Travel, Safari Consultants, Safari Drive, SAR Travel, Tana Travel, Tim Best, Time for Africa, Travel Africa, Union Castle Travel, Wild Africa Safaris **White-water rafting**: Adrift **Wildlife/birdwatching**: Animal Watch, Naturetrek, Sunbird, Wildlife Worldwide

---

INDEPENDENT TRAVEL

SEVERAL DIRECT flights on British Airways and Air Zimbabwe leave London for Harare each week. Flights on a number of other carriers from London via European cities take longer, but are usually cheaper.

Scores of economy buses go from the big cities to virtually every location but are crowded, erratic, none too safe and recommended only for the adventurous. A skeletal but preferable network of luxury coaches links the main centres only. To reach places outside, you must hire a car – arrange rental before you leave to save on the local tax. The main roads are very well-kept and uncongested; driving is on the left.

For covering large distances quickly, Air Zimbabwe's regular and cheap domestic flights serve Bulawayo, Harare and the main tourist areas: Victoria Falls, Hwange National Park and Great Zimbabwe. Much slower, but more romantic, is the overnight train journey from Bulawayo to Victoria Falls, which runs for part of the way along the edge of Hwange National Park.

Among the cheapest and most pleasant places to stay in Zimbabwe are government cottages in national parks. At the other extreme, the most desirable and evocative accommodation is at intimate private safari lodges which come with personalised service, guided game activities, magnificent settings and hefty price tags. In cities, hotels can be pricey, but the number of B&Bs with competitive rates is growing, while the rock-bottom option is dormitories at backpacker lodges.

RED TAPE, HEALTH AND SAFETY

EUROPEAN PASSPORT-HOLDERS do not need visas.

Zimbabwe is a healthy country, and apart from the real hazard of malaria, there's scant danger of contracting 'tropical illnesses' or catching a bug from the local food or water. Anti-malaria pills offering some protection against the disease are advisable. Health professionals also recommend ensuring that your tetanus and polio jabs are up to date; some suggest other inoculations. Get advice from your GP or a travel clinic.

For visitors Zimbabwe has two economies: a moderately expensive tourist one, charged in US dollars, and a cheap local Zimbabwe dollar one. Costs depend largely on which economy you spend most of your time in. Car hire, large hotels and safari lodges tend to be expensive, while B&Bs, backpacker lodges, eating out and transport are cheap.

Generally Zimbabwe is a safe and friendly country, although theft is a potential hazard. The incidence of passport theft is high – carry a photocopy. Driving out of town at night should be avoided because of poorly lit vehicles and badly marked roads. Violent crime is a rarity and lawlessness bears no comparison to the sky-high levels found in parts of neighbouring South Africa. For the latest advice, contact the Foreign Office Travel Advice Unit (see page 11).

MORE INFORMATION Zimbabwe National Tourist Board, Zimbabwe House, 429 Strand, London WC2R 0QE, tel 0171-836 7755

No tourist office web site exists, but you can access information about Zimbabwe at:
http://www.tourist-offices.org.uk/Zimbabwe/index.html

COST OF LIVING £

TOUR OPERATORS

AA Motoring	(01256) 814 433	Anderson's Pacific	
AAT Kings	0181-974 9922	Way	(01932) 222079
Abercrombie &		Anemone	0181-889 9207
Kent	0171-730 9600	Anglers World	(01246) 221717
Acacia	0181-960 5747	Anglo Dutch	0181-289 2808
Ace Study Tours	(01223) 835055	Animal Watch	(01732) 741612
ACT	(01531) 660210	APT International	0181-879 7444
Action Vacances	0161-442 6130	Aquasun	0171-723 2490
Adrift	0181-874 4969	Aquatours	0181-255 8050
Aer Lingus Holidays	0181-899 4747	Arblaster & Clarke	(01730) 893344
Africa Archipelago	0181-780 5838	Archers	0181-466 6745
Africa Exclusive	(01604) 28979	Arctic Experience	(01737) 218800
Africa Travel		Argo	0171-331 7070
Centre	0171-387 1211	Armchair	0181-560 8008
African Experience	0171-630 0100	Art of Travel	0171-738 2038
African Explorations	(01993) 822443	Asean Explorer	(01481) 823417
African Journeys	(01704) 20463	Asian Affair	0171-287 4010
African Safari Club	0181-466 0014	Asiaworld Travel	(01932) 820050
African Safari Trails	0181-941 7400	Aspects of Tunisia	0171-486 4425
Airborne Holidays	0171-836 4646	Aspro Holidays	(01706) 260000
Airglobe Holidays	0171-813 2255	Austral Tours	0171-233 5384
Airtours	(01706) 260000	Australia Flight	
Airwaves	0181-875 1199	Centre	(01772) 727727
All Abroad	0181-458 2666	Australian Affair	0171-734 0927
Allez France	(01903) 742345	Australian Pacific	
All-Ways Pacific	(01494) 875757	Tours	0181-879 7444
Alternative Travel		Austravel	0171-734 7755
Group	(01865) 513333	Austria Travel	0171-222 2430
Amathus	0171-636 9873	Austrian Holidays	0171-434 7394
American		Aztec	0181-882 2999
Adventures	(01892) 511894		
American		Bakers Dolphin	(01934) 636666
Connections	(01494) 473173	Bales Tours	(01306) 885991
American		Balkan Holidays	0171-543 5555
Round-Up	(01404) 881777	Beachcomber Tours	(01483) 33008
AMG Travel	0181-958 3188	Belgium Travel	
Amsterdam Travel		Service	(01992) 456166
Service	(01992) 456066	Belleair	0181-785 3266
Anatolian Sky		Belle France	(01892) 890885
Holidays	0121-633 4018	Bents	(01568) 780800
Andalucian		Best of Greece &	
Safaris	(01572) 821330	Cyprus	0171-255 2320
Andante	(01980) 610 555	Best of Morocco	(01380) 828533

Bike Tours	(01225) 310859	CIE Tours	0181-667 0011
Birding	(01797) 223223	Citalia	0181-686 5533
Bladon Lines	0181-780 8800	Classic Collection	
Blakes Holidays	(01603) 784131	Holidays	(01903) 823088
Bluebird Express	(0990) 320000	Classic Nepal	(01773) 873497
Blue Moon Travel	0171-224 0226	Classic Tours	0171-613 4441
Bonaventure	0181-780 1311	Clipper Voyages	0171-436 2931
Bowens	0121-327 3543	Club Cantabrica	(01727) 866177
Bowhills	(01489) 877627	Club Med	0171-581 1161
Bridge the World	0171-734 6455	Collineige	(01276) 24262
Bridgewater Travel	0161-707 8547	Colour Line	0191-296 1313
British Airways		Concept Express Ltd	0171-493 4243
Holidays	(01293) 723171	Connections	
British Museum		(Red Sea Plus)	0171-355 1234
Traveller	0171-323 8895	Conservation	
Brittany Direct	0181-641 6060	Corporation Africa	0181-398 4464
Bundu Safaris	(01273) 388642	Corfu A La Carte	(01635) 201140
Butterfields	(01262) 470230	Coromandel	(01572) 821330
		Corsican Places	(01424) 774366
Cadogan	(01703) 332661	Cosmos	0161-480 5799
Campfire Adventures	(01980) 620839	Costa Smeralda	0171-493 8303
Canadian		Countrywide	0161-224 2855
Connections	(01494) 473173	Cox & Kings	0171-873 5005
Canterbury Travel		Creative Tours	0171-495 1775
(Lapland only)	(01923) 823470	Cresta	0161-927 7000
Canvas	(01383) 644000	Cricketer	(01892) 664242
Cape Tours	(01908) 231 62	Crusader	(01255) 425453
Caravan Abroad	(01737) 842735	Crystal	0181-399 5144
Carefree Italy	(01293) 552277	CV Travel	0171-581 0851
Carefree Spain	(01689) 848711	Cygnus Wildlife	(01548) 856178
Caribbean		Cyplon Travel	0181-340 7612
Connection	(01244) 341131	Cyprair Tours	0171-388 7515
Caribtours	0171-581 3517		
Carisma	(01923) 284235	DA Tours	(01383) 881700
Carrier	(01625) 582006	Danube Travel	0171-493 0263
Casas Cantabricas	(01223) 328721	David Sayers Travel	(01572) 821330
Castaways	(01737) 812255	Delta Airlines	0171-731 3979
Catherine Secker		Delta Travel	0161-274 4444
(Crete)	0181-460 8022	DER	0171-290 1111
Cathrine Crocker	(01271) 891018	Designer Travel	0161-839 5158
Cathy Matos	0171-267 3787	Destination Pacific	0171-336 7788
Cazenove & Lloyd		Destination Portugal	(01993) 773269
Safaris	0171-376 3746	Destination Provence	(01765) 609091
Cedok	0171-839 4414	Destination Red Sea	0181-440 9900
Celebrity Holidays	0171-439 1961	Discover the World	(01737) 218800
Chevron Air	(01753) 851267	Discovery	0171-602 7444
China Travel Service	0171-836 9911	Dominiques Villas	0171-738 8772

Dragoman	(01728) 861133	Golden Sun	0171-485 9555
Dream Journeys	(01784) 449832	Gozo Holidays	(01923) 262059
Drive France	0181-395 8888	Greece & Cyprus	
Drive Ireland	0151-231 1480	Travel Centre	0121-355 6955
Driveline Europe	(01707) 660011	Greek Islands Club	(01932) 220477
		Greek Sun	(01732) 740317
East Travel	(01473) 214305	Green Services	
Egyptian Encounter	(01590) 623993	Travel	(01934) 612277
EHS Travel	(01993) 700600	Grenadier Travel	(01206) 549585
Elegant Resorts	(01244) 897888	Guerba	(01373) 826611
Elite Vacations	0181-864 9818		
Encounter Overland	0171-370 6845	Hamilton Travel	0171-344 3355
Eurocamp	(01565) 626262	Harlequin	(01708) 852780
European Waterways	0171-436 2931	Hartley's Safaris	(01522) 511577
Eurosites	(01706) 830888	Hawaiian Dream	0181-470 1181
Eurovillages	(01606) 734400	Hayes & Jarvis	0181-748 5050
Excelsior	(01202) 309555	Headwater	(01606) 42220
Exodus	0181-675 5550	Hello Italy	(01483) 284011
Explore Worldwide	(01252) 319448	Hermis	0171-731 3979
Explorers Tours	(01753) 681999	HF Holidays	0181-905 9558
		High Class Travel	0181-933 1000
Far East Dream		Highlife Holidays	0181-452 3388
Journeys	(01784) 449832	Highway Journeys	(01256) 895966
Far East Gateways	0161-945 4321	Himalayan	
Ffestiniog Travel	(01766) 512340	Kingdoms	0117-923 7163
Filoxenia	(01422) 375999	Holiday Place	0171-431 0670
Finlandia	0171-409 7334	Holts' Tours	(01304) 612248
Finman Travel	(01942) 262662	Hoseasons	(01502) 500555
First Choice	0161-745 7000	Hungarian Air Tours	0171-437 9405
Florida Vacations	(01727) 841568		
Fourseasons	0113-256 4374	Ilios Island Holidays	(01403) 259788
French Affair	0171-381 8519	Imaginative Travel	0181-742 8612
French Country		Individual Travellers	
Camping	(01923) 261311	Spain & Portugal	(01798) 869485
French Country		Infinity Tours	0171-978 5212
Cruises	(01572) 821330	Inghams	0181-780 4400
French Golf Holidays	(01277) 374374	Inntravel	(01653) 628811
French Impressions	0181-324 4042	Inscape	(01993) 891726
French Life	0113-239 0077	Insight Holidays	(0990) 143433
Frontiers	0171-629 2044	Inspirations	(01293) 822244
Funway	0181-466 0222	Interchange	0181-681 3612
		Inter-Church Travel	(0800) 300444
Gambia Experience	(01703) 730888	Interhome	0181-891 1294
Garuda Indonesia	(01753) 687676	Intersky Holidays	0181-341 9999
Getaway Vacations	0181-313 0550	Intourist	0171-538 5965
Globespan	0141-353 0699	Intra Travel	0171-323 3305
Goldenjoy	0171-794 9767	Irish Ferries	(0990) 170000

Irish Roamer	(01740) 653169	Longmere	
Israel Travel Service	0161-839 1111	International	0181-655 2112
Italian Affair	0171-381 6636	Longshot Golf	(01730) 268621
Italian Escapades	0181-748 2661	Longwood Holidays	0181-551 4494
Italiatour	0171-371 1114	LSG Theme Holidays	(01509) 231713
ITC			
(Caribbean)	(01244) 355300	Made to Measure	(01243) 533333
(Indian Ocean)	(01244) 355320	Magic of Italy	0181-748 7575
(South Africa)	(01244) 355330	Magic of the Orient	(01293) 537700
(Sports holidays)	(01244) 355390	Magic of Spain	0181-748 4220
		Magnum Travel	0181-360 5353
Japan Experience	(01703) 730830	Malta Direct	0181-785 3233
Jasmin Tours	(01628) 531121	Malta Sun	0181-983 4040
Jetabout	0181-741 3111	Maltatours	0171-821 7000
Jetlife	(01322) 614801	Manos	0171-216 8070
Jetsave Ltd	(01342) 328231	Martin Randall	0181-742 3355
Jetset	0171-436 6757	McCabe Travel	0181-675 6828
Journey Latin		Meon	(01730) 268411
America	0181-747 8315	Metak Holidays	0171-935 6961
Joyce's Hidden		Midas	(01883) 744955
Ireland	(01934) 823017	Minorca Sailing	
Just America	(01730) 266 588	Holidays	0181-948 2106
Just France	0181-780 0303	Moswin	0116-271 9922
		Motours	(01892) 518555
KD Cruises	(01372) 742033	Mundi Color	
KE Adventure	(01768) 773966	Holidays	0171-828 6021
Kerry Holidays	(0800) 393443	Musgrove World	
Kestours	0181-402 1800	Travel	(01753) 648135
Key to America	(01784) 248777	Mysteries of India	0181-574 2727
Keycamp	0181-395 4000		
Kings Angling	(01708) 453043	NAR	(01753) 855031
Kirker	0171-231 3333	Naturetrek	(01962) 733051
Kosmar	0181-368 6833	Nippon Travel	
Kumuka		Agency	0171-437 2424
Expeditions	0171-937 8855	Noble Caledonian	0171-409 0376
Kuoni	(01306) 740888	Nomadic Thoughts	0181-960 1001
		Normandie Vacances	(01922) 721901
Lagrange	0171-371 6111	North American	
Lakes &		Travel Service	0113-243 0000
Mountains	(01329) 844405	North Portugal	
Lanzarote Leisure	0181-449 7441	Travel	(01242) 262159
Lanzotic Travel			
(Prague only)	(01342) 834120	Okavango Tours &	
Laskarina	(01629) 824884	Safaris	0181-343 3283
Latin America Travel	0171-630 0070	Oonas Divers	(01323) 648924
Leger	(01709) 839839	Oriental Magic	(0645) 213141
Limosa	(01263) 578143	Orientours	0181-346 9144

Ornitholidays	(01243) 821230	Savile Row Tours	0171-625 3001
Osprey	0131-557 1555	Scandinavian Seaways	(01255) 241234
		Scandinavian Travel	
PAB Travel	0121-233 1252	Service	0171-930 8189
Page & Moy	0116-254 2000	ScanMeridian	0171-431 5393
Palmer & Parker	(01494) 815411	Scantours	0171-839 2927
Panorama	(01273) 206531	Scott Dunn World	0181-672 1234
Pan Tours	0171-233 8458	Seafarer	0171-234 0500
Passage to South		Select France	(01865) 331350
America	0181-767 8989	Select Sites	(01873) 859876
Paxos	(01580) 765000	Serena	0171-244 8422
Pax Travel	0171-837 3567	Shearings	(01942) 824824
Pearl of the Orient	0171-932 0998	Sherpa	0181-577 2717
Peltours	0181-346 9144	Siesta International	(01642) 227711
Peregrine	(01865) 511642	Silk Cut Travel	(01730) 265211
Petitts India	(01892) 515966	Silverbird	0181-875 9191
Planos	(01225) 744300	Simply Caribbean	(01423) 526887
P & O European		Simply Corsica	0181-747 3580
Ferries	(01992) 456045	Simply Simon	0171-373 1933
Portugala Holidays	0181-444 1857	Simply Travel	0181-995 3883
Portuguese Travel		Simply Tropix	0181-875 1777
Centre	0171-581 3105	Simply Turkey	0181-747 1011
Premier Holidays	(01223) 516677	Simply Tuscany &	
President Holidays	0181-688 7555	Umbria	0181-995 8277
Prestige	(01425) 480400	Skiathos Travel	0181-940 5157
Price Right	0181-444 3030	Skopelos Villas	(01689) 877938
Prospect	0181-995 2151	Skybus	0171-373 6055
Pullman Holidays		Skytours	(0990) 502555
(UK)	0171-630 5111	Solaire	0121-778 5061
Pure Crete	0181-760 0879	Solo's Holidays	0181-951 2800
		Somak	0181-423 3000
Railtours	(01902) 324343	Something Special	(01992) 505500
Ramblers Holidays	(01707) 331133	South African Affair	0171-381 5222
Ranch America	0181-868 2910	South African Airways	0171-312 5000
Regal Holidays	(01353) 778096	South American	
Regent Holidays	0117-921 1711	Experience	0171-976 5511
Reliancetours	0171-437 0503	Sovereign	(01293) 599900
Rendezvous Holidays	0171-266 3399	Sovereign Scanscape	0181-880 8118
Ryan Holidays	(0800) 777377	Spanish Affair	0171-385 8127
		Spanish Harbour	
Safari Consultants	(01787) 228494	Holidays	0117-986 9777
Safari Drive	(01488) 681611	Spearhead Travel	(01883) 732005
Saga	(0800) 300500	Specialised Tours	(01342) 712785
Sally Holidays	0181-395 3030	Speedwing	0181-905 5252
Sandpiper	(01932) 868658	Sri Lanka Holidays	0171-439 0944
SAR Travel	0171-287 1133	Stena Line Holidays	(0990) 747474
SAS Holiday World	0141-951 8988	Steppes East	(01285) 810267

Sunbird	(01767) 682969	Trips Worldwide	0117-987 2626
Sunquest	0171-499 9991	Tropical Places	(01342) 824011
Sunselect	0161-707 8279		
Sunset Travel	0171-622 0777	Ultima Tours	0151-347 1818
Sunsites	(01565) 625555	Unicorn Holidays	(01582) 834400
Sunspot Tours	(01580) 715222	Unijet	(0990) 336336
Sunvil	0181-568 4499	Union Castle Travel	0171-229 1411
Sunward	(01752) 894040	Up and Away	0181-289 5050
Sunworld	0113-255 5222	US Airtours	0141-248 4844
Superstar Holidays	0171-437 9277		
Susi Madron's	0161-248 8282	Vacances en	
Swan Hellenic	0171-800 2300	Campagne	(01798) 869433
Swiss Travel Service	(01992) 456143	Vacanze in Italia	(01798) 869426
		Vacation Canada	0141-332 1511
Taber	(01274) 735611	VFB	(01242) 240340
Tana Travel	(01789) 414200	Vintage Travel	(01954) 261431
Tapestry Holidays	0181-742 0055	Virgin Holidays	(01293) 617181
TCA Holidays	(01453) 835051	Voyages Ilena	0171-924 4440
Temple World	0181-940 4114	Voyages Jules Verne	0171-616 1000
Thermalia	0171-483 1898		
Thomas Cook	(01733) 372255	Wallace Arnold	(01332) 636456
Thomson	(0990) 502555	Waymark	(01753) 516477
Tim Best	0171-591 0300	Welcome Holidays	(01695) 574578
Time for Africa	(01489) 878593	West End Travel	0171-409 0630
Time Off	0171-235 8070	Wild Africa Safaris	0171-259 9909
Titan HiTours	(01737) 760033	Wildlife Worldwide	0181-667 9158
Top Deck	0171-244 8641	Winetrails	(01306) 712111
Tradewinds	(01706) 219111	Worldwide Journeys	0171-381 8638
Trailfinders	0171-938 3366		
Trans Indus	0181-566 2729	Zimgolf	0191-389 1443
Transun	(01865) 798888		
Travel 2	0171-263 8414		
Travel Africa	(01904) 708878		
Travelbag	0171-497 0515		
Travelcoast	0181-891 2222		
Travel Club of			
Upminster	(01708) 225000		
Travel for the Arts	0171-483 4466		
Travel Indochina	0171-937 8855		
Travel South			
America	(01904) 704443		
Travellers Czech	(01959) 540700		
Travelmood	0171-258 0280		
Travelpack	(0990) 747101		
Travelscene	0181-427 4445		
Travelsphere	(01858) 410456		
Trek America	(01295) 256777		

INDEX